Patterns of
Reflection

Patterns of
Reflection
A Reader

———

Fourth Edition

Dorothy U. Seyler
Northern Virginia Community College

ALLYN AND BACON
Boston   London   Toronto   Sydney   Tokyo   Singapore

Vice President, Humanities: Joseph Opiela
Editorial Assistant: Kristen Desmond
Executive Marketing Manager: Lisa Kimball
Editorial Production Service: Marbern House
Manufacturing Buyer: Suzanne Lareau
Cover Administrator: Linda Knowles
Electronic Composition: Omegatype Typography, Inc.

Copyright © 2001, 1998, 1995 by Allyn & Bacon
A Pearson Education Company
160 Gould Street
Needham Heights, MA 02494

Internet: www.abacon.com

Library of Congress Cataloging-in-Publication Data

Patterns of reflection / Dorothy U. Seyler.—4th ed.
    p. cm.
    Includes index.
    ISBN 0-205-31481-3
    1. College readers. 2. English language—Rhetoric—Problems, exercises, etc. 3. Report writing—Problems, exercises, etc. I. Seyler, Dorothy U.
PE1417.P396 2000
808'.0427—dc21

                                    99-059738

Printed in the United States of America

10 9 8 7 6 5 4 3 2   RRD-VA   05 04 03 02 01

It is not enough to have a good mind.
The main thing is to use it well.

René Descartes

I like to find
What's not found
at once, but lies
within something of another nature
in repose, distinct.

Denise Levertov

Contents

4.   Using Comparison and Contrast: Ways of Learning   **121**

5.   Explaining and Illustrating: Examining Media Images   **167**

Preface

Being asked to write a textbook is certainly an enjoyable experience—an editor believes that you may be able to think and write, usefully, about writing. Being asked to prepare a second edition of that text—now there's a truly wonderful experience, because some folks actually used the book and pronounced it helpful. But to do a third edition—what a joy! A great opening for three editions, but here I am preparing a fourth edition. How do I carry forward this introduction? I am at a loss except to say that I am so pleased to offer another edition both to old friends and to those new friends we hope to make.

Patterns of Reflection provides engaging selections on personal, social, and political concerns and issues, selections that also demonstrate varied uses of the major rhetorical strategies or patterns. The organizing of chapters by both rhetorical patterns and topics makes *Patterns of Reflection* a special text, both a practical guide to the various writing patterns and purposes students will use in their college writing and a study of themes generating lively class discussions and personal reflections.

Patterns of Reflection asks students in its opening chapter to think about the challenges and rewards of reading and writing, both in an honest and helpful introduction and in six essays on issues such as writing anxiety and the value of keeping a journal. Each of the subsequent chapters illustrates one specific pattern or purpose, beginning with those strategies students are most comfortable with and then progressing to the more demanding ones: narration, description, comparison and contrast, explaining and illustrating, process analysis, division and classification, definition, causal analysis, and, finally, argument and persuasion. At the same time, each chapter's thematic core allows students to begin by reflecting on what is closest to them—their childhood, the people and places they know, the learning process—and then move beyond their immediate lives to their society—the media, working and playing, interpersonal relations, values, and social issues—and then eventually to reflect on how they want to live as individuals, as members of a group, and as part of an interdependent environment.

Within the two broad organizational patterns are diverse works appealing to readers of varied backgrounds and interests. Instructors can skip some chapters and reorder others to meet the needs of their courses; students will have their favorite selections at the same time that they can be reminded of how much we all share as individuals who must grow up, learn, and prepare for work. Each chapter gains further diversity by the varying of length of essays; by the inclusion of essays, newspaper articles, and a few excerpts from longer works; by the addition of a short story or poem to many chapters; and by the inclusion of four annotated student essays illustrating description, contrast, definition, and argument. *Patterns of Reflection* is indeed a rich storehouse of opportunity.

Although the selections are preeminent, this is not just an anthology; it is a text, and as such it provides many aids to learning. Each chapter begins with a clear explanation of the strategy that includes specific guidelines for writing. Then the student is encouraged to "get started" by engaging in some reflecting and/or writing activity that can be used as a preparation for reading, as a class activity, or as a basis for journal writing. Following each selection are vocabulary exercises and questions that guide students from understanding to analyzing to responding to their reading. After all selections in a chapter, you will find "Making Connections," a section that helps readers to stretch their minds beyond one selection. These are topics for discussion, research, and/or writing that go beyond a particular work to others the author has written or that invite reflection on similarities and differences in approach and attitude among several authors. Each chapter concludes with topics for writing that are based on the chapter's readings and that will give practice in the chapter's rhetorical strategy. Topics are explained at length to help students reflect on and then plan their essays.

The fourth edition of *Patterns,* while retaining the basic plan and apparatus of the original, offers some changes and additions that both instructors and students will appreciate. First, there are thirty-five new essays and twenty-five new authors represented. In seven cases, authors have been represented with new, more current articles, but the authors have been retained because you said that you liked their writing. Second, the greatest number of new works will be found in Chapter 10, on argument, because of the desire to have that chapter address current issues. But, while seven of the eight articles are new, only five of the authors are new. Third, the questions following each work have been organized under new headings, headings that will help to stress the process of reading as both understanding content *and* drawing inferences about that content to reach conclusions about thesis and purpose. The introductory material to each chapter has also been reorganized and, in addition, expanded. The reorganization—with more subheadings and the use of lists and bullets—will aid readability while reducing length so that some additional guidance for students can be added without adding pages to the book. Most of the new material will be found in Chapters 1 and 10. In Chapter 1, one essay has been moved "up front" to serve as material for guided reading. Questions accompany the essay, suggesting the kinds of questions that readers should be asking and answering as they read. In Chapter 10's introduction, there is more discussion of the nature of argument and of logical fallacies. Finally, while most of the text's readings remain relatively brief, a few works have been added that are a bit longer, providing both students and instructors with greater variety.

Patterns of Reflection is a reader that both students and instructors will find a workable text, one that contributes meaningfully to their composition course and is "user friendly," explaining, guiding, and supporting, without dictating to either student or instructor.

No book of value is written alone. I am happy to acknowledge the help of friends and colleagues in preparing this new edition. Once again I am indebted to my daughter Ruth for her always-sound advice on selections. And thanks are due, as always, to the library staff at the Annandale Campus of Northern Virginia Community College, especially to Marian Delmore and Ruth Stanton for their help in solving my research problems. I remain grateful to Scott Rubin and my initial editor Barbara Heinssen for their advice and encouragement through the first edition, and to Tim Julet and Eben Ludlow for their help with the second edition, all formerly of Macmillan Publishing. I would not be writing this preface to the fourth edition if it were not for the continued support, through two editions now, of my editor at Allyn and Bacon, Joe Opiela. I also appreciate the many fine suggestions from the following reviewers: Dr. John Tuttle, Francis Marion University; Syble Smith Davis, Houston Community College-Central Campus; Elizabeth Flores, College of Lake County; Sandra Feldman, Santa Rosa Junior College; and V. Kay Colbert, North Georgia College.

Finally, I want to give a special thank you to the four students who gave me permission to use their essays. They were hardworking, thoughtful writers who should be proud of their achievements. I hope they will find the same joy that I have reaching out to students all over the country.

Patterns of Reflection

1

On Reading and Writing

You have purchased your texts and are ready to begin another English course. What papers will be assigned, you wonder, perhaps somewhat nervously. And why has this text of readings been assigned? After all, writing is difficult enough; must you read, too? Giving these questions some thoughtful analysis is a good place to start your journey through this text and course.

The Challenges and Rewards of Writing

Many people, of all ages, become nervous about writing; they experience what is called writing anxiety. Some are so anxious, as Gail Godwin observes in this chapter (see pp. 17–20), that they dream up all kinds of excuses to put off a writing task. If you have some anxiety about writing, you can take comfort in knowing that others share your nervousness, including professional writers who sometimes go through lengthy periods of writer's block. You can also take some comfort in recognizing the appropriateness of your feelings. When faced with a term of writing compositions, students can expect a degree of anxiety, because writing well is not easy.

Let's consider some realities of the writing process. First, writing is a skill, like dancing or riding a bike or playing tennis. You were not born knowing how to ride a bike. You had to learn, perhaps with some painful bumps and bruises to both bike and ego. To be a competent writer, you must develop your skills the same way tennis players develop a spin serve: good instruction, a strong desire to succeed, and practice, practice, practice. A second fact of writing is that some writers are more talented than others, just as Pete Sampras is a more talented tennis player than most. But Sampras's ability did not come from a genie in a bottle. The best in any field make their abilities look "like magic." You need to remember, however, that they also spend years of study, self-discipline, and practice to achieve their excellence. This text cannot give you a great tennis game, but it can help you to become, with practice and commitment on your part, a competent writer.

Even for those willing to practice, learning to write well is not easy because writing is a complex skill. Topics to write about, audiences to write for, and reasons to write cannot be completely catalogued, and the ways of choosing and combining words into sentences are infinite in their variety. Still, you can, through instruction and practice in this course, develop some good strategies for planning, organizing, drafting, and revising your writing. In addition, this text will provide opportunities for thinking about issues important to all of us and worthy of exploring through writing.

If learning to write well is difficult, why bother to try to develop your skills? For a good answer to this question, ask any student over twenty-five why he or she is now in college. Many "older" students are training for a second career, but many more want to improve basic skills so that they can advance in their current careers. They will assure you, from their experience in the workplace, that all language skills are essential: reading, speaking, listening, and writing. More immediate and personal goals for writing well can also be noted:

- ❑ The more you develop your awareness of the writing process, the better reader you will become. You will understand, from your own experience, how writers select and organize material to achieve their purpose.
- ❑ The more confident a writer you become, the more efficiently you will handle written assignments in your other college courses.
- ❑ Since writing is an act of discovery, the more you write, the more you will learn about who you are and what matters to you. After all, how accurately do you see your parents, your friends, your campus? Writing will sharpen your vision of the world around you and your understanding of the world inside you.

Good Reasons for Reading

Good writers make good readers. It is also true that reading well improves writing. The strong connection between reading and writing skills explains why students in reading courses are asked to write and students in writing courses are asked to read. Here are three specific uses of reading in a composition course.

Reading for Models

At times students are assigned readings to illustrate a type of writing: the personal essay, the book review, the scholarly report. Or, the readings may illustrate a strategy or purpose in writing: description, illustration, argument. Chapters 2 through 10 in this text contain readings grouped by a dominant writing pattern or purpose. If you are assigned Tracy Kidder's description of Mrs. Zajac and then asked to write a descriptive essay of someone you know, you have been asked to use Kidder's essay as a model for your assignment.

Readings can also be studied as models of effective writing. They can illustrate clever openings, the use of transitions, varied sentence patterns, and effective metaphors. Read, then, not just for what the work says but for what kind of writing it represents and for what writing techniques it illustrates. Questions on strategies and style following each reading will guide your study of the work's special merits. Remember: in the broadest sense, reading contributes to language development. You learned your first language by imitating the speech you heard around you. Imitate the readings in this text to improve your writing skills.

Reading for Information and Insight

You may also be asked to read for information: for facts, for new ideas, for startling analyses. Even when you are reading for models, you will have the chance to explore many subjects, some new to you. Reading, as syndicated columnist Robert Samuelson has observed, "allows you to explore new places, new ideas and new emotions." In this text when you read, you can travel with Lance Morrow to Africa, understand with Linda Waite the ways that marriage improves people's lives, and contemplate with John Ciardi the meaning of happiness. When preparing reading assignments, be sure to think about the questions asking for your reactions. Approach each reading assignment as an opportunity to grow in knowledge, understanding, and imagination.

Reading for Writing

One of the interesting effects of reading is that it produces writing, more works to read and react to in a never-ending chain reaction. A columnist writes about assault weapons. A reader responds with a letter to the editor opposing the banning of such guns. A student, to complete an argument assignment, writes a refutation of the letter. At times writing assignments in this course may call for a response to reading. You may be asked to summarize an essay, analyze a writer's use of details, or contrast writers' differing views on a subject. When writing about reading, you will need to show both skill in writing and understanding of the reading, a challenging task.

Guidelines for Active Reading

When first looking over library materials or texts for courses, you are wise to begin by skimming to see how the material is put together and what, in general, it is about. But, once you become engaged in a particular work that you need to know well, accuracy—not speed—is your goal. You can improve your reading skills by becoming an active, engaged reader who follows a clear reading strategy. A good reading strategy calls for the following preparation, reading, and responding steps.

Prepare

1. *Prepare to become a part of the writer's audience.* Not all writers write with each one of us in mind. Some writers prepare scholarly reports for other specialists. Some scholars, such as Linda Waite (see pages 384–395), present the results of research to a more generally educated audience. Writers of the past wrote for readers in their time, readers who may be expected to know their times or other works with which you may be unfamiliar. So, prepare yourself to join the writer's audience by learning as much as you can about each of the following:

   ❑ the writer
   ❑ the time in which the work was written
   ❑ the kind of work it is (a textbook chapter, a newspaper editorial, a personal narrative)
   ❑ the writer's anticipated audience.

For writings in the text, you will be aided in this step by introductory notes. Be sure to study them. *Never start to read words on a page without first knowing what you are reading!*

2. *Prepare to read with an open mind.* Good readers seek new knowledge and ideas. They do not "rewrite" a work to suit themselves. Keep in mind that not all who write will share your views or express themselves as you do. Read what is on the page, giving the writer a fair chance to develop ideas, giving yourself the thoughtful reflection needed to comprehend those ideas. Remember: You are in a college course to learn, not to be entertained. So, stick to the task of reading with understanding, not complaining that you didn't "like" this work or that the assignment was "boring." If the reading is difficult for you, look up words or references you do not know and be prepared to read a second time to really learn the material.

3. *Prepare by prereading.* To be prepared to read with understanding, you need to skim the selection to see what kind of work you are about to read (#1 above), to get some idea of the author's subject, and to start thinking about what you already know on that topic. Follow these steps:

   ❑ Read all introductory notes or biographical notes provided about the author.
   ❑ Consider the title. What clues in the title reveal the work's subject and perhaps the writer's approach to or attitude about that subject?
   ❑ Read the opening paragraph and then skim the rest of the work, noting in particular any subheadings and/or graphics.
   ❑ Ask yourself: "What do I already know about this subject?" and "What do I expect to learn—and what will I need to know—from reading this work?"
   ❑ From your prereading, raise two or three questions about the subject that you hope to find answers to by reading the work.

Read Actively

4. *Read with concentration.* Your goal is understanding, not completing an assignment as quickly as possible, so read as slowly as necessary to achieve comprehension. Maintain concentration. Avoid reading a page and then gazing out the window or getting a snack. You will have to go back to the beginning to really know what you have read if you

keep interrupting the reading process. Read an entire essay or story or poem or chapter (or several related sections in one chapter) at one time.

5. *Use strategies for understanding words and references.* Reading a work containing words you do not know is like trying to play tennis with some of the strings missing from your racket. When you come to a word you do not know, begin by studying the sentence in which it appears. You may be able to guess the word's meaning from its context. If context clues do not help, study the parts that make up the word. Many words are combinations of words or word parts (roots, prefixes, and/or suffixes) that appear in other words that you do know. For example, take the word *autobiography*. This is made up of *auto,* a root meaning self (*auto*mobile), *bio,* a root meaning life (*bio*logy), and *graph,* a root meaning writing (auto*graph*). You can understand many longer words if you think about their parts. These strategies will allow you to keep reading rather than interrupting the process to turn to a dictionary. When reading Joseph Reynolds's essay in this chapter, you may need to look up the meaning of the word *inveterate.* You should also use a dictionary or encyclopedia to look up the writers to whom Reynolds refers. Understanding references to people, places, and other written works is essential for full comprehension.

6. *Be alert to the use of figurative language and other writing strategies.* Figures of speech such as metaphors, irony, and understatement help shape a writer's tone and convey a writer's attitude to his or her topic. Use the Glossary if necessary to check the definitions of these terms.

7. *Annotate or make notes as you read.* Studies have demonstrated that students who *annotate* (underline key passages and make notes in the margin) their texts get higher grades than those who do not annotate. So, to be a successful student, develop the habit of reading with pen in hand. As you read, underline key sentences such as each paragraph's topic sentence and the writer's thesis, if stated. When you look up a definition or reference, write what you learn in the margin so that you can reread that section with understanding. When you underline a writer's thesis, note in the margin that this is the main idea. When you see a series of

examples or a list, label it as examples (exs) or list and then number each one in the margin. If you read that there are *three* reasons for this or *four* ways of doing that, be sure to find all three or all four in the passage and label each one. Put a question mark next to a difficult passage—and then ask about it in class. Pay attention to transition words and phrases; these are designed to show you how the parts of the work fit together. Draw arrows to connect example to idea. Create your own abbreviations and symbols; just use them consistently. Become engaged with the text, as illustrated by the sample annotation in Figure 1.

8. *As you read and annotate, think about the writer's primary purpose in writing and the structures or strategies being used.* Keep in mind the strategies examined in Chapters 2 through 10 in this text as you read and identify the primary strategy that gives the work its structure and/or purpose. Consider, as well, if the writer's primary purpose is to share feelings and experiences, to inform readers, or to argue for a claim. However, also keep in mind that writers can—and usually do—mix strategies and may have more than one purpose. For example, a writer using a contrast pattern can develop the points of contrast by providing examples. The writer's primary purpose may be to persuade, but at the same time readers are informed about a topic.

9. *Keep a reading journal.* In addition to annotating to aid reading comprehension, you may want to develop the habit of writing regularly in a journal. A reading journal records your responses to reading assignments but is more informal and personal than class notes. Keeping a journal gives you the chance to list impressions and feelings in addition to ideas that you may use in your next paper. (Read Reynolds on the advantages of keeping a journal.) Develop the habit of writing regularly and often. Chances are that both your reading and writing skills will improve.

Respond

10. *Review your reading.* To aid memory, review your reading immediately and then periodically. After finishing an assignment in this text, you can review by answering the questions following each selection. Then, look over your annotations and your reading journal shortly before class

Johnson?
Descartes?

Thesis—
advantages
of journal
writing

Thoreau—
example of
journal writer

interesting
simile

"I write, therefore I am," wrote Samuel Johnson, altering 1
Descartes' famous dictum: "I think, therefore I am."

When writing in my journal, I feel keenly alive and some- 2
how get a glimpse of what Johnson meant.

My journal is a storehouse, a treasury for everything in my 3 ①
daily life: the stories I hear, the people I meet, the quotations I
like, and even the subtle signs and symbols I encounter that
speak to me indirectly. Unless I capture these things in writing,
I lose them.

All writers are such collectors, whether they keep a journal 4
or not; they see life clearly, a vision we only recognize when
reading their books. Thoreau exemplifies the best in journal
writing—his celebrated *Walden* grew out of his journal entries.

By writing in my own journal, I often make discoveries. I see 5 ②
connections and conclusions that otherwise would not appear
obvious to me. I become a craftsman, like a potter or a carpenter who makes a vase or a wooden stoop out of parts. Writing
is a source of pleasure when it involves such invention and
creation.   *meaning?*

I want to work on my writing, too, hone it into clear, read- 6 ③
able prose, and where better to practice my writing than in my
journal. Writing, I'm told, is a skill and improves with practice.
I secretly harbor this hope. So my journal becomes the arena
where I do battle with the written word.

Figure 1.   Sample annotation of first six paragraphs of Reynolds's
"I Think (and Write in a Journal), Therefore I Am."

discussion of the assigned selection. *Warning: When you are*
called on, the instructor does not want to hear that you read the
selection but cannot remember enough to answer the question!

11. *Reflect.* In addition to reviewing to check comprehension,
reflect on your reading and connect it to other parts of the
course and other parts of your life. Remember that reading
is not "drill." It is one of the most important ways that we
gain new knowledge and new insights into ourselves and
our world.

Guided Reading

Read the following column (published April 12, 1999), practicing all the guidelines for active reading. Remember to prepare,
to read actively, and then to respond to your reading. Use the

questions to the right of the article to guide your reading and thinking. Add your own annotations to the left.

"An End to Our American Argot?"

WILLIAM RASPBERRY

A graduate of Indiana Central College, William Raspberry (b. 1935) joined the *Washington Post* in 1962. He now writes one local column a week and two syndicated columns on broader topics. He often focuses on urban or race problems, or on changes in our culture.

It can be fascinating to watch young people create and propagate their special codes—slang— to keep us older ones from understanding what they're talking about. Sooner or later, though, we catch on to "da bomb" or "say word" or "waaay jazzed," and the kids coin new formulations.   1

1. Why do young people create their own language? Is this Raspberry's subject?

There's nothing hostile about this trend, which may be almost as old as language itself. But it does separate people into insiders and outsiders while it obstructs successful communication. Indeed, its primary purpose may be to obstruct understanding.   2

I think Americans are building another sort of obstruction to understanding, more insidious than slang because it is unintended, hardly even recognized. We are, I fear, losing a good deal of our common language.   3

2. What else is happening to our language? What seems to be the author's attitude toward the change?

The thought hit me a week or so ago when I compared our intervention in Kosovo and various other crises around the world to Br'er Rabbit and the Tar Baby. Scores of younger readers didn't know what I was talking about, having never come across the wily rabbit, or Uncle Remus or their creator, Joel Chandler Harris.   4

3. What do these examples have in common? How do they aid communication?

It's a small thing, and I don't mean to suggest that the sky is falling . . .   5

6   And there it is again. Did your children read about Chicken Little? Will *their* children? And if they don't, we'll have to find other, wordier and less evocative ways to talk about chronic over-worriers who go around making mountains out of molehills.

7   The American language used to be heavily seasoned with phrases that evoked much fuller messages. Some—"Sodom and Gomorrah," for instance, or "road to Damascus"—were from the Bible. Others—"pound of flesh" or "the past is prologue"—came from Shakespeare's works or other classics, including *Aesop's Fables*. Still others came to us from the stories of national heroes.

8   But one hears fewer biblical references in our public discourse these days, perhaps because we fear too many listeners won't know what we're talking about. Shakespeare is no longer a requirement in some colleges, even for English majors. The heroes have mostly been debunked: There was no cherry tree confession, and Lincoln was less an anti-slavery saint than a political pragmatist. And you know about Jefferson.

9   And that's not all. The canon—official or otherwise—keeps getting expanded to the point that it's increasingly possible for two Americans to be well educated without ever having read the same book.

10   The point is not that we are substituting inferior literature for superior—how can you compare "Beowulf" and "The Bluest Eye"?—but that we are losing much of the common lore on which connotative language is built.

11   For a time, the gap was filled by television. "Father Knows Best," "Amos and Andy," "Laugh-In" and "M*A*S*H" all provided us with images and figures of speech and analogies to aid our communication. More recently, Archie Bunker and Cliff Huxtable—both watched by Americans of every stripe—furnished us with conversational shorthand.

4. Why are TV shows intro-duced?

No more. With the declining dominance of the networks, not even TV binds us together anymore. In a recent survey, "ER" was No. 1 for white viewers but ranked 15th for African Americans. ("Friends" was No. 2 with whites, 88th with blacks.) Conversely, the "Steve Harvey Show," top-ranked for black viewers, was No. 127 with whites. 12

Only six shows, including "60 Minutes," the "CBS Sunday Movie" and "Monday Night Football" made the top 20 for both groups. 13

What does this have to do with language and communication? It is common experience (or at any rate common knowledge of vicarious experience) that enriches language and gives us a shorthand way of talking about things. Imagine having to spell out in words the combination of frustration and mindless bureaucracy that is captured by the phrase "Catch-22." 14

5. *What do we lose when we lose a common language?*

6. *What does "vicarious" mean?*

But when we have no common shorthand— worse, when we, black and white, have two separate shorthands—it isn't just our language that gets weaker. So does some of the glue that binds us together and makes us *American*. 15

7. *Why are these words in quotation marks?*

8. *What is Raspberry's thesis?*

What, if anything, will substitute for that glue? Can it be that only the language of computers and the Internet stands between us and a latter-day Tower of Babel? 16

9. *Reflect on Raspberry's ideas. Do you agree that we have a problem? If so, do you have any solutions?*

"What a revoltin' development" that would be. 17

Looking Ahead

We have explored some ideas about reading and writing in these opening pages. Other issues are examined by the six writers whose essays on reading and writing and language compose the rest of this chapter, some of whom have been referred to in the previous discussion. Before reading selections in this— or in any—chapter, though, turn first to each chapter's "Getting Started" section. These sections can be used in several ways: to start your reflections on some phase of the chapter's topic, to provide a class activity, to give you ideas for journal writing.

Getting Started

Read the following poem by Richard Wilbur; it is not a difficult poem to read, I promise! Enjoy his images and metaphors as you picture the scene he recreates. Then think about what Wilbur has to say about the writing process. Use these questions to guide your reading and thinking:

1. What is his daughter doing in her room? Why are there silences in between the periods of typing?
2. Five stanzas are about a bird trapped in his daughter's room. What does this story have to do with his daughter's current activity?
3. What does he wish for his daughter? Why, at the end of the poem, does he wish her the same thing—but harder?
4. What would you say is the basic meaning or point of the poem?
5. Why has this poem been included in this chapter?

Did you like this poem? If so, do you think you can use it as a useful reminder or as a guide through this writing course? If not, why not? You may want to answer these questions in a journal entry or have answers ready for class discussion.

"The Writer"

RICHARD WILBUR

Born in New York City, Richard Wilbur (b. 1921) attended Amherst College and fought in World War II. He then taught at several colleges, including Harvard and Smith. He has several collections of poetry and has published literary criticism and children's books. His books have led to two Pulitzer Prizes and a National Book Award. The following poem is from his collection *The Mind Reader* (1971).

In her room at the prow of the house
Where light breaks, and the windows are tossed
    with linden,
My daughter is writing a story.

I pause in the stairwell, hearing
From her shut door a commotion of typewriter-keys   5
Like a chain hauled over a gunwale.*

Young as she is, the stuff
Of her life is a great cargo, and some of it heavy:
I wish her a lucky passage.

But now it is she who pauses,   10
As if to reject my thought and its easy figure.
A stillness greatens, in which

The whole house seems to be thinking,
And then she is at it again with a bunched clamor
Of strokes, and again is silent.   15

I remember the dazed starling
Which was trapped in that very room, two years ago;
How we stole in, lifted a sash

And retreated, not to affright it,
And how for a helpless hour, through the crack of   20
   the door,
We watched the sleek, wild, dark

And iridescent creature
Batter against the brilliance, drop like a glove
To the hard floor, or the desk-top,

And wait then, humped and bloody,   25
For the wits to try it again; and how our spirits
Rose when, suddenly sure,

It lifted off from a chair-back,
Beating a smooth course for the right window
And clearing the sill of the world.   30

It is always a matter, my darling.
Of life or death, as I had forgotten. I wish ·
What I wished you before, but harder.

---

*Upper edge of the side of a boat, pronounced gŭn'əl.

"I Think (and Write in a Journal), Therefore I Am"

JOSEPH REYNOLDS

An English and Latin teacher, Joseph Reynolds (b. 1942) is also a freelance writer who has published more than a hundred articles in newspapers and journals. In addition, Reynolds has averaged four entries a week in a journal he has kept for over a dozen years. Thus he writes from experience when he explains the values of keeping a journal. His article on journal writing was first published in 1981 in the *Christian Science Monitor.*

> *For a long time I was a reporter to a journal, of no very wide circulation, whose editor has never yet seen fit to print the bulk of my contributions, and, as is too common with writers, I got only my labor for my pains. However, in this case my pains were their own reward.*
>
> —Henry David Thoreau
> *Walden*

1   "I write, therefore I am," wrote Samuel Johnson, altering Descartes' famous dictum: "I think, therefore I am."

2   When writing in my journal, I feel keenly alive and somehow get a glimpse of what Johnson meant.

3   My journal is a storehouse, a treasury for everything in my daily life: the stories I hear, the people I meet, the quotations I like, and even the subtle signs and symbols I encounter that speak to me indirectly. Unless I capture these things in writing, I lose them.

4   All writers are such collectors, whether they keep a journal or not; they see life clearly, a vision we only recognize when reading their books. Thoreau exemplifies the best in journal writing—his celebrated *Walden* grew out of his journal entries.

5   By writing in my own journal, I often make discoveries. I see connections and conclusions that otherwise would not appear obvious to me. I become a craftsman, like a potter or a carpenter who makes a vase or a wooden stoop out of parts. Writing

is a source of pleasure when it involves such invention and creation.

I want to work on my writing, too, hone it into clear, read- 6
able prose, and where better to practice my writing than in my journal. Writing, I'm told, is a skill, and improves with practice. I secretly harbor this hope. So my journal becomes the arena where I do battle with the written word.

Sometimes when I have nothing to write, I sit idly and thumb 7
back through old entries. I rediscover incidents long forgotten.

During a recent cold midwinter night, for example, I reread 8
an entry dated a summer ago. My wife and I had just returned after a day at the beach. We were both tired and uncomfortable after a long ride home, but our spirits were lifted when we saw our cat come down the driveway to greet us, her tail held high shouting her presence. By reading this entry, I relived the incident, warming with affection for my cat and a sunny day at the beach.

I always try to write something, however, even if it is free 9
writing, writing anything that comes to mind. Often this process is a source of a "core idea" that can later be developed into a more finely polished piece of writing. The articles I've published had their inception in my journal.

Journal writing, in addition, is a time when I need not worry 10
about the rules of spelling and grammar; it provides a relaxed atmosphere in which my ideas and feelings can flow freely onto the page. If I discover an idea worth developing, then my prewriting is done.

My journal becomes a place where I can try different kinds 11
of writing, as well, from prose and poetry to letters to the editor. Attempting different kinds is useful; once I find the inspiring medium, my writing improves.

When I write in my journal, I seek the solitude of my study. 12
With pen in hand, I become omniscient; I am aware of the quiet, damp, night air, or the early-morning sounds of life. My journal is the place where I discover life.

"Usually when a man quits writing in his journal, . . . he has 13
lost interest in life," attests E. B. White, an inveterate journal writer himself.

So for these few moments, at least, I hold myself in hand, 14
I am.

Expanding Vocabulary

1. Reynolds expects readers to be familiar with Thoreau, Johnson, Descartes, and E. B. White. Look up each of these writers in an encyclopedia or biographical dictionary and then write a two-sentence identification of each person.
2. After checking a dictionary for the definition of any word you are unsure of, use each of the following words in a separate sentence. (Numbers in parentheses refer to paragraph numbers.)

   dictum (1)
   keenly (2)
   subtle (3)
   exemplifies (4)
   hone (6)
   omniscient (12)
   inveterate (13)

Understanding Content

1. Reynolds lists eight reasons for keeping a journal. Reread the essay, placing a number in the margin to indicate each reason.
2. Make a list of the reasons, following Reynolds's order, stating each reason as a phrase. (For example: a place to discover life.)
3. In what sense does Reynolds become omniscient (paragraph 12) when he sits in his study, writing in his journal? Explain his point.

Drawing Inferences about Thesis and Purpose

1. What does Reynolds mean when he says that "all writers are such collectors"? Explain.
2. State in your own words Reynolds's main point, or thesis, about journal writing.

Analyzing Strategies and Style

1. Although his organization is simple (listing), Reynolds's style is not. He uses a number of effective comparisons, or metaphors. Find at least three metaphors, state the two items being compared (e.g., Reynolds compares himself to a potter), and then explain the point of the comparison (e.g., like a potter working with clay, Reynolds creates something new when he works with words in his journal). See the Glossary for a definition of *metaphor*.
2. As a part of your vocabulary study, you learned about the four writers Reynolds refers to in his essay. Explain how each writer's

words, quoted by Reynolds, contribute to this essay about journal writing. Why, in other words, does Reynolds quote Thoreau, Johnson, Descartes, and White?

3. Reynolds writes of his own experience, using the pronoun *I* throughout. What techniques help him avoid sounding self-centered or pompous? How does he make his personal experience interesting to many readers?

Thinking Critically

1. Reynolds lists many reasons for journal writing. Which two reasons would you select as most convincing? Why?
2. Which reason is least likely to encourage you to start a journal? Why?
3. Has Reynolds effectively demonstrated the rewards of journal writing? If so, how? If not, why not?

"The Watcher at the Gates"

GAIL GODWIN

With degrees from the Universities of North Carolina and Iowa, Gail Godwin (b. 1937) began her career as a journalist and English instructor before becoming primarily a fiction writer. She has published a collection of short stories and several novels, including her 1982 best-seller *A Woman and Two Daughters.* In the following essay, published in 1977 in the *New York Times Book Review,* Godwin examines the sources of writer's block and offers some solutions to the problem.

I first realized I was not the only writer who had a restraining critic who lived inside me and sapped the juice from green inspirations when I was leafing through Freud's *Interpretation of Dreams* a few years ago. Ironically, it was my "inner critic" who had sent me to Freud. I was writing a novel, and my heroine was in the middle of a dream, and then I lost faith in my own invention and rushed to "an authority" to check whether she could have such a dream. In the chapter on dream interpretation, I came upon the following passage that has helped me free myself, in some measure, from my critic and has led to many pleasant and interesting exchanges with other writers.

2   Freud quotes Schiller, who is writing a letter to a friend. The friend complains of his lack of creative power. Schiller replies with an allegory. He says it is not good if the intellect examines too closely the ideas pouring in at the gates. "In isolation, an idea may be quite insignificant, and venturesome in the extreme, but it may acquire importance from an idea which follows it. . . . In the case of a creative mind, it seems to me, the intellect has withdrawn its watchers from the gates, and the ideas rush in pell-mell, and only then does it review and inspect the multitude. You are ashamed or afraid of the momentary and passing madness which is found in all real creators, the longer or shorter duration of which distinguishes the thinking artist from the dreamer . . . you reject too soon and discriminate too severely."

3   So that's what I had: a Watcher at the Gates. I decided to get to know him better. I discussed him with other writers, who told me some of the quirks and habits of their Watchers, each of whom was as individual as his host, and all of whom seemed passionately dedicated to one goal: rejecting too soon and discriminating too severely.

4   It is amazing the lengths a Watcher will go to keep you from pursuing the flow of your imagination. Watchers are notorious pencil sharpeners, ribbon changers, plant waterers, home repairers and abhorrers of messy rooms or messy pages. They are compulsive looker-uppers. They are superstitious scaredy-cats. They cultivate self-important eccentricities they think are suitable for "writers." And they'd rather die (and kill your inspiration with them) than risk making a fool of themselves.

5   My Watcher has a wasteful penchant for 20-pound bond paper above and below the carbon of the first draft. "What's the good of writing out a whole page," he whispers begrudgingly, "if you just have to write it over again later? Get it perfect the first time!" My Watcher adores stopping in the middle of a morning's work to drive down to the library to check on the name of a flower or a World War II battle or a line of metaphysical poetry. "You can't possibly go on till you've got this right" he admonishes. I go and get the car keys.

Other Watchers have informed their writers that: 6

"Whenever you get a really good sentence you should stop 7 in the middle of it and go on tomorrow. Otherwise you might run dry."

"Don't try and continue with your book till your dental ap- 8 pointment is over. When you're worried about your teeth, you can't think about art."

Another Watcher makes his owner pin his finished pages to 9 a clothesline and read them through binoculars "to see how they look from a distance." Countless other Watchers demand "bribes" for taking the day off: lethal doses of caffeine, alcoholic doses of Scotch or vodka or wine.

There are various ways to outsmart, pacify or coexist with 10 your Watcher. Here are some I have tried, or my writer friends have tried, with success:

Look for situations when he's likely to be off guard. Write 11 too fast for him in an unexpected place, at an unexpected time. (Virginia Woolf captured the "diamonds in the dustheap" by writing at a "rapid haphazard gallop" in her diary.) Write when very tired. Write in purple ink on the back of a Master Charge statement. Write whatever comes into your mind while the kettle is boiling and make the steam whistle your deadline. (Deadlines are a great way to outdistance the Watcher.)

Disguise what you are writing. If your Watcher refuses to let 12 you get on with your story or novel, write a "letter" instead, telling your "correspondent" what you are going to write in your story or next chapter. Dash off a "review" of your own unfinished opus. It will stand up like a bully to your Watcher the next time he throws more obstacles in your path. If you write yourself a good one.

Get to know your Watcher. He's yours. Do a drawing of him 13 (or her). Pin it to the wall of your study and turn it gently to the wall when necessary. Let your Watcher feel needed. Watchers are excellent critics after inspiration has been captured; they are dependable, sharp-eyed readers of things already set down. Keep your Watcher in shape and he'll have less time to keep you from shaping. If he's really ruining your whole working day sit down, as Jung did with his personal demons, and write him a letter. On a very bad day I once wrote my Watcher a letter. "Dear Watcher," I wrote, "What is it you're so afraid I'll do?" Then I held his pen for him, and he replied instantly with a candor that has kept me from truly despising him.

14   "Fail," he wrote back.

Expanding Vocabulary

1. In her essay Godwin refers to four people and one work. She does not identify them because she expects her readers to know them. Find the people and book and identify each one in a sentence. Use your dictionary or a biographical dictionary in your library if necessary.
2. Match each word in column A with its definition in column B. When in doubt, first find the word in the essay and look for context clues to aid your understanding of the word's meaning. Then, if necessary, use your dictionary to complete the matching exercise.

Column A	*Column B*
restraining (1)	note differences
sapped (1)	those who strongly dislike
allegory (2)	deadly
duration (2)	liking
discriminate (2)	holding back
severely (2)	symbolic story
notorious (4)	work
abhorrers (4)	frankness
eccentricities (4)	weakened or cut off
penchant (5)	calm down
begrudgingly (5)	reluctantly
admonishes (5)	length of time in an activity
lethal (9)	famous in a negative way
pacify (10)	warns
opus (12)	seriously or harshly
candor (13)	oddities

Understanding Content

1. Where did Godwin find the idea of a Watcher at the Gates?
2. How did reading about a Watcher make her feel?
3. What two unpleasant traits do most Watchers have?
4. What are some of the tricks Watchers use to keep us from writing?
5. What do Watchers fear? Why do many writers have a Watcher at the Gates problem?
6. What are some ways writers can outsmart their Watchers?

Drawing Inferences about Thesis and Purpose

1. What is a Watcher at the Gates? That is, what problem does the Watcher stand for?
2. What is Godwin's primary purpose in writing? To develop the idea of the Watcher? To offer some understanding of writing anxiety? To explain ways to get rid of writing anxiety?

Analyzing Strategies and Style

1. What strategy does Godwin use when she calls a restraining critic a Watcher at the Gates and suggests that writers get to know him or her? What is effective about this strategy, this approach to her subject?
2. Godwin opens with a metaphor: "sapped the juice from green inspirations." Explain the metaphor.
3. Godwin's piece is a good example of a personal essay. On the basis of your study of this essay, list the characteristics of a personal essay.
4. How would you describe the essay's tone? What elements help to create that tone?

Thinking Critically

1. Does it help you to know that many people, including professional writers, have writing anxiety? Why or why not?
2. Follow Godwin's suggestion about getting to know your Watcher. Begin by drawing, as best you can, a picture of your Watcher. Then write a brief description of this person or thing.
3. What are some of your favorite excuses for avoiding writing? Now pretend that you are Gail Godwin; how might she tell you to get around these excuses and go on to write?
4. Why do so many people suffer from writer's block? Explain.

"On Reading and Becoming a Writer"

TERRY McMILLAN

African-American writer Terry McMillan (b. 1951) has published several novels, including *Disappearing Acts* (1989), *Waiting to Exhale* (1992), and *How Stella Got Her Groove Back* (1996). An instructor in writing at the University of Arizona, McMillan has also edited *Five for Five: The Films of Spike Lee* (1991) and *Breaking Ice: An Anthology of Contemporary African-American Fiction* (1990).

The following excerpt, from the introduction to *Breaking Ice,* recounts McMillan's exciting discovery of black writers and her development as a writer.

1   As a child, I didn't know that African-American people wrote books. I grew up in a small town in northern Michigan, where the only books I came across were the Bible and required reading for school. I did not read for pleasure, and it wasn't until I was sixteen when I got a job shelving books at the public library that I got lost in a book. It was a biography of Louisa May Alcott. I was excited because I had not really read about poor white folks before; her father was so eccentric and idealistic that at the time I just thought he was crazy. I related to Louisa because she had to help support her family at a young age, which was what I was doing at the library.

2   Then one day I went to put a book away, and saw James Baldwin's face staring up at me. "Who in the world is this?" I wondered. I remember feeling embarrassed and did not read his book because I was too afraid. I couldn't imagine that he'd have anything better or different to say than Thomas Mann, Henry Thoreau, Ralph Waldo Emerson, Nathaniel Hawthorne, Ernest Hemingway, William Faulkner, etc. and a horde of other mostly white male writers that I'd been introduced to in Literature 101 in high school. I mean, not only had there not been any African-American authors included in any of those textbooks, but I'd never been given a clue that if we did have anything important to say that somebody would actually publish it. Needless to say, I was not just naïve, but had not yet acquired an ounce of black pride. I never once questioned why there were no representative works by us in any of those textbooks. After all, I had never heard of any African-American writers, and no one I knew hardly read *any* books.

3   And then things changed.

4   It wasn't until after Malcolm X had been assassinated that I found out who he was. I know I should be embarrassed about this, but I'm not. I read Alex Haley's biography of him and it literally changed my life. First and foremost, I realized that there was no reason to be ashamed of being black, that it was ridiculous. That we had a history, and much to be proud of. I began to notice how we had actually been treated as less than human; began to see our strength as a people whereas I'd only

been made aware of our inferiorities. I started thinking about my role in the world and not just on my street. I started *thinking*. Thinking about things I'd never thought about before, and the thinking turned into questions. But I had more questions than answers.

So I went to college. When I looked through the catalog and saw a class called Afro-American Literature, I signed up and couldn't wait for the first day of class. Did *we* really have enough writers to warrant an entire class? I remember the textbook was called *Dark Symphony: Negro Literature in America* because I still have it. I couldn't believe the rush I felt over and over once I discovered Countee Cullen, Langston Hughes, Ann Petry, Zora Neale Hurston, Ralph Ellison, Jean Toomer, Richard Wright, and rediscovered and read James Baldwin, to name just a few. I'm surprised I didn't need glasses by the end of the semester. My world opened up. I accumulated and gained a totally new insight about, and perception of, our lives as "black" people, as if I had been an outsider and was finally let in. To discover that our lives held as much significance and importance as our white counterparts was more than gratifying, it was exhilarating. Not only had we lived diverse, interesting, provocative, and relentless lives, but during, through, and as a result of all these painful experiences, some folks had taken the time to write it down.

Not once, throughout my entire four years as an undergraduate, did it occur to me that I might one day *be* a writer. I mean, these folks had genuine knowledge and insight. They also had a fascination with the truth. They had something to write about. Their work was bold, not flamboyant. They learned how to exploit the language so that readers would be affected by what they said and how they said it. And they had talent.

I never considered myself to be in possession of much of the above, and yet when I was twenty years old, the first man I fell in love with broke my heart. I was so devastated and felt so helpless that my reaction manifested itself in a poem. I did not sit down and say, "I'm going to write a poem about this." It was more like magic. I didn't even know I was writing a poem until I had written it. Afterward, I felt lighter, as if something had happened to lessen the pain. And when I read this "thing" I was shocked because I didn't know where the words came from. I was scared, to say the least, about what I had just experienced, because I didn't understand what had happened.

8   For the next few days, I read that poem over and over in disbelief because *I* had written it. One day, a colleague saw it lying on the kitchen table and read it. I was embarrassed and shocked when he said he liked it, then went on to tell me that he had just started a black literary magazine at the college and he wanted to publish it. Publish it! He was serious and it found its way onto a typeset page. Seeing my name in print excited me. And from that point on, if a leaf moved on a tree, I wrote a poem about it. If a crack in the sidewalk glistened, surely there was a poem in that. Some of these verbose things actually got published in various campus newspapers that were obviously desperate to fill up space. I did not call myself a poet; I told people I wrote poems.

9   Years passed.

10   Those poems started turning into sentences and I started getting nervous. What the hell did I think I was doing? Writing these little go-nowhere vignettes. All these beginnings. And who did I think I was, trying to tell a story? And who cared? Even though I had no idea what I was doing, all I knew was that I was beginning to realize that a lot of things mattered to me, things disturbed me, things that I couldn't change. Writing became an outlet for my dissatisfactions, distaste, and my way of trying to make sense of what I saw happening around me. It was my way of trying to fix what I thought was broken. It later became the only way to explore personally what I didn't understand. The problem, however, was that I was writing more about ideas than people. Everything was so "large," and eventually I had to find a common denominator. I ended up asking myself what I really cared about: it was people, and particularly African-American people.

11   The whole idea of taking myself seriously as a writer was terrifying. I didn't know any writers. Didn't know how you knew if you "had" it or not. Didn't know if I was or would ever be good enough. I didn't know how you went about the business of writing, and besides, I sincerely wanted to make a decent living. (I had read the horror stories of how so few writers were able to live off of their writing alone, many having lived like bohemians.) At first, I thought being a social worker was the right thing to do, since I was bent on saving the world (I was an idealistic twenty-two years old), but when I found out I couldn't do it that way, I had to figure out another way to

make an impact on folks. A positive impact. I ended up majoring in journalism because writing was "easy" for me, but it didn't take long for me to learn that I did not like answering the "who, what, when, where, and why" of anything. I then—upon the urging of my mother and friends who had graduated and gotten "normal" jobs—decided to try something that would still allow me to "express myself" but was relatively safer, though still risky: I went to film school. Of course what was inherent in my quest to find my "spot" in the world was this whole notion of affecting people on some grand scale. Malcolm and Martin caused me to think like this. Writing for me, as it's turned out, is philanthropy. It didn't take years for me to realize the impact that other writers' work had had on me, and if I was going to write, I did not want to write inconsequential, mediocre stories that didn't conjure up or arouse much in a reader. So I had to start by exciting myself and paying special attention to what I cared about, what mattered to me.

Film school didn't work out. Besides, I never could stop 12 writing, which ultimately forced me to stop fighting it. It took even longer to realize that writing was not something you aspired to, it was something you did because you had to. . . .

I've been teaching writing on the university level now for 13 three years, and much to my dismay, rarely have I ever had an African-American student. I wish there were more ways to encourage young people to give writing a shot. Many of them still seem to be intimidated by the English language, and think of writing as "hard"—as in Composition 101–hard. So many of them are set on "making it" (solely in material terms) that we find many of our students majoring in the "guaranteed" professions: the biological sciences, law, engineering, business, etc. If I can make an appeal to those who will read this anthology, I would like to say this to them: If for whatever reason you do not derive a genuine sense of excitement or satisfaction from your chosen field, if you are majoring in these disciplines because of a parent's insistence, if you are dissatisfied with the world to any extent and find yourself "secretly" jotting it down whenever or wherever you can; if you don't understand why people (yourself included) do the things that they do and it plagues you like an itch—consider taking a fiction writing course. Find out if there are African-American writing groups or *any* workshops that are available in your area. Then write.

Read as much "serious" fiction as you can—and not just African-American authors. Then, keep writing. "Push it," says Annie Dillard. "Examine all things intensely and relentlessly. Probe and search . . . do not leave it, do not course over it, as if it were understood, but instead follow it down until you see it in the mystery of its own specificity and strength."

14   Persist.

Expanding Vocabulary

Determine the meaning of each of the following words either from its context in this essay or from studying your dictionary. Then select five of the words and use each one in a separate sentence of your own.

eccentric (1)	bohemians (11)
exhilarating (5)	philanthropy (11)
provocative (5)	inconsequential (11)
flamboyant (6)	mediocre (11)
verbose (8)	conjure (11)
vignettes (10)	specificity (13)

Understanding Content

1. In what way did the author identify with Louisa May Alcott?
2. What writers was McMillan introduced to in high school? What writers were not part of her required reading?
3. What does McMillan confess to lacking when she was young? What book changed her thinking?
4. What did she learn from her college course in Afro-American Literature?
5. How did McMillan come to write and publish her first poem? Why did she not want to call herself a poet? What seems to have been her attitude toward writers and writing?
6. What were her reasons for writing fiction? How did she narrow and focus her writing?
7. Why did she go to film school? What was the result?
8. What dismays McMillan as a college teacher? What reasons does she offer for students' not taking a fiction writing course? What advice does she give to potential African-American writers?

Drawing Inferences about Thesis and Purpose

1. What is McMillan's purpose in writing?
2. From your reading of this essay, what personality emerges? What sort of person do you imagine McMillan to be?

Analyzing Strategies and Style

1. How would you characterize the style in which this essay is written? (Style is shaped from word choice and sentence structure.) List examples of McMillan's word choice and sentence patterns that help to create the essay's style.
2. What is McMillan's tone? That is, what voice do you hear? How does she create that tone?

Thinking Critically

1. McMillan presents a list of writers in paragraph 2 and another list in paragraph 5. How many writers from the first list do you know? How many from the second list? From your own survey (or the class's as a whole), would you conclude that students today are more familiar than McMillan was with African-American authors, or has the situation not changed much?
2. McMillan believes that students think of fiction writing as "hard" in the same way that freshman composition is hard. Which course do you think would be harder for you? Why?
3. The author concludes with advice directed to the expected audience for *Breaking Ice,* African-American students, some of whom may possibly become writers. How can her advice be applied to composition writers as well as to fiction writers? Explain.

"How to Write with Style"

KURT VONNEGUT

Kurt Vonnegut (b. 1922) is one of the most popular contemporary novelists. A former employee of General Electric in public relations, Vonnegut is now famous for such novels as *Cat's Cradle* (1963), *Slaughterhouse Five* (1969), and, most recently, *Timequake* (1993). The following advice on style was published by International Paper Company as one of a series of articles used as ads on the "Power of the Printed Word."

Newspaper reporters and technical writers are trained to reveal almost nothing about themselves in their writings. This makes them freaks in the world of writers, since almost all of the other ink-stained wretches in that world reveal a lot about 1 themselves to readers. We call these revelations, accidental and intentional, elements of style.

2   These revelations tell us as readers what sort of person it is with whom we are spending time. Does the writer sound ignorant or informed, stupid or bright, crooked or honest, humorless or playful—? And on and on.

3   Why should you examine your writing style with the idea of improving it? Do so as a mark of respect for your readers, whatever you're writing. If you scribble your thoughts any which way, your readers will surely feel that you care nothing about them. They will mark you down as an egomaniac or a chowderhead—or worse, they will stop reading you.

4   The most damning revelation you can make about yourself is that you do not know what is interesting and what is not. Don't you yourself like or dislike writers mainly for what they choose to show you or make you think about? Did you ever admire an empty-headed writer for his or her mastery of the language? No.

5   So your own winning style must begin with ideas in your head.

1. Find a Subject You Care About

6   Find a subject you care about and which you in your heart feel others should care about. It is this genuine caring, and not your games with language, which will be the most compelling and seductive element in your style.

7   I am not urging you to write a novel, by the way—although I would not be sorry if you wrote one, provided you genuinely cared about something. A petition to the mayor about a pothole in front of your house or a love letter to the girl next door will do.

2. Do Not Ramble, Though

8   I won't ramble on about that.

3. Keep It Simple

9   As for your use of language: Remember that two great masters of language, William Shakespeare and James Joyce, wrote sentences which were almost childlike when their subjects were most profound. "To be or not to be?" asks Shakespeare's Ham-

let. The longest word is three letters long. Joyce, when he was frisky, could put together a sentence as intricate and as glittering as a necklace for Cleopatra, but my favorite sentence in his short story "Eveline" is this one: "She was tired." At that point in the story, no other words could break the heart of a reader as those three words do.

Simplicity of language is not only reputable, but perhaps 10 even sacred. The *Bible* opens with a sentence well within the writing skills of a lively fourteen-year-old: "In the beginning God created the heaven and the earth."

4. Have the Guts to Cut

It may be that you, too, are capable of making necklaces for 11 Cleopatra, so to speak. But your eloquence should be the servant of the ideas in your head. Your rule might be this: If a sentence, no matter how excellent, does not illuminate your subject in some new and useful way, scratch it out.

5. Sound Like Yourself

The writing style which is most natural for you is bound to 12 echo the speech you heard when a child. English was the novelist Joseph Conrad's third language, and much that seems piquant in his use of English was no doubt colored by his first language, which was Polish. And lucky indeed is the writer who has grown up in Ireland, for the English spoken there is so amusing and musical. I myself grew up in Indianapolis, where common speech sounds like a band saw cutting galvanized tin, and employs a vocabulary as unornamental as a monkey wrench.

In some of the more remote hollows of Appalachia, children 13 still grow up hearing songs and locutions of Elizabethan times. Yes, and many Americans grow up hearing a language other than English, or an English dialect a majority of Americans cannot understand.

All these varieties of speech are beautiful, just as the varieties 14 of butterflies are beautiful. No matter what your first language, you should treasure it all your life. If it happens not to be standard English, and if it shows itself when you write standard English, the result is usually delightful, like a very pretty girl with one eye that is green and one that is blue.

15   I myself find that I trust my own writing most, and others seem to trust it most, too, when I sound most like a person from Indianapolis, which is what I am. What alternatives do I have? The one most vehemently recommended by teachers has no doubt been pressed on you, as well: to write like cultivated Englishmen of a century or more ago.

6. Say What You Mean to Say

16 I used to be exasperated by such teachers, but am no more. I understand now that all those antique essays and stories with which I was to compare my own work were not magnificent for their datedness or foreignness, but for saying precisely what their authors meant them to say. My teachers wished me to write accurately, always selecting the most effective words, and relating the words to one another unambiguously, rigidly, like parts of a machine. The teachers did not want to turn me into an Englishman after all. They hoped that I would become understandable—and therefore understood. And there went my dream of doing with words what Pablo Picasso did with paint or what any number of jazz idols did with music. If I broke all the rules of punctuation, had words mean whatever I wanted them to mean, and strung them together higgledy-piggledy, I would simply not be understood. So you, too, had better avoid Picasso-style or jazz-style writing, if you have something worth saying and wish to be understood.

17   Readers want our pages to look very much like pages they have seen before. Why? This is because they themselves have a tough job to do, and they need all the help they can get from us.

7. Pity the Readers

18 They have to identify thousands of little marks on paper, and make sense of them immediately. They have to *read*, an art so difficult that most people don't really master it even after having studied it all through grade school and high school—twelve long years.

19   So this discussion must finally acknowledge that our stylistic options as writers are neither numerous nor glamorous, since our readers are bound to be such imperfect artists. Our audience requires us to be sympathetic and patient teachers, even willing to simplify and clarify—whereas we would rather soar high above the crowd, singing like nightingales.

That is the bad news. The good news is that we Americans 20
are governed under a unique Constitution, which allows us to
write whatever we please without fear of punishment. So the
most meaningful aspect of our styles, which is what we choose
to write about, is utterly unlimited.

8. For Really Detailed Advice

For a discussion of literary style in a narrower sense, in a more 21
technical sense, I commend to your attention *The Elements of
Style,* by William Strunk, Jr., and E. B. White (Allyn & Bacon,
2000). E. B. White is, of course, one of the most admirable literary stylists this country has so far produced.

You should realize, too, that no one would care how well or 22
badly Mr. White expressed himself, if he did not have perfectly
enchanting things to say.

Expanding Vocabulary

Match each word in column A with its definition in column B. When
in doubt, first find the word in the essay and look for context clues to
aid your understanding of the word's meaning. Then, if necessary, use
your dictionary to complete the matching exercise.

Column A	*Column B*
egomaniac (3)	having many complexly
chowderhead (3)	arranged parts
intricate (9)	moving, expressive language use
reputable (10)	iron or steel with zinc coating
eloquence (11)	appealingly provocative
piquant (12)	one who is pretty dense, like a
galvanized (12)	thick soup
locutions (13)	particular style of speaking
exasperated (16)	angrily impatient
higgledy-piggledy (16)	one who has an obsessive focus
	on the self
	in utter disorder
	esteemed, of good reputation

Understanding Content

1. How will readers respond to you if you "scribble your thoughts
   any which way"?
2. A winning style begins with what?
3. What is the most compelling element in your style?

4. List the specific guidelines Vonnegut provides, each in a separate sentence.
5. Explain Vonnegut's rule for cutting.
6. Why is it best to sound like yourself?
7. What will happen when you break rules, give new meanings to words, or try to create an avant-garde style?

Drawing Inferences about Thesis and Purpose

1. What is Vonnegut's topic?
2. More than anything else, what does your style tell readers?
3. What, for Vonnegut, is the most important "element of style"?

Analyzing Strategies and Style

1. The author has little to say about his second point. What does he gain by his brevity?
2. Find some examples of clever word choice or metaphors. Explain why they are effective.

Thinking Critically

1. Which of Vonnegut's points do you think is most important for writers? Why? Which point is most important for *you* to focus on as you work on your writing? Why?
2. Vonnegut writes that simplicity is "perhaps even sacred." Explain how simple language can be called sacred. Is this a new idea for you? Does it make sense?
3. Vonnegut begins and ends emphasizing the importance of having something to say. Do you agree with him that this is the most important element of style? Why or why not?

"Little Red Riding Hood Revisited"

RUSSELL BAKER

Born in rural Virginia in 1925, Russell Baker is one of the best-known newspaper columnists. He authored his *New York Times* "Observer" column—a thrice-weekly column syndicated in over 400 newspapers—from 1947 until his recent retirement. He has won two Pulitzer Prizes, one for his columns, one for his autobiography *Growing Up* (1982). His most recent memoirs are found in *There's a Country in My Cellar* (1991). In the following column, published January 13, 1980, Baker takes a well-known folk tale and rewrites it, using some of the worst examples of bad modern writing.

In an effort to make the classics accessible to contemporary readers, I am translating them into the modern American language. Here is the translation of "Little Red Riding Hood": 1

Once upon a point in time, a small person named Little Red Riding Hood initiated plans for the preparation, delivery and transportation of foodstuffs to her grandmother, a senior citizen residing at a place of residence in a forest of indeterminate dimension. 2

In the process of implementing this program, her incursion into the forest was in midtransportation process when it attained interface with an alleged perpetrator. This individual, a wolf, made inquiry as to the whereabouts of Little Red Riding Hood's goal as well as inferring that he was desirous of ascertaining the contents of Little Red Riding Hood's foodstuffs basket, and all that. 3

"It would be inappropriate to lie to me," the wolf said, displaying his huge jaw capability. Sensing that he was a mass of repressed hostility intertwined with acute alienation, she indicated. 4

"I see you indicating," the wolf said, "but what I don't see is whatever it is you're indicating at, you dig?" 5

Little Red Riding Hood indicated more fully, making one thing perfectly clear—to wit, that it was to her grandmother's residence and with a consignment of foodstuffs that her mission consisted of taking her to and with. 6

At this point in time the wolf moderated his rhetoric and proceeded to grandmother's residence. The elderly person was then subjected to the disadvantages of total consumption and transferred to residence in the perpetrator's stomach. 7

"That will raise the old woman's consciousness," the wolf said to himself. He was not a bad wolf, but only a victim of an oppressive society, a society that not only denied wolves' rights, but actually boasted of its capacity for keeping the wolf from the door. An interior malaise made itself manifest inside the wolf. 8

9   "Is that the national malaise I sense within my digestive tract?" wondered the wolf. "Or is it the old person seeking to retaliate for her consumption by telling wolf jokes to my duodenum?" It was time to make a judgment. The time was now, the hour had struck, the body lupine cried out for decision. The wolf was up to the challenge. He took two stomach powders right away and got into bed.

10   The wolf had adopted the abdominal-distress recovery posture when Little Red Riding Hood achieved his presence.

11   "Grandmother," she said, "your ocular implements are of an extraordinary order of magnitude."

12   "The purpose of this enlarged viewing capability," said the wolf, "is to enable your image to register a more precise impression upon my sight systems."

13   "In reference to your ears," said Little Red Riding Hood, "it is noted with the deepest respect that far from being underprivileged, their elongation and enlargement appear to qualify you for unparalleled distinction."

14   "I hear you loud and clear, kid," said the wolf, "but what about these new choppers?"

15   "If it is not inappropriate," said Little Red Riding Hood, "it might be observed that with your new miracle masticating products you may even be able to chew taffy again."

16   The observation was followed by the adoption of an aggressive posture on the part of the wolf and the assertion that it was also possible for him, due to the high efficiency ratio of his jaw, to consume little persons, plus, as he stated, his firm determination to do so at once without delay and with all due process and propriety, notwithstanding the fact that the ingestion of one entire grandmother had already provided twice his daily recommended cholesterol intake.

17   There ensued flight by Little Red Riding Hood accompanied by pursuit in respect to the wolf and a subsequent intervention on the part of a third party, heretofore unnoted in the record.

18   Due to the firmness of the intervention, the wolf's stomach underwent ax-assisted aperture with the result that Red Riding Hood's grandmother was enabled to be removed with only minor discomfort.

19   The wolf's indigestion was immediately alleviated with such effectiveness that he signed a contract with the intervening third party to perform with grandmother in a television

commercial demonstrating the swiftness of this dramatic relief
for stomach discontent.

"I'm going to be on television," cried grandmother. 20

And they all joined her happily in crying, "What a 21
phenomena!"

Expanding Vocabulary

Examine the following words in their contexts in the essay and then
write a brief definition or synonym for each one. See how many you
can understand the meaning of by using context and your knowledge
of the original story.

indeterminate (2)	duodenum (9)
incursion (3)	lupine (9)
interface (3)	ocular (11)
perpetrator (3)	elongation (13)
consignment (6)	masticating (15)
malaise (8)	aperture (18)
retaliate (9)	

Understanding Content

1. If you do not know the story "Little Red Riding Hood," find a copy
   in the children's section of your public library and read it.
2. How does Baker's ending differ from the original story?

Drawing Inferences about Thesis and Purpose

1. Baker writes that he wants to make the classic "accessible" to modern readers. What is his actual purpose in writing?
2. What does Baker gain by "retelling" the entire story as a way to
   comment on modern American language?

Analyzing Strategies and Style

1. When Baker writes "Once upon a point in time"—and indeed the
   rest of paragraph 2, what characteristics of writing is he ridiculing?
2. In paragraph 5, what kind of language is he ridiculing with the
   words "you dig"?
3. In paragraph 8, we are assured that the grandmother-eating wolf
   is not really a bad wolf but a victim of "an oppressive society."
   What kind of writing and what attitudes are satirized here?
4. The language and sentence patterns in paragraphs 16 and 17 sound
   like the writing of what professional group?

Thinking Critically

1. What makes Baker's "version" amusing? Why do we chuckle as we read?
2. What group of readers will not be able to laugh much at Baker's cleverness? What does this tell you about one of the reasons why reading a work can be easy for some readers and difficult for others?
3. On a serious note, what elements of language use offend Baker? What kinds of writing can you learn to avoid from him?

MAKING CONNECTIONS

1. Several writers in this chapter refer to other writers in their essays. Select a writer referred to in this chapter whom you do not know much about and read about that writer in at least two sources in your library or online. Then prepare a short biography (that includes a list of the author's major works) for your class.

2. Godwin, Vonnegut, and McMillan are all authors of novels. After becoming acquainted with each of these writers through their essays in this chapter, which one's novels do you most want to read? Be prepared to defend your choice. Alternatively, read a novel by the writer of your choice and prepare a two-page summary and evaluation of the novel for your class.

3. Both Vonnegut and Baker examine writing style. Compare and contrast their observations. Can you defend the assertion that both writers are making similar points, just doing it differently?

TOPICS AND GUIDELINES FOR WRITING

1. Terry McMillan offers some insight into how she creates her literature. How do you get started on a piece of writing? How do ideas come to you? What strategies do you use? In an essay explain the ways you get started on a piece of writing. Your purpose in writing should be either to offer your strategies as a useful way to get started or to offer your ap-

proach as a way to avoid because, on reflection, you have decided that your approach is not very effective.

2. How have you learned to fool your Watcher at the Gates (see Godwin, p. 17)? In an essay give your advice to anxious writers for avoiding writer's block, based on techniques that have worked for you. Think of your essay as possibly a feature article in your college paper. (Remember: If you use the term "Watcher at the Gates," give Godwin credit.)

3. What kind of reading do you enjoy most? Do you like science fiction, romance novels, the newspaper, magazines devoted to a special interest or hobby? In an essay explain why you enjoy the kind of material you usually read. Illustrate your reasons with specific examples from your reading.

4. Terry McMillan advises future writers to read as much fiction as they can. What are good reasons for reading? In an essay explain and support reasons for encouraging college students to read more.

5. This chapter's introduction offers some reasons for writing. Why should adults become competent writers? Why should an engineer, a banker, or a teacher be able to write? In an essay answer these questions. Focus either on the practical considerations of a particular job or on more philosophical reasons having to do with personal growth and discovery or general career needs. Remember to explain and illustrate each reason.

2

Using Narration

Growing Up, Growing Wiser

"Once upon a time there lived a princess"—so the fairy tale begins. A story, or narrative, relates a series of events in time sequence. If the narrative relates events that are made up out of the writer's imagination, then the narrative is *fiction*. If the narrative relates events that have taken place, it is *nonfiction*. Nonfiction narratives are found in histories, biographies, newspaper articles, and essays that use narration as a development strategy.

In some writing, distinction between fiction and nonfiction blurs. The historical novel, for example, is fiction bound by the author's research of a particular time and place. Many feature articles in newspapers and magazines reveal the use of such story elements as conflict and point of view. Fiction is illustrated in this chapter by Sandra Cisneros's "Eleven." Santha Rama Rau's "By Any Other Name" is a good example of nonfiction that strikes us as very much like a story.

When to Use Narration

Your instructor may ask you to write a story, a narrative account drawn, perhaps, from some incident in your life, complete with characters and dialogue. More likely, you will be asked to draw on incidents from your life to develop a narrative essay. This means that narration will be used as a technique for developing a main idea or thesis. Your purpose in writing may be to share experiences or inform readers of a different time, place, or culture, or some blending of both purposes. However you see your primary purpose in writing, the incidents you select, the way you tell about them, and the reflective comments you include will add up to a statement (or strong implication) of the main point you want to make.

How to Use Narration

Purpose and Thesis

The fewer observations you make about the significance of the events you narrate, the more you need to rely on the telling of the events to carry your meaning. Rau, for example, tells her story with only the briefest of comments about the significance of one's first day at school. Gaye Wagner, on the other hand, reflects on the events she narrates, observing in paragraph 4, "With the death of a comrade, I understood that I was inside the fence." Only you can decide just how much comment you want in a given narrative essay and where those comments should be placed to greatest effect. But first, and most important, have a clear sense of purpose and thesis. An unfocused retelling of some event in your life does not become a polished essay.

When thinking about experiences you might use in a narrative essay, reflect on your purpose and subject as a way to decide on a thesis. Ask, "Why do I want to tell readers about a particular incident?" "What insights into human life do I find in the incident?" Try analyzing your experiences as potential stories shaped by a central conflict that is resolved in some way. But remember that resolution does not necessarily mean a happy ending. Often the only resolution to some experiences is a lesson, bitterly learned. Growing up seems, all too often, to be filled with such painful lessons. Fortunately, they can become the topics of good stories and essays.

Organization and Details

After selecting your topic and deciding on a tentative thesis, think about the shape of your essay. The good narrative essay does not include every stray telephone call that you received the day of the big game. Select the details that are truly significant, that will carry the meaning of the experience for readers. Make your writing vivid through the use of concrete details, but be sure that they are details that contribute to the support of your thesis.

Usually narratives are presented in chronological order, but you may want to consider beginning at the end of the event and then going back to recount the events leading up to the key moment. N. Scott Momaday follows chronology strictly in telling of the experience that "ended" his childhood. By contrast, Wagner begins with her feelings after an officer's death and then goes back in time to recount his death and funeral before going forward to tell of the event after his death that altered her thinking. Varying time sequence requires careful attention to verb tenses and transition words and phrases so that readers can follow the shifts in time. Some transition words you may need to use include *first, next, then, after, the following day (week, etc.), meanwhile, at the same time.* You will find other examples in the essays in this chapter.

Another choice you must make is the perspective or point of view from which the incident will be told. Most narrative essays are told in the first person. With strong understatement, Momaday begins: "At Jemez I came to the end of my childhood." Some writers prefer to use the third person (he, she, they) even though they are writing about their own experiences. Another choice to make is the vantage point of the narrator or essayist. Do you want to take your reader into the event at the time it occurred in your life? That is, should you tell it as if it is occurring as you write? Or, should you select the distance of the adult voice reflecting back on a childhood experience? When Elizabeth Wong writes: "At last I was one of you; I wasn't one of them. Sadly, I still am," we hear the voice of the adult thinking back to her experience with Chinese school.

Keep in mind these several steps when planning your narrative essay. We all have stories to tell, experiences worth sharing with others. The key is to shape those experiences into a composition that brings readers into our lives and makes them want to know us and understand us, and thereby to understand better what they share with us.

Getting Started: Reflections on Growing Up

Think back over your growing-up years. What periods in your life, particular events, or individuals come to mind as having had an impact on you, perhaps moving you closer to adulthood, to a clearer understanding of yourself and of life? What, on reflection, was an important period in your life? What was an event that changed you in some way? Who was an influential person? Why was he or she important? Write some of your reflections on these questions in a journal entry. Keep your reflections in mind as you read the essays in this chapter, thinking as you read about ways you might use your experiences in an effective narrative essay.

"Always Running"

LUIS J. RODRIGUEZ

Luis Rodriguez (b. 1954) is a poet, journalist, and community activist who grew up poor in Los Angeles, struggled with drugs and gangs, and held many odd jobs before and during his years at East Los Angeles College, Berkeley, and UCLA. He has served as a facilitator for various writing workshops, particularly with migrant workers and in homeless shelters, and has published two books of poems, *Poems Across the Pavement* (1989) and *The Concrete River* (1991). In the following (an excerpt from Chapter 2 of Rodriguez's memoir *Always Running* [1993]), observe how the author combines descriptive details and dialogue—and uses restraint effectively.

"If you ain't from no barrio, then you ain't born."

—a 10-year-old boy from South San Gabriel

One evening dusk came early in South San Gabriel, with 1
wind and cold spinning to earth. People who had been sitting on porches or on metal chairs near fold-up tables topped with cards and beer bottles collected their things to go inside. Others put on sweaters or jackets. A storm gathered beyond the trees.

Tino and I strolled past the stucco and wood-frame homes 2
of the neighborhood consisting mostly of Mexicans with a sprinkling of poor white families (usually from Oklahoma, Arkansas and Texas). *Ranchera* music did battle with Country & Western songs as we continued toward the local elementary school, an oil-and-grime stained basketball under my arm.

We stopped in front of a chain-link fence which surrounded 3
the school. An old brick building cast elongated shadows over

a basketball court of concrete on the other side of the fence. Leaves and paper swirled in tiny tornadoes.

4   "Let's go over," Tino proposed.

5   I looked up and across the fence. A sign above us read: NO ONE ALLOWED AFTER 4:30 PM, BY ORDER OF THE LOS ANGELES COUNTY SHERIFF'S DEPARTMENT. Tino turned toward me, shrugged his shoulders and gave me a who-cares look.

6   "Help me up, man, then throw the ball over."

7   I cupped my hands and lifted Tino up while the boy scaled the fence, jumped over and landed on sneakered feet.

8   "Come on, Luis, let's go," Tino shouted from the other side.

9   I threw over the basketball, walked back a ways, then ran and jumped on the fence, only to fall back. Although we were both 10 years old, I cut a shorter shadow.

10   "Forget you, man," Tino said. "I'm going to play without you."

11   "Wait!" I yelled, while walking further back. I crouched low to the ground, then took off, jumped up and placed torn sneakers in the steel mesh. I made it over with a big thud.

12   Wiping the grass and dirt from my pants, I casually walked up to the ball on the ground, picked it up, and continued past Tino toward the courts.

13   "Hey Tino, what are you waiting for?"

14   The gusts proved no obstacle for a half-court game of B-ball, even as dark clouds smothered the sky.

15   Boy voices interspersed with ball cracking on asphalt. Tino's lanky figure seemed to float across the court, as if he had wings under his thin arms. Just then, a black-and-white squad car cruised down the street. A searchlight sprayed across the school yard. The vehicle slowed to a halt. The light shone toward the courts and caught Tino in mid-flight of a lay-up.

16   The dribbling and laughter stopped.

17   "All right, this is the sheriff's," a voice commanded. Two deputies stood by the fence, batons and flashlights in hand.

18   "Let's get out of here," Tino responded.

19   "What do you mean?" I countered. "Why don't we just stay here?"

20   "You nuts! We trespassing, man," Tino replied. "When they get a hold of us, they going to beat the crap out of us."

"Are you sure?" 21

"I know, believe me, I know." 22

"So where do we go?" 23

By then one of the deputies shouted back: "You boys get 24
over here by the fence—now!"

But Tino dropped the ball and ran. I heard the deputies yell 25
for Tino to stop. One of them began climbing the fence. I decided to take off too.

It never stopped, this running. We were constant prey, and 26
the hunters soon became big blurs: the police, the gangs, the
junkies, the dudes on Garvey Boulevard who took our money,
all smudged into one. Sometimes they were teachers who
jumped on us Mexicans as if we were born with a hideous
stain. We were always afraid. Always running.

Tino and I raced toward the dark boxes called classrooms. 27
The rooms lay there, hauntingly still without the voices of children, the commands of irate teachers or the clapping sounds of
books as they were closed. The rooms were empty, forbidden
places at night. We scurried around the structures toward a
courtyard filled with benches next to the cafeteria building.

Tino hopped on a bench, then pulled himself over a high 28
fence. He walked a foot or two on top of it, stopped, and proceeded to climb over to the cafeteria's rooftop. I looked over
my shoulder. The deputies weren't far behind, their guns
drawn. I grabbed hold of the fence on the side of the cafeteria.
I looked up and saw Tino's perspiring face over the roof's edge,
his arm extended down toward me.

I tried to climb up, my feet dangling. But then a firm hand 29
seized a foot and pulled at it.

"They got me!" I yelled. 30

Tino looked below. A deputy spied the boy and called out: 31
"Get down here . . . you *greaser!*"

Tino straightened up and disappeared. I heard a flood of 32
footsteps on the roof—then a crash. Soon an awful calm covered us.

"Tino!" I cried out. 33

A deputy restrained me as the other one climbed onto the 34
roof. He stopped at a skylight, jagged edges on one of its sides.
Shining a flashlight inside the building, the officer spotted Tino's
misshapen body on the floor, sprinkled over with shards of glass.

Expanding Vocabulary

Study the contexts in which the following words are used, or study their definitions in your dictionary, and then use each word in a separate sentence.

elongated (3)   smudged (26)
scaled (7)   hauntingly (27)
obstacle (14)   irate (27)
interspersed (15)   scurried (27)

Understanding Content

1. Briefly summarize the situation of the narrative by answering the reporter's questions: who, what, where, when.
2. When the police officers arrive, what does Tino recommend? Why does he choose his course of action?
3. What happens to Tino?

Drawing Inferences about Thesis and Purpose

1. What does the quotation at the opening of the excerpt contribute to the essay?
2. Although both Tino and Luis are 10 years old, their relationship does not seem quite equal. Which one seems to be the leader? How do you know?
3. Since Tino is already on the court, why does Luis say, in paragraph 13, "What are you waiting for?" What does he want to accomplish?
4. What is Rodriguez's purpose in writing? What is his thesis?

Analyzing Strategies and Style

1. Examine the author's opening three paragraphs. What do we learn about the narrator from the opening? What tone do the paragraphs establish?
2. Rodriguez includes several metaphors and images in his writing. Find three and explain each one's meaning and contribution.

Thinking Critically

1. Are you surprised by Tino's assertion that the police will beat the boys if they are caught? Do you think that he overstates and overreacts? If you think so, how would you explain your views to Rodriguez? If you agree with Rodriguez, do you have evidence to support your views?
2. Rodriguez writes that the many "hunters" blur into one. Included are teachers "who jumped on us Mexicans." Does this statement surprise you? Why or why not?

3. What are some strategies young people can use to try to cope with gangs, with drug dealers, and with prejudiced teachers?

"The Struggle to Be an All-American Girl"

ELIZABETH WONG

A native of Los Angeles and graduate of the University of Southern California, Elizabeth Wong (b. 1958) began her career as a journalist in southern California. Now interested in playwriting, Wong lives in New York where she attended New York University's Tisch School of the Arts. She has written several plays and screenplays, including *Kimchee and Chitlins: A Serious Comedy about Getting Along* (1996), and *Letters to a Student Revolutionary* (1996). In the following article, published originally in the *Los Angeles Times,* Wong examines her attitudes toward growing up Chinese in American society.

It's still there, the Chinese school on Yale Street where my brother and I used to go. Despite the new coat of paint and the high wire fence, the school I knew ten years ago remains remarkably, stoically the same.

Every day at 5 P.M., instead of playing with our fourth- and fifth-grade friends or sneaking out to the empty lot to hunt ghosts and animal bones, my brother and I had to go to Chinese school. No amount of kicking, screaming, or pleading could dissuade my mother, who was solidly determined to have us learn the language of our heritage.

Forcibly, she walked us the seven long, hilly blocks from our home to school, depositing our defiant tearful faces before the stern principal. My only memory of him is that he swayed on his heels like a palm tree, and he always clasped his impatient twitching hands behind his back. I recognized him as a repressed maniacal child killer, and knew that if we ever saw his hands we'd be in big trouble.

We all sat in little chairs in an empty auditorium. The room smelled like Chinese medicine, an imported faraway mustiness. Like ancient mothballs or dirty closets. I hated that smell.

I favored crisp new scents. Like the soft French perfume that my American teacher wore in public school.

5   There was a stage far to the right, flanked by an American flag and the flag of the Nationalist Republic of China, which was also red, white and blue but not as pretty.

6   Although the emphasis at the school was mainly language—speaking, reading, writing—the lessons always began with an exercise in politeness. With the entrance of the teacher, the best student would tap a bell and everyone would get up, kowtow, and chant, "Sing san ho," the phonetic for "How are you, teacher?"

7   Being ten years old, I had better things to learn than ideographs copied painstakingly in lines that ran right to left from the tip of a *moc but*, a real ink pen that had to be held in an awkward way if blotches were to be avoided. After all, I could do the multiplication tables, name the satellites of Mars, and write reports on *Little Women* and *Black Beauty*. Nancy Drew, my favorite book heroine, never spoke Chinese.

8   The language was a source of embarrassment. More times than not, I had tried to disassociate myself from the nagging loud voice that followed me wherever I wandered in the nearby American supermarket outside Chinatown. The voice belonged to my grandmother, a fragile woman in her seventies who could outshout the best of the street vendors. Her humor was raunchy, her Chinese rhythmless, patternless. It was quick, it was loud, it was unbeautiful. It was not like the quiet, lilting romance of French or the gentle refinement of the American South. Chinese sounded pedestrian. Public.

9   In Chinatown, the comings and goings of hundreds of Chinese on their daily tasks sounded chaotic and frenzied. I did not want to be thought of as mad, as talking gibberish. When I spoke English, people nodded at me, smiled sweetly, said encouraging words. Even the people in my culture would cluck and say that I'd do well in life. "My, doesn't she move her lips fast," they would say, meaning that I'd be able to keep up with the world outside Chinatown.

10   My brother was even more fanatical than I about speaking English. He was especially hard on my mother, criticizing her, often cruelly, for her pidgin speech—smatterings of Chinese scattered like chop suey in her conversation. "It's not 'What it is,' Mom," he'd say in exasperation. "It's 'What *is* it, what *is* it,

what *is* it!' " Sometimes Mom might leave out an occasional "the" or "a," or perhaps a verb of being. He would stop her in mid-sentence: "Say it again, Mom. Say it right." When he tripped over his own tongue, he'd blame it on her: "See, Mom, it's all your fault. You set a bad example."

What infuriated my mother most was when my brother cor- 11
nered her on her consonants, especially "r." My father had played a cruel joke on Mom by assigning her an American name that her tongue wouldn't allow her to say. No matter how hard she tried, "Ruth" always ended up "Luth" or "Roof."

After two years of writing with a *moc but* and reciting words 12
with multiples of meanings, I finally was granted a cultural divorce. I was permitted to stop Chinese school.

I thought of myself as multicultural. I preferred tacos to egg 13
rolls; I enjoyed Cinco de Mayo more than Chinese New Year.

At last, I was one of you; I wasn't one of them. 14

Sadly, I still am. 15

Expanding Vocabulary

Match each word in column A with its definition in column B. When in doubt, first find the word in the essay and look for context clues to aid your understanding of the word's meaning. Then, if necessary, use your dictionary to complete the matching exercise.

Column A	*Column B*
stoically (1)	insane
dissuade (2)	meaningless talk
defiant (3)	obscene
maniacal (3)	not showing emotion,
kowtow (6)	impassive
phonetic (6)	corresponding to pronunciation
ideographs (7)	convince not to do something
raunchy (8)	agitated
pedestrian (8)	simplified version of one lan-
frenzied (9)	guage with some elements
gibberish (9)	of a second language
fanatical (10)	rebellious
pidgin (10)	intolerant
	lacking distinction
	bow in subservience
	picture symbols used to make
	words

Understanding Content

1. What details of American culture does Wong provide to establish contrast and reveal her preference?
2. What is Wong's attitude toward the Chinese language? What was her brother's attitude toward speaking English?
3. When Wong says that Chinese sounded "pedestrian," "frenzied," and like "gibberish," how are we to understand her statements? Do these judgments tell us about Chinese or about Wong's feelings?
4. Wong was finally freed from attending Chinese school. How did she feel at the time?

Drawing Inferences about Thesis and Purpose

1. Wong does not recount one incident but rather discusses a period in her life. State the subject of her essay.
2. What is Wong's thesis? What point does she establish about her subject? (Wong does not state a thesis; you will have to write one for the essay.)
3. Wong thought of herself as "multicultural." Explain her meaning.
4. Explain the essay's last sentence.

Analyzing Strategies and Style

1. In the opening paragraphs, Wong describes the Chinese school that she attended. List all the words and phrases that express her feelings about the school. (Note: Some are direct, others more subtle. Look at her description of the teacher, for example.)
2. Wong describes her Chinese principal as a "repressed maniacal child killer." How are we to understand her description? What does the author accomplish with this description?
3. In paragraph 4, the author uses two sentence fragments. What do they contribute to the paragraph? How are they effective?
4. Wong also uses several metaphors. Find two, expressed as similes. Explain each one.
5. Examine the sentence patterns (in the second half of paragraph 8) used to discuss the Chinese language. How does Wong vary the sentences to reinforce her point?

Thinking Critically

1. Have you ever been embarrassed by something a parent said or did, or the way he or she spoke or dressed? If so, how old were you? Do children and adolescents usually outgrow these feelings? Why do so many young people experience them? What are some situations in which children embarrass parents?

2. Were you required to do something as a child that was different from what your classmates or friends did? (For example, take violin lessons when none of your friends did, or attend religious instruction after school.) If so, how did you feel about it then? Have your attitudes changed? If so, in what way?
3. Should children be forced to attend a school or participate in an activity that they do not want to attend or participate in? Why or why not?

"The End of My Childhood"

N. SCOTT MOMADAY

An English professor at the University of Arizona, N. Scott Momaday (b. 1934) is an artist, poet (*The Gourd Dancer*), Pulitzer Prize–winning novelist (*House Made of Dawn*), and author of a much-praised autobiography, *The Names: A Memoir*, published in 1976. Momaday, whose father was a Kiowa, explores this heritage in his memoir, capturing the American Indian's sense of harmony with the Earth. The following excerpt from *The Names* recounts Momaday's loss of childhood innocence.

At Jemez I came to the end of my childhood. There were no 1 schools within easy reach. I had to go nearly thirty miles to school at Bernalillo, and one year I lived away in Albuquerque. My mother and father wanted me to have the benefit of a sound preparation for college, and so we read through many high school catalogues. After long deliberation we decided that I should spend my last year of high school at a military academy in Virginia.

The day before I was to leave I went walking across the river 2 to the red mesa, where many times before I had gone to be alone with my thoughts. And I had climbed several times to the top of the mesa and looked among the old ruins there for pottery. This time I chose to climb the north end, perhaps because I had not gone that way before and wanted to see what it was. It was a difficult climb, and when I got to the top I was spent. I lingered among the ruins for more than an hour, I judge, waiting for my strength to return. From there I could see the whole valley below, the fields, the river, and the village. It was all very beautiful, and the sight of it filled me with longing.

3   I looked for an easier way to come down, and at length I found a broad, smooth runway of rock, a shallow groove winding out like a stream. It appeared to be safe enough, and I started to follow it. There were steps along the way, a stairway, in effect. But the steps became deeper and deeper, and at last I had to drop down the length of my body and more. Still it seemed convenient to follow in the groove of rock. I was more than halfway down when I came upon a deep, funnel-shaped formation in my path. And there I had to make a decision. The slope on either side was extremely steep and forbidding, and yet I thought that I could work my way down on either side. The formation at my feet was something else. It was perhaps ten or twelve feet deep, wide at the top and narrow at the bottom, where there appeared to be a level ledge. If I could get down through the funnel to the ledge, I should be all right; surely the rest of the way down was negotiable. But I realized that there could be no turning back. Once I was down in that rocky chute I could not get up again, for the round wall which nearly encircled the space there was too high and sheer. I elected to go down into it, to try for the ledge directly below. I eased myself down the smooth, nearly vertical wall on my back, pressing my arms and legs outward against the sides. After what seemed a long time I was trapped in the rock. The ledge was no longer there below me; it had been an optical illusion. Now, in this angle of vision, there was nothing but the ground, far, far below, and jagged boulders set there like teeth. I remember that my arms were scraped and bleeding, stretched out against the walls with all the pressure that I could exert. When once I looked down I saw that my legs, also spread out and pressed hard against the walls, were shaking violently. I was in an impossible situation: I could not move in any direction, save downward in a fall, and I could not stay beyond another minute where I was. I believed then that I would die there, and I saw with a terrible clarity the things of the valley below. They were not the less beautiful to me. It seemed to me that I grew suddenly very calm in view of that beloved world. And I remember nothing else of that moment. I passed out of my mind, and the next thing I knew I was sitting down on the

ground, very cold in the shadows, and looking up at the rock where I had been within an eyelash of eternity. That was a strange thing in my life, and I think of it as the end of an age. I should never again see the world as I saw it on the other side of that moment, in the bright reflection of time lost. There are such reflections, and for some of them I have the names.

Expanding Vocabulary

Examine the following words in their contexts in the essay and then write a brief definition or synonym for each one. (Do not use a dictionary; try to guess the word's meaning from its context.)

mesa (2)
negotiable (3)
chute (3)
optical illusion (3)

Understanding Content

1. What were the circumstances that led Momaday to the event at Jemez?
2. Momaday presents dramatic details of the incident. Where was he climbing? What could he see at the top of his climb? How did the view make him feel?
3. Why did Momaday choose to come down a different way? After starting down, what decision did he have to make?
4. How did that decision turn out to be critical? What situation did it lead to?
5. When stretched across the rocky chute, what does Momaday think about initially? Then what happens to him?

Drawing Inferences about Thesis and Purpose

1. Momaday says that this experience marked "the end of an age." Why? Why will he "never again see the world as I [he] saw it on the other side of that moment"? What did Momaday have to face on the rocky chute?
2. What is Momaday's thesis?

Analyzing Strategies and Style

1. Describe Momaday's presentation. How is his narrative organized? What is the point of view? Does the author take us back to the time of the incident or keep us in the perspective of the adult

writer? Why do the choices of the author seem the right ones for this narrative?

2. Analyze Momaday's style of writing. Is his word choice mostly informal or formal, concrete or abstract? Are his sentences mostly simple or complex, short or long, straightforward or highly qualified? Again, why do the choices seem right for the telling of this narrative? What does he gain by his choice of style?

3. Momaday uses an effective metaphor in the middle of paragraph 3: "jagged boulders set there like teeth." Explain the comparison and its emotional effect.

Thinking Critically

1. Momaday took his climb "to be alone with my [his] thoughts" before his move to a new state and school. Why is it good to take time for reflection before major changes in our lives? Do you take time for reflection, for time alone, on a regular basis? Why or why not?

2. Many people like to test themselves physically, believing that such activities build character as well as muscles. Do you enjoy some strenuous physical activity? If so, what are your reasons for the activity? What do you think you have gained?

3. Have you ever experienced a situation of physical danger? If so, what were your thoughts and feelings at the time? What were your reactions to the event after the danger had passed? Did the experience change you in any way? If so, how?

"By Any Other Name"

SANTHA RAMA RAU

Santha Rama Rau (b. 1923) was born in India and lived her early years there, during British colonial rule of India. She has also been educated in England and at Wellesley College in the United States. A novelist, essayist, and travel writer, Rama Rau's books include *Home to India* (1945) and *Gifts of Passage* (1961). "By Any Other Name," a recounting of her experience at a British-run school in India, was first published in 1951 in *The New Yorker*.

1   At the Anglo-Indian day school in Zorinabad to which my sister and I were sent when she was eight and I was five and a half, they changed our names. On the first day of school, a hot, windless morning of a north Indian September, we stood in the

headmistress's study and she said, "Now you're the *new* girls. What are your names?"

My sister answered for us. "I am Premila, and she"—nodding in my direction—"is Santha." 2

The headmistress had been in India, I suppose, fifteen years or so, but she still smiled her helpless inability to cope with Indian names. Her rimless half-glasses glittered, and the precarious bun on the top of her head trembled as she shook her head. "Oh, my dears, those are much too hard for me. Suppose we give you pretty English names. Wouldn't that be more jolly? Let's see, now—Pamela for you, I think." She shrugged in a baffled way at my sister. "That's as close as I can get. And for *you*," she said to me, "how about Cynthia? Isn't that nice?" 3

My sister was always less easily intimidated than I was, and while she kept a stubborn silence, I said, "Thank you," in a very tiny voice. 4

We had been sent to that school because my father, among his responsibilities as an officer of the civil service, had a tour of duty to perform in the villages around that steamy little provincial town, where he had his headquarters at that time. He used to make his shorter inspection tours on horseback, and a week before, in the stale heat of a typically postmonsoon day, we had waved good-by to him and a little procession—an assistant, a secretary, two bearers, and the man to look after the bedding rolls and luggage. They rode away through our large garden, still bright green from the rains, and we turned back into the twilight of the house and the sound of fans whispering in every room. 5

Up to then, my mother had refused to send Premila to school in the British-run establishments of that time, because, she used to say, "you can bury a dog's tail for seven years and it still comes out curly, and you can take a Britisher away from his home for a lifetime and he still remains insular." The examinations and degrees from entirely Indian schools were not, in those days, considered valid. In my case, the question had never come up, and probably never would have come up if Mother's extraordinary good health had not broken down. For the first time in my life, she was not able to continue the lessons she had been giving us every morning. So our Hindi books were put away, the stories of the Lord Krishna as a little boy were left in mid-air, and we were sent to the Anglo-Indian school. 6

7   That first day at school is still, when I think of it, a remarkable one. At that age, if one's name is changed, one develops a curious form of dual personality. I remember having a certain detached and disbelieving concern in the actions of "Cynthia," but certainly no responsibility. Accordingly, I followed the thin, erect back of the headmistress down the veranda to my classroom feeling, at most, a passing interest in what was going to happen to me in this strange, new atmosphere of School.

8   The building was Indian in design, with wide verandas opening onto a central courtyard, but Indian verandas are usually white-washed, with stone floors. These, in the tradition of British schools, were painted dark brown and had matting on the floors. It gave a feeling of extra intensity to the heat.

9   I suppose there were about a dozen Indian children in the school—which contained perhaps forty children in all—and four of them were in my class. They were all sitting at the back of the room, and I went to join them. I sat next to a small, solemn girl who didn't smile at me. She had long, glossy-black braids and wore a cotton dress, but she still kept on her Indian jewelry—a gold chain around her neck, thin gold bracelets, and tiny ruby studs in her ears. Like most Indian children, she had a rim of black kohl around her eyes. The cotton dress should have looked strange, but all I could think of was that I should ask my mother if I couldn't wear a dress to school, too, instead of my Indian clothes.

10   I can't remember too much about the proceedings in class that day, except for the beginning. The teacher pointed to me and asked me to stand up. "Now, dear, tell the class your name."

11   I said nothing.

12   "Come along," she said, frowning slightly. "What's your name, dear?"

13   "I don't know," I said, finally.

14   The English children in the front of the class—there were about eight or ten of them—giggled and twisted around in their chairs to look at me. I sat down quickly and opened my eyes very wide, hoping in that way to dry them off. The little girl with the braids put out her hand and very lightly touched my arm. She still didn't smile.

15   A lot of that morning I was rather bored. I looked briefly at the children's drawings pinned to the wall, and then concentrated on a lizard clinging to the ledge of the high, barred win-

dow behind the teacher's head. Occasionally it would shoot out its long yellow tongue for a fly, and then it would rest, with its eyes closed and its belly palpitating, as though it were swallowing several times quickly. The lessons were mostly concerned with reading and writing and simple numbers—things that my mother had already taught me—and I paid very little attention. The teacher wrote on the easel black-board words like "bat" and "cat," which seemed babyish to me; only "apple" was new and incomprehensible.

When it was time for the lunch recess, I followed the girl 16 with braids out onto the veranda. There the children from the other classes were assembled. I saw Premila at once and ran over to her, as she had charge of our lunchbox. The children were all opening packages and sitting down to eat sandwiches. Premila and I were the only ones who had Indian food—thin wheat chapatties, some vegetable curry, and a bottle of buttermilk. Premila thrust half of it into my hand and whispered fiercely that I should go and sit with my class, because that was what the others seemed to be doing.

The enormous black eyes of the little Indian girl from my 17 class looked at my food longingly, so I offered her some. But she only shook her head and plowed her way solemnly through her sandwiches.

I was very sleepy after lunch, because at home we always 18 took a siesta. It was usually a pleasant time of day, with the bedroom darkened against the harsh afternoon sun, the drifting off into sleep with the sound of Mother's voice reading a story in one's mind, and, finally, the shrill, fussy voice of the ayah waking one for tea.

At school, we rested for a short time on low, folding cots on 19 the veranda, and then we were expected to play games. During the hot part of the afternoon we played indoors, and after the shadows had begun to lengthen and the slight breeze of the evening had come up we moved outside to the wide courtyard.

I had never really grasped the system of competitive games. 20 At home, whenever we played tag or guessing games, I was always allowed to "win"—"because," Mother used to tell Premila, "she is the youngest, and we have to allow for that." I had often heard her say it, and it seemed quite reasonable to me, but the result was that I had no clear idea of what "winning" meant.

21   When we played twos-and-threes that afternoon at school, in accordance with my training, I let one of the small English boys catch me, but was naturally rather puzzled when the other children did not return the courtesy. I ran about for what seemed like hours without ever catching anyone, until it was time for school to close. Much later I learned that my attitude was called "not being a good sport," and I stopped allowing myself to be caught, but it was not for years that I really learned the spirit of the thing.

22   When I saw our car come up to the school gate, I broke away from my classmates and rushed toward it yelling, "Ayah! Ayah!" It seemed like an eternity since I had seen her that morning—a wizened, affectionate figure in her white cotton sari, giving me dozens of urgent and useless instructions on how to be a good girl at school. Premila followed more sedately, and she told me on the way home never to do that again in front of the other children.

23   When we got home we went straight to Mother's high, white room to have tea with her, and I immediately climbed onto the bed and bounced gently up and down on the springs. Mother asked how we had liked our first day in school. I was so pleased to be home and to have left that peculiar Cynthia behind that I had nothing whatever to say about school, except to ask what "apple" meant. But Premila told Mother about the classes, and added that in her class they had weekly tests to see if they had learned their lessons well.

24   I asked, "What's a test?"

25   Premila said, "You're too small to have them. You won't have them in your class for donkey's years." She had learned the expression that day and was using it for the first time. We all laughed enormously at her wit. She also told Mother, in an aside, that we should take sandwiches to school the next day. Not, she said, that *she* minded. But they would be simpler for me to handle.

26   That whole lovely evening I didn't think about school at all. I sprinted barefoot across the lawns with my favorite playmate, the cook's son, to the stream at the end of the garden. We quarreled in our usual way, waded in the tepid water under the lime trees, and waited for the night to bring out the smell of the jasmine. I listened with fascination to his stories of ghosts and demons, until I was too frightened to cross the garden alone in

the semidarkness. The ayah found me, shouted at the cook's son, scolded me, hurried me in to supper—it was an entirely usual, wonderful evening.

It was a week later, the day of Premila's first test, that our lives changed rather abruptly. I was sitting at the back of my class, in my usual inattentive way, only half listening to the teacher. I had started a rather guarded friendship with the girl with the braids, whose name turned out to be Nalini (Nancy, in school). The three other Indian children were already fast friends. Even at that age it was apparent to all of us that friendship with the English or Anglo-Indian children was out of the question. Occasionally, during the class, my new friend and I would draw pictures and show them to each other secretly. 27

The door opened sharply and Premila marched in. At first, the teacher smiled at her in a kindly and encouraging way and said, "Now, you're little Cynthia's sister?" 28

Premila didn't even look at her. She stood with her feet planted firmly apart and her shoulders rigid, and addressed herself directly to me. "Get up," she said. "We're going home." 29

I didn't know what had happened, but I was aware that it was a crisis of some sort. I rose obediently and started to walk toward my sister. 30

"Bring your pencils and your notebook," she said. 31

I went back for them, and together we left the room. The teacher started to say something just as Premila closed the door, but we didn't wait to hear what it was. 32

In complete silence we left the school grounds and started to walk home. Then I asked Premila what the matter was. All she would say was "We're going home for good." 33

It was a very tiring walk for a child of five and a half, and I dragged along behind Premila with my pencils growing sticky in my hand. I can still remember looking at the dusty hedges, and the tangles of thorns in the ditches by the side of the road, smelling the faint fragrance from the eucalyptus trees and wondering whether we would ever reach home. Occasionally a horse-drawn tonga passed us, and the women, in their pink or green silks, stared at Premila and me trudging along on the side of the road. A few coolies and a line of women carrying baskets of vegetables on their heads smiled at us. But it was nearing the hottest time of day, and the road was almost deserted. I walked more and more slowly, and shouted to Premila, from time to 34 time, "Wait for me!" with increasing peevishness. She spoke to me only once, and that was to tell me to carry my notebook on my head, because of the sun.

35   When we got to our house the ayah was just taking a tray of lunch into Mother's room. She immediately started a long, worried questioning about what are you children doing back here at this hour of the day.

36   Mother looked very startled and very concerned, and asked Premila what had happened.

37   Premila said, "We had our test today, and She made me and the other Indians sit at the back of the room, with a desk between each one."

38   Mother said, "Why was that, darling?"

39   "She said it was because Indians cheat," Premila added. "So I don't think we should go back to that school."

40   Mother looked very distant, and was silent a long time. At last she said, "Of course not, darling." She sounded displeased.

41   We all shared the curry she was having for lunch, and afterward I was sent off to the beautifully familiar bedroom for my siesta. I could hear Mother and Premila talking through the open door.

42   Mother said, "Do you suppose she understood all that?"

43   Premila said, "I shouldn't think so. She's a baby."

44   Mother said, "Well, I hope it won't bother her."

45   Of course, they were both wrong. I understood it perfectly, and I remember it all very clearly. But I put it happily away, because it had all happened to a girl called Cynthia, and I never was really particularly interested in her.

Expanding Vocabulary

Determine the meaning of each of the following words either from its context in this essay or from studying your dictionary. Then select five of the words and use each one in a separate sentence of your own.

precarious (3)	ayah (18)
intimidated (4)	wizened (22)
insular (6)	sari (22)
kohl (9)	tepid (26)
palpitating (15)	tonga (34)
incomprehensible (15)	coolies (34)
chapatties (16)	peevishness (34)

Understanding Content

1. Why did Rama Rau and her sister start attending the Anglo-Indian day school? What was the author's mother's view of the British?
2. What happened to the author and her sister at the beginning of their first day?
3. What did Rama Rau have to learn about games?
4. What happened the day her sister had a test?
5. What was Rama Rau's reaction, at five, to her school experience?

Drawing Inferences about Thesis and Purpose

1. How did the author feel when she was asked to tell the class her name? How do you know?
2. What was her reaction to her first day of school?
3. What is the author's purpose in writing? What does she want readers to understand from her experience? Write a thesis for the essay.

Analyzing Strategies and Style

1. Look at Rama Rau's description of the headmistress (paragraph 3). What do the details tell us about the author's view of this woman?
2. What differences in cultures are revealed by the details of afternoons at schools and afternoons and evenings at home?
3. How would you describe the tone of this essay? Is the author angry or bitter or nostalgic or happy or something else? Support your choice.

Thinking Critically

1. What, if any, details of Indian culture are new to you? Has Rama Rau captured the Indian—and Anglo-Indian—life effectively? What details are most important in creating this glimpse of Indian culture?
2. How important are names? Do our names help to shape our characters? Do you know people whose names do not seem to fit them? Be prepared for a class discussion of these issues.
3. Santha and Premila respond differently to the discrimination they experience. Do you think that one strategy is better than the other? Defend your views.
4. Should students from other cultures change their names—or the pronunciation of their names—to fit in better in U.S. schools? Why or why not?

"Death of an Officer"

GAYE WAGNER

Gaye Wagner (b. 1955) is a detective with the child abuse unit in the San Diego Police Department. She holds a master's degree and previously worked in children and youth services in New Hampshire. "Death of an Officer" was first published in *The American Enterprise* magazine in May 1995. Through narration Wagner examines issues of a police officer's commitment and perspective and shows us how we can learn and grow through reflection on telling moments in our lives, regardless of our age.

1   When Officer Ron Davis was shot in the dark, foggy pre-dawn of September 17, 1991, I momentarily lost my perspective on why I've chosen to do what I'm doing. For a time, I focused on just one dimension of my job as a police officer: the possibility of a violent death, for me or people I care about.

2   Despite the graphic slides and blow-by-blow descriptions of on-duty deaths that we sat through in the Academy, I still must have believed deep down that I, and those alongside me, were invincible. Then the faceless gloom of mortality took the place of a fallen comrade. The streets became an evil, threatening place.

3   Before I felt the blow of a co-worker's death, I looked on each shooting, stabbing, and act of violence as any rubber-necker would—with a certain detachment. I was living the ultimate student experience: Social Wildlife 101. What better way to understand problems of crime and justice than to immerse yourself in the 'hood. I was there, but I was still an onlooker peering inside some kind of fence. I watched, probed each tragic or bizarre incident with curiosity, and pondered the problems I faced.

4   With the death of a comrade, I understood that I was inside the fence. I'm no longer an outsider looking in. The shadow of death stalks all of us who walk in the valley of drugs, guns, alcohol, hopelessness, and hate. Police, addicts, hustlers, parents trying to build futures for their children, good people struggling—we all risk falling into the firing line of desperation, apathy, or corruption.

For a while, my response to the new threats I saw around me 5
was to treat all people like they were the enemy. Since an "us"
and "them" mentality can be a self-fulfilling prophecy, some of
my contacts with people were a little bumpy. Normally my approach is courteous, in one of several variations: either as sym-
pathizer, "just the facts, Bud" chronicler, or all-ears naive
airhead who can hardly believe that you, yes you, could do a
dastardly deed . . . ("how did this all happen my friend?").

But suddenly I just wasn't as enamored with this job as I had 6
been. Let's face it, a sense of contributing to society, the excitement of racing cars with lights and sirens, helping folks, and the
drama of never knowing what's next place a poor second to living long enough to count grey hairs and collect Social Security.

I had trouble getting an impersonal all-units bulletin about 7
someone I knew out of my head. I read these bulletins every
day, but the words now stung: "187 Suspect . . . Arrest in Public
for 187 P.C.—Homicide of a Police Officer . . . Suspect Description: Castillo, Arno . . . On September 17, 1991, at 05:15 hours,
Castillo was contacted by two officers in regard to a domestic
violence call. As the officers approached, Castillo opened fire
with a .45 cal. automatic weapon, fatally wounding one officer."

It was a routine incident that any one of us could have gone 8
to, in an apartment complex that we've all been to. A victim
mired in her own problems—a broken collar bone and a life
crushing down around her—forgot to tell officers that her
crazed, abusive boyfriend had fled with a gun. What followed
happened fast. Thick fog and darkness shrouded the complex
parking lot where Davis and his partner stopped to contact a
driver backing out of the lot.

Ron took a bullet in the neck as he stepped out of his passen- 9
ger side door. The bullet bled him faster than any resuscitating
efforts could counteract. He died while his partner hopelessly
tried to breathe life back into his bloody, weakening body.
Medics said that even if they'd been there when it happened,
there would have been nothing they could do to save his life.

The next week brought a crush of support for our division. 10
The chief, the field operations commander, psychological services counselors, and peer support counselors all came to our
lineups to say we're here man, and we know it doesn't feel
good. The lineup room looked like a wake with its display of

food, flowers, and cards that showered in from other divisions, other departments, and the citizens of our division.

11   Ron's squad was placed on leave, so officers came from other divisions to help us cover manpower shortages. And on the day of the funeral, officers volunteered from all over the city to cover our beats so that everyone in our division could go to the service.

12   The funeral procession filled the three miles from Jack Murphy Stadium to the church with bumper-to-bumper police units flashing red and blue overhead lights. Police cars came from San Diego, the Border Patrol, the U.S. Marshals, El Cajon, La Mesa, Chula Vista, National City, Riverside, Los Angeles, seemingly everywhere. The sight we made sent chills up my spine.

13   For the breadth of that three-mile procession, for a few minutes at least, drivers couldn't keep racing in their usual preoccupied frenzy. Traffic had to stop. In those frozen freeway moments, a tiny corner of the world had to take time out to notice our mourning at the passing of Ronald W. Davis, age 24, husband, father of two, San Diego police officer. The citizens held captive by the procession responded with heart. There was no angry beeping, there were no cars nosing down breakdown lanes. Drivers turned off ignitions in anticipation of a long wait and watched patiently. Many got out of their cars and waved or yelled words of sympathy.

14   The pastor's words at the funeral have stayed with me, because he began stretching my perspective back to a more fruitful, hopeful size. "Life is not defined by the quantity of years that we are on this earth, but by the quality of the time that we spend here."

15   I never cried at the funeral. I cried three weeks later in front of a second grade class.

16   Staring at the bulletin board one day drinking my coffee, I noticed a sheaf of papers with big, just-learned-to-write letters on them. The papers were letters to the Officers of Southeastern from Ms. Matthews's second grade class at Boone Elementary:

Dear Friends of Officer Davis,

We hope this letter will make you feel better. We feel sad about what happened to Officer Davis. We know he was a nice man and a good cop. We thank you for protecting our neighborhood. We know you try to protect every one of us. We know Officer Davis was a good father. We're sorry.

Your friend, Jeffrey

Dear Friends of Officer Davis,

We feel sorry about Officer Davis. I know you feel sorry for what happened when the bad guy killed your friend, Officer Davis. Thank you for protecting us. I know that he's dead and I know you feel sorry about it. I'm glad you got the bad guy. Do you think this would happen again? I'm sure not. Please protect yourself.

Your friend,

Henry

P.S. I live in Meadowbrook apartments.

Thank you.

Dear Friends of Officer Davis,

We feel sad about Officer Davis being killed. The man that killed Officer Davis got killed right behind our house. We live in front of Meadowbrook apartments. It is really sad that Officer Davis got killed. Last year when my brother was in sixth grade and he was playing basketball with his friends, two kids came and took the ball away. They broke his basketball hoop. Officers helped find the two kids. We are thankful you are trying to protect us.

Your friend,

Travis

Dear Friends,

I hope you will feel better. I know how you feel, sad. Was Officer Davis your friend? Well, he was my friend, too. When I saw the news I felt very sad for him. When I grow up, I might be a police officer. I'll never forget Officer Davis. I know how losing a friend is. When you lose a friend you feel very sad. I know how losing a friend is cause my best friend moved away to Virginia. They wrote to me once and I still miss her and I miss Officer Davis, too.

Your Friend,

Jennifer L.

Dear Officers,

I hope you feel a little better with my letter. We feel sorry that Officer Davis was killed. I heard that he got shot on his neck when he was just getting out of his car. I also heard that Officer Davis was an officer for two years and that he has two children. That one is one years old and the other five years old. I want to say thank you for protecting us and for helping us. We all wish that Officer Davis was still alive.

Your friend always,

Arlene

Dear Officers,

We were so sad that your friend Officer Davis died. Last night on 9-17-91 I couldn't sleep because I was thinking all about your friend Officer Davis. When I heard about Officer Davis getting shot I was so sad. I know how it feels when a friend is gone. I wish that Officer Davis could hear this but he can't right now. Officer Davis and the rest of the force do a great job.

Sincerely,

Jasper

17   Those letters brought feelings up from my gut. The next day I visited Room B-17 to deliver thank you notes to the authors. Ms. Matthews was so excited with my visit that she asked me to speak to the class. She explained that the letters were a class exercise to help the students deal with fears they had expressed to her after the shooting. Because many of her students lived in the apartments where Ron was shot, the shooting was very

personal to them. Some couldn't sleep, others were afraid to walk to school, and some were shocked at the realization that the "good guys" get killed too.

I hadn't expected to give a speech, and wasn't really ready to give one on this particular topic. When I faced the class, I saw 32 sets of Filipino, Latino, white, and African-American eyes fixed on me. Their hands all sat respectfully in their laps. In those young faces, I saw an innocence and trust that I didn't want to shake. I thought of the sympathy in their letters; I pictured them passing by the large, dark stain of Officer Davis's blood that still scarred the parking lot pavement; and I wondered what young minds must think when a force of blacked-out SWAT officers sweeps through nearby homes in search of the "bad guy" who shot the "good guy." 18

I wondered how many of the children had been home looking out their windows when the suspect, Arnanda Castillo, was shot by a volley of officers' gunfire as he sprung out of his hiding place in the late afternoon of September 17. I couldn't imagine what these children must be thinking, because a second grader growing up in rural New Hampshire in 1962 didn't witness such events. I could only think that second graders of any generation in any place in the world shouldn't have to witness or ponder the senselessness of human violence. 19

When I finally opened my mouth to speak, my eyes watered and no words would come out. I could say nothing. Each time I tried to push my voice, my eyes watered more. I looked helplessly at Ms. Matthews and the vice principal, who had come to listen to me. Ms. Matthews came to my rescue by starting to talk to the class about strong feelings and the importance of letting feelings out so we don't trap sadness inside ourselves. "Even police officers know that crying can be a strong thing to do." Her reassurances to them reassured me and made me smile at the image of myself, "the big, brave cop" choked up by a second grade class. 20

We talked for a time about the shooting, about having someone to talk to about scary things, and about how important their thoughtful letters had been in a time of sadness. By the time I left, they were more enchanted with my handcuffs and nunchakus than they were concerned by death. Ahhh, the lure for us kids of all ages conjured up by cops and robbers, catching 21 bad guys, rescuing good guys, and having a belt full of cop toys. Through Ron's death, I grew to have a more mature, realistic view of my job.

22   Through the eyes of the pastor at the funeral and Ms. Matthews's second grade class, I recovered perspective and belief in the value of what I do. It's important for me to live my life doing something I believe is important for this thing we call humanity. And I believe that what I do is important because of people like Henry, Jasper, Jennifer L., Jeffrey, Travis, Arlene, Ms. Matthews, and all of the kids in Room B-17.

Expanding Vocabulary

Examine the following words in their contexts in the essay and then write a brief definition or synonym for each one. (Do not use a dictionary; try to guess the word's meaning from its context.)

invincible (2)   shrouded (8)
rubbernecker (3)   resuscitating (9)
bizarre (3)   nunchakus (21)
dastardly (5)   conjured (21)
enamored (6)

Understanding Content

1. Where does the author work, and what does she do?
2. What event had led to her writing?
3. What was her initial response to the event?
4. What did she do in response to reading the students' letters? Then what happened?

Drawing Inferences about Thesis and Purpose

1. How did Officer Wagner feel after Officer Davis's death? What was the difference between her training experience and this experience?
2. What did the author receive from the young students? How did they help her change her thinking?
3. What is Wagner's thesis?

Analyzing Strategies and Style

1. Describe Wagner's chronology. How could the order be altered? What does Wagner gain with her chronology?
2. Why does the author include many of the students' letters? What do they contribute to the essay?

3. Near the end, Wagner writes that the students seem most interested in her "cop toys." What does she gain by including this detail?

Thinking Critically

1. Have you experienced violence in your family, neighborhood, or school? If so, how did the experience make you feel? If not, can you describe how you think the second graders from the neighborhood where Officer Davis was shot may have felt?
2. Has it occurred to you that police officers may doubt their commitment or fear for their safety? Should officers express their feelings as Wagner has? Why or why not?
3. Is it fair to say that there are some truths we have to "learn" several times before we really understand? Is there any age limit to learning tough truths? How hard is it to learn, to gain perspective, to grow wiser? Be prepared to discuss your answers to these questions.

"Eleven"

SANDRA CISNEROS

Sandra Cisneros (b. 1954) is the daughter of a Mexican-American mother and Mexican father. A graduate of Loyola University and the writing program at the University of Iowa, Cisneros is the author of *Bad Boys* (1980) and *My Wicked Wicked Ways* (1987), two books of poetry; *The House on Mango Street* (1984), a novel; and *Woman Hollering Creek* (1991), a collection of short stories, from which the story "Eleven" is taken. Although written in simple language, her lyrical prose and the voice of an oral storyteller combine into Cisneros's innovative style. Her brief story "Eleven" painfully captures the self-consciousness of the eleven-year-old.

What they don't understand about birthdays and what they   1
never tell you is that when you're eleven, you're also ten, and nine, and eight, and seven, and six, and five, and four, and three, and two, and one. And when you wake up on your eleventh birthday you expect to feel eleven, but you don't. You open your eyes and everything's just like yesterday, only it's today. And you don't feel eleven at all. You feel like you're still ten. And you are—underneath the year that makes you eleven.

2   Like some days you might say something stupid, and that's the part of you that's still ten. Or maybe some days you might need to sit on your mama's lap because you're scared, and that's the part of you that's five. And maybe one day when you're all grown up maybe you will need to cry like if you're three, and that's okay. That's what I tell Mama when she's sad and needs to cry. Maybe she's feeling three.

3   Because the way you grow old is kind of like an onion or like the rings inside a tree trunk or like my little wooden dolls that fit one inside the other, each year inside the next one. That's how being eleven years old is.

4   You don't feel eleven. Not right away. It takes a few days, weeks even, sometimes even months before you say Eleven when they ask you. And you don't feel smart eleven, not until you're almost twelve. That's the way it is.

5   Only today I wish I didn't have only eleven years rattling inside me like pennies in a tin Band-Aid box. Today I wish I was one hundred and two instead of eleven because if I was one hundred and two I'd have known what to say when Mrs. Price put the red sweater on my desk. I would've known how to tell her it wasn't mine instead of just sitting there with that look on my face and nothing coming out of my mouth.

6   "Whose is this?" Mrs. Price says, and she holds the red sweater up in the air for all the class to see. "Whose? It's been sitting in the coatroom for a month."

7   "Not mine," says everybody. "Not me."

8   "It has to belong to somebody," Mrs. Price keeps saying, but nobody can remember. It's an ugly sweater with red plastic buttons and a collar and sleeves all stretched out like you could use it for a jump rope. It's maybe a thousand years old and even if it belonged to me I wouldn't say so.

9   Maybe because I'm skinny, maybe because she doesn't like me, that stupid Sylvia Saldívar says, "I think it belongs to Rachel." An ugly sweater like that, all raggedy and old, but Mrs. Price believes her. Mrs. Price takes the sweater and puts it right on my desk, but when I open my mouth nothing comes out.

10   "That's not, I don't, you're not . . . Not mine," I finally say in a little voice that was maybe me when I was four.

11   "Of course it's yours," Mrs. Price says. "I remember you wearing it once." Because she's older and the teacher, she's right and I'm not.

Not mine, not mine, not mine, but Mrs. Price is already turn-   12
ing to page thirty-two, and math problem number four. I don't
know why but all of a sudden I'm feeling sick inside, like the
part of me that's three wants to come out of my eyes, only I
squeeze them shut tight and bite down on my teeth real hard
and try to remember today I am eleven, eleven. Mama is making a cake for me for tonight, and when Papa comes home
everybody will sing Happy birthday, happy birthday to you.

But when the sick feeling goes away and I open my eyes, the   13
red sweater's still sitting there like a big red mountain. I move
the red sweater to the corner of my desk with my ruler. I move
my pencil and books and eraser as far from it as possible. I even
move my chair a little to the right. Not mine, not mine, not mine.

In my head I'm thinking how long till lunchtime, how long   14
till I can take the red sweater and throw it over the schoolyard
fence, or leave it hanging on a parking meter, or bunch it up
into a little ball and toss it in the alley. Except when math period ends Mrs. Price says loud and in front of everybody,
"Now, Rachel, that's enough," because she sees I've shoved the
red sweater to the tippy-tip corner of my desk and it's hanging
all over the edge like a waterfall, but I don't care.

"Rachel," Mrs. Price says. She says it like she's getting mad.   15
"You put that sweater on right now and no more nonsense."

"But it's not—"   16

"Now!" Mrs. Price says.   17

This is when I wish I wasn't eleven, because all the years in-   18
side of me—ten, nine, eight, seven, six, five, four, three, two,
and one—are pushing at the back of my eyes when I put one
arm through one sleeve of the sweater that smells like cottage
cheese, and then the other arm through the other and stand
there with my arms apart like if the sweater hurts me and it
does, all itchy and full of germs that aren't even mine.

That's when everything I've been holding in since this   19
morning, since when Mrs. Price put the sweater on my desk, finally lets go, and all of a sudden I'm crying in front of everybody. I wish I was invisible but I'm not. I'm eleven and it's my
birthday today and I'm crying like I'm three in front of everybody. I put my head down on the desk and bury my face in my
stupid clown-sweater arms. My face all hot and spit coming
out of my mouth because I can't stop the little animal noises
from coming out of me, until there aren't any more tears left in

my eyes, and it's just my body shaking like when you have the hiccups, and my whole head hurts like when you drink milk too fast.

20 But the worst part is right before the bell rings for lunch. That stupid Phyllis Lopez, who is even dumber than Sylvia Saldívar, says she remembers the red sweater is hers! I take it off right away and give it to her, only Mrs. Price pretends like everything's okay.

21 Today I'm eleven. There's a cake Mama's making for tonight, and when Papa comes home from work we'll eat it. There'll be candles and presents and everybody will sing Happy birthday, happy birthday to you, Rachel, only it's too late.

22 I'm eleven today. I'm eleven, ten, nine, eight, seven, six, five, four, three, two, and one, but I wish I was one hundred and two. I wish I was anything but eleven, because I want today to be far away already, far away like a runaway balloon, like a tiny *o* in the sky, so tiny-tiny you have to close your eyes to see it.

Understanding Content

1. Why is this a special day for the story's narrator?
2. What happens at school to ruin the day for her?
3. Why does the narrator have trouble convincing the teacher that the sweater is not hers? What can you infer (conclude from evidence) about the personality of the narrator?
4. Describe the teacher, Mrs. Price. What kind of teacher does she seem to be?

Drawing Inferences about Theme

1. Why doesn't the narrator want to be associated with the sweater?
2. Explain the story's idea that when you are eleven you are also ten and nine and so on. Also, why don't you feel eleven when you first have your eleventh birthday?

Analyzing Strategies and Style

1. Cisneros's main character uses several comparisons. Find three and explain the idea of each one.
2. Look at the examples in paragraph 2 of the idea that you are all the years you have already lived. What makes these examples effective?
3. Describe Cisneros's style of writing. Does her narrator talk like an eleven-year-old? Is this approach to telling the story effective?

Thinking Critically

1. Have you experienced a time when you felt that you behaved younger than your years? Or older than your years? If so, how did you behave? How do you think someone your actual age should have or would have behaved? How did your behavior make you feel?
2. Have you been embarrassed in front of a group? If so, how did you feel at the time? On reflection, do you think your embarrassment was what most people would have felt, or do you think you were too easily embarrassed? What can you learn about yourself from reflecting on your response?
3. Is it normal and understandable that people sometimes behave younger than their years? Should we be accepting of such behavior as part of human growth and development? Why or why not?
4. Is it normal and understandable that young people are more often and more easily embarrassed in front of a group than adults? If so, why?

MAKING CONNECTIONS

---

1. Luis Rodriguez and N. Scott Momaday write of dangerous experiences that lead to greater awareness and a loss of innocence. Most of us, though, do not face such dramatic moments. We need to learn and grow from being made to feel different (Rau), or from experiences on the job (Wagner), or from embarrassment at school (Cisneros). Reflect on how we gain insight and mature from seemingly insignificant encounters with life. Why do some young people seem more grown up than others? What is required of us to grow from our experiences? What do the authors suggest on this subject? What can you add from your experience and reflection?

2. Elizabeth Wong, Santha Rama Rau, and Sandra Cisneros write of the important role of language in fitting in or being in control of one's life. Compare their views and then reflect on the significance of language skills in growing up.

3. Luis Rodriguez, Santha Rama Rau, and N. Scott Momaday have written autobiographies. Select one from your library and read it. Think about what more you learn about the writer's life from reading the complete memoir. Prepare a two-page summary of the memoir.

TOPICS AND GUIDELINES FOR WRITING

1. Think of a situation, or period in your life, in which you felt unattractive or physically different from others in some way. (For example, you were big for your age, or short for your age, or had to wear braces.) How did the situation affect you at the time? Later? Reflect on what you might share from that time with readers and then plan your narrative essay to develop and support those reflections. Select significant details of the event or time, select a point of view, and use time words (e.g., *then, later*) to guide your reader through the situation. You may want to use metaphors that capture your emotions at the time.

2. Think of your years in school. Was there a special teacher who made a difference in your attitude toward education or about yourself? If so, reflect on the incidents involving that teacher and then select either several important moments in that teacher's class or one particular event to serve as a narrative basis for your reflections. Decide whether you want to take your reader back to that time to present only your understanding then, or whether you want to blend your emerging awareness at the time with your greater understanding as an adult.

3. If you came to America as a young person or were born here of parents who were recent immigrants, think of the stories you might tell of growing up in the midst of two cultures. Did you experience discrimination in any way? Did you experience feeling torn between two cultures? How did these situations make you feel then? Now? If you maintained elements of your family's culture, how has that benefited you? If you rejected your family's culture, what, from your perspective now, do you think you have lost? Reflect on these questions as a way to select your essay's subject and thesis. Resist the urge to write in general about your childhood. Rather, focus on one incident or short period and have one clear thesis.

4. Can you recall an incident in which one of your parents embarrassed you, or in which you embarrassed your parent? If you have experienced either one of these situations, think

about your feelings both at the time and now. If you were embarrassed by a parent, do you think, on reflection, that you should have felt embarrassment? If you embarrassed a parent, were you aware of it at the time or only on looking back? What insights into the parent/child relationship or into the problems of growing up have you gained from reflecting on these incidents? Those insights can serve as the thesis of your narrative essay. Focus your retelling only on the important elements of the incident, those parts that will guide your reader to the insight you have gained.

5. Recall an event in your life from which you learned a lesson, perhaps a painful one. What was the lesson? How much did you understand at the time? Did you try to deny the lesson, or did you accept it? Construct your narrative so that your retelling carries your point. Offer some reflection but avoid stating the lesson as a simple moral, such as "I learned that one shouldn't steal."

6. Recall a particular event or period in your life that resulted in your losing some of your innocence, in your rather suddenly becoming much more grown up. What romantic or naive view of life did you lose? What more adult view was forced on you? You will probably want to place your reader back in that time of your growing up. Use chronological order and focus your attention on the key stages in the event that moved you from innocence to awareness.

3

Using Description

Reflecting on People and Places

Good writing is concrete writing. Good writers *show* readers what they mean; they do not just tell them. Vague and abstract words may be confusing and often fail to engage readers. "The tawny-colored cocker spaniel with big, floppy ears" has our attention in ways that "The dog" will never achieve. We can see the "spaniel"; what "dog" are we to imagine? Thus, descriptive details are a part of all good writing, whatever its primary purpose or form.

When to Use Description

Sometimes writers use description to make the general concrete and to engage readers. But sometimes, a writer's primary purpose is to describe, to tell us—to show us—what a particular person, place, or thing looks like. Many instructors like to assign descriptive essays both because they are fun to write and because they provide good practice for using concrete language in other essays.

The descriptive essay can be viewed as a painting in words. (Not surprisingly, you will find some paintings reproduced in this chapter.) Like the artist who draws or paints, the artist working with words must be a perceptive observer. Some people actually see more than others. Can you close your eyes and "see" your writing classroom? The college library? Your history instructor? How carefully have you looked at the world around you? Some people go to a restaurant because they are hungry. The food critic goes to a restaurant not just to have din-

ner but to observe the color of the walls, the politeness of the
waiters, the taste of the food. The food critic does not want to
write, in her Sunday column, that the service was "okay." She
needs to decide whether the waiters were formally polite,
chatty, intrusive, uninformed. To generate details for good essays you will need to see more of the world around you and to
store those visual impressions in your memory.

How to Use Descriptive Details
Descriptive Language

Really seeing what you want to describe is the necessary first
step to writing a good descriptive essay. But, just as the artist
must transfer impressions into forms and colors on canvas, so
you must transfer your impressions into words. To help your
reader see what you see, you need to choose words that are accurate, concrete, and vivid. If you are describing your backyard, for example, you want descriptive details so precise that
a reader could easily draw a picture of your yard. If you were
to write that your yard is "a large yard that goes to a creek,"
you would not be helping your reader to see much. How large
is large? To an apartment dweller, the fifteen-by-twelve-foot
deck of a townhouse might seem large. Better to describe your
backyard as "gently sloping seventy feet from the screened-in
back porch to a narrow creek that marks the property line."
Now we can begin to see—really to see—your yard.

Take time to search for just the right word. The food critic
will soon lose her column if she writes that the walls of a restaurant are "a kind of beige with pink." She needs to write, instead,
that they are "salmon-colored." Do not settle for describing a
lake as "bluish green." Is the water aquamarine? Or a deeper
turquoise? Is its surface mirror-like or opaque? You might notice that some of these examples are actually metaphors:
"salmon-colored" and "mirror-like." Fresh, vivid comparisons
(not worn-out clichés) will help readers see your world and will
leave a lasting impression on them. Lance Morrow, describing
an East African wildlife preserve, writes that "a herd of elephants moves like a dense gray cloud . . . a mirage of floating
boulders" and "a lion prowls in lion-colored grasses."

Finding Unity

When your primary purpose is to write a description, one way
to get started is to list all the details that come to mind. However, to shape those details into a unified essay, you will eventually want to eliminate some and develop others. Remember
that a list of details, no matter how vivid, does not make an
essay. First, select the *telling details*, the specifics that really
work to reveal your subject. Second, be sure that your essay
has a thesis. Select the details that, taken together, create a unified impression, that make a point. In an essay on her father,
British novelist Doris Lessing wants to show that war kills the
spirit if not the body of those who have to fight. To support her
thesis, she first draws the portrait of her father as a vigorous
young man, full of life, and then presents the unpleasant details of the angry, sick, shattered man whom she knew after the
war.

Organization

Remember to organize details according to some principle so
that readers can follow the developing picture and so that you
convey your desired impression. You need to decide on a perspective from which the details will be "seen" by the reader. In
describing a classroom, for example, you could create the impression of someone standing at the door by presenting details
in the order in which the person's eyes move around the room.
Spatial patterns are numerous. You can move from foreground
to background, from the center out, from left to right. Descriptions of people are sometimes more challenging to organize,
because in addition to physical details you need possessions,
activities, and ways of speaking—the telling details of character. You could take the perspective of a new acquaintance, presenting what one would see first and then what details of
personality emerge as a relationship develops. Whatever pattern you choose, develop it consistently and use connecting
words (e.g., *from* the left, *below* the penetrating eyes, *next* to the
rose bushes) to guide your reader. It's your canvas; get to know
your subject well, select your colors with care, and pay close attention to each brushstroke.

Francisco de Goya y Lucientes, *Third of May, 1808,* 1814. Approximately 8'8" x 11'3". Museo del Prado, Madrid, Spain. Scala/Art Resource, NY.

A Spaniard, Goya (1746–1828) lived and painted at the Spanish court of Charles II. His paintings reveal an unsentimental, tough-minded observation of human life.

Jan Vermeer, *Young Woman with a Water Jug*. Oil on canvas, 18" x 16" (45.7 x 40.6 cm). The Metropolitan Museum of Art, Gift of Henry G. Marquand, 1889. Marquand Collection. Copyright © 1993 The Metropolitan Museum of Art.

Vermeer (1632–1675) is the best known and most highly regarded of the seventeenth-century Dutch masters. His paintings of middle-class people going about their daily lives have a quiet, dignified beauty.

Frédéric Bazille, *Young Woman with Peonies,* Collection of Mr. and Mrs. Paul Mellon, © 1997 Board of Trustees, National Gallery of Art, Washington, 1870, oil on canvas, 23-3/4" x 29-3/4".

One of the pioneers of Impressionism, Bazille (1841–1870) shared a studio in Paris with Monet and Renoir but then died, in the Franco-Prussian War, before realizing his full potential as a painter.

Edgar Degas, *The Dance Class,* c. 1874. Oil on canvas, 85 x 75 cm.
Musée d'Orsay, Paris, France. Erich Lessing/Art Resource, NY.

*One of the best known of the French Impressionists, Degas
(1834–1917) is known for his interest in capturing movement, an
interest that led to many studies of dancers and racehorses.*

and at sentimental movies, but she never cried in front of students, except once a few years ago when the news came over the intercom that the Space Shuttle had exploded and Christa McAuliffe had died—and then she saw in her students' faces that the sight of Mrs. Zajac crying had frightened them, and she made herself stop and then explained.

At home, Chris laughed at the antics of her infant daughter 5
and egged the child on. She and her first-grade son would sneak up to the radio when her husband wasn't looking and change the station from classical to rock-and-roll music. "You're regressing, Chris," her husband would say. But especially on the first few days of school, she didn't let her students get away with much. She was not amused when, for instance, on the first day, two of the boys started dueling with their rulers. On nights before the school year started, Chris used to have bad dreams: her principal would come to observe her, and her students would choose that moment to climb up on their desks and give her the finger, or they would simply wander out the door. But a child in her classroom would never know that Mrs. Zajac had the slightest doubt that students would obey her.

The first day, after going over all the school rules, Chris 6
spoke to them about effort. "If you put your name on a paper, you should be proud of it," she said. "You should think, This is the best I can do and I'm proud of it and I want to hand this in." Then she asked, "If it isn't your best, what's Zajac going to do?"

Many voices, most of them female, answered softly in uni- 7
son, "Make us do it over."

"Make you do it over," Chris repeated. It sounded like a chant. 8

"Does anyone know anything about Lisette?" she asked 9
when no one answered to that name.

Felipe—small, with glossy black hair—threw up his hand. 10
"Felipe?" 11

"She isn't here!" said Felipe. He wasn't being fresh. On those 12
first few days of school, whenever Mrs. Zajac put the sound of a question in her voice, and sometimes before she got the question out, Felipe's hand shot up.

In contrast, there was the very chubby girl who sat nearly 13
motionless at her desk, covering the lower half of her face with her hands. As usual, most of their voices sounded timid the first day, and came out of hiding gradually. There were twenty

children. About half were Puerto Rican. Almost two-thirds of the twenty needed the forms to obtain free lunches. There was a lot of long and curly hair. Some boys wore little rattails. The eyes the children lifted up to her as she went over the rules—a few eyes were blue and many more were brown—looked so solemn and so wide that Chris felt like dropping all pretense and laughing. Their faces ranged from dark brown to gold, to pink, to pasty white, the color that Chris associated with sunless tenements and too much TV. The boys wore polo shirts and T-shirts and new white sneakers with the ends of the laces untied and tucked behind the tongues. Some girls wore lacy ribbons in their hair, and some wore pants and others skirts, a rough but not infallible indication of religion—the daughters of Jehovah's Witnesses and Pentecostals do not wear pants. There was a lot of prettiness in the room, and all of the children looked cute to Chris.

Expanding Vocabulary

Examine the following words in their contexts in the essay. Then write a brief definition or synonym for each one. (Do not use a dictionary; try to guess the word's meaning from its context.)

projection (2)	egged . . . on (5)
karate (3)	unison (7)
maneuvers (3)	pretense (13)
perpetrated (3)	infallible (13)
holsters (3)	

Understanding Content

1. The excerpt you have read comes from the first four pages of Kidder's book. Why does Kidder begin his study in this way? What, exactly, does he accomplish in these opening pages?
2. What specific details do we get about Mrs. Zajac? List them. (Consider age, physical appearance, personality traits, values.)
3. Why does Mrs. Zajac go to school in a skirt or dress?
4. What details do we get about the children? List them.

Drawing Inferences about Thesis and Purpose

1. What is effective about Kidder's last sentence? What does it tell us about Mrs. Zajac's attitude toward teaching?

2. What can you conclude about the Kelly School neighborhood from details about the children?
3. What is the author's attitude toward his subject? Does he present Mrs. Zajac in a positive or negative way? As a good or bad teacher?

Analyzing Strategies and Style

1. Why is the first paragraph in italics? What is the italic print designed to represent?
2. What is effective about beginning with this opening paragraph?
3. Kidder offers some contrasts between Mrs. Zajac's classroom behavior and her behavior at home and with her children. How do these contrasts help us to understand Mrs. Zajac?
4. What are three details that you would consider *telling* details? Why are they especially effective?
5. Can you find any sentences that contain general or abstract ideas?
6. What does your answer to question 5 tell you about Kidder's style of writing? Is this writing primarily general or specific? Abstract or concrete?

Thinking Critically

1. Would you have enjoyed being in Mrs. Zajac's fifth-grade class? Why or why not?
2. Mrs. Zajac emphasizes being proud of work you sign your name to. Is it ever too early to teach this idea? Is it ever too late?
3. Are you usually proud of the work you hand in? If not, why do you hand it in that way?
4. Under what conditions and at what age levels should students be allowed to redo work that isn't right or isn't their best effort? Why?
5. Mrs. Zajac believes in dressing properly for her job. Should students have a dress code or wear uniforms? How can clothes make a difference in the classroom or on the job?

"Lost Lives of Women"

AMY TAN

Amy Tan (b. 1952) was born in California shortly after her parents immigrated to the United States from China. Tan started a career in consulting on programs for disabled children and then turned to writing short stories, some of which became part of her first and best-selling novel *The Joy Luck Club.* Her second novel, *The Kitchen God's Wife,* appeared in 1991. In the following article, which appeared in the April 1991 issue of *Life* magazine, Tan captures the stories of several women, relatives of hers, grouped in an old photo.

1   When I first saw this photo as a child, I thought it was exotic and remote, of a faraway time and place, with people who had no connection to my American life. Look at their bound feet! Look at that funny lady with the plucked forehead!

2   The solemn little girl is, in fact, my mother. And leaning against the rock is my grandmother, Jingmei. "She called me Baobei," my mother told me. "It means Treasure."

3   The picture was taken in Hangzhou, and my mother believes the year was 1922, possibly spring or fall, judging by the clothes. At first glance, it appears the women are on a pleasure outing.

4   But see the white bands on their skirts? The white shoes? They are in mourning. My mother's grandmother, known to the others as Divong, "The Replacement Wife," has recently died. The women have come to this place, a Buddhist retreat, to perform yet another ceremony for Divong. Monks hired for the occasion have chanted the proper words. And the women and little girl have walked in circles clutching smoky sticks of

incense. They knelt and prayed, then burned a huge pile of spirit money so that Divong might ascend to a higher position in her new world.

This is also a picture of secrets and tragedies, the reasons   5
that warnings have been passed along in our family like heirlooms. Each of these women suffered a terrible fate, my mother said. And they were not peasant women but big city people, very modern. They went to dance halls and wore stylish clothes. They were supposed to be the lucky ones.

Look at the pretty woman with her finger on her cheek. She   6
is my mother's second cousin, Nunu Aiyi, "Precious Auntie." You cannot see this, but Nunu Aiyi's entire face was scarred from smallpox. Lucky for her, a year or so after this picture was taken, she received marriage proposals from two families. She turned down a lawyer and married another man. Later she divorced her husband, a daring thing for a woman to do. But then, finding no means to support herself or her young daughter, Nunu eventually accepted the lawyer's second proposal— to become his number two concubine. "Where else could she go?" my mother asked. "Some people said she was lucky the lawyer still wanted her."

Now look at the small woman with a sour face *(third from left)*.   7
There's a reason that Jyou Ma, "Uncle's Wife," looks this way. Her husband, my great-uncle, often complained that his family had chosen an ugly woman for his wife. To show his displeasure, he often insulted Jyou Ma's cooking. One time Great-Uncle tipped over a pot of boiling soup, which fell all over his niece's four-year-old neck and nearly killed her. My mother was the little niece, and she still has that soup scar on her neck. Great-Uncle's family eventually chose a pretty woman for his second wife. But the complaints about Jyou Ma's cooking did not stop.

Doomma, "Big Mother," is the regal-looking woman seated   8
on a rock. (The woman with the plucked forehead, far left, is a servant, remembered only as someone who cleaned but did not cook.) Doomma was the daughter of my great-grandfather and Nu-pei, "The Original Wife." She was shunned by Divong, "The Replacement Wife," for being "too strong," and loved by Divong's daughter, my grandmother. Doomma's first daughter was born with a hunchback—a sign, some said, of Doomma's own crooked nature. Why else did she remarry, disobeying her

family's orders to remain a widow forever? And why did Doomma later kill herself, using some mysterious means that caused her to die slowly over three days? "Doomma died the same way she lived," my mother said, "strong, suffering lots."

9   Jingmei, my own grandmother, lived only a few more years after this picture was taken. She was the widow of a poor scholar, a man who had the misfortune of dying from influenza when he was about to be appointed a vice-magistrate. In 1924 or so, a rich man, who liked to collect pretty women, raped my grandmother and thereby forced her into becoming one of his concubines. My grandmother, now an outcast, took her young daughter to live with her on an island outside of Shanghai. She left her son behind, to save his face. After she gave birth to another son she killed herself by swallowing raw opium buried in the New Year's rice cakes. The young daughter who wept at her deathbed was my mother.

10   At my grandmother's funeral, monks tied chains to my mother's ankles so she would not fly away with her mother's ghost. "I tried to take them off," my mother said. "I was her treasure. I was her life."

11   My mother could never talk about any of this, even with her closest friends. "Don't tell anyone," she once said to me. "People don't understand. A concubine was like some kind of prostitute. My mother was a good woman, high-class. She had no choice."

12   I told her I understood.

13   "How can you understand?" she said, suddenly angry. "You did not live in China then. You do not know what it's like to have no position in life. I was her daughter. We had no face! We belonged to nobody! This is a shame I can never push off my back." By the end of the outburst, she was crying.

14   On a recent trip with my mother to Beijing, I learned that my uncle found a way to push the shame off his back. He was the son my grandmother left behind. In 1936 he joined the Communist party—in large part, he told me, to overthrow the society that forced his mother into concubinage. He published a story about his mother. I told him I had written about my grandmother in a book of fiction. We agreed that my grandmother is the source of strength running through our family. My mother cried to hear this.

My mother believes my grandmother is also my muse, that   15
she helps me write. "Does she still visit you often?" she asked
while I was writing my second book. And then she added
shyly, "Does she say anything about me?"

"Yes," I told her. "She has lots to say. I am writing it down."   16

This is the picture I see when I write. These are the secrets I   17
was supposed to keep. These are the women who never let me
forget why stories need to be told.

Expanding Vocabulary

Define each of the following words and then use each one in a
sentence.

exotic (1)
heirlooms (5)
concubine (6)
shunned (8)
muse (15)

Understanding Content

1. When and where was the picture taken?
2. Who are the women in the photo? That is, what is their relationship
   to the author?
3. Why are the women together? What have they gathered to do?
4. What was the author's initial reaction to the photo?

Drawing Inferences about Thesis and Purpose

1. What reaction does Tan want readers to have after they read her
   descriptions of the women? What do the women share, other than
   family connections? What is Tan's purpose in writing about them?
2. Explain the last line of the essay.
3. What is Tan's thesis?

Analyzing Strategies and Style

1. Tan tells us in paragraph 5 that the women in the photo "were not
   peasant women but big city people, very modern." Why does she
   include this comment? Why is this a telling detail?
2. What other details do you consider to be especially important?
   Why do you select them?

3. Tan gives each woman's Chinese name and then its meaning in English. What does she gain from this strategy?
4. Tan uses a metaphor in paragraph 5. Explain the metaphor.

Thinking Critically

1. Do you have stories to tell about your family? If you have a family album, find a picture in it that you think holds a secret or tells a story, and write that story in your journal.
2. Why is it important to write the stories of these women? What does Tan gain for herself? For others?
3. Why is it important for humans generally to tell stories? What does each culture, each age, gain from making stories?

"Poetic Passage"

MAYA ANGELOU

A versatile writer, Maya Angelou (b. 1928) has several volumes of poetry, including *All God's Children Need Traveling Shoes,* children's books such as *Kofi and His Magic-Globe,* and her famous autobiography, *I Know Why the Caged Bird Sings* (1985). Angelou was asked by President Clinton to write—and then read—a poem for his inaugural ceremony. "Poetic Passage," from a collection of essays titled *Even the Stars Look Lonesome* published in 1997, offers a moving portrait of Oprah Winfrey.

1   Before beginning a long and arduous journey the prudent traveler checks her maps, clocks and addressbook entries and makes certain that her clothes will suit the weather she plans to encounter. If the trip includes crossing national boundaries, she examines her travel documents for their validity and, to the best of her ability, furnishes her wallet with the appropriate currency for her destination. This traveler urges us toward sober deliberation and stolid concentration. The second traveler is less careful, not so meticulous in planning the trip and, as a result, will encounter delays, disruptions and even despair. When disappointments mount to intolerable proportions, this traveler may even give up and return home, defeated. We learn from this example to either prepare well or stay at home.

It is the third, the desperate traveler who teaches us the most 2
profound lesson and affords us the most exquisite thrills. She
touches us with her boldness and vulnerability, for her sole
preparation is the fierce determination to leave wherever she is
and her only certain destination is somewhere other than
where she has been. An old blues describes this eager traveler:

I got the key to the Highway,
Booked down and I'm bound to go
I'm going to leave here running
'cause walkings most too slow.

Oprah Winfrey belongs to the third group of wanderers. She 3
has been in voluntary transit since entering her teens. We know
some sparse details of Oprah's passage, and stand in wonder
at the awful inheritance that she had to either carry with her or
jettison:

She was born poor and powerless in a land where
power is money and money is adored.

Born black in a land where might is white
and white is adored.

Born female in a land where decisions are masculine
and masculinity controls.

With such burdensome baggage it would seem that travel was
unlikely if not downright impossible. Yet, among the red-clay
hills of Mississippi the small, plain black girl with the funny
name decided that she would travel and she would be her own
conductor and porter. She would make the journey and carry
her own baggage.

Today, even in the triumphal atmosphere that surrounds 4
her, the keen observer can detect a steely determination in her
voice and the resoluteness in her dark eyes.

She used faith, fate and a smile whose whiteness rivals a flag 5
of truce to bring her from the dirt roads of the South to the
world's attention. The Creator's blessings—intelligence, lively
imagination and a relentless drive—have brought Oprah from
the poignancy of a lonely childhood to the devotion of millions.

6   One loyal fan has said, "We can thank Oprah for some of the sanity in our country. She is America's most accessible and honest psychiatrist."

7   Oprah, as talk-show host, tries to maintain a calm façade as she lends an ear to brutes, bigots and bagmen, but her face often betrays her. Her eyes will fill with tears when she listens to the lament of mothers mistreated by their offspring, and they dart indignantly at the report of cruelty against children and savagery against the handicapped. The full lips spread into a wide, open smile when a guest or audience member reveals a daring spirit or a benevolent wit.

8   She is everyone's largehearted would-be sister who goes where the fearful will not tread. She asks our questions and waits with us for the answers.

9   The road has been long and the path has been stony. After her parents separated from each other and from her, she was left in the care of a grandmother who believed in the laying on of hands in all ways. She learned behavior from her grandmother, which she still honors today. She kneels nightly to thank God for His protection and generosity, for His guidance and forgiveness. She has a genuine fear of sin and sincerely delights in goodness. Unheralded success has not robbed her of her sense of wonder, nor have possessions made her a slave to property.

10   The little-girl laughter that erupts unexpectedly midsentence should not lure any observer into believing her to be childish, nor should the direct glance encourage any to feel that she is a hardened sophisticate. She is an honest, hardworking woman who has developed an unusual degree of empathy and courage. Oprah is making her journey at what might seem to be a dizzying pace, but it is her pace and she alone has set her tempo.

Expanding Vocabulary

Match each word in Column A with its definition in Column B. When in doubt, first find the word in the essay and look for context clues to aid your understanding of the word's meaning. Then, if necessary, use the dictionary to complete the matching exercise.

Column A	Column B
arduous (1)	revealing little emotion
prudent (1)	discard
stolid (1)	surface impression
meticulous (1)	quite moving
profound (2)	refined, worldly person
exquisite (2)	full of hardships
jettison (3)	identification with the feelings of
poignancy (5)	others
façade (7)	deep, insightful
sophisticate (10)	pace
empathy (10)	careful, wise in practical issues
tempo (10)	beautifully designed
	extremely careful and precise

Understanding Content

1. What kind of traveler was Oprah?
2. What was the "inheritance" she had either to carry or jettison?
3. What traits does Angelou attribute to Oprah?
4. What did she learn from her grandmother?

Drawing Inferences about Thesis and Purpose

1. What, for Angelou, are Oprah's *telling* details of character?
2. What does the author imply about how character develops or is shaped?
3. What are readers to learn from this portrait of Oprah?

Analyzing Strategies and Style

1. Reread Angelou's opening two paragraphs. What do they accomplish as an introduction to her character sketch of Oprah?
2. What metaphor runs throughout the essay? Where does the author use it? How is it effective in developing her ideas?
3. Angelou is a poet as well as an essayist. Where do you find her almost breaking into poetic lines? What does she gain by her choice of expression?

Thinking Critically

1. What have you learned about Oprah that you did not know before? How has it affected your image of her?

2. If you already knew most of what Angelou tells us about Oprah, do you think she has presented her portrait accurately and fairly? Why or why not?
3. Angelou is not the first writer to assert that the worst is to be born poor, black, and female in America. What makes these three burdens so difficult in American culture? Do you agree with this assessment of American society? Why or why not?

"Africa"

LANCE MORROW

Journalist Lance Morrow (b. 1939) is a senior writer at *Time* magazine who contributes to cover stories and the *Time* essay section. Morrow has also written several books, including *The Chief: A Memoir of Fathers and Sons* (1985), a study of the author's relationship with his famous journalist father Hugh Morrow. In 1981, Morrow received the National Magazine Award for his *Time* essays. In "Africa," published in the February 23, 1987, issue of *Time*, Morrow re-creates in words what he saw, felt, and reflected about while on safari in East Africa.

1   The animals stand motionless in gold-white grasses—zebras and impala, Thomson's gazelles and Cape buffalo and hartebeests and waterbuck and giraffes, and wildebeests by the thousands, all fixed in art naïf, in a smiting equatorial light. They stand in the shadowless clarity of creation.

2   Now across the immense African landscape, from the distant escarpment, a gray-purple rainstorm blows. It encroaches upon the sunlight, moving through the air like a dark idea. East Africa has a genius for such moments. Wildlife and landscape here have about them a force of melodrama and annunciation. They are the *Book of Genesis* enacted as an afternoon dream.

3   In Amboseli,[1] under the snow-covered dome of Mount Kilimanjaro, a herd of elephants moves like a dense gray cloud,

---

[1]A game reserve in Kenya.—Ed.

slow motion, in lumbering solidity: a mirage of floating boulders. Around them dust devils rise spontaneously out of the desert, like tornadoes that swirl up on the thermals and go jittering and rushing among the animals like evil spirits busy in the primal garden.

Later, in the sweet last light of the afternoon, a lion prowls in   4
lion-colored grasses and vanishes into the perfect camouflage—setting off for the hunt, alert, indolent and somehow abstracted, as cats are. A rhinoceros disappears: the eye loses it among gray boulders and thorn trees. . . .

To the human eye, the animals so often seem mirages: now   5
you see them, now you don't. Later, just after dusk, Abyssinian nightjars discover the magic wash of the headlight beams. The birds flit in and out of the barrels of light, like dolphins frisking before a boat's prow. The Land Cruiser jostles, in four-wheel drive, across black volcanic stones toward the camp, the driver steering by the distant light-speck of the cooking fire.

And then the African night, which, more than elsewhere,   6
seems an abnegation of the conscious world. MMBA, "miles and miles of bloody Africa," and it all falls into black magic void.

The world stills, for the longest time. Then, at the edge of   7
sleep, hyenas come to giggle and whoop. Peering from the tent flap, one catches in the shadows their sidelong criminal slouch. Their eyes shine like evil flashlight bulbs, a disembodied horror-movie yellow, phosphorescent, glowing like the children of the damned. In the morning, one finds their droppings: white dung, like a photographic negative. Hyenas not only eat the meat of animals but grind up and digest the bones. The hyenas' dung is white with the calcium of powdered bones.

Africa has its blinding clarities and its shadows. The clarities   8
proclaim something primal, the first days of life. The shadows lie at the other extreme of time: in the premonition of last days, of extinction. Now you see the animals. Soon, perhaps, you won't.

Africa is comprehensive: great birth, great death, the begin-   9
ning and the end. The themes are drawn, like the vivid, abstract hide of the zebra, in patterns of the absolute.

The first question to ask is whether the wildlife of Africa can   10
survive.

11   The second question is this: If the wild animals of Africa vanish from the face of the earth, what, exactly, will have been lost?

12   The Africa of the animals is a sort of dream kingdom. Carl Jung traveled to East Africa in 1925 and wrote of a "most intense sentiment of returning to the land of my youth," of a "recognition of the immemorially known." Africa, he said, has "the stillness of the eternal beginning."

13   Earliest man lived in these landscapes, among such animals, among these splendid trees that have personalities as distinct as those of the animals: the aristocratic flat-topped acacia, the gnarled and magisterial baobab. Possibly scenes from that infancy are lodged in some layer of human memory, in the brilliant but preconscious morning. . . .

14   It is easy to fall in love not only with the shapes and colors of the animals but with their motions, their curving and infinitely varied gaits. The zebra moves with a strong, short-muscled stride. It is a sleek, erotic beast with vigorous bearing. The zebra's self-possession is a likable trait. It is human habit to sort the animals almost immediately into orders of preference. The animals are arranged in people's minds as a popularity contest. Some animals are endearing, and some repulsive. One wants to see the lion first, and then the elephant and after that the leopard, then rhino . . . and so on. One wants to see some animals because they are fierce, and some because they are lovable and soft. It is hard to explain the attractions and preferences. It is possible that human feelings about wild animals reflect the complexities of sexual attractions. Certain animals are admired for their majestic aggressions, and others for softer qualities. The lion is a sleek piece of violence, the waterbuck a sweet piece of grace.

15   Some of the animals move in deep slow motion, as if traversing another medium, previous to air, and thicker—an Atlantis of time. The elephant goes sleeping that way across the spaces. The medium through which it moves can be seen as time itself, a thicker, slower time than humans inhabit, a prehistoric metabolism. The giraffe goes with undulous slow motion, a long waving that starts with the head and proceeds dreamily, curving down the endless spine. The giraffe is motion as process through time. It is delicate, intelligent and ec-

centric, and as Karen Blixen said, so much a lady. Each of the animals has its distinct gait. The Grant's gazelle's tail never stops switching, like a nervous windshield wiper. The hartebeest moves off, when startled, in an undulous hallumph. For days in Masai Mara,[2] the visitor watched the wilde- 16 beests. Ungainly and pewter colored, they are subject to sudden electric jolts of panic, to adrenal bursts of motion that can make them seem half crazed as a tribe. Now they were engaged not so much in migration as in vagrancy, wandering across the plain on strange but idiotically determined vectors. Wildebeests smell monsters on the afternoon breeze, take sudden fear and bolt for Tanzania or Uganda or the Indian Ocean, anywhere to get away.

Sometimes, of course, the monsters are there. The veldt is lit- 17 tered with the corpses that the lion or cheetah has killed and dined on. But sometimes the herding wildebeests seem to be caught in a collective shallow madness. A fantasy of terror shoots through a herd, and all the beasts are gone: hysteria of hooves. The wildebeests thunder by the thousands across rivers and plains, moving like a barbarian invasion. They follow their instinct for the rains, for better grass. And they mow the grass before them. If they know where rain is, the wildebeests are relentless. Otherwise, they march with an undirected rigor, without destination, like cadets on punishment, beating a trail in the parade ground. The wildebeest's bisonlike head is too large for its body, its legs too thin and ungainly. It looks like a middle-aged hypochondriac, paltry in the loins and given to terrible anxiety attacks, the sort of creature whose hands (if it had hands) would always be clammy. God's genius for design may have faltered with the wildebeest.

In Masai Mara, vultures wheel dreamily in the air, like a 18 slow motion tornado of birds. Below the swirling funnel, a cheetah has brought down a baby wildebeest. The cheetah, loner and fleet aristocrat, the upper-class version of the hyena, has opened up the wildebeest and devoured the internal organs. The cheetah's belly is swollen and its mouth is ringed with blood as it breathes heavily from the exertion of gorging.

[2]A game reserve in Kenya.—Ed.

A dozen vultures flap down to take their turn. They wait 20 yards away, then waddle in a little toward the kill to test the cheetah. The cheetah, in a burst, rushes the vultures to drive them off, and then returns to the baby wildebeest. The vultures grump and readjust their feathers and wait their turn, the surly lumpen-carrion class.

19   The skeleton of an elephant lies out in the grasses near a baobab tree and a scattering of black volcanic stones. The thick-trunked, gnarled baobab gesticulates with its branches, as if trying to summon help. There are no tusks lying among the bones, of course; ivory vanishes quickly in East Africa. The elephant is three weeks dead. Poachers. Not far away, a baby elephant walks alone. That is unusual. Elephants are careful mothers and do not leave their young unattended. The skeleton is the mother, and the baby is an orphan. . . .

20   The wild animals fetch back at least 2 million years. They represent, we imagine, the first order of creation, and they are vividly marked with God's eccentric genius of design: life poured into pure forms, life unmitigated by complexities of consciousness, language, ethics, treachery, revulsion, reason, religion, premeditation or free will. A wild animal does not contradict its own nature, does not thwart itself, as man endlessly does. A wild animal never plays for the other side. The wild animals are a holiday from deliberation. They are sheer life. To behold a bright being that lives without thought is, to the complex, cross-grained human mind, profoundly liberating. And even if they had no effect upon the human mind, still the wild animals are life—other life.

21   John Donne asked, "Was not the first man, by the desire of knowledge, corrupted even in the whitest integrity of nature?" The animals are a last glimpse of that shadowless life, previous to time and thought. They are a pure connection to the imagination of God.

Expanding Vocabulary

1. Match each word in column A with its definition in column B. When in doubt, first find the word in the essay and look for context clues to aid your understanding of the word's meaning. Then, if necessary, use your dictionary to complete the matching exercise.

Column A	Column B
naïf (1)	original
escarpment (2)	sensual
annunciation (2)	irregular
thermals (3)	luminous
primal (3)	directions
abnegation (6)	open grassland
phosphorescent (7)	excessively worried about
premonition (8)	health
gnarled (13)	current of warm air
magisterial (13)	unqualified or unaffected
erotic (14)	natural simplicity
Atlantis (15)	authoritative
metabolism (15)	meager
undulous (15)	forewarning
eccentric (15)	expresses through gestures
adrenal (16)	twisted and knotty
vectors (16)	mythical island
veldt (17)	worthless
hypochondriac (17)	religious significance
paltry (17)	process of generating energy in
lumpen-carrion (18)	an organism
gesticulates (19)	sudden charge of energy
unmitigated (20)	rejection
	clifflike ridge of land or rock
	wavelike

2. Morrow mentions three people he expects his readers to know. After checking a dictionary or encyclopedia, add a one-sentence biographical statement to your text for Carl Jung, Karen Blixen, and John Donne.

Understanding Content

1. In the first thirteen paragraphs, Morrow paints the East Africa game preserve landscape. What are the predominant colors of this landscape? What does the land look like?
2. Morrow devotes paragraph 7 to the hyenas. What image of this animal emerges? How does the detail of the hyenas romping in the darkness help to create Morrow's view of the hyenas?
3. In paragraphs 14 through 19 Morrow describes the animals' movements. Read these paragraphs again, picturing each animal's

movements as Morrow presents them. Which animals would you want to see first? Why?

4. Morrow notes what others have also experienced when on safari in a group: members of the group have animal favorites. Morrow suggests that preferences may be connected to sexual attractions. Is this a new idea for you? Does it seem to make sense?

5. Morrow ends the section on movement with nonmovement: a dead elephant and lonely baby elephant. How does this detail contribute to the image of East Africa that he seeks to develop? If the animals become extinct, what will we have lost?

Drawing Inferences about Thesis and Purpose

1. What is Morrow's subject?

2. What is his purpose in writing—or does he have several purposes? What would he like readers to see? To understand?

3. Is there one sentence in the essay that could stand as Morrow's thesis? If you don't think so, then state the essay's thesis in your own words.

4. After several paragraphs about the wildebeests, Morrow concludes that "God's genius . . . may have faltered." Why? What details lead to this conclusion?

5. Why, in Morrow's view, are the animals "pure forms" and "sheer life"? How do they differ from humans? What do they represent in the development of life forms?

Analyzing Strategies and Style

1. Look at Morrow's opening paragraphs. What does the first paragraph accomplish? As the camera rolls on, what is added in paragraph 2? How do these two scenes announce the complex world of the game preserve that Morrow develops in the rest of the essay?

2. Examine Morrow's organization. Is it appropriate to say that Morrow first shows us photographs of his trip and then a videotape? Why?

3. How many paragraphs at the beginning of the essay give us photographs? How many separate photos are needed? What is the organizing principle of the photos?

4. Morrow works with images of light and dark: "blinding clarities" and "shadows" (paragraph 8). How do these images help him develop his reflections on what this landscape and its animal inhabitants represent?

5. In addition to the play of light and dark, Morrow presents other details as contrasts, almost contradictions. Find some examples. Is a

landscape of contrasts simple or complex? Boring or awesome? What sense of this world does the author give us?

6. Morrow uses some striking metaphors to develop his description. Find three that you particularly like and explain why they are effective.

Thinking Critically

1. Has Morrow rekindled, or awakened, in you an interest in the wildlife of East Africa? If so, but you cannot afford to go on safari, what can you do to see these animals and learn more about them? List as many sources of information and experience as you can.
2. On the basis of Morrow's description—or your experiences— which of the big game is your favorite animal? Why? What attracts you to that animal? List the characteristics that you find appealing.
3. Closer to home, what domestic animal is or would be your favorite pet? Why? List the characteristics that you find appealing.
4. Should we be concerned about the possible extinction of the African elephant or rhino, the two most seriously threatened of the big game in East Africa? Why or why not? Be prepared to defend your position.

"The Autumn Garden"

LAUREN SPRINGER

With a master's degree in horticulture, Lauren Springer (b. 1959) gardens for pleasure and professionally. She has written a gardening column for *The Denver Post* and is currently a contributing editor to *Horticulture* magazine. She is also a designer of public gardens in several cities and is the author of several books on gardening. The following description of gardens in autumn is a chapter from her book *The Undaunted Garden,* published in 1994.

Fresh, vibrant June passes to a languid, slow July. Then comes a turning point, when summer suddenly feels utterly tiresome. Some years, late summer weather is kind and merciful, indulging the gardener in a quick turn to cool nights and days filled with a mellow, amber sunlight that actually feels

1

good on the face, totally unlike the prickling and piercing rays of high summer. Other years, the wait is interminable, summer's heat oozing on well into months traditionally autumnal.

2   Autumn has become my favorite time of the year. It took a while for negative associations with the beginning of the school year to wane, for the golden sunlight and foliage to stop conjuring up the intestinal butterflies that went along with similarly toned school buses lurching down the street. While some find spring with all its optimistic beginnings the finest season in the garden, I much prefer the unfrenzied pace of fall. In the spring, it is easy to feel overwhelmed by the sudden demands of the garden. A long winter has a way of creating such great yearnings and high expectations that I could almost say I feel a bit pressured by the new season, not to mention out of shape after a lazy winter spent fattening up by the fire. By autumn, I'm synchronized with the garden, lean and mean, realistic about my expectations. The garden requires much less of me—weeds are well under control and careful deadheading has long been abandoned. As a friend once described so well, the autumn garden is a machete garden. Anyone still trying to control or tame it in September is either hopelessly deluded or has a strange need to use large cutting tools from the jungle. The season transforms the garden and the gardener. While a similar scene in June might send one scrambling for stakes and twine, come September, it is a wonderful sense of release to watch plants collapse slowly on each other, soft and heavy with the weight of a full season's growth. Leaves begin to yellow and brown. Flowers become seeds. Everything is soft, large, ripe. As I walk among the plants, they reflect my mood—placid and self-satisfied.

3   Fall isn't all retrospective mellowness. It is also a time for renewed activity. As the oppressive heat wanes, rediscovered energy can be put to great use, and not just for the traditional autumnal rite of bulb planting. Seed collecting kicks into high gear. Autumn is also the best time to assess the garden and decide which plants need to be moved, divided or tossed out altogether. Plants are at their largest, and crowding is painfully evident. A plant from which one waited patiently for some sign of beauty can now be given the old heave-ho without reservations if it has failed to perform. Integrating new plants is eas-

ier than ever; a full, live picture lies before the gardener, helping inspire good combinations as compared to the spring, when tiny, barely awakened leaf rosettes require calling upon strong imaging powers to visualize what may develop later. Most plants relish the chance to put out good roots without the competition of top growth and moisture-sapping heat. The soil stays warm much longer than the air, giving fall-planted individuals a long season of underground growth and establishment. If it weren't for the fact that some plants are not available in the fall, I would probably stop almost all my spring planting. Even small transplanted seedlings, given the benefit of some mulch around their base, have done remarkably well when planted in the fall.

Autumn is a time when warm color and rustling sounds resonate throughout the plant world. In the deciduous woodlands of the East and Midwest, winter spreads down the land from north to south, from highland to lowland, rolling a carpet of foliage color over the landscape before it. The land, so serenely green for all those months, suddenly looks like an infrared photograph. On the grasslands of the prairie and plains, the tired gray-green and buff of late summer take on richer amber, sienna and rust tones as the foliage and seedheads of the grasses ripen. Late-blooming wildflowers, predominantly deep golds and purples, attract sleepy butterflies and bees, while more energetic birds frenetically gorge themselves on seeds before the first snow cover blankets the land. 4

The sun arcs lower in the sky, softening and burnishing the light. All colors seem to emanate an inner warmth as if the heat of the summer were stored within them. The most mundane scenes—an empty concrete basketball court alive with whirling, wind-blown leaves, a chocolate-brown field spiked with tawny corn stubble—take on the qualities of gold leaf, the light of a Venetian Renaissance painting. 5

The lower sun also creates lovely lighting effects in the garden. While in summer it would be suppertime before any similar effect might be possible, now mid- and late afternoon becomes a time for backlit drama. Grass panicles glisten and shimmer when touched by the slanted light; foliage reds and golds are intensified as the sun passes through them; fragile petals resemble halos given this autumnal spotlight. 6

7   Just as fall is a time for letting go, for riding with the slow, melancholy yet beautiful decline toward the inevitability of winter, it is also a time for loosening up rigid color rules. What may jar in the May and June garden is a welcome sight in October. Colors have richened and deepened with the cooler temperatures and golden light. The sunlight of autumn softens the boundaries that in spring and summer define orange, red, magenta and purple. The gardener should soften as well. Just as a person living out his or her last years should be indulged some special extravagances and not judged harshly for them, so should an autumnal garden be allowed a grand finale of wild color fireworks without too many "tasteful" restraints. Nature combines cobalt skies, red and yellow leaves and purple asters; the gardener does well to take inspiration from these stunning scenes.

8   Form and texture take on their most important roles this time of the year—seedheads, flower stalks and the mature size of the plants create a sense of fullness, of tactile and visual abundance. Grasses hiss and rattle in the breezes like so many whispering crones. I chuckle thinking of the overexcited Halloweeners soon to pass by the ravenna grass and miscanthus clumps. Not only are the grasses large enough to hide a menacing creature, their wind-borne voices are sure to strike fear in the more imaginative and suggestible trick-or-treaters. The sweet civility of Christmas, with its parade of guests to kiss and horrible velvet jumpers to wear, scored a distant second on my childhood holiday rankings, far behind the front-runner, Halloween. Those seemingly interminable dark walks between houses, long before street-lit safety became an issue, were more adrenalizing than the mountains of candy filling the sack. Sadly Halloween, with our good-natured attempts to protect the little ones from the increasingly dangerous traffic and increasingly sick adults, has become an utter bore. Children show up listlessly at the door with parents in tow. Well-lit malls and gymnasiums filled with high-tech scary props that now often host the event will never equal those unchaperoned nights spent running from whispering, chattering, cackling plant life.

9   Back in the garden, a frosty morning transforms all things hairy, spiny, silver. Prickly pear, snowball and claret-cup cactus are caught in a crystalline net of hoary spines. Lambs ears, san-

tolina and *Salvia argentea* glisten in the weak early sunlight. The artemisias, a frosty sight even in the heat of summer, take on an ethereal quality. *Artemisia caucasica,* a four-inch shrublet, and huge four-foot *A.* x 'Powis Castle' are the laciest. Whitest are ground-hugging *A. stellerana* and 18-inch *A.* x 'Valerie Finnis'. Prettiest of all, though, is the sparkling silver skeleton of 'Silver King' artemisia's flower panicles. The foliage of this plant is nice, but I can find silver in many other plants less inclined to bossiness in the garden. The only reason I tolerate this spreading garden thug (and only in one small, isolated spot) is for those delicate flower stalks that appear late in the summer and remain until the first heavy snow flattens them. Their airy effect is intensified on those mornings when hoarfrost transforms the landscape and they look like white plumes of chilled breath from the garden.

Two very distinct autumn scenes dominate my garden. The 10 east-facing rose garden offers lingering pastel perennials and frost-tolerant annuals among the last cabbagy heads of various peach, pink, yellow and white ever-blooming David Austin roses. On the other side of the house, in the warm western sun, grasses, late-blooming perennials and tough annuals in hot colors—indigo-blue, red, orange, gold, purple—burn brightly until well into November when a pummeling of successive hard frosts and snowy dustings finally extinguish them. The two areas couldn't be any more different in mood.

The rose garden acquiesces, its billowing denizens bowing 11 slowly to the end of the season. Some of the rose blossoms tend to ball, not opening fully, yet their colors are deeper than any other time of the season. The gallica roses' foliage takes on burgundy overtones. Pearl-like buds of Japanese anemones—pink 'September Charm' and large white 'Honorine Jobert'—begin to open. These aristocrats of the fall-blooming perennials raise their flowers on sturdy yet wire-thin stems high above the lush, grapelike foliage. Their blossoms, so simple of face—a yellow center surrounded by five or so oblong petals just as a child would draw—have a charm unmatched by the most intricate orchid. Companion to them are the white bottlebrush spikes of foul-smelling *Cimicifuga simplex* 'White Pearl', placed well in the back between the larger rose shrubs. Seen and not smelled from a distance, the flowers resemble fine white tapers, slightly bent as if they had been stored in too hot a place over the summer.

12   Small patches of color appear here and there against the tangle of fading greens. A persistent panicle of white 'Miss Lingard' phlox, much appreciated for its long bloom and resistance to mildew, stands out, almost blindingly pristine, like a beacon from the muted background. A spangle of fluorescent pale yellow *Coreopsis verticillata* 'Moonbeam' daisies flirt with hardy ageratum (*Eupatorium coelestinum*), a tough, foot-tall spreader with fuzzy, periwinkle blue flower heads that, like 'Moonbeam' coreopsis, take on extra luminescence late in the day. Various nicotianas, surprisingly frost-tolerant given their leafy, tropical appearance, weave in and about the roses. Graceful white dusk-blooming *Nicotiana alata* attracts the last hawk- and hummingbird moths of the season to its fragrant, tubular flowers. Lanky *Nicotiana langsdorfii* dangles small lime green bells over a spray of apricot 'Bredon' roses. *N. sylvestris*, in all its bulk, still opens a few white blossoms in its starburst of a flowerhead, and the few solitary chartreuse stars of an unknown nicotiana seedling frame the last blooms of fragrant pink damask rose 'Comte de Chambord'.

13   While I appreciate these soft remnants of the lush, heady bloom that drew my attention to the rose garden in June, now I am drawn to the west side. Early shadows encase the east side; the warmth of the season lingers on the west. The plantings here are grown hotter and drier, staying smaller and less apt to tumble. Many perennials are still flowering or just peaking. Self-sown annuals abound, starting their bloom later than transplants and giving a prolonged show well into fall.

Expanding Vocabulary

Match each word in column A with its definition in column B. When in doubt, first find the word in the essay and look for context clues to aid your understanding of the word's meaning. Then, if necessary, use your dictionary to complete the matching exercise.

Column A	*Column B*
vibrant (1)	residents
indulging (1)	arranged to happen at the same time
interminable (1, 8)	

conjuring (2)	issue from
synchronized (2)	ordinary
machete (2)	conclusion
placid (2)	gray or white as if with age
retrospective (3)	beating
emanate (5)	in a pure state
mundane (5)	yielding to desires or whims
panicles (6, 9)	delicate, airy
finale (7)	light produced without heat
crystalline (9)	performing magic
hoary (9)	consents without protest
ethereal (9)	contemplation of past events
thug (9)	like clear glass
pummeling (10)	full of energy and vigor
acquiesces (11)	ruffian
denizens (11)	large, broad-bladed knife
pristine (12)	tiresomely long
luminescence (12)	branched clusters of flowers
	with flowers arranged along
	each branch
	calm, composed, at ease

Understanding Content

1. What is the author's favorite season?
2. What are the advantages of autumn over spring for the gardener?
3. What are the gardener's activities in autumn? Why can fall be a good time to plant?
4. What is Springer's favorite holiday? Why? What has happened to the holiday today?
5. Which of her gardens does she prefer in autumn? Why?

Drawing Inferences about Thesis and Purpose

1. What is Springer's purpose in writing? Is it appropriate to say that she has several purposes? (How does she want readers to feel? What would she like them to do?)
2. What is Springer's thesis?

Analyzing Strategies and Style

1. Springer evokes the beauty of the autumn garden. Examine paragraphs 6 and 7 and then explain how she does it.
2. The author appeals to many senses. Find passages that appeal to different senses. See how many senses she appeals to.

3. Springer brings in two holidays. How does her discussion of them fit into her general subject?

Thinking Critically

1. Was the author able to make you see her garden in autumn? If so, what makes her description effective? If not, why not?
2. Do you like gardening? Why or why not? Has Springer changed your thinking in any way?
3. Will you look at autumn differently now?
4. Why do we sometimes give more value to spring or summer than to autumn? Has Springer convinced you to appreciate autumn too?

"My Father"

DORIS LESSING

Born in Persia (now Iran) but reared in Southern Rhodesia (now Zimbabwe), Doris Lessing (b. 1919) left school at fourteen, took various odd jobs, and began to write, first in Africa and now in London. She has steadily published short stories, plays, and novels since 1950 and is considered by critics to be one of the most significant contemporary writers. She has several short story collections, including *A Man and Two Women* (1963); several short novels, including *The Grass Is Singing* (1950); and many novels, including her most celebrated one, *The Golden Notebook* (1962). A number of essays and reviews are collected in *A Small Personal Voice* (1975). In "My Father," first published in 1963 in the London *Sunday Telegraph,* we see Lessing's commitment to portraying her father clearly and honestly, and accepting the figure in the portrait.

1   We use our parents like recurring dreams, to be entered into when needed; they are always there for love or for hate; but it occurs to me that I was not always there for my father. I've written about him before, but novels, stories, don't have to be "true." Writing this article is difficult because it has to be "true." I knew him when his best years were over.

2   There are photographs of him. The largest is of an officer in the 1914–18 war. A new uniform—buttoned, badged, strapped, tabbed—confines a handsome, dark young man who holds

himself stiffly to confront what he certainly thought of as his duty. His eyes are steady, serious, and responsible, and show no signs of what he became later. A photograph at sixteen is of a dark, introspective youth with the same intent eyes. But it is his mouth you notice—a heavily-jutting upper lip contradicts the rest of a regular face. His moustache was to hide it: "Had to do something—a damned fleshy mouth. Always made me uncomfortable, that mouth of mine."

Earlier a baby (eyes already alert) appears in a lace waterfall 3 that cascades from the pillowy bosom of a fat, plain woman to her feet. It is the face of a head cook. "Lord, but my mother was a practical female—almost as bad as you!" as he used to say, or throw at my mother in moments of exasperation. Beside her stands, or droops, arms dangling, his father, the source of the dark, arresting eyes, but otherwise masked by a long beard.

The birth certificate says: Born 3rd August, 1886, Walton 4 Villa, Creffield Road, S. Mary at the Wall, R.S.D. Name, Alfred Cook. Name and surname of Father: Alfred Cook Tayler. Name and maiden name of Mother: Caroline May Batley. Rank or Profession: Bank Clerk. Colchester, Essex.

They were very poor. Clothes and boots were a problem. 5 They "made their own amusements." Books were mostly the Bible and *The Pilgrim's Progress*. Every Saturday night they bathed in a hip-bath in front of the kitchen fire. No servants. Church three times on Sundays. "Lord, when I think of those Sundays! I dreaded them all week, like a nightmare coming at you full tilt and no escape." But he rabbited with ferrets along the lanes and fields, bird-nested, stole fruit, picked nuts and mushrooms, paid visits to the blacksmith and the mill and rode a farmer's carthorse.

They ate economically, but when he got diabetes in his for- 6 ties and subsisted on lean meat and lettuce leaves, he remembered suet puddings, treacle puddings, raisin and currant puddings, steak and kidney puddings, bread and butter pudding, "batter cooked in the gravy with the meat," potato cake, plum cake, butter cake, porridge with treacle, fruit tarts and pies, brawn, pig's trotters and pig's cheek and home-smoked ham and sausages. And "lashings of fresh butter and cream and eggs." He wondered if this diet had produced the diabetes, but said it was worth it.

7   There was an elder brother described by my father as: "Too damned clever by half. One of those quick, clever brains. Now I've always had a slow brain, but I get there in the end, damn it!"

8   The brothers went to a local school and the elder did well, but my father was beaten for being slow. They both became bank clerks in, I think, the Westminster Bank, and one must have found it congenial, for he became a manager, the "rich brother," who had cars and even a yacht. But my father did not like it, though he was conscientious. For instance, he changed his writing, letter by letter, because a senior criticised it. I never saw his unregenerate hand, but the one he created was elegant, spiky, careful. Did this mean he created a new personality for himself, hiding one he did not like, as he hid his "damned fleshy mouth"? I don't know.

9   Nor do I know when he left home to live in Luton or why. He found family life too narrow? A safe guess—he found everything too narrow. His mother was too down-to-earth? He had to get away from his clever elder brother?

10   Being a young man in Luton was the best part of his life. It ended in 1914, so he had a decade of happiness. His reminiscences of it were all of pleasure, the delight of physical movement, of dancing in particular. All his girls were "a beautiful dancer, light as a feather." He played billiards and ping-pong (both for his county); he swam, boated, played cricket and football, went to picnics and horse races, sang at musical evenings. One family of a mother and two daughters treated him "like a son only better. I didn't know whether I was in love with the mother or the daughters, but oh I did love going there; we had such good times." He was engaged to one daughter, then, for a time, to the other. An engagement was broken off because she was rude to a waiter. "I could not marry a woman who allowed herself to insult someone who was defenceless." He used to say to my wryly smiling mother: "Just as well I didn't marry either of *them*; they would never have stuck it out the way you have, old girl."

11   Just before he died he told me he had dreamed he was standing in a kitchen on a very high mountain holding X in his arms. "Ah, yes, that's what I've missed in my life. Now don't you let yourself be cheated out of life by the old dears. They take all the colour out of everything if you let them."

But in that decade—"I'd walk 10, 15 miles to a dance two or   12
three times a week and think nothing of it. Then I'd dance
every dance and walk home again over the fields. Sometimes
it was moonlight, but I liked the snow best, all crisp and fresh.
I loved walking back and getting into my digs just as the sun
was rising. My little dog was so happy to see me, and I'd feed
her, and make myself porridge and tea, then I'd wash and
shave and go off to work."

The boy who was beaten at school, who went too much to   13
church, who carried the fear of poverty all his life, but who
nevertheless was filled with the memories of country plea-
sures; the young bank clerk who worked such long hours for
so little money, but who danced, sang, played, flirted—this naturally vigorous, sensuous being was killed in 1914, 1915, 1916.
I think the best of my father died in that war, that his spirit was
crippled by it. The people I've met, particularly the women,
who knew him young, speak of his high spirits, his energy, his
enjoyment of life. Also of his kindness, his compassion and—a
word that keeps recurring—his wisdom. "Even when he was
just a boy he understood things that you'd think even an old
man would find it easy to condemn." I do not think these people would have easily recognized the ill, irritable, abstracted,
hypochondriac man I knew.

He "joined up" as an ordinary soldier out of a characteristi-   14
cally quirky scruple: it wasn't right to enjoy officers' privileges
when the Tommies had such a bad time. But he could not stick
the communal latrines, the obligatory drinking, the collective
visits to brothels, the jokes about girls. So next time he was offered a commission he took it.

His childhood and young man's memories, kept fluid, were   15
added to, grew, as living memories do. But his war memories
were congealed in stories that he told again and again, with the
same words and gestures, in stereotyped phrases. They were
anonymous, general, as if they had come out of a communal
war memoir. He met a German in no-man's-land, but both
slowly lowered their rifles and smiled and walked away. The
Tommies were the salt of the earth, the British fighting men the
best in the world. He had never known such comradeship. A
certain brutal officer was shot in a sortie[1] by his men, but the

---

[1]A rapid movement of besieged troops to take the offensive.—Ed.

other officers, recognizing rough justice, said nothing. He had known men intimately who saw the Angels at Mons.[2] He wished he could force all the generals on both sides into the trenches for just one day, to see what the common soldiers endured—*that* would have ended the war at once.

16   There was an undercurrent of memories, dreams, and emotions much deeper, more personal. This dark region in him, fate-ruled, where nothing was true but horror, was expressed inarticulately, in brief, bitter exclamations or phrases of rage, incredulity, betrayal. The men who went to fight in that war believed it when they said it was to end war. My father believed it. And he was never able to reconcile his belief in his country with his anger at the cynicism of its leaders. And the anger, the sense of betrayal, strengthened as he grew old and ill.

17   But in 1914 he was naïve, the German atrocities in Belgium inflamed him, and he enlisted out of idealism, although he knew he would have a hard time. He knew because a fortuneteller told him. (He could be described as uncritically superstitious or as psychically gifted.) He would be in great danger twice, yet not die—he was being protected by a famous soldier who was his ancestor. "And sure enough, later I heard from the Little Aunties that the church records showed we were descended the backstairs way from the Duke of Wellington, or was it Marlborough? Damn it, I forget. But one of them would be beside me all through the war, she said." (He was romantic, not only about this solicitous ghost, but also about being a descendant of the Huguenots, on the strength of the "e" in Tayler; and about "the wild blood" in his veins from a great uncle who, sent unjustly to prison for smuggling, came out of a ten-year sentence and earned it, very efficiently, along the coasts of Cornwall until he died.)

18   The luckiest thing that ever happened to my father, he said, was getting his leg shattered by shrapnel ten days before Passchendaele.[3] His whole company was killed. He knew he was going to be wounded because of the fortuneteller, who had said he would know. "I did not understand what she meant, but both times in the trenches, first when my appendix burst

[2]A Belgian town, site of a World War I battle.—Ed.
[3]A town in Belgium, site of a bloody World War I battle.—Ed.

and I nearly died, and then just before Passchendaele, I felt for some days as if a thick, black velvet pall was settled over me. I can't tell you what it was like. Oh, it was awful, awful, and the second time it was so bad I wrote to the old people and told them I was going to be killed."

His leg was cut off at mid-thigh, he was shell-shocked, he 19 was very ill for many months, with a prolonged depression afterwards. "You should always remember that sometimes people are all seething underneath. You don't know what terrible things people have to fight against. You should look at a person's eyes, that's how you tell. . . . When I was like that, after I lost my leg, I went to a nice doctor man and said I was going mad, but he said, don't worry, everyone locks up things like that. You don't know—horrible, horrible, awful things. I was afraid of myself, of what I used to dream. I wasn't myself at all."

In the Royal Free Hospital was my mother, Sister McVeagh. 20 He married his nurse which, as they both said often enough (though in different tones of voice), was just as well. That was 1919. He could not face being a bank clerk in England, he said, not after the trenches. Besides, England was too narrow and conventional. Besides, the civilians did not know what the soldiers had suffered, they didn't want to know, and now it wasn't done even to remember "The Great Unmentionable." He went off to the Imperial Bank of Persia, in which country I was born.

The house was beautiful, with great stone-floored high- 21 ceilinged rooms whose windows showed ranges of snow-streaked mountains. The gardens were full of roses, jasmine, pomegranates, walnuts. Kermanshalhi[4] he spoke of with liking, but soon they went to Teheran, populous with "Embassy people," and my gregarious mother created a lively social life about which he was irritable even in recollection.

Irritableness—that note was first struck here, about Persia. 22 He did not like, he said, "the graft and the corruption." But here it is time to try and describe something difficult—how a man's good qualities can also be his bad ones, or if not bad, a danger to him.

My father was honourable—he always knew exactly what 23 that word meant. He had integrity. His "one does not do that

---

[4]A city in western Iran (formerly Persia).—Ed.

sort of thing," his "no, it is *not* right," sounded throughout my childhood and were final for all of us. I am sure it was true he wanted to leave Persia because of "the corruption." But it was also because he was already unconsciously longing for something freer, because as a bank official he could not let go into the dream-logged personality that was waiting for him. And later in Rhodesia, too, what was best in him was also what prevented him from shaking away the shadows: it was always in the name of honesty or decency that he refused to take this step or that out of the slow decay of the family's fortunes.

24   In 1925 there was leave from Persia. That year in London there was an Empire Exhibition, and on the Southern Rhodesian stand some very fine maize cobs and a poster saying that fortunes could be made on maize at 25/- a bag. So on an impulse, turning his back forever on England, washing his hands of the corruption of the East, my father collected all his capital, £800, I think, while my mother packed curtains from Liberty's, clothes from Harrods,[5] visiting cards, a piano, Persian rugs, a governess and two small children.

25   Soon, there was my father in a cigar-shaped house of thatch and mud on the top of a kopje that overlooked in all directions a great system of mountains, rivers, valleys, while overhead the sky arched from horizon to empty horizon. This was a couple of hundred miles south from the Zambesi,[6] a hundred or so west from Mozambique,[7] in the district of Banket, so called because certain of its reefs were of the same formation as those called *banket* on the Rand. Lomagundi[8]—gold country, tobacco country, maize country—wild, almost empty. (The Africans had been turned off it into reserves.) Our neighbours were four, five, seven miles off. In front of the house . . . no neighbours, nothing; no farms, just wild bush with two rivers but no fences to the mountains seven miles away. And beyond these mountains and bush again to the Portuguese border, over which "our boys" used to escape when wanted by the police for pass or other offences.

[5]Both Liberty's and Harrods are British department stores.—Ed.
[6]A river in southeastern Africa that flows to the Indian Ocean.—Ed.
[7]A southeastern African nation that borders Zimbabwe (formerly Southern Rhodesia).—Ed.
[8]A district in Zimbabwe west of Salisbury.—Ed.

And then? There was bad luck. For instance, the price of 26 maize dropped from 25/- to 9/- a bag. The seasons were bad, prices bad, crops failed. This was the sort of thing that made it impossible for him ever to "get off the farm," which, he agreed with my mother, was what he most wanted to do.

It was an absurd country, he said. A man could "own" a 27 farm for years that was totally mortgaged to the Government and run from the Land Bank, meanwhile employing half-a-hundred Africans at 12/- a month and none of them knew how to do a day's work. Why, two farm labourers from Europe could do in a day what twenty of these ignorant black savages would take a week to do. (Yet he was proud that he had a name as a just employer, that he gave "a square deal.") Things got worse. A fortuneteller had told him that her heart ached when she saw the misery ahead for my father: this was the misery.

But it was my mother who suffered. After a period of neu- 28 rotic illness, which was a protest against her situation, she became brave and resourceful. But she never saw that her husband was not living in a real world, that he had made a captive of her common sense. We were always about to "get off the farm." A miracle would do it—a sweepstake, a goldmine, a legacy. And then? What a question! We would go to England where life would be normal with people coming in for musical evenings and nice supper parties at the Trocadero after a show. Poor woman, for the twenty years we were on the farm, she waited for when life would begin for her and for her children, for she never understood that what was a calamity for her was for them a blessing.

Meanwhile my father sank towards his death (at 61). Every- 29 thing changed in him. He had been a dandy and fastidious, now he hated to change out of shabby khaki. He had been sociable, now he was misanthropic. His body's disorders—soon diabetes and all kinds of stomach ailments—dominated him. He was brave about his wooden leg, and even went down mine shafts and climbed trees with it, but he walked clumsily and it irked him badly. He greyed fast, and slept more in the day, but would be awake half the night pondering about. . . .

It could be gold divining. For ten years he experimented on 30 private theories to do with the attractions and repulsions of metals. His whole soul went into it but his theories were wrong or he was *unlucky*—after all, if he had found a mine he would have had to leave the farm. It could be the relation between the minerals of the earth and of the moon; his decision to make infusions of all the plants on the farm and drink them himself in the interests of science; the criminal folly of the British Government in not realising that the Germans and the Russians were conspiring as Anti-Christ to . . . the inevitability of war because no one would listen to Churchill, but it would be all right because God (by then he was a British Israelite) had destined Britain to rule the world; a prophecy said 10 million dead would surround Jerusalem—how would the corpses be cleared away?; people who wished to abolish flogging should be flogged; the natives understood nothing but a good beating; hanging must not be abolished because the Old Testament said "an eye for an eye and a tooth for a tooth. . . ."

31   Yet, as this side of him darkened, so that it seemed all his thoughts were of violence, illness, war, still no one dared to make an unkind comment in his presence or to gossip. Criticism of people, particularly of women, made him more and more uncomfortable till at last he burst out with: "It's all very well, but no one has the right to say that about another person."

32   In Africa, when the sun goes down, the stars spring up, all of them in their expected places, glittering and moving. In the rainy season, the sky flashed and thundered. In the dry season, the great dark hollow of night was lit by veld fires: the mountains burned through September and October in chains of red fire. Every night my father took out his chair to watch the sky and the mountains, smoking, silent, a thin shabby flyaway figure under the stars. "Makes you think—there are so many worlds up there, wouldn't really matter if we did blow ourselves up—plenty more where we came from."

33   The Second World War, so long foreseen by him, was a bad time. His son was in the Navy and in danger, and his daughter a sorrow to him. He became very ill. More and more often it was necessary to drive him into Salisbury with him in a coma, or in danger of one, on the back seat. My mother moved him into a pretty little suburban house in town near the hospitals, where he took to his bed and a couple of years later died. For the most part he was unconscious under drugs. When awake he talked obsessively (a tongue licking a nagging sore place)

about "the old war." Or he remembered his youth. "I've been dreaming—Lord, to see those horses come lickety-split down the course with their necks stretched out and the sun on their coats and everyone shouting.... I've been dreaming how I walked along the river in the mist as the sun was rising.... Lord, lord, lord, what a time that was, what good times we all had then, before the old war."

Expanding Vocabulary

Match each word in column A with its definition in column B. When in doubt, first find the word in the essay and look for context clues to aid your understanding of the word's meaning. Then, if necessary, use your dictionary to complete the matching exercise.

Column A	*Column B*
introspective (2)	friendly, pleasant personality
ferrets (5)	ironically humorous
diabetes (6)	person who worries about his or her health
congenial (8)	
conscientious (8)	lacking clear expression
wryly (10)	nonrationally or supernaturally aware
hypochondriac (13)	
quirky (14)	doubt, skepticism
scruple (14)	boiling with agitation or anger
congealed (15)	variety of polecat used to catch rabbits
inarticulately (16)	
incredulity (16)	view of life that questions the motives of others
cynicism (16)	
psychically (17)	disease that limits the body's use of sugar
seething (19)	
gregarious (21)	especially careful, neat
kopje (25)	peculiar, unusual behavior
fastidious (29)	honest and scrupulous
misanthropic (29)	outgoing with people
veld (32)	examining one's own mental state
	fixed, no longer fluid
	hating, distrusting people
	a restraint on action because of moral considerations
	open, bush country
	a small hill

Understanding Content

1. What is most striking about her father's physical appearance?
2. What feature most distressed her father? What did he do about it? How does this feature and his reaction to it become a telling detail of character?
3. Why, according to Lessing, did her father leave home when he was young? What specific motives does she suggest? What general motive?

Drawing Inferences about Thesis and Purpose

1. Lessing begins by asserting that although stories do not have to be "true," essays do. Both times she puts the word *true* in quotation marks. What is her point? In what sense is a novel true? Not true? In what sense is biography true? Not true? What is the difference between truth and fact?
2. In what ways did the war "kill" Lessing's father? How did the experience change him?
3. Lessing contrasts her father's accounts of his early life with his accounts of World War I. How did these tales differ? What do these differences reveal about her father?
4. What reason did her father give for leaving Persia? What other reasons might be found in his personality? Deriving from his war experiences?
5. What details of his final years in Africa can be explained by personality? By his early family life? By the war?

Analyzing Strategies and Style

1. In general, what characteristics of her writing make Lessing's portrait of interest to readers who may not already be interested in her or her father?
2. Observe Lessing's opening strategies. What does she accomplish by her opening paragraph? How does she begin her portrait? What does she not begin with? What make her strategies effective?
3. What does the author do in paragraph 6? What is effective about her strategy? What can you learn about good writing from studying this paragraph?
4. How would you describe the tone of this biographical essay? What seems to be the author's attitude toward her father? Toward the war?

Thinking Critically

1. Have you thought before about Lessing's distinctions between fiction and biography and between truth and fact? Do Lessing's distinctions make sense to you? If so, why? If not, why not?
2. Do you know anyone who is a war veteran? If so, how has the person been affected by his or her war experience? Does Lessing's father's change seem fairly typical or unusual?
3. Reflect on the nature of personality or character. Are we one person consistently, or are we continually reshaped (or new-shaped) by our life experiences? How stable, or how fluid, is personality?

STUDENT ESSAY: DESCRIPTION

A RELAXING RETREAT
Kim Lavecchia

For me, living in Northern Virginia is incredibly hectic. Dealing with the pressures of a demanding course load, a nonstop daily routine, and a nightmare commute all add up to that one word: stress. But when I need an escape from the troubles of daily life, Meadowlark Gardens is my own relaxing retreat. As I walk through these gardens they surround me with the quiet beauty of colorful vegetation which gradually tapers as it approaches the ponds where many migratory birds like to swim. If I plan my visit late in the day, I may be able to view a serene sunset that, when joined with the

Opening uses personal details.

Paragraph 1 ends with the thesis.

brilliant foliage and playful animals, takes my cares away.

Walking through the gardens, I enjoy the multicolored bedding plants that line the asphalt paths. As I enter the azalea woods my eye is immediately caught by a decagonal, latticework wedding gazebo made of redwood and landscaped by magenta coleus, fuschia and white impatiens, and assorted azaleas and holly bushes. Visible through the thicket are the rays of sunlight as they penetrate the thinning canopy ahead. Gradually the light becomes more intense as I journey along the path towards the open lawn at the edge of the forest. A rolling hill of green grass accented by rust-colored chrysanthemums and an array of lavender proceed to the floodplain where the lakes are nestled. Each contoured lake is bordered by colorful cherry and dogwood trees as well as brown-mulched bulb beds that resemble bull rushes. Standing in the midst of the pond basin I look towards the horizon and see a wild-life knoll filled with cypress trees serving as the habitat for many indigenous animal species.

Description begins with the gardens and paths leading to the lakes.

While I stroll around the lake, families of mallard ducks, Canadian geese, and mute swans glide through the misty

Writer draws on many sense impressions to describe the lake.

green water, waiting for passersby to toss them scraps of day-old bread. Enthusiastic tots loft bread onto the water, causing competition among the pondfish and the birds for every last morsel. A leisurely wind blows through the trees, cooling my arms and legs. If I stop and listen, the wind sounds like the slow hiss of air leaking from an inner tube. The scent of mulch assails my nostrils as I enjoy the scenery and listen to the honking and quacking of the waterfowl.

The day concludes with a brilliant display of orange and yellow rays of light filtering through the clouds as the sun approaches the horizon. An iridescent path of golden light reaches across the lake like an outstretched hand. The gentle warmth of the setting sun fills me with a peaceful glow that renews my faith in myself.

Last are the descriptive details of the sunset.

After a day of demanding activities, I take comfort in knowing I can retreat to a private oasis. The combination of the vivid vegetation, frolicking animals, and picturesque sunset mute the faint sounds of civilization in the background, making Meadowlark Gardens my own relaxing retreat.

Conclusion restates the thesis.

MAKING CONNECTIONS
---

1. Degas and Picasso both depict dancers in their paintings. (See reproductions following p. 76.) How do their paintings differ? How do the differences in presentation change the viewer's "picture" of dancers? Can one painting be said to be more realistic than the other? If so, what is meant by *realistic*?

2. Both Vermeer and Bazille present women at work. (See reproductions following p. 76.) How do their presentations differ? How does each artist want viewers to feel, or respond, to the woman in his painting?

3. In their essays both Tracy Kidder and Maya Angelou create a "portrait" of a woman at work. How do the writers feel about their subjects? How do you know?

4. Study the essays of Kidder, Angelou, and Lessing. What conclusions can you draw about effective strategies for presenting telling details of character?

5. Lessing's father was shaped both by his childhood and by World War I. Santha Rama Rau (pp. 52–58) was shaped by where she grew up and also because of her ethnicity. Elizabeth Wong (pp. 45–47) and Luis Rodriguez (pp. 41–43) are influenced by growing up as minorities in American culture. Think about what these writers say—or imply—about the shaping of personality. Reflect: What are the strongest forces in the molding of character?

TOPICS AND GUIDELINES FOR WRITING
---

1. Describe a place you know well and that has a special significance for you. (Possibilities include your backyard, the path you walked to school, a favorite park, playground, vacation spot, city street.) Give the details that will let your reader see this place clearly, as Lauren Springer lets us see her autumn garden. But also provide the telling details that will let your reader understand why this place has (or had)

significance for you, why it is (or was) special. Organize details according to some spatial pattern.

2. Describe a place you have visited that produced a strong reaction in you, a place that you fell in love with (e.g., Fifth Avenue the week before Christmas), heartily disliked (e.g., Los Angeles in heavy smog), found incredibly beautiful or awe-inspiring or special in some way (e.g., the Florida Everglades, Niagara Falls, the green hills of Vermont). Give enough details to let readers who have not been there see the place, but concentrate on presenting those details so that readers will want to visit—or never visit—depending on your thesis.

3. Describe a room on your campus to develop and support the thesis that the room fulfills—or fails to fulfill—its purpose or function. Possibilities include a classroom, science lab, learning lab, writing center, cafeteria, or library. If your library is a large and separate building, select one section of it, such as the periodicals room. Resist the urge to describe a large building, such as the entire student center. Instead, focus on one place and present details to support your thesis. Organize details according to some spatial pattern.

4. Lance Morrow offers readers some detailed and moving descriptions of animals he saw in the East Africa game preserves. If you enjoy wildlife, either in the wild or in a nearby zoo, take some time to watch one of your favorite animals. Or, if you have a pet, reflect on that animal. Then write a description of the animal you have selected, giving many details but also the telling details that will support a thesis about the animal. Reflect on what is central to the animal's way of life or personality to arrive at your thesis. Is the animal funny? Endearing? Inspiring? Mean? Intelligent or clever? These are some possible ideas around which you can build your thesis.

5. How well do you see someone close to you—a family member, friend, colleague, teacher? Select telling physical and biographical details to create an interesting and thoughtful portrait of the person you select. Pay close attention to the details that shape personality.

6. Select one of the paintings reproduced in this text (including *Homage to Monet* on the cover), or find a color reproduction of a favorite painting in your library's art book collection. Explain how the details in the painting work to create the painting's dominant effect. You will need to reflect on the painting's effect, or the artist's attitude toward the subject. Then ask yourself: How is that effect achieved by the details—the objects, composition, color, and brushwork—that make up the painting? Organize thoughtfully and use spatial terms (e.g., "in the foreground," "to the left of the main figure") to guide your reader through your description.

4

Using Comparison and Contrast

Ways of Learning

When we compare we examine similarities; when we contrast we examine differences. These are strategies frequently used—whether in thinking for ourselves or communicating with others—to organize information or ideas about two (or more) similar subjects. When you think about why you like your biology course more than your chemistry course, you begin to note points of difference between them. You begin to use contrast. When shopping for a stereo system, you might read a consumer guide or gather information from friends so that you can contrast several models for cost, reliability, and sound.

When to Use Comparison and Contrast

Let's see what we have said about thinking comparatively. First, it is a strategy for organizing information and ideas. You may be able to think more clearly about problems in your chemistry course if you contrast those problems with your successes in biology. Second, you have a reason to examine similarities or differences between subjects. Your goal, in our example, is to understand why you are doing better in biology than in chemistry. Perhaps you came to college thinking that you would major in chemistry. Rethinking career goals may be aided by a careful listing of specific differences in your study of chemistry and biology. (One difference is the amount of math needed in the study of chemistry. Could that be the problem?) Third, we compare or contrast items that are similar. There seems to be little purpose in contrasting your chemistry course with doing your laundry. We compare or contrast two cities, two schools, two jobs, two dorms. We probably do not contrast living in Louisville with living in a frat house because there is no point to such a contrast. (You might have good reason, though, to contrast living at home with living away at school.) Finally, a useful comparison or contrast focuses on important similarities or differences. If you have plenty of space for your new stereo, then contrasting the sizes of different systems is unimportant. But unless you have unlimited funds, the cost of each unit is quite important, important to your purpose for choosing the best stereo for you.

Remember that an organizing principle such as comparison or contrast does not supply a purpose for writing. Rather it is a strategy that needs to grow logically out of your topic and purpose. Jonathan Kozol contrasts two schools in the Chicago area to reveal great inequalities within our public school system. Students attending the suburban school have better facilities and more academic choices than those in the urban school. Kozol uses contrast to provide readers with information that may lead to questioning the fairness of these differences. The contrast is a strategy, not an end in itself.

How to Use Comparison and Contrast

Sometimes writers combine comparison and contrast, but more often their goal is to show either similarities or differences. Thus the student who asserts that there are good reasons for parents to move their children from McLean to Langley High School has a thesis that announces a contrast purpose. Although the schools certainly have some similarities—both are high schools in northern Virginia—readers will expect to learn about the significant differences between the two schools.

Organization

How should points of difference between two high schools (or any two items) be organized in an essay? You have two basic plans from which to choose. Suppose you want to show differences in the two buildings, in the courses offered, and in the extracurricular activities. If we assign "A" to McLean and "B" to

Langley and number the points of difference 1, 2, and 3, we can diagram the two patterns as follows:

<table>
<tr><td>*Whole by Whole*</td><td>*Part by Part*</td></tr>
<tr><td>A. McLean</td><td>A. Physical Plant</td></tr>
<tr><td>   1. McLean Physical Plant</td><td>   1. McLean</td></tr>
<tr><td>   2. McLean Courses</td><td>   2. Langley</td></tr>
<tr><td>   3. McLean Activities</td><td>B. Courses</td></tr>
<tr><td>B. Langley</td><td>   1. McLean</td></tr>
<tr><td>   1. Langley Physical Plant</td><td>   2. Langley</td></tr>
<tr><td>   2. Langley Courses</td><td>C. Activities</td></tr>
<tr><td>   3. Langley Activities</td><td>   1. McLean</td></tr>
<tr><td></td><td>   2. Langley</td></tr>
</table>

Observe that the whole-by-whole pattern organizes the essay first by school and then by points of difference, whereas the part-by-part pattern organizes the paper by the three (in this example) points of difference.

As you will see in the essays in this chapter, professional writers do not always strictly follow one plan or the other. Your instructor, however, may want you to practice using either the whole-by-whole or part-by-part structure. In fact, many instructors believe that, for most contrast topics, the part-by-part pattern is the best choice because it keeps writers focused on the business of explaining points of difference.

Transitions

When you read articles that have a comparison or contrast purpose, you may want to label the two subjects A and B and then, in the margin of your book, assign a number to each point of similarity or difference as you read. Then remember when you are writing a contrast essay that you want your reader to be able to recognize the parts of your contrast structure. This means that you will need to use appropriate transitions to mark the parts of your contrast structure. Consider these possibilities and other similar expressions to guide your reader:

by contrast	on the other hand
another difference	a third similarity

Metaphors and Analogies

When we think about the strategies of comparison and contrast, two related terms come to mind: metaphor (or simile) and analogy. We have said that we compare or contrast similar items: two schools, two courses, and so on. A *metaphor* (or a *simile*) differs in that it compares two items that are essentially unlike. When the poet writes the simile: "My love is like a red, red rose," he asks us to consider the ways that love (a feeling) can be like a rose (a flower). (To express the idea as a metaphor, the poet can write: "My love blooms.") In either case, we understand that a feeling isn't really like a flower. This is why a metaphor or a simile is called a *figure of speech*—we are speaking figuratively, not literally. The cleverness of a fresh metaphor delights us, sometimes surprises us, and affects us emotionally. You will find the poet Linda Pastan and the essayist E. B. White using metaphors effectively to express feelings about their subjects.

In the chapter's sixth essay, Liane Ellison Norman compares students to squirrels. That sounds like a metaphor because people and squirrels are not like items. But since Norman uses this figurative comparison as a way to develop her entire essay, to make a point about students, we call this strategy neither comparison nor metaphor but *analogy*. Think of an analogy as fanciful (like a metaphor) but developing a number of points of similarity or difference to support a thesis. Both metaphors and analogies, when original and thoughtful, enrich our writing. Some of this chapter's exercises will give you a chance to practice both strategies.

Getting Started: Reflecting on Expectations of College

Although you may not have been at college for long, still you have probably had some experiences that were not what you expected. Reflect on what you expected college to be like and how your experiences have, in part, differed from those expectations. In your journal or class notebook make two columns— one of expectations and one of what you have actually experienced. Have most of your expectations been met? Only some of them? Is there one important difference that is bothering you? You may want to write about that difference in another journal entry, or perhaps in an essay.

"Conversational Ballgames"

NANCY MASTERSON SAKAMOTO

American-born Sakamoto (b. 1931) lived with her Japanese husband in Osaka and taught English to Japanese students. She is currently a professor at Shitennoji Gakuen University in Hawaii. "Conversational Ballgames" is a chapter from her textbook on conversational English, *Polite Fictions,* published in 1982. Her contrasts of English and Japanese styles of conversation and her strategy for developing that contrast make us aware of the effect of cultural conditioning on the ways we learn to use language.

After I was married and had lived in Japan for a while, my 1
Japanese gradually improved to the point where I could take part in simple conversations with my husband and his friends and family. And I began to notice that often, when I joined in, the others would look startled, and the conversational topic would come to a halt. After this happened several times, it became clear to me that I was doing something wrong. But for a long time, I didn't know what it was.

Finally, after listening carefully to many Japanese conversa- 2
tions, I discovered what my problem was. Even though I was speaking Japanese, I was handling the conversation in a western way.

Japanese-style conversations develop quite differently from 3
western-style conversations. And the difference isn't only in the languages. I realized that just as I kept trying to hold western-style conversations even when I was speaking Japanese, so my English students kept trying to hold Japanese-style conversations even when they were speaking English. We were unconsciously playing entirely different conversational ballgames.

A western-style conversation between two people is like a 4
game of tennis. If I introduce a topic, a conversational ball, I expect you to hit it back. If you agree with me, I don't expect you simply to agree and do nothing more. I expect you to add something—a reason for agreeing, another example, or an elaboration to carry the idea further. But I don't expect you always to agree. I am just as happy if you question me, or challenge me,

or completely disagree with me. Whether you agree or disagree, your response will return the ball to me.

5   And then it is my turn again. I don't serve a new ball from my original starting line. I hit your ball back again from where it has bounced. I carry your idea further, or answer your questions or objections, or challenge or question you. And so the ball goes back and forth, with each of us doing our best to give it a new twist, an original spin, or a powerful smash.

6   And the more vigorous the action, the more interesting and exciting the game. Of course, if one of us gets angry, it spoils the conversation, just as it spoils a tennis game. But getting excited is not at all the same as getting angry. After all, we are not trying to hit each other. We are trying to hit the ball. So long as we attack only each other's opinions, and do not attack each other personally, we don't expect anyone to get hurt. A good conversation is supposed to be interesting and exciting.

7   If there are more than two people in the conversation, then it is like doubles in tennis, or like volleyball. There's no waiting in line. Whoever is nearest and quickest hits the ball, and if you step back, someone else will hit it. No one stops the game to give you a turn. You're responsible for taking your own turn.

8   But whether it's two players or a group, everyone does his best to keep the ball going, and no one person has the ball for very long.

9   A Japanese-style conversation, however, is not at all like tennis or volleyball. It's like bowling. You wait for your turn. And you always know your place in line. It depends on such things as whether you are older or younger, a close friend or a relative stranger to the previous speaker, in a senior or junior position, and so on.

10   When your turn comes, you step up to the starting line with your bowling ball, and carefully bowl it. Everyone else stands back and watches politely, murmuring encouragement. Everyone waits until the ball has reached the end of the alley, and watches to see if it knocks down all the pins, or only some of them, or none of them. There is a pause, while everyone registers your score.

11   Then, after everyone is sure that you have completely finished your turn, the next person in line steps up to the same starting line, with a different ball. He doesn't return your ball,

and he does not begin from where your ball stopped. There is no back and forth at all. All the balls run parallel. And there is always a suitable pause between turns. There is no rush, no excitement, no scramble for the ball.

No wonder everyone looked startled when I took part in 12 Japanese conversations. I paid no attention to whose turn it was, and kept snatching the ball halfway down the alley and throwing it back at the bowler. Of course the conversation died. I was playing the wrong game.

This explains why it is almost impossible to get a western- 13 style conversation or discussion going with English students in Japan. I used to think that the problem was their lack of English language ability. But I finally came to realize that the biggest problem is that they, too, are playing the wrong game.

Whenever I serve a volleyball, everyone just stands back and 14 watches it fall, with occasional murmurs of encouragement. No one hits it back. Everyone waits until I call on someone to take a turn. And when that person speaks, he doesn't hit my ball back. He serves a new ball. Again, everyone just watches it fall.

So I call on someone else. This person does not refer to what 15 the previous speaker has said. He also serves a new ball. Nobody seems to have paid any attention to what anyone else has said. Everyone begins again from the same starting line, and all the balls run parallel. There is never any back and forth. Everyone is trying to bowl with a volleyball.

And if I try a simpler conversation, with only two of us, then 16 the other person tries to bowl with my tennis ball. No wonder foreign English teachers in Japan get discouraged.

Now that you know about the difference in the conversa- 17 tional ballgames, you may think that all your troubles are over. But if you have been trained all your life to play one game, it is no simple matter to switch to another, even if you know the rules. Knowing the rules is not at all the same thing as playing the game.

Even now, during a conversation in Japanese I will notice a 18 startled reaction, and belatedly realize that once again I have rudely interrupted by instinctively trying to hit back the other person's bowling ball. It is no easier for me to "just listen" during a conversation than it is for my Japanese students to "just relax" when speaking with foreigners. Now I can truly sympathize with how hard they must find it to try to carry on a western-style conversation.

19   If I have not yet learned to do conversational bowling in Japanese, at least I have figured out one thing that puzzled me for a long time. After his first trip to America, my husband complained that Americans asked him so many questions and made him talk so much at the dinner table that he never had a chance to eat. When I asked him why he couldn't talk and eat at the same time, he said that Japanese do not customarily think that dinner, especially on fairly formal occasions, is a suitable time for extended conversation.

20   Since westerners think that conversation is an indispensable part of dining, and indeed would consider it impolite not to converse with one's dinner partner, I found this Japanese custom rather strange. Still, I could accept it as a cultural difference even though I didn't really understand it. But when my husband added, in explanation, that Japanese consider it extremely rude to talk with one's mouth full, I got confused. Talking with one's mouth full is certainly not an American custom. We think it very rude, too. Yet we still manage to talk a lot and eat at the same time. How do we do it?

21   For a long time, I couldn't explain it, and it bothered me. But after I discovered the conversational ballgames, I finally found the answer. Of course! In a western-style conversation, you hit the ball, and while someone else is hitting it back, you take a bite, chew, and swallow. Then you hit the ball again, and then eat some more. The more people there are in the conversation, the more chances you have to eat. But even with only two of you talking, you still have plenty of chances to eat.

22   Maybe that's why polite conversation at the dinner table has never been a traditional part of Japanese etiquette. Your turn to talk would last so long without interruption that you'd never get a chance to eat.

Expanding Vocabulary

Study definitions of each of the following words and then use each one in a separate sentence.

elaboration (4)	belatedly (18)
murmuring (10)	customarily (19)
registers (10)	etiquette (22)

Understanding Content

1. When Sakamoto first participated in Japanese conversations, what happened? What was the cause of her problem?
2. What are the characteristics of an American-style conversation?
3. What are the characteristics of a Japanese-style conversation?
4. How do the Japanese feel about conversing during dinner? How do Americans feel about dinner conversation?

Drawing Inferences about Thesis and Purpose

1. How hard is it to converse in another language after one has "learned" the language?
2. What is Sakamoto's thesis? Where is it stated?

Analyzing Strategies and Style

1. What strategy does Sakamoto use as an opening? What makes it effective?
2. What strategy does the author use to explain conversation patterns in English and in Japanese?
3. Explain each analogy; that is, how is American-style conversation like a tennis game, and how is Japanese-style conversation like bowling? What other game comparison does the author use?
4. Who is Sakamoto's primary audience? (Be sure to read the head-note.) What makes her writing style appropriate for her audience and purpose?

Thinking Critically

1. Did the author's analogies help you to see the differences between American and Japanese conversational styles? If not, why not? If the analogies did help you, can you explain why?
2. Had you thought before about the way we carry on conversations? If not, have you learned something about your own patterns of speech interaction? After reflection, do you agree with the author's description of American conversation patterns? Why or why not?
3. What differences between American culture and Japanese culture are suggested in Sakamoto's discussion of conversation?
4. What might we conclude about the relationship between language and cultural traits and values? What do we learn when, as children, we learn our primary language?

"Education"

E. B. WHITE

One of the finest of modern essayists, E. B. White (1899–1985) was born in New York, graduated from Cornell University, and made his name as a writer for the *New Yorker*. He also published many of his best-loved essays, including "Education," from 1938 to 1943 in *Harper's* and then collected them in *One Man's Meat* (1943). White the essayist may be best known for his now-classic children's stories: *Stuart Little, Charlotte's Web,* and *The Trumpet of the Swan*. You can learn much about essay writing by observing White's variation of contrast organization to reinforce thesis and by his use of examples and metaphors.

1   I have an increasing admiration for the teacher in the country school where we have a third-grade scholar in attendance. She not only undertakes to instruct her charges in all the subjects of the first three grades, but she manages to function quietly and effectively as a guardian of their health, their clothes, their habits, their mothers, and their snowball engagements. She has been doing this sort of Augean task for twenty years, and is both kind and wise. She cooks for the children on the stove that heats the room and she can cool their passions or warm their soup with equal competence. She conceives their costumes, cleans up their messes, and shares their confidences. My boy already regards his teacher as his great friend, and I think tells her a great deal more than he tells us.

2   The shift from city school to country school was something we worried about quietly all last summer. I have always rather favored public school over private school, if only because in public school you meet a greater variety of children. This bias of mine, I suspect, is partly an attempt to justify my own past (I never knew anything but public schools) and partly an involuntary defense against getting kicked in the shins by a young ceramist on his way to the kiln. My wife was unacquainted with public schools, never having been exposed (in her early life) to anything more public than the washroom of Miss Winsor's. Regardless of our backgrounds, we both knew

that the change in schools was something that concerned not us but the scholar himself. We hoped it would work out all right. In New York our son went to a medium-priced private institution with semi-progressive ideas of education, and modern plumbing. He learned fast, kept well, and we were satisfied. It was an electric, colorful, regimented existence with moments of pleasurable pause and giddy incident. The day the Christmas angel fainted and had to be carried out by one of the Wise Men was educational in the highest sense of the term. Our scholar gave imitations of it around the house for weeks afterward, and I doubt if it ever goes completely out of his mind.

His days were rich in formal experience. Wearing overalls and an old sweater (the accepted uniform of the private seminary), he sallied forth at morn accompanied by a nurse or a parent and walked (or was pulled) two blocks to a corner where the school bus made a flag stop. This flashy vehicle was as punctual as death: seeing us waiting at the cold curb, it would sweep to a halt, open its mouth, suck the boy in, and spring away with an angry growl. It was a good deal like a train picking up a bag of mail. At school the scholar was worked on for six or seven hours by half a dozen teachers and a nurse, and was revived on orange juice in mid-morning. In a cinder court he played games supervised by an athletic instructor, and in a cafeteria he ate lunch worked out by a dietician. He soon learned to read with gratifying facility and discernment and to make Indian weapons of a semi-deadly nature. Whenever one of his classmates fell low of a fever the news was put on the wires and there were breathless phone calls to physicians, discussing periods of incubation and allied magic.

In the country all one can say is that the situation is different, and somehow more casual. Dressed in corduroys, sweatshirt, and short rubber boots, and carrying a tin dinner-pail, our scholar departs at crack of dawn for the village school, two and a half miles down the road, next to the cemetery. When the road is open and the car will start, he makes the journey by motor, courtesy of his old man. When the snow is deep or the motor is dead or both, he makes it on the hoof. In the afternoons he walks or hitches all or part of the way home in fair weather, gets transported in foul. The schoolhouse is a two-room frame building, bungalow type, shingles stained a burnt brown with weather-resistant stain. It has a chemical toilet in the basement and two teachers above stairs. One takes the first three grades, the other the fourth, fifth, and sixth. They have little or no time for individual instruction, and no time at all for the esoteric. They teach what they know themselves, just as fast and as hard as they can manage. The pupils sit still at their desks in class, and do their milling around outdoors during recess.

5   There is no supervised play. They play cops and robbers (only they call it "Jail") and throw things at one another— snowballs in winter, rose hips in fall. It seems to satisfy them. They also construct darts, pinwheels, and "pick-up sticks" (jackstraws), and the school itself does a brisk trade in penny candy, which is for sale right in the classroom and which contains "surprises." The most highly prized surprise is a fake cigarette, made of cardboard, fiendishly lifelike.

6   The memory of how apprehensive we were at the beginning is still strong. The boy was nervous about the change too. The tension, on that first fair morning in September when we drove him to school, almost blew the windows out of the sedan. And when later we picked him up on the road, wandering along with his little blue lunch-pail, and got his laconic report "All right" in answer to our inquiry about how the day had gone, our relief was vast. Now, after almost a year of it, the only difference we can discover in the two school experiences is that in the country he sleeps better at night—and *that* probably is more the air than the education. When grilled on the subject of school-in-country *vs.* school-in-city, he replied that the chief difference is that the day seems to go so much quicker in the country. "Just like lightning," he reported.

Expanding Vocabulary

Study the definitions of each of the following words in your dictionary and then write the definition that fits the word's use in White's essay. Select five words and write a sentence for each word, using it in the same way that White does.

Augean (1)	kiln (2)
conceives (1)	giddy (2)
involuntary (2)	seminary (3)
ceramist (2)	sallied (3)

dietician (3)   allied (3)
facility (3)   esoteric (4)
discernment (3)   laconic (6)
incubation (3)

Understanding Content

1. Using "A" for the country school and "B" for the city school, outline White's organization paragraph by paragraph. Which contrast
structure does White most closely follow?
2. How does White vary the contrast structure he has selected? What
does he gain by this variation?
3. List the specific points of difference between the two school experiences (including travel, recess, etc.).

Drawing Inferences about Thesis and Purpose

1. Because White's son has attended only one city school and one country school, White cannot claim to be contrasting all (or most) city and
country schools. What, then, is he contrasting about education?
2. White does not state his thesis in the essay. We have to understand
his main point from his details, organization, and style. What is
White's thesis; that is, what point does he want to make about
education?

Analyzing Strategies and Style

1. The boy remembers the fainting Christmas angel from his city-
school days. Why does White give us this detail? What is its
significance?
2. White reveals his implied thesis in part through contrasting details.
Find several sentences that express differences between the schools.
How are the sentences similar? How do they differ? How do the differences in wording emphasize the differences between the schools?
3. White's metaphors may be his best strategy for expressing attitude.
Find two metaphors in paragraph 3, state the two items being compared, and explain how these metaphors express White's attitude
toward the city school.
4. In his second sentence, White lists various activities over which the
country school teacher is guardian. Does this list seem an odd combination to you? What is White's point here? Why is his list of
specifics more effective than a general statement would be?
5. White chooses words carefully, not only for meaning but for
sound—and the emphasis gained by repeating sounds. List all the

words in paragraph 1 that begin with the same first letter. (This technique is called *alliteration*.) What does White accomplish by having these words connected through sound?

Thinking Critically

1. Which school described by White do you think you would have preferred? Why?
2. White is contrasting elementary schools. Do you think his attitude would be different if he were contrasting an old, rural high school (without a gym, cafeteria, science labs, specialized teachers) and a modern, well-equipped suburban high school with specially trained teachers? Should his attitude be different?
3. In your view, how important are a school's facilities? How important are the teachers?
4. What are the most important traits for a teacher to have?

"A Tale of Two Schools"

JONATHAN KOZOL

A graduate of Harvard University and a Rhodes Scholar, Jonathan Kozol (b. 1936) has been an educator, a writer, and an activist on behalf of the poor. He has directed the National Literacy Coalition and written on the problems of illiteracy in *Illiterate America* (1988). He addressed the problems of the homeless in *Rachel and Her Children: Homeless Families in America* (1988) and of education for the poor in *Savage Inequalities: Children in America's Schools* (1991). Kozol's contrast of poor urban and rich suburban schools comes from *Savage Inequalities*.

1   New Trier's[1] physical setting might well make the students of Du Sable High School[2] envious. The *Washington Post* describes a neighborhood of "circular driveways, chirping birds and white-columned homes." It is, says a student, "a maple land of beauty and civility." While Du Sable is sited on one crowded city block, New Trier students have the use of 27 acres. While Du Sable's science students have to settle for makeshift equipment, New Trier's students have superior labs and up-to-

[1]Suburban Chicago high school.—Ed.
[2]Inner-city Chicago school.—Ed.

date technology. One wing of the school, a physical education center that includes three separate gyms, also contains a fencing room, a wrestling room and studios for dance instruction. In all, the school has seven gyms as well as an Olympic pool.

The youngsters, according to a profile of the school in *Town and Country* magazine, "make good use of the huge, well-equipped building, which is immaculately maintained by a custodial staff of 48." [2]

It is impossible to read this without thinking of a school like Goudy,[3] where there are no science labs, no music or art classes and no playground—and where the two bathrooms, lacking toilet paper, fill the building with their stench. [3]

"This is a school with a lot of choices," says one student at New Trier; and this hardly seems an overstatement if one studies the curriculum. Courses in music, art and drama are so varied and abundant that students can virtually major in these subjects in addition to their academic programs. The modern and classical language department offers Latin (four years) and six other foreign languages. Elective courses include the literature of Nobel winners, aeronautics, criminal justice, and computer languages. In a senior literature class, students are reading Nietzsche, Darwin, Plato, Freud and Goethe. The school also operates a television station with a broadcast license from the FCC, which broadcasts on four channels to three counties. [4]

Average class size is 24 children; classes for slower learners hold 15. This may be compared to Goudy—where a remedial class holds 39 children and a "gifted" class has 36. [5]

Every freshman at New Trier is assigned a faculty adviser who remains assigned to him or her through graduation. Each of the faculty advisers—they are given a reduced class schedule to allow them time for this—gives counseling to about two dozen children. At Du Sable, where the lack of staff prohibits such reduction in class schedules, each of the guidance counselors advises 420 children. [6]

The ambience among the students at New Trier, of whom only 1.3 percent are black, says *Town and Country*, is "wholesome and refreshing, a sort of throwback to the Fifties." It is, we are told, "a preppy kind of place." In a cheerful photo of the faculty and students, one cannot discern a single nonwhite face. [7]

[3]Inner-city Chicago school.—Ed.

8   New Trier's "temperate climate" is "aided by the homogeneity of its students," *Town and Country* notes. " . . . Almost all are of European extraction and harbor similar values."

9   "Eighty to 90 percent of the kids here," says a counselor, "are good, healthy, red-blooded Americans."

10   The wealth of New Trier's geographical district provides $340,000 worth of taxable property for each child; Chicago's property wealth affords only one-fifth this much. Nonetheless, *Town and Country* gives New Trier's parents credit for a "willingness to pay enough . . . in taxes" to make this one of the state's best-funded schools. New Trier, according to the magazine, is "a striking example of what is possible when citizens want to achieve the best for their children." Families move here "seeking the best," and their children "make good use" of what they're given. Both statements may be true, but giving people lavish praise for spending what they have strikes one as disingenuous. "A supportive attitude on the part of the families in the district translates into a willingness to pay . . . ," the writer says. By this logic, one would be obliged to say that "unsupportive attitudes" on the part of . . . the parents of Du Sable's children translate into fiscal selfishness, when, in fact, the economic options open to the parents in these districts are not even faintly comparable. *Town and Country* flatters the privileged for having privilege but terms it aspiration.

11   "Competition is the lifeblood of New Trier," *Town and Country* writes. But there is one kind of competition that these children will not need to face. They will not compete against the children who attended . . . Du Sable. They will compete against each other and against the graduates of other schools attended by rich children. They will not compete against the poor. . . .

12   Conditions at Du Sable High School, which I visited in 1990, seem in certain ways to be improved. Improvement, however, is a relative term. Du Sable is better than it was three or four years ago. It is still a school that would be shunned—or, probably, shut down—if it were serving a white middle-class community. The building, a three-story Tudor structure, is in fairly good repair and, in this respect, contrasts with its immediate surroundings, which are almost indescribably despairing. The school, whose student population is 100 percent black, has no campus and no schoolyard, but there is at least a full-sized playing field and track. Overcrowding is not a problem at the

school. Much to the reverse, it is uncomfortably empty. Built in 1935 and holding some 4,500 students in past years, its student population is now less than 1,600. Of these students, according to data provided by the school, 646 are "chronic truants."

The graduation rate is 25 percent. Of those who get to senior 13 year, only 17 percent are in a college-preparation program. Twenty percent are in the general curriculum, while a stunning 63 percent are in vocational classes, which most often rule out college education.

A vivid sense of loss is felt by standing in the cafeteria in 14 early spring when students file in to choose their courses for the following year. "These are the ninth graders," says a supervising teacher; but, of the official freshman class of some 600 children, only 350 fill the room. An hour later the eleventh graders come to choose their classes: I count at most 170 students.

The faculty includes some excellent teachers, but there are 15 others, says the principal, who don't belong in education. "I can't do anything with them but I'm not allowed to fire them," he says, as we head up the stairs to visit classes on a day in early June. Entering a biology class, we find a teacher doing absolutely nothing. She tells us that "some of the students have a meeting," but this doesn't satisfy the principal, who leaves the room irate. In a room he calls "the math headquarters," we come upon two teachers watching a soap opera on TV. In a mathematics learning center, seven kids are gazing out the window while the teacher is preoccupied with something at her desk. The principal again appears disheartened.

Top salary in the school, he says, is $40,000. "My faculty is 16 aging. Average age is 47. Competing against the suburbs, where the salaries go up to $60,000, it is very, very hard to keep young teachers. That, you probably know, is an old story. . . . I do insist," he says, "that every student has a book." He says this with some pride and, in the context of Chicago, he has reason to be proud of this; but, in a wealthy nation like America, it is a sad thing to be proud of.

In a twelfth grade English class, the students are learning to 17 pronounce a list of words. The words are not derived from any context; they are simply written on a list. A tall boy struggles hard to read "fastidious," "gregarious," "auspicious," "fatuous." Another reads "dour," "demise," "salubrious," "egregious" and "consommé." Still another reads "aesthetic," "schism," "heinous," "fetish," and "concerto." There is something poignant, and embarrassing, about the effort that these barely literate kids put into handling these odd, pretentious words. When the tall boy struggles to pronounce "egregious," I ask him if he knows its meaning. It turns out that he has no idea. The teacher never asks the children to define the words or use them in a sentence. The lesson baffles me. It may be that these are words that will appear on one of those required tests that states impose now in the name of "raising standards," but it all seems dreamlike and surreal.

18   After lunch I talk with a group of students who are hoping to go on to college but do not seem sure of what they'll need to do to make this possible. Only one out of five seniors in the group has filed an application, and it is already April. Pamela, the one who did apply, however, tells me she neglected to submit her grades and college-entrance test results and therefore has to start again. The courses she is taking seem to rule out application to a four-year college. She tells me she is taking Spanish, literature, physical education, Afro-American history and a class she terms "job strategy." When I ask her what this is, she says, "It teaches how to dress and be on time and figure your deductions." She's a bright, articulate student, and it seems quite sad that she has not had any of the richness of curriculum that would have been given to her at a high school like New Trier.

19   The children in the group seem not just lacking in important, useful information that would help them to achieve their dreams, but, in a far more drastic sense, cut off and disconnected from the outside world. In talking of some recent news events, they speak of Moscow and Berlin, but all but Pamela are unaware that Moscow is the capital of the Soviet Union or that Berlin is in Germany. Several believe that Jesse Jackson is the mayor of New York City. Listening to their guesses and observing their confusion, I am thinking of the students at New Trier High. These children live in truly separate worlds. What do they have in common? And yet the kids before me seem so innocent and spiritually clean and also—most of all—so vulnerable. It's as if they have been stripped of all the armament—the words, the reference points, the facts, the reasoning, the elemental weapons—that suburban children take for granted. . . .

"It took an extraordinary combination of greed, racism, po- 20
litical cowardice and public apathy," writes James D. Squires,
the former editor of the *Chicago Tribune*, "to let the public schools
in Chicago get so bad." He speaks of the schools as a costly result of "the political orphaning of the urban poor . . . daytime
warehouses for inferior students . . . a bottomless pit."

The results of these conditions are observed in thousands of 21
low-income children in Chicago who are virtually disjoined
from the entire world view, even from the basic reference
points, of the American experience. A 16-year-old girl who has
dropped out of school discusses her economic prospects with
a TV interviewer.

"How much money would you like to make in a year?" asks 22
the reporter.

"About $2,000," she replies. 23

The reporter looks bewildered by this answer. This teen-age 24
girl, he says, "has no clue that $2,000 a year isn't enough to sur-
vive anywhere in America, not even in her world."

Expanding Vocabulary

Match each word in column A with its definition in column B. When
in doubt, first find the word in the essay and look for context clues to
aid your understanding of the word's meaning. Then, if necessary, use
your dictionary to complete the matching exercise.

Column A	*Column B*
immaculately (2)	crafty, not straightforward
ambience (7)	showy
disingenuous (10)	obtained from, or originated
truants (12)	from
irate (15)	especially cleanly
derived (17)	profoundly moving or
poignant (17)	distressing
pretentious (17)	incongruous blending of
surreal (17)	images
vulnerable (19)	open to hurt
disjoined (21)	students absent without
	permission
	separated from
	atmosphere of a place
	extremely angry

Understanding Content

1. What, specifically, are the two items Kozol contrasts?
2. List the specific points of contrast. Include physical facilities, curriculum, class size, teachers and staff, and types of students.
3. What is the difference in tax base in the two communities? What are Kozol's views on the role of community income in education? Should families sending children to poor schools be considered unsupportive of education?
4. When Kozol writes that New Trier students "will not compete against the poor," what is his point?
5. What percentage of Du Sable students graduate? Are chronic truants? Are in vocational programs? Why does Kozol provide these numbers?
6. How do Du Sable and New Trier students differ in their understanding of current events and of the world they live in?

Drawing Inferences about Thesis and Purpose

1. What, more generally, is Kozol contrasting?
2. What is the point of Kozol's contrast? Of what does he want readers to be aware? Write a thesis statement for the essay.

Analyzing Strategies and Style

1. Kozol provides details about, and a general sense of, New Trier in part by quoting from a newspaper and a magazine. What does he accomplish by using the quotations? What impression is created?
2. What does Kozol accomplish by taking readers into a Du Sable biology class and English class? What is the effect of the list of words students are studying in the English class?
3. Examine Kozol's organization. Is it primarily whole by whole, or part by part, or some combination? What makes the organization effective?
4. Examine the ending. What makes it effective?

Thinking Critically

1. Are you surprised (shocked?) by any of the characteristics of either school? If so, which characteristics caught your attention? Why?
2. Would you describe your high school as similar to either New Trier or Du Sable, or is it unlike either one of these schools? Are New Trier and Du Sable typical of good and bad schools? Why or why not?
3. Kozol suggests that affluent students acquire knowledge and understanding that poor students do not learn. What are some exam-

ples of kinds of knowledge Kozol has in mind? What are some
ways of acquiring this knowledge as adults?
4. Should public schools be funded differently so that they provide
greater equality to students?

"Girls Are Beneficiaries of Gender Gap"

DIANE RAVITCH

Holding a doctorate from Columbia University, Diane Ravitch
(b. 1938) was an undersecretary for education in the Bush administration and is currently a research professor of education
at New York University and a senior fellow at Brookings Institution. She is the author of many articles and books on education, including *The State of American Education* (1980). In the
following article, which appeared in *The Wall Street Journal* on
December 17, 1998, Ravitch examines opposing studies of differences in school performance by gender.

Some of us grew up with the image of reporters as tough-   1
minded skeptics. Yet there were no tough-minded reporters in
sight in 1992, when the American Association of University
Women released its report "How Schools Shortchange Girls."
Every newsmagazine, newspaper and network television program did a major story on it, without making any attempt to
examine the underlying evidence for the AAUW's charge that
the schools were harming girls.

The schools, we were told, were heedlessly crushing girls'   2
self-esteem while teachers (70% of them female) were shower-
ing attention on boys. Worst among their faults, according to
the report, was that the schools discouraged girls from taking
the math and science courses that they would need to compete
in the future. The report unleashed a plethora of gender-equity
programs in the schools and a flood of books and articles about
the maltreatment of girls in classrooms and textbooks.

Now the U.S. Department of Education has released a report   3
on high school transcripts that demolishes the AAUW's claim

that girls were not taking as many courses in mathematics and science as boys. This new report shows that in both 1990 and 1994, female high school graduates had higher enrollments than boys in first- and second-year algebra and in geometry; among the graduates of 1994, there were essentially no differences between boys and girls in their participation in precalculus, trigonometry, statistics and advanced placement calculus.

4   In science courses, the picture was much the same. Female graduates in both 1990 and 1994 had higher enrollments than boys in both biology and chemistry; the only course that had a higher male enrollment was physics, studied by 27% of the boys but only 22% of the girls. In every other science course, the differences between boys and girls were slight or favored girls. Overall, girls are much better prepared by the schools than are boys: The latest figures show that 43% of female graduates were taking a rigorous college-preparatory program in 1994, compared with only 35% of boys.

5   To make matters worse for the AAUW, all of its other charges have been definitively refuted in a careful review of the research by Judith Kleinfeld of the University of Alaska. Prof. Kleinfeld found, for example, that there is little evidence that girls have lower self-esteem than boys or that boys get more attention in the classroom than girls.

6   Far from shortchanging girls, the schools have been the leading edge in creating gender equity in the past generation. Girls get better grades than boys; have higher scores in reading and writing; are more likely than boys to take advanced placement examinations; and are likelier to go to college. In 1970, women were only 41% of all college students. Today, female students receive 55% of all bachelor's degrees and 55% of all master's degrees. Indeed, many university campuses have begun to worry about gender imbalance, since men are a decided minority on virtually every campus.

7   Men still get a majority of professional degrees, but even here the numbers are changing fast. In 1970, women earned only 8% of medical degrees; by 1995, that number had increased to 39%. In 1970, women received only 5% of law degrees; in 1995, 43%.

8   At the same time that the AAUW ginned up a nonexistent crisis about girls, the press totally ignored the data on boys. In school, boys are 50% more likely to repeat a grade than girls

and represent more than two-thirds of the children placed in special education with physical, social and emotional problems. Boys are far more likely to be given Ritalin for attention deficit disorder. And talk about a crisis in self-esteem: young men (ages 15 to 24) are five times more likely to commit suicide than young women.

The shameful aspect of the AAUW's phony crisis—and of the media's gullibility in turning it into conventional wisdom—is that it diverted attention from the large and genuine gaps in American education, which are not between boys and girls, but among racial groups. African-Americans and Hispanics are far behind their white peers on every measure of school achievement. On the tests administered by the National Assessment of Educational Progress, average black and Hispanic 17-year-olds score at the same level as average white 13-year-olds. African-American boys, in particular, are at high risk of dropping out without graduating high school; among black college students, nearly two-thirds are female.

Alarmist rhetoric about the schools solves no problem, especially when the problem itself was invented for use in national advertisements and direct mail campaigns as a fund-raising tactic. One can only dream about what might have happened if the AAUW had focused the same amount of energy on recruiting talented women to teach in schools where minority kids are concentrated or on sponsoring charter schools for needy children.

Expanding Vocabulary

Study definitions of each of the following words and then use each one in a separate sentence.

skeptics (1)   refuted (5)
plethora (2)   ginned up (8)
demolishes (3)   gullibility (9)
rigorous (4)

Understanding Content

1. What did the AAUW's report, "How Schools Shortchange Girls," say? List the key points made by this report.
2. What does the Department of Education's report say? How does it contrast with the AAUW report?

3. What does Kleinfeld's research reveal? How does her research contrast with the AAUW report?
4. What negative statistics about boys are provided?
5. Where are the significant gaps in education to be found, according to Ravitch?

Drawing Inferences about Thesis and Purpose

1. What is Ravitch's topic?
2. Ravitch seems to have several purposes in writing. Can you isolate three separate—but related—purposes? (Think about the essay's opening, middle, and conclusion.)
3. After thinking about the relative importance of each of her purposes, state Ravitch's thesis. The thesis should focus on her primary purpose but can be worded to suggest her other purposes as well.

Analyzing Strategies and Style

1. Ravitch opens with negative comments about the media—and returns to this issue near the end. Do you see this as another purpose of her essay or an additional attention-getting strategy? Explain your choice.
2. The essay actually contains two sets of contrasts. What are they? (This question may be best answered if you think about her several purposes in writing.) Which is the more important contrast? On what basis did you decide?
3. Ravitch provides many specifics to develop her article. In what form are most specifics presented? How does this strategy affect the style and tone of the essay?

Thinking Critically

1. Which statistic do you find most surprising? Which is the most upsetting? Which is the best news in your view? Explain each of your answers.
2. Does the information convincingly refute the AAUW report? Why or why not?
3. Ravitch gives a reason for the AAUW's report. Are you disturbed by the explanation? Would you like to hear a defense of the report by the organization? What *should* a critical thinker do after reading this essay?
4. Pick one problem referred to or implied in this essay and then offer suggestions for addressing this problem in our schools.

"Boys and Girls: Anatomy and Destiny"

JUDITH VIORST

Judith Viorst (b. 1931) is a poet, journalist, and author of books for both children and adults. She has published several volumes of poetry and more than a dozen books, both fiction and non-fiction. Viorst may be best known as a contributing editor to *Redbook* magazine; she has received several awards for her *Redbook* columns. Her book *Necessary Losses* (1986) is an important book for adults about coping with the changes we experience at different times in our lives. The following is an excerpt from *Necessary Losses*.

It is argued that sex-linked limits have been culturally pro- 1
duced. It is argued that sex-linked limits are innate. What gender-identity studies seem to strongly suggest, however, is that—from the moment of birth—both boys and girls are so clearly treated as boys or as girls, that even very early displays of "masculine" or "feminine" behavior cannot be detached from environmental influences.

For parents make a distinction between boys and girls. 2
They have different ways of holding boys and girls. 3
They have different expectations for boys and girls. 4
And as their children imitate and identify with their atti- 5
tudes and activities, they encourage or discourage them, depending on whether or not they are boys or girls.

Are there, in actual fact, *real* sex-linked limits? Is there an in- 6
born male or female psychology? And is there any possible way of exploring such tricky questions unbiased by culture, upbringing or sexual politics? . . .

Sigmund Freud . . . went on record as saying that women 7
are more masochistic, narcissistic, jealous and envious than men, and also less moral. He saw these qualities as the inevitable consequences of the anatomical differences between the sexes—the result of the fact (fact?) that the original sexuality of the little girl is masculine in character, that her clitoris is merely an undeveloped penis and that she correctly

perceives herself as nothing more than a defective boy. It is the girl's perception of herself as a mutilated male that irrevocably damages her self-esteem, leading to resentments and attempts at reparation which produce all the subsequent defects in her character.

8　Well, as his friends say, who can be right about everything?

9　For in the years since this was written, science has established that while genetic sex is determined at fertilization by our chromosomes (XX for girls; XY for boys), all mammals, including humans, *regardless of their genetic sex,* start out female in nature and in structure. This female state persists until the production, some time later in fetal life, of male hormones. It is only with the appearance of these hormones, at the right time and in the right amount, that anatomical maleness and postnatal masculinity become possible.

10　While this may not tell us much about the psychology of femaleness and maleness, it does put a permanent crimp in Freud's phallocentricity. For, far from little girls starting out as incomplete little boys, in the beginning all human beings are female.

11　Despite his phallocentricity, however, Freud was smart enough to note at the time that his comments on the nature of women were "certainly incomplete and fragmentary."

12　He also said: "If you want to know more about femininity, enquire from your own experiences of life, or turn to the poets, or wait until science can give you deeper and more coherent information."

13　Two Stanford psychologists have tried to do just that in a highly regarded book called *The Psychology of Sex Differences.* Surveying and evaluating a broad range of psychological studies, authors Eleanor Maccoby and Carol Jacklin conclude that there are several widely held but dead-wrong beliefs regarding the ways in which males and females differ:

14　That girls are more "social" and more "suggestible" than boys. That girls have lower self-esteem. That girls are better at rote learning and simple repetitive tasks and boys more "analytic." That girls are more affected by heredity and boys by environment. That girls are auditory and boys are visual. And that girls lack achievement motivation.

15　Not true, say authors Maccoby and Jacklin. These are myths.

Some myths, however—or are they myths?—have not yet 16
been dispelled. Some sexual mysteries remain unsolved:
Are girls more timid? Are they more fearful? More anxious? 17
Are boys more active, competitive and dominant? 18
And is it a female quality—in contrast to a male quality—to 19
be nurturing and compliant and maternal?
The evidence, the authors say, is either too ambiguous or too 20
thin. These tantalizing questions are still open.

There are, however, four differences which they believe to be 21
fairly well established: That girls have greater verbal ability.
That boys have greater math ability. That boys excel in visual-
spatial ability. And that verbally and physically, boys are more
aggressive.

Are these innate differences, or are they learned? Maccoby 22
and Jacklin reject this distinction. They prefer to talk in terms
of biological predispositions to learn a particular skill or kind
of behavior. And talking in these terms, they designate only
two sexual differences as clearly built upon biological factors.

One is boys' better visual-spatial ability, for which there is 23
evidence of a recessive sex-linked gene.

The other is the relationship that exists between male hor- 24
mones and the readiness of males to behave aggressively.

However, even that has been disputed. Endocrinologist Es- 25
telle Ramey, professor of physiology and biophysics at Georgetown Medical School, told me:

"I think hormones are great little things and that no home 26
should be without them. But I also think that virtually all the
differences in male and female behavior are culturally, not hor-
monally, determined. It's certainly true that *in utero* sex hormones play a vital role in distinguishing male from female
babies. But soon after birth the human brain takes over and
overrides *all* systems, including the endocrine system. It is said,
for instance, that men are innately more aggressive than
women. But conditioning, not sex hormones, makes them that
way. Anyone seeing women at a bargain-basement sale—
where aggression is viewed as appropriate, even endearing—
sees aggression that would make Attila the Hun turn pale."

Although Maccoby and Jacklin's survey also concludes that 27
little girls are no more dependent than boys, the female-
dependency issue will not go away. A few years ago Colette

Dowling's best-selling book *The Cinderella Complex* struck a responsive chord in women everywhere with its theme of a female fear of independence.

> Here it was—the Cinderella Complex. It used to hit girls of sixteen or seventeen, preventing them, often, from going to college, hastening them into early marriages. Now it tends to hit women after college—after they've been out in the world a while. When the first thrill of freedom subsides and anxiety rises to take its place, they begin to be tugged by that old yearning for safety: the wish to be saved.

28   Dowling argues that women, in contrast to men, have a deep desire to be taken care of and that they are unwilling to accept the adult reality that they alone are responsible for their lives. This tendency toward dependency, Dowling maintains, is bred into them by the training of early childhood, which teaches boys that they're on their own in this difficult, challenging world and which teaches girls that they need and must seek protection.

29   Girls are trained *into* dependency, says Dowling.

30   Boys are trained *out* of it.

31   Even in the mid-1980s, at an Eastern liberal-elite private school where the mothers of students are doctors and lawyers and government officials and the students themselves are full of feminist rhetoric, there are echoes of the Cinderella Complex. One of the teachers, who gives a course in human behavior to the high school seniors, told me that he has asked them, for the last several years, where they expect to see themselves at age thirty. The answers, he said, are consistently the same. Both boys and girls expect that the girls will be bearing and rearing children, while also engaged in some interesting *part-time* work. And although the boys express a desire to have a great deal of freedom at that age, the girls routinely place the boys in successful *full-time* jobs, supporting their families.

32   Now it surely is true that a great many women live with a someday-my-prince-will-take-care-of-me fantasy. It is true that the way girls are raised may help explain why. But we also need to consider that the source of female dependence may run deeper than the customs of early child care. And we also need to remember that dependence isn't always a dirty word.

For female dependence appears to be less a wish to be pro- 33
tected than a wish to be part of a web of human relationships,
a wish not only to get—but to give—loving care. To need other
people to help and console you, to share the good times and
bad, to say "I understand," to be on your side—*and also to need
the reverse, to need to be needed*—may lie at the heart of women's
very identity. Dependence on such connections might be described as "mature dependence." It also means, however, that
identity—for women—has more to do with intimacy than with
separateness.

In a series of elegant studies, psychologist Carol Gilligan 34
found that while male self-definitions emphasized individual
achievement over attachment, women repeatedly defined
themselves within a context of responsible caring relationships. Indeed, she notes that "male and female voices typically
speak of the importance of different truths, the former of the
role of separation as it defines and empowers the self, the latter of the ongoing process of attachment that creates and sus-
tains the human community." It is only because we live in a
world where maturity is equated with autonomy, argues Gilligan, that women's concern with relationships appears to be a
weakness instead of a strength.

Perhaps it is both.   35

Claire, an aspiring physician, finds essential meaning in at- 36
tachment. "By yourself, there is little sense to things," she says.
"It is like the sound of one hand clapping. . . . You have to love
someone else, because while you may not like them, you are in-
separable from them. In a way, it is like loving your right hand.
They are part of you; that other person is part of that giant collection of people that you are connected to."

But then there is Helen who, talking about the end of a rela- 37
tionship, reveals the risks inherent in intimacy. "What I had to
learn . . . ," she says, "wasn't only that I had a Self that could
survive it when Tony and I broke up; but that I had a Self *at all!*
I wasn't honestly sure that, when we two were separate, there
would be anything there that *was me.*"

Freud once observed that "we are never so defenseless 38
against suffering as when we love, never so helplessly unhappy
as when we have lost our loved object or its love." Women will
find these words particularly true. For women, far more often

than men, succumb to that suffering known as depression when important love relationships are through. The logic thus seems to be that women's dependence on intimacy makes them, if not the weaker sex, the more vulnerable one.

Expanding Vocabulary

Match each word in column A with its definition in column B. When in doubt, first find the word in the essay and look for context clues to aid your understanding of the word's meaning. Then, if necessary, use your dictionary to complete the matching exercise.

Column A	*Column B*
masochistic (7)	impossible to retract or change
narcissistic (7)	held together, logically
mutilated (7)	connected
irrevocably (7)	to have a hampering effect on
reparation (7)	idea of the central role of the
crimp (10)	penis—or lack of one—in
phallocentricity (10)	shaping one's psychology
coherent (12)	tending to yield to others
auditory (14)	independence, self-directed
compliant (19)	getting pleasure from being
predispositions (22)	dominated or abused
autonomy (34)	submit or yield to something
inherent (37)	overwhelming
succumb (38)	easily affected
vulnerable (38)	deprived of a limb or essential
	part
	existing as an essential
	characteristic
	process of making amends
	advance inclinations to
	something
	excessive love of oneself
	related to sense of hearing

Understanding Content

1. What do gender-identity studies suggest about how we become masculine or feminine?
2. How did Freud explain the "defects" in women's characters?
3. How do all mammals begin their development?

4. What are the incorrect beliefs about males and females, according to Maccoby and Jacklin?
5. For what myths about males and females is there still inadequate evidence?
6. What are the four differences that the researchers consider to be established? Which two may be biological in origin? What is Professor Ramey's view on the origin of male aggression?
7. What is the "Cinderella Complex"?
8. How can dependency be seen as a strength? What seems to matter more to women than to men?

Drawing Inferences about Thesis and Purpose

1. What is Viorst's attitude toward Freud's views of women? Why does she devote space to his views?
2. What is Viorst's subject? What is her purpose in writing?
3. What is her position on differences between males and females and on the source(s) of those differences?

Analyzing Strategies and Style

1. Examine Viorst's opening. How does it both establish her subject and get reader interest?
2. The author uses many brief paragraphs. When does she use them? What does she gain by using them?

Thinking Critically

1. How many of the myths about male and female differences have you believed? Has Viorst convinced you that most are unsupported by evidence? Why or why not?
2. Observe how the author introduces the specialists on whom she draws. Are you prepared to accept them as reliable sources? Can they be reliable and still leave readers with questions and concerns? If so, why?
3. Diane Ravitch (see pp. 141–143) reports on the performances of girls and boys in school. Read her article and then answer this question: Which of the myths listed by Viorst does Ravitch's evidence help to discredit?
4. Do you see female "dependence" or desire for close relationships as a weakness or strength? Explain your views.
5. Why do we have so much trouble sorting out similarities and differences among males and females? What are some of the issues that get in the way of understanding?

"Pedestrian Students and High-Flying Squirrels"

LIANE ELLISON NORMAN

Liane Ellison Norman (b. 1937), now a peace educator and author of *Hammer of Justice: Molly Rush and the Plowshares Eight* (1990), obtained a Ph.D. in literature from Brandeis University and taught journalism and literature at the University of Pittsburgh. In her essay, published in 1978 in *Center* magazine, Norman reflects on her journalism students by drawing an analogy with squirrels.

1   The squirrel is curious. He darts and edges, profile first, one bright black eye on me, the other alert for his enemies on the other side. Like a fencer, he faces both ways, for every impulse toward me an impulse away. His tail is airy. He flicks and flourishes it, taking readings of some subtle kind.

2   I am enjoying a reprieve of warm sun in a season of rain and impending frost. Around me today is the wine of the garden's final ripening. On the zucchini, planted late, the flagrant blossoms flare and decline in a day's time.

3   I am sitting on the front porch thinking about my students. Many of them earnestly and ardently want me to teach them to be hacks. Give us ten tricks, they plead, ten nifty fail-safe ways to write a news story. Don't make us think our way through these problems, they storm (and when I am insistent that thinking *is* the trick, "You never listen to us," they complain). Who cares about the First Amendment? they sneer. What are John Peter Zenger and Hugo Black to us? Teach us how to earn a living. They will be content, they explain, with know-how and jobs, satisfied to do no more than cover the tedium of school board and weather.

4   Under the rebellion, there is a plaintive panic. What if, on the job—assuming there is a job to be on—they fearlessly defend the free press against government, grand jury, and media monopoly, but don't know how to write an obituary. Shouldn't obituaries come first?

I hope not, but even obituaries need good information and firm prose, and both, I say, require clear thought.

The squirrel does not share my meditation. He grows tired of inquiring into me. His dismissive tail floats out behind as he takes a running leap into the tree. Up the bark he goes and onto a branch, where he crashes through the leaves. He soars from slender perch to slender perch, shaking up the tree as if he were the west wind. What a madcap he is, to go racing from one twig that dips under him to another at those heights!

His acrobatic clamor loosens buckeyes in their prickly armor. They drop, break open, and he is down the tree in a twinkling, picking, choosing. He finds what he wants and carries it, an outsize nut which is burnished like a fine cello, across the lawn, up a pole, and across the tightrope telephone line to the other side, where he disappears in maple foliage.

Some inner clock or calendar tells him to stock his larder against the deep snows and hard times that are coming. I have heard that squirrels are fuzzy-minded, that they collect their winter groceries and store them, and then forget where they are cached. But this squirrel is purposeful; he appears to know he'd better look ahead. Faced with necessity, he is prudent, but not fearful. He prances and flies as he goes about his task of preparation, and he never fails to look into whatever startles his attention.

Though he is not an ordinary pedestrian, crossing the street far above, I sometimes see the mangled fur of a squirrel on the street, with no flirtation left. Even a high-flying squirrel may zap himself on an aerial live wire. His days are dangerous and his winters are lean, but still he lays in provisions the way a trapeze artist goes about his work, with daring and dash.

For the squirrel, there is no work but living. He gathers food, reproduces, tends the children for a while, and stays out of danger. Doing these things with style is what distinguishes him. But for my students, unemployment looms as large as the horizon itself. Their anxiety has cause. And yet, what good is it? Ten tricks or no ten tricks, there are not enough jobs. The well-trained, well-educated stand in line for unemployment checks with the unfortunates and the drifters. Neither skill nor virtue holds certain promise. This being so, I wonder, why should these students not demand, for the well-being of their souls, the liberation of their minds?

11   It grieves me that they want to be pedestrians, earthbound and always careful. You ask too much, they say. What you want is painful and unfair. There are a multitude of pressures that instruct them to train, not free, themselves.

12   Many of them are the first generation to go to college; family aspirations are in their trust. Advisers and models tell them to be doctors, lawyers, engineers, cops, and public-relations people; no one ever tells them they can be poets, philosophers, farmers, inventors, or wizards. Their elders are anxious too; they reject the eccentric and the novel. And, realism notwithstanding, they cling to talismanic determination; play it safe and do things right and I, each one thinks, will get a job even though others won't.

13   I tell them fondly of my college days, which were a dizzy time (as I think the squirrel's time must be), as I let loose and pitched from fairly firm stands into the space of intellect and imagination, never quite sure what solid branch I would light on. That was the most useful thing I learned, the practical advantage (not to mention the exhilaration) of launching out to find where my propellant mind could take me.

14   A luxury? one student ponders, a little wistfully.

15   Yes, luxury, and yet necessity, and it aroused that flight, a fierce unappeasable appetite to know and to essay. The luxury I speak of is not like other privileges of wealth and power that must be hoarded to be had. If jobs are scarce, the heady regions of treetop adventure are not. Flight and gaiety cost nothing, though of course they may cost everything.

16   The squirrel, my frisky analogue, is not perfectly free. He must go on all fours, however nimbly he does it. Dogs are always after him, and when he barely escapes, they rant up the tree as he dodges among the branches that give under his small weight. He feeds on summer's plenty and pays the price of strontium in his bones. He is no freer of industrial ordure than I am. He lives, mates, and dies (no obituary, first or last, for him), but still he plunges and balances, risking his neck because it is his nature.

17   I like the little squirrel for his simplicity and bravery. He will never get ahead in life, never find a good job, never settle

down, never be safe. There are no sure-fire tricks to make it as a squirrel.

Expanding Vocabulary

1. Norman writes with an interesting blend of colloquial or slang words and metaphors or similes. For each of the following passages, explain the word or phrase in italics.

   want me to teach them to be *hacks* (3)
   ten *nifty fail-safe* ways to write (3)
   His *dismissive* tail (6)
   What a *madcap* he is (6)
   His *acrobatic clamor* loosens buckeyes in their *prickly armor* (7)
   not an ordinary pedestrian, *crossing the street far above* (9)
   squirrel may *zap* himself on an *aerial live wire* (9)
   unemployment looms as large as the horizon itself (10)
   they cling to *talismanic determination* (12)
   luxury . . . not like other privileges of wealth and power that must *be hoarded to be had* (15)

2. Examine the following words in their contexts in the essay and then write a brief definition or synonym for each one. (Do not use a dictionary; try to guess the word's meaning from its context.)

profile (1)	cached (8)
impulse (1)	eccentric (12)
reprieve (2)	essay (15)
impending (2)	analogue (16)
tedium (3)	strontium (16)
plaintive (4)	ordure (16)
obituary (4)	

Understanding Content

1. Is this essay about squirrels? At what point in the essay do you know the answer to this question?
2. What seems to be the biggest concern in the minds of today's students? How do they feel about job opportunities?
3. Outline the contrasts that make up Norman's analogy. Using "A" for squirrels and "B" for students, list their points of difference.
4. What do squirrels and people have in common living in this world? (See paragraphs 15 through 17.)
5. Norman also introduces herself as once a student. Does she present herself as more like her students today or more like the squirrel?

6. What does Norman gain by using herself as an example? How does this help to advance her thesis?

Drawing Inferences about Thesis and Purpose

1. What, precisely, is Norman's subject?
2. What is her main point or thesis? What is she asserting about students?
3. What does the author think education is—or should be—all about?

Analyzing Strategies and Style

1. What does Norman accomplish with her opening description of the squirrel? Why not begin by announcing her subject and thesis?
2. In paragraph 1, the squirrel is described through a comparison with what athlete? Describe the squirrel's movements in your own words. Does the comparison (metaphor) work well to depict the squirrel's movements?
3. What does the writer gain by introducing herself into the scene in paragraphs 2 and 3?
4. Why does Norman choose the writing of obituaries as her example of what her journalism students want to know how to do? How important is this writing to newspapers? How glamorous is the task?
5. Norman describes the squirrel in part by comparing it to what circus performer? List all the words and phrases that add to this metaphor.
6. Explain the metaphor in paragraph 13 that Norman uses to describe her college experience. What is she comparing herself to? What ideas about the educational experience are suggested by this comparison?
7. Look up the word *pedestrian* in your dictionary. What are its two main meanings? How does the writer use both meanings in her essay?

Thinking Critically

1. Would you describe yourself as a pedestrian student or a high-flying squirrel? If you chose the first category, are you content with that label? If you are not content, what can you do to change? If you are content, explain why.
2. In paragraph 15, Norman says that "flight and gaiety cost nothing, though of course they may cost everything." This statement is a *paradox:* It seems at first to be contradictory, but actually isn't. How can you explain the statement? In what sense are flight and gaiety free? In what sense can they "cost everything"?

3. Norman shows us how metaphors can enrich our writing by providing concrete images and by suggesting much in a few words. To practice writing an *extended* metaphor (developing several points from one comparison), complete the following sentence about someone you know and then write at least three more sentences developing the metaphor.

   If _____ were an object, he/she would be a _____.

   Example: If my mother were an object, she would be a table. My mother is solid and sturdy, always there, feeding us and ready to help. She can be casual or dressed, just like the dining room table, for sometimes it wears a checkered tablecloth and simple pottery, and sometimes it puts on white linen and sparkling china and crystal. Even if she is scraped or banged up, she will not collapse.

You may want to try several of these extended metaphors.

"Marks"

LINDA PASTAN

A graduate of Radcliffe College and Brandeis University, Linda Pastan (b. 1932) is the author of eight books of poetry. Many of her poems, such as the one that follows from *The Five Stages of Grief Poems* (1978), examine the complexity and problems of family life.

> My husband gives me an A
> for last night's supper,
> an incomplete for my ironing,
> a B plus in bed.
> My son says I am average,   5
> an average mother, but if
> I put my mind to it
> I could improve.
> My daughter believes
> in Pass/Fail and tells me   10
> I pass. Wait 'til they learn
> I'm dropping out.

Understanding Content and Strategies

1. Who is speaking (or more accurately, thinking) the words of the poem? In other words, what do we know about the speaker? What relationships does the speaker refer to in the poem?
2. What does the poem's title refer to?
3. What marks does the speaker receive? For what activities? Who does the speaker's son sound like when he says that she "could improve" if she put her "mind to it"?
4. The poem is organized and developed, then, by using what extended metaphor? The speaker is being compared to what?
5. What is the speaker's attitude toward her situation? What lines reveal her attitude?

Drawing Inferences about Theme

1. What observations about family life is Pastan making? Whose perspective on family responsibilities and chores are we given in the poem?

Thinking Critically

1. Do you think the views of family life expressed here are fairly widespread? What evidence do you have for your opinions?
2. Have you ever felt as though you were being graded by family members or rated on a scale from 1 to 10? If so, how did that make you feel?
3. Try your hand at a short, free-verse poem similar to Pastan's. In your poem create a speaker who is a teenager being "graded" by other family members.

STUDENT ESSAY: CONTRAST

"THE FADED STAIN"
Denisse M. Bonilla

"The plantain stain on a 'jíbaros' back can never be erased," says an old Puerto Rican proverb. "Jíbaros," or Puerto Rican peasants, is what my compatriots fondly call each other. The proverb is most com-

Student uses a proverb as an attention-getting opening.

monly used to illustrate their feeling
that, regardless of where a Puerto Rican
lives, a Puerto Rican always remains a
Puerto Rican. But reflecting on my own
experiences, I have read a different
meaning into the old proverb. My compatriots could be saying that once a Puerto
Rican has lived on the island, she or he
can never forget it. However, in saying
this, one must ponder what happens to the
stain itself. Does it look like a plantain for the rest of the jíbaros' life,
or does it change over time? Perhaps it
starts resembling a banana, looking similar but not exactly the same.

Coming back to Puerto Rico as an adult,
I found a place quite different from the
one I thought I had left behind. The memories I had were those of a child who had
never lived outside the island. Because
I lived in Puerto Rico as an insular
child, I had the memories of such a
child. Youth had shaped my perception
when I lived there; then time further
confused my memory, neutralizing the colors of the countryside, creating indis-
tinguishable Puerto Rican cities,
sharpening the soft accent of the people. When I came back as an adult, what
I saw was not what I expected to see.

Thesis stated: What I saw on a return visit to Puerto Rico was different from my youthful memories. The thesis clearly emphasizes contrast.

I remembered the trip from San Juan to Ponce, a trip crossing the island from north to south, as an incredibly long and painful ordeal. Impatient to get to my grandmother's house in Ponce, I would look out the car window, sometimes noticing the small towns or the way the sea peeked out from in-between the mountains. The mountains that I saw during the beginning of the trip were green, seeming to remain in the landscape for hours. I would anxiously await the golden mountains to the south, which to me were an indication of the end of our trip.

When I returned as an adult, I remembered and expected the same grueling and unexciting trip, but was happily disappointed. The trip south was not as long as I remembered; it was over in two hours. Perhaps it did not seem as long as it did in my youth because I had become accustomed to driving longer distances in the large North American continent. But I accredited my newfound tolerance to the enchanting beauty of the Caribbean countryside! The vegetation in the north was a lush shade of green, growing profusely and becoming a tangle of startling color. The houses on the outskirts of the small towns we passed

First difference: the trip to Ponce was not as long or unpleasant as it seemed in her memories.

Student analyzes causes for the differences between youthful memories and adult realities.

seemed to blossom out of the foliage, their old-fashioned charm reminiscent of a bygone time when the Puerto Rican economy was more dependent on agriculture. In what seemed like a short distance, the mountains changed to golden hues and a softer green. The Caribbean Sea appeared to be a watercolor painting framed by the dry southern mountains. The beauty of the trip bewildered me, causing me to recollect in disbelief the impatience I had felt as a young girl. Had I been colorblind when I was young?

The Puerto Rican cities I remembered from my youth were **also different** when viewed through my adult eyes. I remembered Old San Juan as a beautiful old city, <u>comparing</u> it in my memory to places such as Old Town Alexandria. I <u>also</u> saw generic streets in my recollections, remembering how as a young girl I used to imagine that the bigger roads looked exactly like the ones in the United States. <u>But in contrast to my recollections,</u> neither Old San Juan nor the streets of the other cities were similar to those in the U.S. Taking a stroll down the narrow, cobblestoned streets of Old San Juan, I often discovered hidden parks and nicely shaded plazas in which old gentlemen sat

Second difference: cities and streets were different than remembered.

Observe transition words and phrases.

to chat, play dominoes, or feed doves. Wooden fruit stands brimming with delectable tropical fruits stood on many corners. The pastel-colored ambiance of Old San Juan, bespeaking Spanish ancestry and Caribbean sensibility, <u>could not be compared</u> to the somber ambiance of the old American cities in the north. As for my recollections of Puerto Rican streets that looked exactly like the ones in the United States, to my eyes accustomed to the large, smooth highways of North America, the streets of Puerto Rico looked humble and in need of repair.

The people of Puerto Rico proved to be equally changed to my adult eyes and ears. In the memories of a young insular child, Puerto Rican manners were just like American manners and Puerto Rican Spanish was bland, without any distinguishable accent. In contrast, I found my people to be more physically demonstrative than Americans. Their faces and bodies would remain mobile through an entire conversation, allowing someone standing a few feet away to guess what they were talking about. They spoke Spanish with a funny melodic sound, characterized by relaxed pronunciation. The Puerto Rican people were more flamboyant than I had noticed as a child.

Third difference: the people—and their way of speaking Spanish—are different than remembered.

Although the plantain stain on my back faded after I left my country, the experience of rediscovering its many hues left me with an even bigger impression. To notice the essence of a country, one must spend time outside it. My recollections were bland when compared to what I later saw. What I saw when I came back to Puerto Rico left a moist, green, ripe plantain stain on my back, a stain that will never fade.

Conclusion refers again to the proverb and extends the thesis to suggest that one's country is best understood when one spends time away from it.

MAKING CONNECTIONS

1. Ravitch and Viorst examine gender differences. Ravitch provides the statistics on performance, and Viorst gives some explanations of behavioral differences. Study both articles and see if you find any connections between the two discussions. Make a list of all connections you find.

2. Sakamoto discusses differences in American and Japanese conversational styles, and Kozol observes that poor urban students and affluent suburban students do not have the same points of reference and understanding of their world. What are some of the ways that cultural and class differences may affect students in the classroom? What are some things that instructors and students can do to ease some of the problems created by cultural and class differences?

3. White contrasts ways of teaching and attitudes toward how students best learn, whereas the differences Kozol discovers seem to be more about what money can buy than about educational theory. On balance, are students likely to be more damaged by ineffective educational theories or by inadequate facilities? Explain your position.

4. Norman raises the issue of student attitude toward education. How important are effort and desire to succeed? How

important is intellectual curiosity? (Compare Norman and Reid, pp. 340–342, on curiosity.) How much difference can facilities and dedicated teachers make if students are unmotivated to learn? If parents and society do not place a high value on education?

5. We know that Asian (and European) students regularly outscore American students in math and science. We also know that, as a group, students from more affluent school districts outscore students from less affluent districts. What are four strategies for improving American education that you would seek to implement if you were appointed "Education Czar"? What might be some political problems you would have trying to implement your four-point plan?

TOPICS AND GUIDELINES FOR WRITING

1. In an essay, contrast two stories, two movies, or two TV shows you know well. Select two works that have something in common but differ in important and/or interesting ways so that you have a clear purpose in writing. Organize points of difference in the part-by-part pattern *before* you draft your essay. Illustrate points of difference with details from the two works.

2. If you have attended two schools that differed significantly or if you have lived in two quite different places, draw on one of these experiences for a contrast essay. Organize by specific points of difference that together support a thesis statement that announces your contrast purpose. (Example: California and Virginia are not just miles apart; they are worlds apart.) The chapter's introduction gives guidelines for contrasting two schools. If you contrast two places, be sure to use details that *show* the reader how the places differ.

3. Do you know a neighborhood, city, or area of the country that has changed significantly for better or worse? If so, develop an essay that contrasts specific differences between the place you once knew and the place as it is now. Your purpose is to demonstrate that the changes have made the place either better or worse. (Example: The _____

neighborhood of _____ is no longer the attractive, family-oriented community in which I grew up.)

4. You have had many teachers during your years of schooling. Think of ones you liked and ones you didn't like. Think about why you enjoyed some but not others. Then select two to contrast for the purpose of revealing traits that make a good teacher. Write about specific traits (e.g., knowledge of field, energy, clarity, fairness, humor), not just generalizations (e.g., she was nice). Illustrate each teacher's traits with examples.

5. Norman contrasts her college students with squirrels—and the squirrels win because they are more curious and daring, traits Norman would like to see in her students. How do you view today's college students—or some portion of them? What traits, characteristics, attitudes toward learning, and reasons for being in school do you see? Can you think of an animal, fantasy creature, individual, or group from history who in your view has the traits that are more appropriate for college students? If so, then you can develop an analogy along the lines of Norman's essay. Remember to have specific differences between students and the animal, creature, or historical figure you are using.

6. As a variation of topic 5, develop an analogy that compares rather than contrasts today's students with some animal, fantasy creature, or historical figure. Use specific points of similarity and establish a point to the comparison, a thesis about students that is supported through the fanciful comparison.

7. Most of us have had at least one experience that did not turn out as we thought it would. Sometimes, nervous about a new situation, we expect the worst only to discover that we are happy or successful participating in the actual experience. Probably more often we look forward to an upcoming event only to be disappointed. Or, we have childhood memories that are inconsistent with our re-experiencing a place or person from the past. Reflect about any experience you have had that fits the pattern of contrast between perception (expectation) and reality. (Possible experiences include a first date, a special event such as Thanksgiving or a wedding, a first

experience with a new sport, a recent reunion with a child-hood friend, or a return to your childhood home.)

Organize your thoughts into specific points of difference and use the part-by-part structure so that you avoid writing only an autobiographical narrative. The point of your contrast is to offer some insight into why we so often have expectations that do not match reality. Why do we think it will be easy to learn to ski? Why do we remember our grand-parents' old house as larger and more exciting than it appears to us today? The student essay in this chapter is an example of one student's response to this topic.

5

Explaining and Illustrating

Examining Media Images

"How do you know that?" "Where is your evidence?" "Can you be specific?" These questions are raised by the avid dinner companion who wants you to illustrate and support your ideas. As a writer, you need to keep in mind that the engaged reader is going to ask the same kinds of questions. For you to be an effective writer, you must answer these questions; you must provide examples.

Illustrating ideas and opinions with examples seems so obvious a way to develop and support views that you may wonder why the strategy warrants its own chapter. Even though providing examples may be the most frequently used writing technique, as with many "obvious truths," we can all benefit from being reminded of its importance.

When to Use Examples

The smart writer searches for examples as part of the process of generating ideas. Indeed, when brainstorming or in other ways inventing ideas for an essay, you may find that specifics come to mind more easily than general points. Whether you are a generalizer who needs to find illustrations for ideas or a generator of specifics who needs to reflect on what the examples illustrate, the end result will be a blend of general points and concrete examples. When should you select the use of examples as your primary strategy of development? When you are presenting information or discussing ideas that can best be understood and absorbed by readers with the aid of specifics.

How to Use Examples

To use examples effectively, think about what kinds of examples are needed to develop your thesis, about how many you need, and about how to introduce and discuss them effectively. First, the *kinds* of examples. You will need to find illustrations that clearly and logically support your generalizations. When Gloria Steinem asserts that advertisers give orders to women's magazines, we expect her to explain and illustrate those orders. And this is exactly what Steinem does. If she had not used five major companies' demands as examples, we may have doubted her claim of advertisers' control over women's magazines.

We also expect *enough* examples. If John Skow mentioned only one Web site devoted to environmental issues, we would probably conclude that he was overreacting to a minor issue. Occasionally, a writer will select one *extended* example rather than a number of separate examples. Jack McGarvey uses one extended example, his and his students' experience of being on TV, to show the celebrity-making power of television. To develop his example, McGarvey uses techniques of narration and description, reminding us that few pieces of writing are developed using only one strategy. Typically, though, the writer who develops a thesis primarily through illustration presents a goodly number of appropriate examples. How many make a "goodly" number will vary with each essay, but be assured that few writers include too many examples.

How many examples an essay needs depends in part on how they are introduced and discussed and on how many facets of a topic need to be covered. Pico Iyer gives brief examples, mentioning just a title or an author, expecting readers to recognize and complete the examples. Steinem, on the other hand, does not just list five advertisers but gives details of their demands. After all, if all the examples were so obvious that just a brief listing would work, we would already have reached the writer's conclusions and would not need to read the article. As common to our lives as advertising, television, movies, and song lyrics are, we still have much to learn from this chapter's writers because they are the ones who have looked closely at and listened intently to the swirl of words and images bombarding us through the media. Sometimes examples are startling enough to speak for themselves. Usually the writer's task is not only to present good illustrations but to explain how they support the essay's main ideas.

When presenting and explaining illustrations, give some thought to ordering them and to moving smoothly from one to another. Look first for some logical basis for organizing your examples. If there is no clear reason to put one example before another, then you are probably wise to put your most important example last. Examples that add to your point can be connected by such transitions as

for instance	in addition
also	next
another example	moreover
further	finally

Brief examples, such as those in Iyer's "In Fact, We're Dumbing Up," can be listed as a series in one sentence. Examples that offer contrast need contrast connectors:

by contrast	on the other hand
however	instead

Remember that a list does not make an essay. Good writing comes from clear thinking about your topic and then attention to organization and word choice.

Getting Started: Thinking about Advertising

1. Here are eight questions to help you think about advertising, one of the topics examined in this chapter. Select three ads from a magazine of your choice and reflect on these examples of current advertising by answering the following questions for each ad.
   a. What are the ad's purposes? To sell a product? An idea? An image of the company?
   b. What audience is the ad designed to reach?
   c. What kind of relationship does it establish with its audience?
   d. What social values does it express?
   e. To what degree are those values held by the target audience? To what degree are they the values of a different social class or group?

    f. Does the ad use metaphors? Puns? Rhyme? Does the company establish and repeat a logo or slogan for the product? How effectively do these techniques work?

    g. Does the ad use symbols? To what extent do the symbols help express the ad's social values? How effective are the symbols? Does their association with the product seem appropriate?

    h. Is the ad's appeal primarily direct and explicit or indirect and associative? That is, is the message stated or implied, or is one message stated while others are implied?

2. Consider the issue of responsibility in advertising. Should a company be responsible only for the truth of its literal language, or for the truth of the ad's implications as well? Write some of your ideas on this issue in a journal entry or prepare your thoughts for class discussion.

"To Be or Not to Be as Defined by TV"

JACK McGARVEY

Jack McGarvey (b. 1937) completed his master's degree at the University of Connecticut and has taught in the Westport, Connecticut, school system for twenty-one years. He has also published many articles, short stories, and poems in the *New York Times*, *McCall's*, *Parents*, and other newspapers and magazines. The following article, a report on his experience with the power of television, appeared in 1982 in the journal *Today's Education*.

1   A couple of years ago, a television crew came to film my ninth grade English class at Bedford Junior High School in Westport, Connecticut. I'm still trying to understand what happened.

2   I was doing some work with my students, teaching them to analyze the language used in television commercials. After dissecting the advertising claims, most of the class became upset over what they felt were misleading—and in a few cases, untruthful—uses of language. We decided to write to the companies that presented their products inaccurately or offensively.

Most of them responded with chirpy letters and cents-off coupons. Some did not respond at all.

I then decided to contact *Buyline*, a consumer advocate program aired on New York City's WNBC-TV at the time. The show and its host, Betty Furness, were well-known for their investigation of consumer complaints. I sent off a packet of the unanswered letters with a brief explanation of the class's work. 3

About a week later, the show's producer telephoned me. She said that she'd seen the letters and was interested in the class's project. Could she and her director come to Westport to have a look? 4

I said sure and told her about a role-playing activity I was planning to do with my students. I said I was going to organize my class of 24 students into four committees—each one consisting of two representatives from the Federal Trade Commission (FTC), the agency that monitors truth in advertising; two advertising executives anxious to have their material used; and two TV executives caught somewhere in the middle—wanting to please the advertisers while not offending the FTC. Then, I would ask each committee to assume that there had been a complaint about the language used in a TV commercial, and that the committees had to resolve the complaint. "That sounds great! I'll bring a crew," she said. 5

I obtained clearance from my school district's office, and the next morning, as I was walking into the school, I met one of my students and casually let out the word: "WNBC's coming to film our class this afternoon." 6

I was totally unprepared for what happened. Word spread around school within five minutes. Students who barely knew me rushed up to squeal, "Is it true? Is it really, really true? A TV crew is coming to Bedford to film?" A girl who was not in my class pinned me into a corner near the magazine rack in the library to ask me whether she could sit in my class for the day. Another girl went to her counselor and requested an immediate change in English classes, claiming a long-standing personality conflict with her current teacher. 7

Later, things calmed down a bit, but as I took my regular turn as cafeteria supervisor, I saw students staring wide-eyed at me, then turning to whisper excitedly to their friends. I'd become a 8 celebrity simply because I was the one responsible for bringing a TV crew to school.

9   Right after lunch, the show's producer and director came to my class to look it over and watch the role-playing activity; they planned to tape near the end of the school day. The two women were gracious and self-effacing, taking pains not to create any disturbance; but the students, of course, knew why they were there. There were no vacant stares, no hair brushes, no gum chewers, and no note scribblers. It was total concentration, and I enjoyed one of my best classes in more than 15 years of teaching.

10   After the class, I met with the producer and director to plan the taping. They talked about some of the students they'd seen and mentioned Susan. "She's terribly photogenic and very, very good with words." They mentioned Steve. "He really chaired his committee well. Real leadership there. Handsome boy, too." They mentioned Jim, Pete, Randy, and Jenny and their insights into advertising claims. Gradually I became aware that we were engaged in a talent hunt; we were looking for a strong and attractive group to be featured in the taping.

11   We continued the discussion, deciding on the players. We also discussed the sequencing of the taping session. First, I'd do an introduction, explaining the role-playing activity as if the class had never heard of it. Then, I'd follow with the conclusion—summarizing remarks ending with a cheery "See you tomorrow!"—and dismiss the class. The bit players would leave the school and go home. We'd then rearrange the set and film the photogenic and perceptive featured players while they discussed advertising claims as a committee. Obviously, this is not the way I'd conduct an actual class, but it made sense. After all, I wanted my students to look good, and I wanted to look good.

12   "It'll be very hard work," the producer cautioned. "I trust your students understand that."

13   "It's already been hard work," I remarked as I thought of possible jealousies and bruised feelings over our choices of featured players.

14   About a half hour before school's end, the crew set up cameras and lights in the hall near the classroom we'd be working in, a room in an isolated part of the building. But as the crew

began filming background shots of the normal passing of students through the hall, near chaos broke out.

Hordes of students suddenly appeared. A basketball star 15 gangled through the milling mob to do an imitation of Nureyev,[1] topping off a pirouette by feigning a couple of jump shots. A pretty girl walked back and forth in front of the cameras at least a dozen times before she was snared by a home economics teacher. Three boys did a noisy pantomime of opening jammed lockers, none of which were theirs. A faculty member, seen rarely in this part of the building, managed to work his way through the crowd, smiling broadly. And as members of my class struggled through the press of bodies, they were hailed, clutched at, patted on the back, and hugged.

"Knock 'em dead!" I heard a student call. 16

It took the vice-principal and five teachers 10 minutes to 17 clear the hall.

We assembled the cast, arranged the furniture, erased sev- 18 eral mild obscenities from the chalkboard, and pulled down the window shades—disappointing a clutch of spectators outside. The producers then introduced the crew and explained their work.

I was wired with a mike and the crew set up a boom micro- 19 phone, while the girls checked each other's make-up and the boys sat squirming.

Finally, the taping began. It was show business, a perfor- 20 mance, a total alteration of the reality I know as a teacher. As soon as I began the introduction, 26 pairs of eyes focused on me as if I were Billy Joel about to sing. I was instantly startled and self-conscious. When I asked a question, some of the usually quieter students leaped to respond. This so unsettled me that I forgot what I was saying and had to begin again.

The novelty of being on camera, however, soon passed. We 21 had to do retakes because the soundman missed student responses from the rear of the room. The director asked me to rephrase a question and asked a student to rephrase a response. There were delays while technicians adjusted equipment.

We all became very much aware of being performers, and 22 some of the students who had been most excited about making

[1]Famous ballet star.—Ed.

their TV debut began to grumble about the hard work. That pleased me, for a new reality began to creep in: Television is not altogether glamorous.

23   We taped for almost five hours, on more than 3,200 feet of videotape. That is almost an hour-and-a-half's worth, more than double a normal class period. And out of that mass of celluloid the producer said she'd use seven minutes on the program!

24   Two days later, five students and I went to the NBC studios at Rockefeller Center to do a taping of a final segment. The producer wanted to do a studio recreation of the role-playing game. This time, however, the game would include real executives—one from advertising, one from the NBC network, and one from the FTC. We'd be part of a panel discussion moderated by Betty Furness. My students would challenge the TV and the advertising executives, asking them to justify some of the bothersome language used in current commercials.

25   This was the most arduous part of the experience. The taping was live, meaning that the cameras would run for no longer than eight minutes. As we ate turkey and ham during a break with Ms. Furness and the guest executives, I realized that we were with people who were totally comfortable with television. I began to worry. How could mere 14-year-olds compete in a debate with those to whom being on television is as ordinary as riding a school bus?

26   But my concern soon disappeared. As Ms. Furness began reading her TelePrompTer, Susan leaned over and whispered, "This is fun!" And it was Susan who struck first. " 'You can see how luxurious my hair feels' is a perfect example of the silly language your ad writers use," she said with all the poise of a Barbara Walters. "It's impossible to *see* how something feels," she went on.

27   That pleased me, for as an English teacher, I've always emphasized the value of striving for precision in the use of language. The work we'd done with TV commercials, where suggestibility is the rule, had taken hold, I thought, as the ad executive fumbled for a response. The tension vanished, and we did well.

28   The show aired two weeks later, and I had it taped so the class could view it together. It was a slick production, complete with music—"Hey, Big Spender"—to develop a theme for Ms. Furness' introduction. "Teens are big business these days," she

said. "Does television advertising influence how they spend their money?" Then followed a shot of students in the hall—edited to show none of the wildness that actually occurred. Next, three of my students appeared in brief clips of interviews. They were asked, "Have you ever been disappointed by television advertising?" The responses were, "Yes, of course," and I was pleased with their detailed answers. Finally, the classroom appeared, and there I was, lounging against my desk, smiling calmly. I looked good—a young, unrumpled Orson Bean, with a cool blue-and-brown paisley tie. My voice was mellifluous. Gee, I thought as I saw the tape, I could have been a TV personality.

Now, I am probably no more vain than most people. But 29 television does strange things to the ego. I became so absorbed in studying the image of myself that the whole point of the show passed me by. I didn't even notice that I'd made a goof analyzing a commercial until I'd seen the show three times. The students who participated were the same; watching themselves on videotape, they missed what they had said. I had an enormous struggle to get both them and me to recall the hard work and to see the obvious editing. It was as if reality had been reversed: The actual process of putting together the tape was not real, but the product was.

I showed the tape again last year to my ninth grade class. I 30 carefully explained to this delightful gang of fault-finders how the taping had been done. I told them about the changed sequence, the selection of the featured players, the takes and retakes. They themselves had just been through the same role-playing activity, and I asked them to listen carefully to what was said. They nodded happily and set their flinty minds to look at things critically. But as the tape ended, they wanted to tease me about how ugly and wrinkled I looked. They wanted to say, "That's Randy! He goes to Compo Beach all the time." "Jenny's eye shadow—horrible!" "When will you get us on TV?"

The visual image had worked its magic once again: They 31 had missed the point of the show altogether. And, as I dismissed them, I felt something vibrating in their glances and voices—the celebrity image at work again. I was no longer their mundane English teacher: I was a TV personality.

I decided to show the tape again the next day. I reviewed 32 the hard work, the editing, the slick packaging. I passed out questions so we could focus on what had been said on the program. I turned on the recorder and turned off the picture to let them hear only the sound. They protested loudly, of course. But I was determined to force them to respond to how effectively the previous year's class had taken apart the language used in the claims of commercials. This was, after all, the point of the program. And it worked, finally.

33   As class ended, one of the students drifted up to me. "What are we going to do next?" she asked.

34   "We're going to make some comparisons between TV news shows and what's written in newspapers," I replied.

35   "Do they put together news shows the way they filmed your class?"

36   "It's similar and usually much quicker," I answered.

37   She smiled and shook her head. "It's getting hard to believe anything anymore."

38   In that comment lies what every TV viewer should have—a healthy measure of beautiful, glorious skepticism. But as I said, I'm still trying to understand that taping session. And I'm aware of how hard it is to practice skepticism. Every time I see the *Buyline* tape, I'm struck by how good a teacher TV made me. Am I really that warm, intelligent, creative, and good looking? Of course not. But TV made me that way. I like it, and sometimes I find myself still hoping that I am what television defined me to be.

39   I sometimes think children have superior knowledge of TV. They know, from many years of watching it, that the product in all its edited glory is the only reality. Shortly after the program aired on that February Saturday two years ago, our telephone rang. The voice belonged to my daughter's 11-year-old friend. She said, "I just saw you on TV. May I have your autograph?"

40   I was baffled. After all, this was the boisterous girl who played with my daughter just about every day and who mostly regarded me as a piece of furniture that occasionally mumbled something about lowering your voices. "Are you serious?" I croaked.

41   "May I have your autograph?" she repeated, ignoring my question. "I can come over right now." Her voice was without guile.

42   She came. And I signed while she scrutinized my face, her eyes still aglow with Chromacolor.

To Stephanie, television had transformed a kindly grump 43
into something real. And there is no doubt in my mind what-
soever that in the deepest part of her soul is the fervent dream
that her being, too, will someday be defined and literally af-
firmed by an appearance on television.

Lately, my ninth grade class has been growing restless. Shall 44
I move up the TV unit and bring out the tape again? Shall I remind them what a great teacher they have? Shall I remind myself what a fine teacher I am? Shall I renew their—and
my—hope?

To be or not to be as defined by TV? Does that question sug- 45
gest what makes television so totally unlike any other medium?

Expanding Vocabulary

Match each word in column A with its definition in column B. When
in doubt, first find the word in the essay and look for context clues to
aid your understanding of the word's meaning. Then, if necessary, use
your dictionary to complete the matching exercise.

Column A	*Column B*
dissecting (2)	smoothly flowing
advocate (3)	attractive when photographed
photogenic (10)	examined carefully
sequencing (11)	walked with long-legged
gangled (15)	awkwardness
pirouette (15)	careless mistake
snared (15)	separating, analyzing
pantomime (15)	ordinary
arduous (25)	full spin of the body on the
mellifluous (28)	toes or ball of the foot (in
goof (29)	ballet)
flinty (30)	speak in favor of
mundane (31)	act of communicating with
skepticism (38)	bodily or facial expressions
boisterous (40)	and gestures
guile (41)	trapped, caught
scrutinized (42)	cunning, deceit
fervent (43)	very difficult
	emotional, zealous
	arranging in a series
	hard, tough
	loud, unrestrained
	doubting, questioning attitude

Understanding Content

1. What had McGarvey's English class been studying before the TV crew came? What response did the class receive from their letters to companies?
2. Why did a TV crew come to Bedford Junior High?
3. What was the response of students to the news of the coming crew? How did McGarvey's students behave with the crew watching their classes?
4. How did the TV producer want to sequence the class discussion? On what basis did they select students to tape? How long did the taping take? How representative of a typical class would the taped version be?
5. How did McGarvey respond when he watched the finished tape? How did his class respond? And future classes?

Drawing Inferences about Thesis and Purpose

1. What attitude, according to McGarvey, should we hold toward what we see on TV? Why did he, and his students, have trouble maintaining that attitude?
2. What is McGarvey's thesis, the main points he wants to make about television?

Analyzing Strategies and Style

1. What is the source of part of the author's title? What does he gain by his reference to the work from which part of his title comes?
2. McGarvey develops his observations about TV through one example, one event that he recounts at length. Can one long example also be an effective way to illustrate an idea?
3. The author combines narration with some quoted passages— dialogue with the producer and comments by students. What makes this an effective strategy?
4. McGarvey includes a clever description of students (and teachers) showing off for the TV cameras in the school hallway. Examine this passage again (paragraphs 14 and 15). What makes this an effective description? What strategies does the author use here?

Thinking Critically

1. Do you agree with the author and his students that TV commercials use imprecise and suggestive language? If not, why not?
2. Are you skeptical about everything you see on television? That is, do you understand that much of what is presumably "live" has been taped and carefully edited? If you aren't skeptical, should you be?

3. Do you want to be on TV? If so, why? If not, why not?
4. Reflect on the author's idea that television creates or defines reality. And that reality is more "real," more powerful, than the limited reality of our mundane lives. Is this why TV is so powerful, so mesmerizing for many viewers?
5. Is there something wrong with a society in which a seven-minute TV segment can suddenly turn an ordinary person into a celebrity? Why are celebrities so appealing? Do we put too much emphasis on them?

"Caution: Children Watching"

SUZANNE BRAUN LEVINE

A graduate of Radcliffe College, Suzanne Levine (b. 1941) has held various reporting and editorial positions with magazines. She has edited the *Columbia Journalism Review* since 1989 and is co-editor of *The Decade of Women, a Ms. History of the Seventies* (1989). The following article appeared in the July/August 1994 issue of *Ms.* magazine. Here Levine combines her experience as a mother with the results of research to explore the problem of violence on television.

I am very proud of the fact that I have never (well, hardly 1 ever) actually sent my kids off to watch TV just to get them out of my hair. I'm less proud of the fact that I don't exert very strong controls over what they watch; and there have even been times when I have caught an image of a horrendous act of violence out of the corner of my eye . . . and kept walking. When they were little, they were content to mellow out over endless reruns of *Mister Rogers' Neighborhood*, but as they got older— they are now eight and ten—and once we acquired a remote control, they began to graze around the dial and learned to snap back to something safe at the sound of an approaching adult.

Hours vs. Content

I do try to limit the number of hours they watch, and I'm 2 pretty good at enforcing the no-TV-before-homework rule; overall my children certainly watch less than the national average of three and a half hours a day. (That is probably due as much to full-time child care as to my moral authority. Parents caught between the demands of a workday and the obscenely outdated 3:00 P.M. school dismissal time have every reason to argue that watching TV—any kind of TV—is preferable to most of the alternatives.) But I must confess it makes me tired just to achieve that level of control; so when it comes to restricting content, I don't always have it in me to take on the philosophical questions of why violence is bad (because it rarely solves anything; because innocent people get hurt; because it is damaging to the soul) and why violence on TV is also bad, but in a different way (because by making it entertaining, TV shows trivialize it; because on TV violence is both glorified and simplified; and because it even gives people ideas).

3   When I have tried to engage them in dialogue over the issue, I find my children's sophistry daunting: *Teenage Mutant Ninja Turtles* is not violent, they claim, because it is a cartoon, and cartoons are funny; *MacGyver* is not harmful, because the hero doesn't carry a gun; and, besides, they argue, both of the above are hard to distinguish from the news shows grownups watch. They would not be impressed, although I am, by statistics assembled in a 1992 *TV Guide* study, that put cartoons at the top of the list of violent fare, followed by toy commercials(!). And although MacGyver may be unarmed, the promotions for his show were cited as having among the highest number of incidents of gunplay and physical assault; the newscasts aired only a tame fraction of the same.

The Connection between Television and Violence

4   The National Center for Juvenile Justice estimates that there were 247,000 violent crimes committed by minors in 1992 (the most recent year for which data are available). We know that before they are out of grade school, most of our children have seen some 8,000 murders and 100,000 acts of violence on television. Any parent can tell you that there is a connection between these numbers, regardless of the ongoing debate among experts. In a poll of 71,000 *USA Weekend* readers, 86 percent said that they "notice changes in [their] kids' behavior after they've seen a violent show." While some parents I know wit-

ness increased aggressiveness, there are other responses; I have found that sometimes my kids become more passive, detached, "spaced out." It seems that boys are more drawn to the shows and more agitated by them; girls, for the most part, are repelled, even saddened by them.

Whether these differences in children's responses are a function of nature or environment is a perplexing issue for parents, one that highlights the gray area between cause and effect—and therefore complicates the debate over suggested remedies. For example, a bill proposed by Senators Daniel Inouye (D.-Hawaii) and Ernest Hollings (D.-S.C.) to limit the kinds of shows broadcast during peak viewing hours for children raises important questions about freedom and responsibility. Proponents of the bill point to studies that show children exposed to a heavy diet of blood and guns become desensitized to real violence and, at the same time, excessively fearful of becoming victims. But the very persuasive arguments against such legislation center around the risks of censorship. Television's First Amendment protection *is* limited by a federal statute that instructs the Federal Communications Commission to make sure that TV stations operate in the "public interest." But any further effort to restrict content opens a Pandora's box.[1] Whenever I say to myself, "Children shouldn't be allowed to see this stuff!" I am reminded that the same motives were behind efforts I deplored to remove from library shelves such "offensive material" as *The Diary of Anne Frank*, *The Adventures of Tom Sawyer*, and *Our Bodies, Ourselves*.

Necessary Violence

Efforts to explain the relationship between violence imagined and violence committed lead into other mazes. World-renowned child psychologist Bruno Bettelheim made the disturbing observation that the ghoulish fairy tales that show up in every culture are necessary vehicles for children to work out their violent impulses and to come to terms with their own hearts of darkness.

---

[1] In Greek myth, Pandora opened a box containing all the evils of human life.—Ed.

7   My own childhood experience with grim fairy tales (Hans
Christian Andersen, in my case) has made me leery of parental
prudishness. I remember my mother reading me a story called
"The Girl Who Trod on a Loaf." It went something like this:
"There was a very vain girl who loved her beautiful clothes.
One muddy day she went out to buy bread, and on the way
home, she came across a big puddle. She didn't want to get her
party shoes dirty so she put the loaf down and stepped on it instead . . . " And? And nothing. I must have seen that there were
more pages to the story, or perhaps I sensed my mother's internal censor cutting the narrative off, because soon after I was
able to read, I went back to that story and found that indeed it
goes on into a horrendous climax in which the girl is sucked
through the mud puddle into a subterranean hell where she is
punished for her vanity. To this day it is the only fairy tale I remember, and the horror of the story is compounded by the dis-
tress I felt at uncovering my mother's subterfuge.

8   The Television Violence Reduction Through Parental Em-
powerment Act—better known as the V-Chip Bill[2]—proposed
by Edward Markey (D.-Mass.) would do just what my mother
tried to do: banish the bad stuff. There is something too neat
and clean about putting a microchip in the TV that would alert
parents to violent programming and allow them to block it out.
It has obvious immediate appeal, but does it give parents the
false confidence that by pushing a button, they have fulfilled
their responsibility to articulate and "sell" their values to their
children? And how would you protect your children from the
promos for the off-limits violent movies and series that, according to the *TV Guide* study, "have become a major source of
televised violence"? On a strictly pragmatic level, I know that
the Girl-Who-Trod-on-a-Loaf principle will ensure that my
children will ultimately see the proscribed show—most likely
at a friend's house—at which time they will probably pay
closer attention than usual because of the taboo at home.

9   The instructive power of violent images is evoked by Walter
Wink, a professor of biblical interpretation at Auburn Theolog-
ical Seminary in New York City. In his book *Engaging the Pow-*

[2]The V-Chip bill has been passed. A ratings system has also been established.—Ed.

ers, Wink writes that "violence is so successful as a myth precisely because it does not appear to be mythic in the least. Violence simply appears to be the nature of things." Children's entertainment, says Wink, reflects the "myth of redemptive violence" as played out in the classic plot line:

> Children identify with the good guys so that they can think of themselves as good. This enables them to project out onto the bad guy their own repressed anger, violence, rebelliousness, or lust and then vicariously to enjoy their own evil by watching the bad guy initially prevail. . . . When the good guy finally wins, viewers are then able to reassert control over their own inner tendencies, repress them, and reestablish a sense of goodness. Salvation is guaranteed through identification with the hero.

The redemptive value of this morality play is challenged by 10 such real-life findings as those of Leonard Eron, a professor of psychology at the University of Michigan who monitored a group of kids for over 20 years. He concluded that the more frequently they watched violent television at age 8, the more serious were the crimes they were convicted of by 30, the more aggressive their behavior when drinking, and the harsher the punishment they inflicted on their own children.

The crusading founder of Action for Children's Television, 11 Peggy Charren, responds to such studies with characteristic directness: "Poverty is what you fix if you want to do something about violence." She spoke at a *TV Guide* symposium on television violence and children, where she described the work she has done to bring about changes in children's programming; although her group no longer exists, its mission has been picked up by the Washington, D.C.–based Center for Media Education. Meanwhile, public anxiety is rising to a desperate level. A Times Mirror Center for the People & the Press study has found that 80 percent of those interviewed felt violence on TV was "harmful to society." I am among that 80 percent. What can we do?

What the Public Can Do

First of all, we can protest—to the stations, the producers, 12 the advertisers. (We should also praise, with equal vigor, shows that please us.) We can urge them to adopt a rating system that will alert parents to particularly lethal shows—ABC announced an 800-number to call for parental advisories on specific programming. We can try harder to monitor the programs that our kids watch. And we can try to put simulated violence into a larger moral context.

13   A recurrent worry expressed at the congressional hearings was that young viewers are seeing a sanitized kind of punching, stabbing, and killing. How to reconnect violence with pain and suffering in their minds? "Make it grisly," advises TV critic Marvin Kitman. When Gloucester is blinded in the 1983 Granada TV production of *King Lear,* Kitman reminds us, we are forced to focus on "those bloody rags" he uses to cover the ravaged eye sockets, which "said something special about the enormity of the violence wrought." Kitman may have identified a positive use for the "if it bleeds, it leads" format embraced by most local TV news programs: a reality fix on violence. When we invite our children to join us watching the news (after stressing to them that the world is not a uniformly violent place, that good and peaceful deeds are taking place all the time, only not on camera) we might be able to use the litany of crime and cruelty as "bloody rags"—reminders that when violence strikes, real people bleed and suffer and die, and real people mourn them. One local television station—WCCO in Minneapolis—is trying out a "family sensitive" five o'clock news broadcast that reports crime but saves the pictures for eleven. This format has possibilities, but it remains to be seen whether newswriters will take the opportunity to create an instructive context that could help families deal with the crime stories.

14   In the opposite vein, we can find ways to heighten a child's awareness of the artifice that makes a pretend punch look real and a real actor appear to be blown apart by a submachine gun. I would welcome a violence counterpart to a very effective aid I have found for explaining advertising to my kids. I taped an HBO special called *Buy Me That* that demystifies the techniques used by makers of commercials for children's toys. One segment begins by showing an ad in which several kids are hopping happily on a sort of pogo stick, as if it were the easiest thing in the world; then the toy is given to a group of real kids who try to hop. They fall off; they hurt themselves; many give

up. In another segment, the maker of cereal commercials explains that glue is poured onto cereal (yuk!) because it looks whiter than milk. My kids watch the show over and over and are experts at detecting similar gimmicks in TV commercials. The spell has clearly been broken.

Remedial Programming

It would certainly be possible to do the same with scenes of 15 violence: to explain exactly how blood shows up on the clean white shirt of a victim or how the noise of a punch is made or how a retractable knife blade simulates a stabbing; and it would be great to interview a stunt man or woman about the athletic expertise it takes to jump from a building or simply to fall down dead.

Another kind of remedial programming would dramatize 16 convincing alternatives to a body blow. We know that, in the same way that violent families produce violent children, a limited vocabulary of alternatives for conflict resolution produces a reflexive use of violence. Elizabeth Thoman, executive director of the Center for Media Literacy in Los Angeles, advises parents to explore with their children alternatives to stories that focus on violence as the solution to interpersonal conflict. In the same vein, Kitman proposes a policy modeled on the fairness doctrine, which used to require giving equal airtime to conflicting political points of view. It would mandate a balance of programs that deal with conflict and anger in ways that are nonviolent.

Kitman's suggestion recalls the truism that television's 17 weakness is also its strength: it is one of the most effective teaching tools we have. Dr. Deborah Prothrow-Stith of the Harvard School of Public Health is thinking of ways to use the best of the medium to combat the worst. She suggests the campaign against smoking as an analogy. "We went from thinking it was the most glamorous thing in the world to finding it offensive and unhealthy," she points out at the *TV Guide* symposium. "How did we do that? It was education in the classroom. It was working with the media. We banned the advertising of cigarettes on television." She thinks we can perform a similar change of attitudes about violence. So does Charren, who has an imaginative suggestion of her own, a "media-literacy merit badge" for Girl and Boy Scouts. "It's a way to teach kids that the violence you see on television is not the solution to problems," she says.

18   While such ideas are building toward a nationwide campaign to heal the bruised hearts and minds of our children, I take my hat off to one innovative father I have heard about. He would let his child watch *Teenage Mutant Ninja Turtles* cartoons, but only if the child would imagine a fifth turtle named Gandhi. Later they would discuss how "Ninja Gandhi" might get the turtles out of trouble without violence. I am equally impressed by the legendary parent who lures her kids away from the evil box with an invitation to an impromptu spring picnic. But my true (and secret) role model is the one who can effectively command "Turn the TV off—*now* . . . because I say so!" I am none of the above. But I'm trying. And I believe that as long as we keep struggling with the system and with our children, we are teaching at the only level that really counts—by what we do, not what we say.

Expanding Vocabulary

Match each word in column A with its definition in column B. When in doubt, first find the word in the essay and look for context clues to aid your understanding of the word's meaning. Then, if necessary, use your dictionary to complete the matching exercise.

Column A	*Column B*
horrendous (1)	capable of causing death
trivialize (2)	capable of being drawn back
sophistry (3)	upset, disturbed
agitated (4)	prohibited by social custom
desensitized (5)	hideous, terrible
deplored (5)	gruesome, horrifying
ghoulish (6)	make insignificant
leery (7)	expressed strong
subterfuge (7)	disapproval of
proscribed (8)	expert knowledge, skill
taboo (8)	believable but faulty argument
vicariously (9)	morbid
lethal (12)	condemned, prohibited
simulated (12)	made less sensitive

grisly (13)	make less mysterious
litany (13)	trickery, deception
artifice (14)	feeling as if one is
demystifies (14)	experiencing what another
retractable (15)	is experiencing
expertise (15)	suspicious, wary
	repetitive recital
	deceptive strategy
	pretended, feigned

Understanding Content

1. What does Levine have trouble doing with her own children?
2. How do her children try to justify their watching some violent shows?
3. What is Levine's attitude toward government control of television programming? What problem does she see with the V-Chip?
4. Briefly summarize the various views toward television and violence covered by Levine. Where does she stand on the connection between violent television and violence in society?
5. List the author's proposals for coping with violence on television.

Drawing Inferences about Thesis and Purpose

1. What is Levine's subject?
2. What is her purpose in writing? What does she want to accomplish with her article?
3. State the essay's thesis so that the author's purpose is clear.

Analyzing Strategies and Style

1. What opening strategy does Levine use? What does she gain by her opening to the topic of television violence?
2. Are the particular TV shows mentioned familiar ones most readers would know? (Think about her audience.)
3. In addition to mentioning three books that some people have wanted to censor, Levine refers to a story her mother read her. What is the point of her reference to "The Girl Who Trod on a Loaf"? What makes this an effective example?
4. Besides references to TV shows and books, what other kind of detail does Levine use to develop her thesis? Why are these details important to any discussion of violence on television?
5. Examine Levine's three "role model" parents in her closing paragraph. What does she accomplish by admitting that she is "none of the above"? What makes her final paragraph an effective conclusion?

Thinking Critically

1. When expressing her understanding of how parents can use the TV as a babysitter, Levine refers to "the obscenely outdated 3:00 P.M. school dismissal time." Should the school day be extended to more closely match parents' work schedules? Why or why not?
2. Is Levine right in asserting that a V-Chip would give parents "false confidence" that they have fulfilled their responsibility? Is she right that children will find a way to see prohibited shows at a friend's house? Do these statements "ring true" based on your experience?
3. Levine argues that censorship is more damaging than being exposed to violent TV shows. Do you agree? Why or why not?
4. Review Levine's suggestions for coping with television violence. What ideas seem most sensible, most likely to be effective? Explain your position.

"Sex, Lies, and Advertising"

GLORIA STEINEM

Editor, writer, and lecturer, Gloria Steinem (b. 1934) has been cited in *World Almanac* as one of the twenty-five most influential women in America. She is the co-founder of *Ms.* magazine and was its editor from 1972 to 1987. She continues her association with *Ms.* as a consulting editor, is the co-founder of the National Women's Political Caucus, and is the author of a number of books, including *Outrageous Acts and Everyday Rebellions* (1983), *Revolution from Within: A Book of Self-Esteem* (1992), and *Moving Beyond Words* (1993). In "Sex, Lies, and Advertising," first published in *Ms.* in 1990, Steinem "tells all" about the strategies advertisers use to control much of the content and appearance of women's magazines.

1   When *Ms.* began, we didn't consider *not* taking ads. But we wanted to ask advertisers to come in *without* the usual quid pro quo of "complementary copy"—editorial features praising their product area.

2   We knew this would be hard. Food advertisers have always demanded that women's magazines publish recipes and arti-

cles on entertaining (preferably ones that name their products) in return for their ads; clothing advertisers expect to be surrounded by fashion spreads (especially ones that credit their designers); and shampoo, fragrance, and beauty products insist on positive editorial coverage of beauty subjects, plus photo credits besides. That's why women's magazines look the way they do.

Advertisers who demand such "complementary copy" clearly are operating under a double standard. The same food companies place ads in *People* with no recipes. Cosmetics companies support *The New Yorker* with no regular beauty columns. 3

In recent years, advertisers' control over the editorial content of women's magazines has become so institutionalized that it is sometimes written into "insertion orders" or dictated to ad salespeople as official policy. The following are typical orders given to women's magazines: 4

❏ Dow's Cleaning Products stipulated that ads for its Vivid and Spray 'n Wash products should be adjacent to "children or fashion editorial"; ads for Bathroom Cleaner should be next to "home furnishings/family" features; and so on. "If a magazine fails for ½ the brands or more," the Dow order warns, "it will be omitted from further consideration." 5

❏ S. C. Johnson & Son, makers of Johnson Wax, lawn and laundry products, insect sprays, hair sprays, and so on, insisted that its ads *"should not be opposite extremely controversial features or material antithetical to the nature/copy of the advertised product."* (Italics theirs.) 6

❏ Maidenform, manufacturer of bras and other women's apparel, left a blank for the particular product and stated: "The creative concept of the ___ campaign, and the very nature of the product itself appeal to the positive emotions of the reader/consumer. Therefore, it is imperative that all editorial adjacencies reflect that same positive tone. The editorial must not be negative in content or lend itself contrary to the ___ product imagery/message (e.g. *editorial relating to illness, disillusionment, large size fashion, etc.*)." (Italics mine.) 7

❏ The De Beers diamond company, a big seller of engagement rings, prohibited magazines from placing its ads with "adjacencies to hard news or anti/love-romance themed editorial." 8

❏ Procter & Gamble, one of this country's most powerful and diversified advertisers, stands out in the memory of Anne Summers and Sandra Yates [who ran the company that published *Ms.* in the late 1980s]: its products were not to be placed in *any* issue that included 9 *any* material on gun control, abortion, the occult, cults, or the disparagement of religion. Caution was also demanded in any issue that included articles on sex or drugs, even for educational purposes.

10   Those are the most obvious chains around women's magazines. There are also rules so understood they needn't be written down: for instance, an overall "look" compatible with beauty and fashion ads. Even "real" nonmodel women photographed for a women's magazine are usually made up, dressed in credited clothes, and retouched out of all reality. When editors do include articles on less-than-cheerful subjects (for instance, domestic violence), they tend to keep them short and unillustrated. The point is to be "upbeat." Just as women in the street are asked, "Why don't you smile, honey?" women's magazines acquire an institutional smile.

11   Within the text itself, praise for advertisers' products has become so ritualized that fields like "beauty writing" have been invented. One of its frequent practitioners explained seriously that "It's a difficult art. How many new adjectives can you find? How much greater can you make a lipstick sound? The FDA restricts what companies can say on labels, but we create illusion. And ad agencies are on the phone all the time pushing you to get their product in."

12   Often, editorial becomes one giant ad. An issue of *Lear's* featured an elegant woman executive on the cover. On the contents page, we learn she is wearing Guerlain makeup and Samsara, a new fragrance by Guerlain. Inside are full-page ads for Samsara and Guerlain antiwrinkle cream. In the article about the cover subject, we discover she is Guerlain's director of public relations and is responsible for launching, you guessed it, the new Samsara. When the *Columbia Journalism Review* cited this example in one of the few articles to include women's magazines in a critique of ad influence, editor Frances Lear was quoted as defending her magazine because "this kind of thing is done all the time."

13   Advertisers are also adamant about where in a magazine their ads appear. When Revlon was not placed as the first beauty ad in one Hearst magazine, for instance, Revlon pulled its ads from *all* Hearst magazines. Ruth Whitney, editor in chief of *Glamour*, attributes some of these demands to "ad agencies wanting to prove to a client that they've squeezed the last drop

of blood out of a magazine." She also is, she says, "sick and tired of hearing that women's magazines are controlled by cigarette ads." Relatively, speaking, she's right. To be as censoring as are many advertisers for women's products, tobacco companies would have to demand articles in praise of smoking and expect glamorous photos of beautiful women smoking their brands.

I don't mean to imply that the editors I quote here share my 14 objections to ads: most assume that women's magazines have to be the way they are. But it's also true that only former editors can be completely honest. "Most of the pressure came in the form of direct product mentions," explains Sey Chassler, who was editor in chief of *Redbook* from the sixties to the eighties. "We got threats from the big guys, the Revlons, blackmail threats. They wouldn't run ads unless we credited them.

"But it's not fair to single out the beauty advertisers because 15 these pressures come from everybody. Advertising wants to know two things: What are you going to charge me? What *else* are you going to do for me? It's a holdup. For instance, management felt that fiction took up too much space. They couldn't put any advertising in that. For the last ten years, the number of fiction entries into the National Magazine Awards has declined.

"I also think advertisers do this to women's magazines es- 16 pecially," he concluded, "because of the general disrespect they have for women."

What could women's magazines be like if they were as edi- 17 torially free as books? as realistic as newspapers? as creative as films? as diverse as women's lives? We don't know.

We'll only find out if we take women's magazines seriously. 18 If readers were to act in a concerted way to change traditional practices of *all* women's magazines and the marketing of *all* women's products, we could do it. After all, they are operating on our consumer dollars; money that we now control. You and I could:

❑ refuse to buy products whose ads have clearly dictated their sur- 19 roundings, and write to tell the manufacturers why;
❑ write to editors and publishers (with copies to advertisers) that 20 we're willing to pay *more* for magazines with editorial independence, but will *not* continue to pay for those that are just editorial extensions of ads;

21 ❑ write to advertisers (with copies to editors and publishers) that we want fiction, political reporting, consumer reporting—whether it is, or is not, supported by their ads;

22 ❑ put as much energy into breaking advertising's control over content as into changing the images in ads, or protesting ads for harmful products like cigarettes;

23 ❑ support only those women's magazines and products that take us seriously as readers and consumers.

24 Those of us in the magazine world can also use the carrot-and-stick technique. The stick: if magazines were a regulated medium like television, the demands of advertisers would be against FCC rules. Payola and extortion would be penalized. As it is, there are potential illegalities. A magazine's postal rates are determined by the ratio of ad-to-edit pages, and the former costs more than the latter. Counting up all the pages that are *really* ads could make an interesting legal action.

25 The carrot means appealing to enlightened self-interest. Many studies show that the greatest factor in determining an ad's effectiveness is the credibility of its surroundings. The "higher the rating of editorial believability," concluded a 1987 survey by the *Journal of Advertising Research,* "the higher the rating of the advertising." Thus, an impenetrable wall between edit and ads would also be in the best interest of advertisers.

26 Even as I write this, I get a call from a writer from *Elle,* who is doing a whole article on where women part their hair. Why, she wants to know, do I part mine in the middle?

27 It's all so familiar. A writer trying to make something of a nothing assignment; an editor laboring to think of new ways to attract ads; readers assuming that other women must want this ridiculous stuff; more women suffering for lack of information, insight, creativity, and laughter that could be on these same pages.

28 I ask you: Can't we do better than this?

Expanding Vocabulary

Examine the following words in their contexts in the essay and then write a brief definition or synonym of each one. Avoid using a dictionary; try to guess each word's meaning from its context.

stipulated (5)   adjacencies (7)
antithetical (6)   diversified (9)

ritualized (11)	extensions (20)
launching (12)	Payola (24)
critique (12)	extortion (24)
adamant (13)	impenetrable (25)
concerted (18)	

Understanding Content

1. What do advertisers expect—or demand—in women's magazines?
2. Do advertisers make similar demands with other kinds of magazines?
3. What are some of the more subtle "understood" "rules" of advertisers in women's magazines?
4. What have advertisers done to get their way?
5. What does the author want readers to do about the control advertisers have?
6. What can those in the magazine business do?

Drawing Inferences about Thesis and Purpose

1. Explain the idea of using a carrot-and-stick approach.
2. What is Steinem's purpose in writing? Does she have more than one? What does she want to accomplish?
3. What is Steinem's thesis?

Analyzing Strategies and Style

1. Steinem uses bullets in two places. What does she gain by using this organizational strategy?
2. The author concludes by mentioning a call from an *Elle* writer. What is effective about this example as a way to conclude?

Thinking Critically

1. How many of the controlling strategies of advertisers are new to you? What one is the most surprising or shocking to you? Why?
2. Steinem suggests that advertisers place their extreme demands on women's magazines because they lack respect for women. Does this seem a good explanation of their double standard? If you disagree, how would you account for the advertisers' demands on women's magazines?
3. Steinem lists several actions we can take to change advertisers' mistreatment of women's magazines. Which suggestion do you think is the best one? Why? Are there other suggestions you would make? Explain.

"The Issue Isn't Sex, It's Violence"

CARYL RIVERS

A graduate of Trinity College and Columbia University, Caryl Rivers (b. 1937) has taught journalism at Boston University and is a freelance writer. She is the author of several novels and nonfiction books, the latter including *For Better or Worse* (humorous essays on marriage with her journalist husband Alan Lupo, 1981) and *Lifeprints* (1984). The focus of her concern has been with the experiences and issues of contemporary women, as the following article, published in the *Boston Globe* September 15, 1985, demonstrates.

1   After a grisly series of murders in California, possibly inspired by the lyrics of a rock song, we are hearing a familiar chorus: Don't blame rock and roll. It's all just adolescent rebellion. Kids will be kids. They love to rebel, and the more shocking the stuff, the better they like it.

2   There's some truth in this, of course. I loved to watch Elvis shake his torso when I was a teenager, and it was even more fun when Ed Sullivan wouldn't let the cameras show him below the waist. I snickered at the forbidden "Rock with Me, Annie" lyrics by a black Rhythm and Blues group, which were deliciously naughty. But I am sorry, rock fans, that is not the same thing as hearing lyrics about how a man is going to force a woman to perform oral sex on him at gunpoint in a little number called "Eat Me Alive." It is not in the same league with a song about the delights of slipping into a woman's room while she is sleeping and murdering her, the theme of an AC/DC ballad that allegedly inspired the California slayer.

3   Make no mistake, it is not sex we are talking about here, but violence. Violence against women. Most rock songs are not violent—they are funky, sexy, rebellious and sometimes witty. Please do not mistake me for a Mrs. Grundy. If Prince wants to leap about wearing only a purple jock strap, fine. Let Mick Jagger unzip his fly as he gyrates, if he wants to. But when either one of them starts garroting, beating or sodomizing a woman in their number, that is another story.

I always find myself annoyed when "intellectual" men dis- 4
miss violence against women with a yawn, as if it were beneath
their dignity to notice. I wonder if the reaction would be the
same if the violence were directed against someone other than
women. How many people would yawn and say, "Oh, kids
will be kids," if a rock group did a nifty little number called
"Lynchin," in which stringing up and stomping on black people were set to music? Who would chuckle and say, "Oh, just a
little adolescent rebellion" if a group of rockers went on MTV
dressed as Nazis, desecrating synagogues and beating up Jews
to the beat of twanging guitars?

I'll tell you what would happen. Prestigious dailies would 5
thunder on editorial pages; senators would fall over each
other to get denunciations into the *Congressional Record*. The
president would appoint a commission to clean up the music
business.

But violence against women is greeted by silence. It shouldn't 6
be.

This does not mean censorship, or book (or record) burning. 7
In a society that protects free expression, we understand a lot
of stuff will float up out of the sewer. Usually, we recognize the
ugly stuff that advocates violence against any group as the
garbage it is, and we consider its purveyors as moral lepers. We
hold our nose and tolerate it, but we speak out against the values it proffers.

But images of violence against women are not staying on 8
the fringes of society. No longer are they found only in tattered, paper-covered books or in movie houses where winos
snooze and the scent of urine fills the air. They are entering the
mainstream at a rapid rate. This is happening at a time when
the media, more and more, set the agenda for the public debate. They are a powerful legitimizing force—especially television. Many people regard what they see on TV as the truth;
Walter Cronkite once topped a poll as the most trusted man in
America.

Now, with the advent of rock videos and all-music channels, 9
rock music has grabbed a big chunk of legitimacy. American
teenagers have instant access, in their living rooms, to the messages of rock, on the same vehicle that brought them "Sesame
Street." Who can blame them if they believe that the images

they see are accurate reflections of adult reality, approved by adults? After all, Big Bird used to give them lessons on the same little box. Adults, by their silence, sanction the images. Do we really want our kids to think that rape and violence are what sexuality is all about?

10   This is not a trivial issue. Violence against women is a major social problem, one that's more than a cerebral issue to me. I teach at Boston University, and one of my most promising young journalism students was raped and murdered. Two others told me of being raped. Recently, one female student was assaulted and beaten so badly she had $5,000 worth of medical bills and permanent damage to her back and eyes.

11   It's nearly impossible, of course, to make a cause-and-effect link between lyrics and images and acts of violence. But images have a tremendous power to create an atmosphere in which violence against certain people is sanctioned. Nazi propagandists knew that full well when they portrayed Jews as ugly, greedy and powerful.

12   The outcry over violence against women, particularly in a sexual context, is being legitimized in two ways: by the increasing movement of these images into the mainstream of the media in TV, films, magazines, albums, videos, and by the silence about it.

13   Violence, of course, is rampant in the media. But it is usually set in some kind of moral context. It's usually only the bad guys who commit violent acts against the innocent. When the good guys get violent, it's against those who deserve it. Dirty Harry blows away the scum, he doesn't walk up to a toddler and say, "Make my day." The A Team does not shoot up suburban shopping malls.

14   But in some rock songs, it's the "heroes" who commit the acts. The people we are programmed to identify with are the ones being violent, with women on the receiving end. In a society where rape and assaults on women are endemic, this is no small problem, with millions of young boys watching on their TV screens and listening on their Walkmans.

15   I think something needs to be done. I'd like to see people in the industry respond to the problem. I'd love to see some women rock stars speak out against violence against women. I would like to see disc jockeys refuse air play to records and

videos that contain such violence. At the very least, I want to see the end of the silence. I want journalists and parents and critics and performing artists to keep this issue alive in the public forum. I don't want people who are concerned about this issue labeled as bluenoses and book-burners and ignored.

And I wish it wasn't always just women who are speaking out. Men have as large a stake in the quality of our civilization as women do in the long run. Violence is a contagion that infects at random. Let's hear something, please, from the men.   16

Expanding Vocabulary

Match each word in column A with its definition in column B. When in doubt, first find the word in the essay and look for context clues to aid your understanding of the word's meaning. Then, if necessary, use your dictionary to complete the matching exercise.

Column A	*Column B*
funky (3)	copulating anally
gyrates (3)	with a high reputation
garroting (3)	suppliers
sodomizing (3)	intellectual
desecrating (4)	those who spread ideas to support a cause or group
prestigious (5)	unconventional, offbeat
purveyors (7)	approved
proffers (7)	typical of a people or region
cerebral (10)	prudes
sanctioned (11)	whirls or spins
propagandists (11)	spread of contagious disease
endemic (14)	offers
bluenoses (15)	strangling, using a collarlike instrument
contagion (16)	marring or defacing sacred objects

Understanding Content

1. How does Rivers characterize much rock music?
2. What characterizes some current music?
3. How, according to the author, do some men react to violence against women?

4. How does Rivers characterize the men who annoy her with their dismissal of the problem of violence against women? In what situations does she think these men would react differently? What would be their reactions?
5. In addition to music lyrics, where do we find images of violence against women?
6. Why is the answer to the previous question significant? What attitude toward television do kids hold?
7. What responses to the problem does Rivers want? What response is she not calling for?

Drawing Inferences about Thesis and Purpose

1. Why should we be concerned about lyrics or images approving of violence against women? What impact do they have? How widespread are they?
2. What is Rivers's subject? What is her thesis? Where does she state it?

Analyzing Strategies and Style

1. Examine Rivers's opening; what strategy does she use?
2. As a part of her opening, the author tells us that she "loved to watch Elvis shake his torso" when she was young. What does she accomplish by including this biographical detail?
3. In paragraph 4, the author places the word *intellectual* in quotation marks. Why?
4. Rivers refers to a number of people throughout her essay. Are there any names you do not recognize? What does the list suggest to you about Rivers's expected audience?
5. Paragraph 4 concludes with two long questions. Do we know how we are supposed to answer these questions? What are such questions called?

Thinking Critically

1. Are you familiar with some of the lyrics and TV images that depict violence against women? If so, what has been your reaction to them?
2. Whether familiar with them or not, what is your reaction now to such lyrics and TV images? Is this a serious problem that "intellectual" men and other people fail to appreciate? Support your answer.
3. Look at what Rivers wants people to do about the problem. Which, if any, of her suggestions may be helpful? If any of the suggestions are bad ideas, explain why.

4. Are there other actions you would like to see? Should some lyrics and videos be banned? Should companies refuse to produce works that attack women?
5. What do you think of a society that "grooves" on violence of all kinds? What image of ourselves is reflected in the lyrics of a 2-Live Crew song or on many MTV videos? Reflect on these questions.

"In Fact, We're Dumbing Up"

PICO IYER

Pico Iyer (b. 1957) is an Englishman educated at Oxford University (B.A. and M.A. in English) and at Harvard (M.A. in English). He is the author of three books: *The Recovery of Innocence,* (1984), *Video Night in Katmandu: And Other Reports from the Not-So-Far East* (1988), and *The Lady and the Monk: Four Seasons in Kyoto* (1991). Iyer is also a contributing editor and essayist for *Time.* In the following, one of his *Time* essays, published May 24, 1999, Iyer looks at some of the current (1999) popular books and movies.

The obvious point to make about American culture today is that it's going to the dogs. That is, of course, the obvious point to make about every culture every day. Still, the indicators are alarming: magazines read more and more like tabloids, and newspapers treat foreign affairs as if they referred to overseas friendships. The Internet bombards us with more data than knowledge of how to make sense of them, and in certain parts of Los Angeles, 89% of the citizens at age 18 can't read. I am often to be found on street corners declaiming about the days before speed-of-light machines confined our minds to the space of a tiny screen and left us lost in terms of the big picture.

The only trouble is, if anyone's losing touch, it's me. The most striking thing about our culture, to an outsider today, may be that Harold Bloom's 745-page scholarly exegesis of Shakespeare's plays is on the best-seller list (joining a history of the makers of the *Oxford English Dictionary*), and an updated version of *Les Liaisons Dangereuses* is at the cineplex. In certain respects the country around us seems to be dumbing up, presenting us on a daily basis with texts and thoughts that give no indication of a nation suffering from attention deficit disorder.

3   Every time I return to California, for example, from my sometime home in Japan, I find that every current movie not based on Thomas Hardy seems to be derived from Henry James. The only reason not to catch Victor Hugo onscreen is that we caught him on Broadway a few years ago. This week sees Ally McBeal venturing into an "Athenian" forest in *A Midsummer Night's Dream*. Indeed, the hottest writer of treatments in Hollywood (as he was three years ago) is that high-concept old guy Shakespeare. Keanu Reeves in *Shamela*? Bette Midler and Stephen Dorff in *The Merry Wives of Windsor*? Who knows where it will end?

4   Now the simple response to this is that the very explosion of ancient literary props in Hollywood shows just how impoverished our contemporary imagination has become: the only way we can find good stories is by going back to *Titus Andronicus*. *Clueless* directors find their inspiration in Jane Austen. But this doesn't get around the fact that we're seeing full-dress, four-hour versions of *Hamlet* now, with Dostoevsky's life story, in *The Gambler*, on its way this August. And these are not just the playthings of the black berets in art houses; to my alarm, the Academy Awards for three straight years now have gone to films I've actually liked for their classical power, humanity and intelligence.

5   I wonder sometimes if there may not in fact be a correlation between the tyranny of the instant, in our accelerated, data-filled information culture, and the longing for those graces that belong to a more spacious time. Perhaps people crave, and are demanding, a return to something deeper, or less of the moment. The surprise best seller of two years ago—a serious literary novel by a first timer, no less—was a retelling of *The Odyssey* in the culture of the Civil War (with a flavor directly taken from the Taoist hermits of old China). It was replaced by another debut novel set, for nearly all its 428 pages, in the teahouses of Kyoto in the 1930s. Just as last year, during the Capitol soap opera, the American public showed itself wiser than its rulers, so in our free time, it's proving itself more discerning than those who would wish to take it to the cleaners.

6   This is not to say the culture is growing smarter or more sophisticated for having 800-page novels written in 18th century English on the best-seller list (Thomas Pynchon's *Mason &*

Dixon is more often on the coffee table than the bedside table anyway); only, perhaps, that there are certain human standards that are not so easily compromised or exploited. Los Angeles' most glittery new attraction is neither a theme park nor a movie studio but a home for fine art. The latest places people go for vacation are monasteries and retreats that offer stillness. Left to its own devices, the American public is seeking Romeo and Juliet stories set in Kerala (courtesy of Arundhati Roy) and unvarnished accounts of Shackleton's exploration of the South Pole.

Perhaps, in an age of speed, there is a special appeal to slow- 7 ness; and perhaps in a time of special effects, we long more than ever for classical stories that take us somewhere else. Something in us rebels against being turned too quickly into surfaces. And it's worth remembering too that when the Brontë Sisters brought out a book of poems 150 years ago, it sold all of two copies. I'm sure I'll continue yelling that the culture's going to the dogs—but when I do so, I should probably bear in mind that that's what people were saying when first they saw the clunky puns of *The Taming of the Shrew*, or filed out of the sex- and violence-filled soap opera that was the latest from the scriptwriter called Aeschylus.

Expanding Vocabulary

Select the five words you are least familiar with, study their contexts in the essay (and your dictionary if necessary) and then use each one in a separate sentence.

bombards (1)	correlation (5)
declaiming (1)	discerning (5)
exegesis (2)	exploited (6)
impoverished (4)	

Understanding Content

1. What evidence does the author give to show that "American culture today is . . . going to the dogs"?
2. In what two media does Iyer find evidence that we are "dumbing up"?
3. What does Iyer mean by the expression "dumbing up"?
4. What is one explanation for Hollywood's use of Shakespeare and Jane Austen? Why does Iyer reject this explanation?
5. What is Iyer's explanation for the appeal of many of today's successful books and movies?

Drawing Inferences about Thesis and Purpose

1. What does Iyer mean when he writes that the American public is "more discerning than those who would wish to take it to the cleaners"? Who wants to take us to the cleaners? How do we show that we are more discerning?
2. What are Iyer's many examples designed to show about our contemporary culture; in other words, what is his thesis?
3. Is Iyer saying that our culture has become more "cultured," more sophisticated? How does he limit and focus what he is saying in this essay?

Analyzing Strategies and Style

1. What is the source of Iyer's title? What expression is he echoing?
2. Iyer uses many examples of books and movies to support his thesis. Some are more fully identified than others. When either a title or author is not given, what can you conclude about Iyer's expectations of readers?
3. Examine the author's conclusion. What point is he making with his last two examples?

Thinking Critically

1. How do you react to the specifics in paragraph one? Are you surprised? Shocked? Unconcerned? Explain.
2. How many of Iyer's books, authors, and movies do you recognize? How many have you read or seen? How important is it for readers to know a writer's examples?
3. Iyer writes of the "tyranny of the instant" in our "data-filled information culture." Explain his point in your own words. Do you agree with his analysis of our time? Why or why not? Do you agree that we are unfulfilled by this culture and long for the insights and grace of more intelligent books and movies? Why or why not?
4. How can you explain the apparent discrepancy between the "dumbing down" and the "dumbing up" of our culture?

"Lost In Cyberspace"

JOHN SKOW

A freelance writer, John Skow (b. 1932) has been a contributing editor to *Time* magazine and has published widely in popular magazines, mostly on environmental and sports topics. His article exploring environmental sites on the Internet appeared in *Time* on April 26, 1999.

This environment reporter's idea of interactive technology   1
was to tap the computer case with a 12-in. adjustable-end wrench to correct vapor lock and improve e-mail reception. Mostly on instinct, he patrolled the environment outdoors and avoided the World Wide Web. The information superhighway vanished last year, he noticed, at least as an annoying metaphor, and maybe the World Wide Web would go away too.

But no. The Web is still here, and without it, journalistic obsolescence looms (yawns? festers? creeps in petty pace? click one). So this reporter sets out (urls forth?) onto the Internet. And what does he discover?

There appears to be more virtual environment on the Web   2
than there remains real environment in the actual, tattered, nonvirtual world itself. Or nearly. Yet doing research on the Internet is like taking a two-year-old for a walk. Pretty pebbles and deeply meaningful small sticks present themselves, but enlightenment seldom proceeds in a straight line. There is always some beguiling irrelevancy to be clicked, which is good. Often, however, the environmental pilgrim discovers to his surprise that there is not much depth of information. A surprising number of green websites are little more than 16-bit fund-raising brochures.

The Web is praised as a wondrous educational tool, and in   3
some respects it is. Mostly, though, it appears to be a stunning advance in the shoring up of biases, both benign (one's own views) and noxious (other views). Whether anyone's opinion is changed by the Web is an open question, though of course the same could be said of Balkan politics and air strikes. A six-month debate on an Environmental News Network forum (*www.enn.com/community/forum*), about agribusiness, organic farming and Monsanto's genetic engineering of plants, began in September with sweet reason: "In the U.S. only 10.9% of the average American's income is spent on food. Compare this to Britain at 11.5%, Sweden 14.5%." Fairly quickly the discourse descended to a mudball fight. A farmer who thinks chemical fertilizers and pesticides are fine dismissed an organic farmer

as a gardener and added, "Man, you drip of liberalism; it almost stinks." Another nonorganic disputant offered, "More than anything, I cannot STAND ignorant hysterics seeking to ban or destroy whatever technological innovation currently threatens their precarious emotional stability." From the other side came this: "You are a vile individual who licks the boots of the well-heeled, and you'll never see the light about the virtues of unspoiled nature and wildlife . . . You are just full of technocrap!" The mudballs still fly, and all are welcome. Park your chewing gum and razors at the door.

4   Or punch in another Internet address, like *www.swcenter.org,* which brings up a useful activist group I know, Arizona's Southwest Center for Biological Diversity. As usual, the Southwest Center is tormenting the U.S. Fish and Wildlife Service to add deserving beasts and plants to the Endangered Species List (the beluga whale in Alaska's Cook Inlet is a candidate). There's good information here, on a wide array of eco-skirmishing, but what I print out is something I've never laid hands on, a copy of the Endangered Species Act itself, the great Magna Charta of U.S. environmentalism. Yes, the Interior Department probably would have sent a copy of the ESA if I had phoned and asked. But the Web is right there: reach up and pick the overhanging mangos.

5   A friend recommends *www.envirolink.org,* a widely used green portal, and this leads across the Atlantic to the Danish Wind Turbine Manufacturers Association, which offers detailed text on wind power in Dansk, Deutsch or English. I am glad to see that the Danes, my forebears, are hoisting a wetted finger toward nonpollutive electricity, but the download time is more than an hour, and that is too windy. Click the "back" button.

6   Returned from Denmark, but still on Envirolink, I stumble on controversy. It seems that last spring, Lycos, a prominent Internet search engine, promised support to Envirolink, which was started in 1991 by Josh Knauer, then a freshman at Carnegie Mellon University, and is chronically underfunded. Envirolink was to get financing, and Lycos would be allowed to look green. (So says news analysis downloaded from the New Haven *Advocate* newspaper. Stealing good stuff is what the Web is for.) For three months, if you clicked on "Lycos saves

the planet," you reached Envirolink. Then Lycos canceled the contract. Norm Lenhart, a senior editor at something called *Off-Road.com*, had complained that Envirolink offered entry to such activist groups as Earth First and the Animal Liberation Front. Norm who? At what? *Off-Road.com* is an Internet site for fans of off-road vehicles, with ties to the anti-environmental "wise-use" movement. The website is a click away from *Blue Ribbon* magazine, another off-road lobbying outfit, sponsored by Honda, Yamaha, Skidoo and Polaris, whose motto is "preserving our natural resources FOR the public instead of FROM the public."

Here is one of the back alleys in which the Web can be brilliantly educational. Will enough high school kids, rummaging for term-paper material, find this alley and see what it means? Which is, perhaps, that virtual power, not real size, is often what's important. Envirolink has few staff members and little money, but it has power, because it is an entry to 400 enviro and animal-rights websites. *Off-Road.com* is an unknown, except to its communicants, who are mostly Western motorheads determined to keep Forest Service logging roads open at a time when rising environmental awareness makes it clear to the wider society that they should be closed. Lycos, briefly eager to save the planet with Envirolink, is a real business with real funding. Did Lycos, which now carries the Environmental News Service in place of Envirolink, cave in to an insignificant squawk from the far reaches of Webland? Lycos execs say no, and it is true that Envirolink shows up among the search engines top-rated enviro websites. But the conservative American Land Rights Association seems to think yes, and offers a Web address (*www.lycos.com*) at which Lycos may be thanked for right thinking. What's a Web crawler to believe? Well, for one thing, that Japanese car, motorcycle and snowmobile manufacturers—the power here is quite real, not virtual—are trying, through *Blue Ribbon* magazine and its parent, Blue Ribbon Coalition, to defeat U.S. environmental policy.

An innocent enviro wandering the Web—or an innocent black-hearted polluter—learns to click skeptically. Brave souls who reach *www.radio4all.org/anarchy/fakes* get a list of "anti-environmental" groups, most of them with wonderfully benign-sounding names: the Abundant Wildlife Society of

North America, the California Desert Coalition, the Evergreen Foundation, the Environmental Conservation Organization, Mothers' Watch. Maybe most of these really are benign. Dunno. I check out the National Wetlands Coalition, a big-biz coalition against wetlands, and the Global Climate Coalition. The cover of this last org has been blown for some time. It's a consortium including oil and car companies that are mightily interested in stalling enactment of the Kyoto accords on carbon-dioxide emissions. Will a high school student patching together a paper on global warming buy the GCC'S line, which says go slow because scientists disagree? Or click further and discover that, no, scientists really don't disagree; that 2,500 of them say Earth is in a period of potentially dangerous warming, to which human activities contribute to an alarming degree?

9   The wanderer learns a lot about prairie dogs, which are in sharp decline and should be listed as threatened, says the World Wildlife Fund (*www.panda.org*). And about the last Congress, which was insufficiently environmental, according to the League of Conservation Voters (*www.lcv.org*). I download a superb four-part, college-level course on the ozone hole from the University of Cambridge (*www.atm.ch.cam.ac.uk/tour/index. html*). And I am assured by *www.eco.freedom.org/unibomb.htm* that Bill Clinton and Al Gore are environmentalists (a deniable charge, surely) and in league with Earth First! and the Unabomber.

10   And . . . it's 4 A.M.; do I know where my eyeballs are? So— oxymoron alert—a beginner's conclusion. The Web's strongest suit, at least as it deals with the environment, is serendipity, random walking. Search engines only pretend to sort out the jumbled and expanding Internet universe. Which, as has been widely noted, is unedited, unowned, unsanitized—though Congress continues to try—and, like the worldwide world itself, decidedly not guaranteed. Likewise for its environmental subset. Run barefoot through its meadows, but be careful where you put your feet.

Expanding Vocabulary

Match each word in column A with its definition in column B. When in doubt, first find the word in the essay and look for context clues to aid your understanding of the word's meaning. Then, if necessary, use your dictionary to complete the matching exercise.

Column A	*Column B*
obsolescence (1)	damaging to health or morals
tattered (2)	raising up, lifting
beguiling (2)	dangerously lacking stability
benign (3)	temporary alliance
noxious (3)	diverting or amusing
disputant (3)	figure of speech joining two
precarious (3)	contradictory or incongruous
hoisting (5)	words
squawk (7)	condition of being outmoded
coalition (8)	cooperative arrangement among
consortium (8)	institutions
oxymoron (10)	making fortunate discoveries
serendipity (10)	by accident
	one who argues or debates
	torn and ragged
	complain noisily
	gentle, mild, not dangerous

Understanding Content

1. What do Internet Web sites on the environment often contain? What do they often lack?
2. What kind of debate did Skow find on Environmental News Network? What important document did he find on Southwest Center for Biological Diversity's Web page?
3. Why did Lycos promise support to Envirolink? Why, apparently, did it withdraw support? What does Lycos carry now?
4. Who seems to be trying to hurt U.S. environmental policy?
5. What organization with a Web site is owned by a group trying to stall tougher guidelines on car emissions?

Drawing Inferences about Thesis and Purpose

1. Skow writes that the best part of the Web on the environment can be found through serendipity. What does he mean by this statement; what is he saying about the Web?
2. What is Skow's subject? (Do not say the Web; be more precise.)
3. What is the author's thesis?
4. Are there implications from Skow's explorations that go beyond environmental sites?

Analyzing Strategies and Style

1. The author either is—or is pretending to be—a beginner using the Web. How does he use this strategy effectively in the essay?

2. What does Skow gain by providing the Internet addresses of the sites he finds?

Thinking Critically

1. Has Skow's exploration taught you anything new about the Internet? If so, what have you learned?
2. Are you surprised at all by Skow's study? What key point about who owns Web sites may be surprising to many Internet users?
3. What strategies can Internet users employ to learn about the sponsors of particular Web sites? What questions do we always need to ask about possible sources of information?
4. Pico Iyer (see pp. 199–201) and John Skow are both suggesting that the Internet is a source of data, not insight. Are we too impressed by statistics to recognize that we may still lack understanding? Explain your answer.

"The Barbie Problem"

DAVE BARRY

A humor columnist for the *Miami Herald* since 1983, Dave Barry (b. 1947) is now syndicated in more than 150 newspapers. A Pulitzer Prize winner in 1988 for commentary, Barry has several books, including *Dave Barry Slept Here* (1989), a collection of his columns. The following column appeared in 1998.

1   If you're a man, at some point a woman will ask you how she looks.

2   "How do I look?" she'll ask.

3   You must be careful how you answer this question. The best technique is to form an honest yet sensitive opinion, then collapse on the floor with some kind of fatal seizure. Trust me, this is the easiest way out. Because you will never come up with the right answer.

4   The problem is that women generally do not think of their looks in the same way that men do. Most men form an opinion of how they look in seventh grade, and they stick to it for the rest of their lives. Some men form the opinion that they are irresistible stud muffins, and they do not change this opinion

even when their faces sag and their noses bloat to the size of eggplants and their eyebrows grow together to form what appears to be a giant forehead-dwelling tropical caterpillar.

Most men, I believe, think of themselves as average-looking. 5 Men will think this even if their faces cause heart failure in cattle at a range of 300 yards. Being average does not bother them; average is fine, for men. This is why men never ask anybody how they look. Their primary form of beauty care is to shave themselves, which is essentially the same form of beauty care that they give to their lawns. If at the end of his four-minute daily beauty regimen, a man has managed to wipe most of the shaving cream out of his hair and is not bleeding too badly, he feels that he has done all he can, so he stops thinking about his appearance and devotes his mind to more critical issues, such as the Super Bowl.

Women do not look at themselves this way. If I had to ex- 6 press, in three words, what I believe most women think about their appearance, those words would be: "not good enough."

Why do women have such low self-esteem? There are many 7 complex psychological and societal reasons, by which I mean Barbie. Girls grow up playing with a doll proportioned such that, if it were a human, it would be seven feet tall and weigh 81 pounds, of which 53 pounds would be bosoms. This is a difficult appearance standard to live up to, especially when you contrast it with the standard set for little boys by their dolls . . . excuse me, by their action figures. Most of the action figures that my son played with were hideous-looking. For example, he was very fond of an action figure called "Buzz Off," who was part human, part flying insect. Buzz Off was not a looker. But he was extremely self-confident. You could not imagine Buzz Off saying to the other action figures: "Do you think these wings make my hips look big?"

But women grow up thinking they need to look like Barbie, 8 which for most women is impossible, although there is a multi-billion-dollar beauty industry devoted to convincing women that they must try. I once saw an "Oprah" show wherein supermodel Cindy Crawford dispensed makeup tips to the studio audience. Cindy had all these middle-aged women applying beauty products to their faces; she stressed how important it was to apply them in a certain way, using the tips of their fingers. All the woman dutifully did this, even though it was obvious to any sane observer that, no matter how carefully they applied these products, they would never look remotely like Cindy Crawford, who is some kind of genetic mutation.

9   I'm not saying that men are superior. I'm just saying that you're not going to get a group of middle-aged men to sit in a room and apply cosmetics to themselves under the instruction of Brad Pitt, in hopes of looking more like him. Men would realize that this task was pointless and demeaning. They would find some way to bolster their self-esteem that did not require looking like Brad Pitt. They would say to Brad: "Oh YEAH? Well what do you know about LAWN CARE, pretty boy?"

10   Of course many women will argue that the reason they become obsessed with trying to look like Cindy Crawford is that men, being as shallow as a drop of spit, WANT women to look that way. To which I have two responses:

11   1. Hey, just because WE'RE idiots, that doesn't mean YOU have to be; and

12   2. Men don't even notice 97 percent of the beauty efforts you make anyway. Take fingernails. The average woman spends 5,000 hours per year worrying about her fingernails; I have never once, in more than 40 years of listening to men talk about women, heard a man say, "She has a nice set of fingernails!" Many men would not notice if a woman had upward of four hands.

13   Anyway, to get back to my original point: If you're a man, and a woman asks you how she looks, you're in big trouble. Obviously, you can't say she looks bad. But you also can't say that she looks great, because she'll think you're lying, because she has spent countless hours, with the help of the multibillion-dollar beauty industry, obsessing about the differences between herself and Cindy Crawford. Also, she suspects that you're not qualified to judge anybody's appearance. This is because you have shaving cream in your hair.

Expanding Vocabulary

Examine the following words in their contexts in the essay and then write a brief definition or synonym for each one. Do not use a dictionary; try to guess the word's meaning from its context.

irresistible (4)
stud muffin (4)
regimen (5)
dutifully (8)

mutation (8)
demeaning (9)
bolster (9)
obsessing (13)

Understanding Content

1. According to Barry, how do most men view themselves?
2. What does their beauty care consist of?
3. According to Barry, how do most women see themselves?
4. Why do women have low self-esteem, according to Barry?
5. Why is it difficult for men to find a good answer when women ask how they look?

Drawing Inferences about Thesis and Purpose

1. What is Barry's subject?
2. What strategy, beyond using examples, does he use to develop his subject?
3. Barry says that men do not notice women's fingernails, but he also says that just because men are idiots, there is no reason for women to be. Is he conceding that men do influence women's concerns about their appearance?
4. What is Barry's thesis?

Analyzing Strategies and Style

1. At what point in your reading are you aware that Barry is using humor? What are some examples of his humor?
2. When Barry writes that Cindy Crawford is "some kind of genetic mutation," is he being unkind or complimentary? How do you know?
3. Barry write of boys' "dolls . . . excuse me, . . . their action figures." What is he saying by this wording?
4. Has Barry selected good examples in Cindy Crawford and Brad Pitt? Would you guess that almost all readers would know these two examples?

Thinking Critically

1. Do you agree with Barry that men and women see themselves—and judge their appearances—differently? Why or why not?
2. Do you think that Barbie has had a significant influence on women's views of themselves? How important are toys in shaping children's images of themselves and their world? Explain your response.

3. Which of the media have the greatest influence in setting standards of appearance for both men and women? Give examples to support your answer.

MAKING CONNECTIONS

---

1. Levine and Rivers are both concerned about violence in the media, whether in song lyrics or on television. Because children and teenagers are big listeners and watchers, they are growing up exposed to a considerable amount of violence. Levine does point out that fairy tales also contain much violence, but some experts believe that their violence is healthy for children. Are there different kinds or levels of violence? Should distinctions be made, and some kinds of violence banned or available to adults only? Consider the examples these writers use and those you know, and then try to define the kinds of violence that may be tolerated and the kinds that should be controlled in some way.

2. If violence in lyrics and on television should be controlled, who should do the controlling? Is the task one for parents, for education through the schools and TV, for voluntary control by the media, for federal guidelines and restrictions? Review the recommendations made by Levine and Rivers and then decide on the approaches you would take if you were "media czar."

3. Levine, Rivers, McGarvey, and Steinem are all stating or implying the power of the media. The media create images that sanction the dress, language, and behavior presented in those images. And children are not the only ones influenced by those images, as McGarvey's experience demonstrates. How should children be instructed to understand the media, especially television, movies, and advertising, so that they can distinguish between image and reality? Consider the suggestions stated or implied in this chapter and reflect on other possibilities as well.

4. Both Gloria Steinem and John Skow examine the ways that advertising misleads. Steinem focuses on all the material

throughout a magazine that advertisers seek to control, Skow on the number of "information" Web sites that are actually created to control users' views of issues. How can we know what is accurate and reliable? Think about strategies readers can use to guide their reading of both magazines and Web sites.

TOPICS AND GUIDELINES FOR WRITING

1. What makes your favorite type of television program so good, or what makes your least favorite type of program so bad? Do you most enjoy (or least enjoy) watching news, sports, sitcoms, soaps, a movie channel? Select your most (or least) favorite type and then support a thesis with specific examples from particular shows.

2. The columnist George Will has described the names of some foods as "printed noise." (Think of the names of ice cream flavors, for example.) Are there other words or pictures that should be labeled verbal or visual litter—words or pictures that are silly, inaccurate, overstated, childish? Think about product commercials; political advertising; repeated coverage of particular issues in the media; repeated "lectures" from teachers, parents, friends that you now simply tune out. Select your topic, decide on your thesis, and then support your thesis with plenty of examples.

3. Examine current political campaigns to see whether any use negative advertising that distorts the issues and misleads voters. For evidence, listen to radio and TV ads for specific examples with which to develop your essay. Your thesis will be that the _____ campaign uses misleading negative tactics, or the _____ campaign uses only fair and accurate campaign tactics.

4. Caryl Rivers is concerned about violence against women presented in song lyrics and television images. Are you? Examine examples of lyrics and/or TV images (e.g., MTV videos), decide on your point of view, and then support it with plenty of examples.

214 Explaining and Illustrating

5. In this chapter you have read some articles about the power of advertising and image making. When a product's name is clever, that name becomes an ongoing advertisement for the product. Many product names are highly connotative or suggestive, such as *Lestoil* cleaner. Think about the names used for one type of product, such as cleaning materials, perfumes, diet foods, or cigarettes. (You may want to explore your favorite grocery store or shopping mall for ideas.) In an essay, explain the effects of the various product names, grouping the names by their different effects (their purpose or the desired impact on buyers), and illustrate those effects with specific examples. Be sure to work with enough examples to support your thesis, probably at least fifteen specific items (e.g., White Shoulders) in the product category (e.g., perfumes).

6. Writing fables or parables to make a point about human character traits or about morality can be fun. Try writing one to make some point about advertising or about what motivates humans to buy particular products. Think, for example, about the many different car models—what types of people are drawn to each model—or the array of sports equipment or kinds of drinks. When planning your story, follow these guidelines: (a) keep your story short, no more than two or three pages; (b) make it a story—not an essay—with characters, dialogue, and a sequence of events; (c) remember that characters do not have to be human; (d) fill your story with specific details; (e) avoid any direct statement of your story's point; (f) consider using humor as a way to imply your point.

6

Using Process Analysis
How We Work and Play

How does it work? How do we do it? How did it happen? These questions are answered when you provide a process analysis. You live with process analysis every day. The directions to the library that you give to a visitor, the mechanic's explanation of how your car engine is supposed to be working, your history text's account of the planning and execution of the D-Day invasion of Normandy, the biology instructor's explanation of the steps to follow in dissecting a frog: All of these directions, accounts, and instructions are examples of process analysis.

When to Use Process Analysis

The label "process analysis" tells us about this kind of writing. It is, first, *process* because we are talking about an activity or procedure that takes us from one situation to another, that results in some change, some goal reached. You follow the instructions on the recipe card to produce the desired carrot cake, or on the box to put together the new bookcase. You listen to the instructor's guidelines carefully so that you will end with a properly dissected frog. Process is also a type of *analysis* because the good writer of process breaks down the activity into a clear series of steps or stages. Getting the steps in a process right—absolutely right!—is essential. You have come to value the person who gives clear directions, the instructor whose guidelines help you through the intricate stages that shaped an important period in history. You value those who write process analyses well because you have probably experienced more than one occasion of frustration over directions that were unclear, incomplete, or just plain wrong. When you have a topic that can most logically be developed as steps or stages in a process, then you will want to be one of those writers who presents the steps or stages clearly and completely for your readers.

How to Use Process Analysis

To write a clear, effective process analysis you need to keep several points in mind. First, when you are assigned a process analysis—or, more accurately, topics that can best be developed by using process analysis—you are not writing a *list* of instructions. You are writing an essay. This means that you must begin the way you begin any essay—with decisions about audience and purpose. You would not give the same directions for using a camera to a fifth-grade class that you would give to an advanced photography class at an adult education center. Similarly, when planning a process essay, you must assess your readers' knowledge of the subject as a basis for deciding how much background information and explanation are appropriate. These are really two separate decisions. One answers the question: Where do I start? The other answers the question: How detailed is my discussion of each step or stage in the process? Many "how-to" books are not really written for beginners, as you may have discovered. Instead, the author assumes more background than the beginner has.

When the process is complex, the writing challenge lies in giving sufficient explanation of each step so that readers are not too confused with step one to comprehend step two. Unless you are given an assignment that calls for a particular audience, think of directing your essays to a general adult audience made up of people like your classmates. Few of them are likely to be as knowledgeable as you are about a topic you select for your process analysis. When planning the essay, take time to include the background and explanations needed by readers who are not likely to have your knowledge and expertise.

The good essay is not only directed to a clearly defined audience; it is also unified around a clear thesis. In those instructions with the bookcase pieces, the implied thesis is: If you follow these directions you will put the bookcase together correctly. In a process essay, the thesis extends beyond the completing of the process. You must ask yourself why a reader should be interested in learning about the process topic you have selected. Ernest Hemingway wants to keep inexperienced campers from having so miserable a time that they will swear never to camp again. John Aigner explains a process for preparing for a job interview so that readers will be able to do well in their interviews and get the job.

Finally, the good essay is the interesting essay. The Word-Perfect manual doesn't have to be interesting; it just has to be clear so that the computer user can complete the desired documents. But the essay, whatever its purpose or organizational strategy, needs to engage its reader, to make an audience for itself through clear explanations and interesting details. Be sure to guide your reader through the time sequence that is your basic organizational strategy. Search for transitions that are more lively than "the first step," "the second step," and so on. Here are some transition words that often appear in process essays:

after	following	last	second
before	later	next	then
finally	last	now	when

In addition, when you present each step or stage, provide vivid details and concrete examples. Hemingway does not tell us in general terms to fry in the frying pan and boil in the kettle. He prepares trout and pancakes and macaroni, and an apple pie. The reader, mouth watering, is ready to start packing. Make your analysis right, make it clear, but, above all, make it interesting.

Getting Started: Reflections on Your Favorite Game

If you were going to teach some element of your favorite game or sport to a beginner, how would you break down the element into steps to be taught in sequence? For example, if you were to teach the tennis serve, you might go through the following steps: the stance, the toss, the backswing, contact with the ball, and the follow-through. List steps in the process of teaching some movement, play, or strategy in your favorite game. Try this process analysis in your journal or prepare it for class discussion.

"Putting Your Job Interview into Rehearsal"

JOHN P. AIGNER

A graduate of City College of New York, John Aigner (b. 1937) is the founder and president of Network Résumés, a New York City career services firm. Aigner teaches courses for career counselors in addition to running his company, which helps job seekers with the process of finding desired positions. His article on preparing for a job interview was originally published in the *New York Times* on August 16, 1983.

1   No actor would be so foolish as to walk onto a stage in front of a first-night audience without weeks of rehearsal. Yet every day thousands of job seekers at all stages of their careers walk into interviews without even a minimum of preparation. Hours of effort and expense invested in an effective résumé that successfully obtained the interview are thrown away through lack of preparation.

2   There are three key areas in which preparation can pay big dividends:

❑ Creating and rehearsing a personal script.
❑ Developing a "power vocabulary."
❑ Researching information about the job, company and industry.

3   Creation of a script and a power vocabulary are essentially one-time projects that will likely remain useful with only minor variations throughout a job search. General industry-oriented information also has an extended utility during a search. The gathering of information about the company or opportunity will need to be repeated for each occasion.

4   Persons who might be uncertain about the basic shoulds and shouldn'ts preliminary to successful interviewing—proper dress, on-time arrival, appropriate greeting—might try reading

"Sweaty Palms," by Anthony Medley, or "How to Win in a Job Interview," by Nason Robertson.

Preparing the Script

Devising a strategy for handling difficult questions will enable you to answer them calmly and with confidence. A particularly successful approach is to make a list of the most feared questions (some excellent examples may be found in "How to Turn an Interview Into a Job," by Jeffrey G. Allen, or "Outinterviewing the Interviewer," by Steven Merman and John McLaughlin), and prepare a written answer to each. Then record your answers on a cassette, listen to yourself and practice, practice, practice.

Be aware that most interviewers cover the same ground, and the same basic questions will appear in most interviews. This makes it relatively simple to prepare your answers. Following are some difficult questions that job-seekers may encounter, with suggestions for answering them:

❏ "Why did you leave your last job?" or "Why do you want to leave your present job?" Remember to be positive, not defensive. Acceptable answers are: greater opportunity, changing conditions, seeking greater responsibility. The best answers are both honest and brief.

❏ "Why should we hire you?" You may say that from your research you have learned that the interviewer's company is a leader in your field and you believe that your skills and its needs are well matched.

❏ "What are your strengths and weaknesses?" For many interviewees this question is the most intimidating. This is where preparation and a positive approach are most rewarding. One of the best ways to deal with a weakness is to refer to it as "an area in which I am working to strengthen my skills." Some career advisers suggest responding with, "Well, I don't really have any major weaknesses, but . . . " This is not a satisfactory answer, and would annoy me if I were the interviewer.

One general rule is never to answer a serious or really difficult question off the top of your head. Ask for an opportunity to think the question over, and promise to get back to the interviewer the next day. This approach has the added benefit of giving you a follow-up, second opportunity to sell yourself.

8   Have a friend or relative ask you the questions as many times as necessary for you to feel comfortable with the answers. Three to six hours spent practicing in this way will result in greatly improved confidence during interviews. If you think of additional questions later or if an interviewer throws you a curve, you can update your recorded answers.

9   The interviewer controls the flow of an interview, but the interviewee controls the content. If you know what you want to say, you will be more likely to say it, and you will have provided yourself with a powerful tool to maintain control of even a difficult interview.

The Power Vocabulary

10   A survey conducted among personnel executives by the Bureau of National Affairs concluded that the interview was the single most important factor in landing a job and that most applicants were rejected because they didn't promote themselves well during the interview. They frequently preface their description of an experience with, "Well, I only . . . " or "That wasn't a major part of my job." By such a deprecating phrase, they devalue their experience.

11   This lack of confidence about self-promotion is particularly true of women, an American Management Association study has concluded. Men, it seems, have had more practice at competition and are less reticent when it comes to advertising their accomplishments.

12   You should consider the interviewer to be in the same category as the tax auditor. He or she is not your friend, and you are under no obligation to volunteer any information that won't help you. In short, telling the truth and telling everything are not the same thing. If you performed well at a project, such as setting up a computer installation or devising a new method of taking inventory, it is not necessary to volunteer, for example, that the project lasted only a short while. If asked directly, of course answer honestly.

13   The words you select to describe yourself during the interview will have a powerful effect on the outcome. These words can be planned in advance. In the same way that you planned a script for the interview, you can also plan a vocabulary of

"power" words that will create an accumulation of positive impressions about you and your accomplishments.

Consider this example: "I reduced costs" versus "I trimmed 14 costs." The word "reduce" conjures up a fat person who is trying to lose weight. The word "trim" brings to mind someone who is fit and healthy.

Or: "While at company X, I . . . " versus "I am proud of the 15 fact that while at company X, I . . . " The latter approach is much stronger and more positive.

Use only positive words, ones that create strong mental im- 16 ages, adjectives such as accurate, dynamic, proficient, reliable, thorough, and verbs such as expedite, generate, improve, motivate, persuade, solve. These descriptors will add spice if you pepper your interview with them.

You can learn to develop a winning interview style by se- 17 lecting ten winning words each week and writing them on index cards. Practice using them in sentences about yourself, using one word per sentence. Select words with which you feel comfortable and work them into phrases within your script. You'll quickly discover that these words affect your self-image and the image that others have of you.

Avoid complaints of any kind. Do not criticize your previ- 18 ous company, supervisor or position. A complaint is always negative, and that is not the impression you wish to create.

Gathering Information

Valuable information about an industry, and about particular 19 companies within it, can be acquired through a library source such as Standard & Poor's, or annual reports, or through the trade press. This is an excellent way to learn the jargon of an industry. These special-interest professional and business publications have mushroomed like cable channels, and are frequently overlooked by job seekers because most are not available on newsstands and are not sold to the general public. There are thousands of these publications—privately circulated newsletters, weekly newspapers, slick monthlies, annual directories and everything in between. They contain a wealth of insider information—for example, industrywide trends and concerns, corporate plans, new-product announcements, trade jargon.

20   A sample copy or even a free subscription is generally available for the asking. To track down the trade press in your industry, check the *Standard Periodical Directory, Gebbe Press All-in-One Directory, The Encyclopedia of Business Information Sources, Ayers Guide to Periodicals* or *Standard Rate and Data.* For articles on particular business subjects, check the *Business Periodicals Index.*

21   Being current on industry concerns in general and company problems in particular can go a long way toward making an interview successful.

Expanding Vocabulary

Examine the following words in their contexts in the essay and then write a brief definition or synonym of each one. (Do not use a dictionary; try to guess each word's meaning from its context.)

preliminary (4)	accumulation (13)
intimidating (6)	descriptors (16)
deprecating (10)	jargon (19)
devalue (10)	mushroomed (19)
reticent (11)	

Understanding Content

1. What are the three broad steps in preparation for a job interview? What characteristic do the first two share? How does the third step differ somewhat from the first two?
2. List the specific steps within the first step: preparing the script. Why is it possible to prepare basically one script?
3. List the specific steps for developing a power vocabulary.
4. Why does it help to think of the interviewer as similar to a tax auditor?
5. What is the procedure for gathering information? What are the advantages beyond preparation for a specific interview?

Drawing Inferences about Thesis and Purpose

1. What is Aigner's subject; that is, what process is he analyzing?
2. What is Aigner's thesis—what is the point of his process analysis?
3. When advising people on how to sell themselves, one invites the charge of encouraging misrepresentation, of "packaging" the interviewee. How does Aigner seek to avoid this charge? How does he try to balance polishing one's interview skills with a fair presentation of one's qualifications?

Analyzing Strategies and Style

1. What analogy does Aigner use throughout his article? Where does he introduce the comparison? Where does he refer to it again? Is this an effective analogy? Why or why not?
2. Aigner's introduction runs to several paragraphs, but his conclusion is only one paragraph containing one sentence. Does it seem too abrupt to you? Can you make the case that it is an effective ending?
3. Examine Aigner's metaphors in paragraphs 1, 8, and 16. How are they effective? What do they contribute to the article?

Thinking Critically

1. If you have interviewed for a job, did you think at the time to prepare in any of the ways Aigner suggests? If so, do you think the process helped you in the interview? If not, would you follow Aigner's steps the next time? Why or why not?
2. Is there one step in Aigner's process that would be especially important in your career field? If so, why? How would it make you a better interviewee in your career field?
3. Aigner emphasizes the similarity of most job interviews. Had you thought about this point before? Does the idea seem sensible? How can understanding this characteristic of interviews help to make the interview process a little easier?
4. Aigner gives the most space to developing a power vocabulary. Is there some good advice here that extends beyond the interview process? How important are positive attitudes about ourselves?

"How to Give Orders Like a Man"

DEBORAH TANNEN

Deborah Tannen (b. 1945) holds a Ph.D. in linguistics from the University of California at Berkeley and is University Professor of Linguistics at Georgetown University. Dr. Tannen's interest in how "ordinary" people use language to communicate—or fail to communicate—has resulted in many articles, a number of popular books, and many calls for speaking engagements. Among her books are *Conversational Style* (1984), *That's Not What I Meant!* (1986), and *Talking from 9 to 5* (1994). The following article, adapted from her latest book, appeared in the *New York Times* in August 1994.

1   A university president was expecting a visit from a member of the board of trustees. When her secretary buzzed to tell her that the board member had arrived, she left her office and entered the reception area to greet him. Before ushering him into her office, she handed her secretary a sheet of paper and said: "I've just finished drafting this letter. Do you think you could type it right away? I'd like to get it out before lunch. And would you please do me a favor and hold all calls while I'm meeting with Mr. Smith?"

2   When they sat down behind the closed door of her office, Mr. Smith began by telling her that he thought she had spoken inappropriately to her secretary. "Don't forget," he said. *"You're* the president!"

3   Putting aside the question of the appropriateness of his admonishing the president on her way of speaking, it is revealing —and representative of many Americans' assumptions—that the indirect way in which the university president told her secretary what to do struck him as self-deprecating. He took it as evidence that she didn't think she had the right to make demands of her secretary. He probably thought he was giving her a needed pep talk, bolstering her self-confidence.

4   I challenge the assumption that talking in an indirect way necessarily reveals powerlessness, lack of self-confidence or anything else about the character of the speaker. Indirectness is a fundamental element in human communication. It is also one of the elements that varies most from one culture to another, and one that can cause confusion and misunderstanding when speakers have different habits with regard to using it. I also want to dispel the assumption that American women tend to be more indirect than American men. Women and men are both indirect, but in addition to differences associated with their backgrounds—regional, ethnic and class—they tend to be indirect in different situations and in different ways.

5   At work, we need to get others to do things, and we all have different ways of accomplishing this. Any individual's ways will vary depending on who is being addressed—a boss, a peer or a subordinate. At one extreme are bald commands. At the other are requests so indirect that they don't sound like requests at all, but are just a statement of need or a description of a situation. People with direct styles of asking others to do

things perceive indirect requests—if they perceive them as requests at all—as manipulative. But this is often just a way of blaming others for our discomfort with their styles.

The indirect style is no more manipulative than making a telephone call, asking "Is Rachel there?" and expecting whoever answers the phone to put Rachel on. Only a child is likely to answer "Yes" and continue holding the phone—not out of orneriness but because of inexperience with the conventional meaning of the question. (A mischievous adult might do it to tease.) Those who feel that indirect orders are illogical or manipulative do not recognize the conventional nature of indirect requests.

Issuing orders indirectly can be the prerogative of those in power. Imagine, for example, a master who says "It's cold in here" and expects a servant to make a move to close a window, while a servant who says the same thing is not likely to see his employer rise to correct the situation and make him more comfortable. Indeed, a Frenchman raised in Brittany tells me that his family never gave bald commands to their servants but always communicated orders in indirect and highly polite ways. This pattern renders less surprising the finding of David Bellinger and Jean Berko Gleason that fathers' speech to their young children had a higher incidence than mothers' of both direct imperatives like "Turn the bolt with the wrench" *and* indirect orders like "The wheel is going to fall off."

The use of indirectness can hardly be understood without the cross-cultural perspective. Many Americans find it self-evident that directness is logical and aligned with power while indirectness is akin to dishonesty and reflects subservience. But for speakers raised in most of the world's cultures, varieties of indirectness are the norm in communication. This is the pattern found by a Japanese sociolinguist, Kunihiko Harada, in his analysis of a conversation he recorded between a Japanese boss and a subordinate.

The markers of superior status were clear. One speaker was a Japanese man in his late 40's who managed the local branch of a Japanese private school in the United States. His conversational partner was a Japanese-American woman in her early 20's who worked at the school. By virtue of his job, his age and his native fluency in the language being taught, the man was

6

7

8

9

in the superior position. Yet when he addressed the woman, he frequently used polite language and almost always used indirectness. For example, he had tried and failed to find a photography store that would make a black-and-white print from a color negative for a brochure they were producing. He let her know that he wanted her to take over the task by stating the situation and allowed her to volunteer to do it: (This is a translation of the Japanese conversation.)

10   *On this matter, that, that, on the leaflet? This photo, I'm thinking of changing it to black-and-white and making it clearer. . . . I went to a photo shop and asked them. They said they didn't do black-and-white. I asked if they knew any place that did. They said they didn't know. They weren't very helpful, but anyway, a place must be found, the negative brought to it, the picture developed.*

11   Harada observes, "Given the fact that there are some duties to be performed and that there are two parties present, the subordinate is supposed to assume that those are his or her obligation." It was precisely because of his higher status that the boss was free to choose whether to speak formally or informally, to assert his power or to play it down and build rapport—an option not available to the subordinate, who would have seemed cheeky if she had chosen a style that enhanced friendliness and closeness.

12   The same pattern was found by a Chinese sociolinguist, Yuling Pan, in a meeting of officials involved in a neighborhood youth program. All spoke in ways that reflected their place in the hierarchy. A subordinate addressing a superior always spoke in a deferential way, but a superior addressing a subordinate could either be authoritarian, demonstrating his power, or friendly, establishing rapport. The ones in power had the option of choosing which style to use. In this spirit, I have been told by people who prefer their bosses to give orders indirectly that those who issue bald commands must be pretty insecure; otherwise why would they have to bolster their egos by throwing their weight around?

13   I am not inclined to accept that those who give orders directly are really insecure and powerless, any more than I want to accept that judgment of those who give indirect orders. The conclusion to be drawn is that ways of talking should not be

taken as obvious evidence of inner psychological states like insecurity or lack of confidence. Considering the many influences on conversational style, individuals have a wide range of ways of getting things done and expressing their emotional states. Personality characteristics like insecurity cannot be linked to ways of speaking in an automatic, self-evident way.

Those who expect orders to be given indirectly are offended 14 when they come unadorned. One woman said that when her boss gives her instructions, she feels she should click her heels, salute, and say "Yes boss!" His directions strike her as so imperious as to border on the militaristic. Yet I received a letter from a man telling me that indirect orders were a fundamental part of his military training. He wrote:

Many years ago, when I was in the Navy, I was training to be a 15 *radio technician. One class I was in was taught by a chief radioman, a regular Navy man who had been to sea, and who was then in his third hitch. The students, about 20 of us, were fresh out of boot camp, with no sea duty and little knowledge of real Navy life. One day in class the chief said it was hot in the room. The students didn't react, except perhaps to nod in agreement. The chief repeated himself: "It's hot in this room." Again there was no reaction from the students.*

Then the chief explained. He wasn't looking for agreement or dis- 16 *cussion from us. When he said that the room was hot, he expected us to do something about it—like opening the window. He tried it one more time, and this time all of us left our workbenches and headed for the windows. We had learned. And we had many opportunities to apply what we had learned.*

This letter especially intrigued me because "It's cold in here" 17 is the standard sentence used by linguists to illustrate an indirect way of getting someone to do something—as I used it earlier. In this example, it is the very obviousness and rigidity of the military hierarchy that makes the statement of a problem sufficient to trigger corrective action on the part of subordinates.

A man who had worked at the Pentagon reinforced the view 18 that the burden of interpretation is on subordinates in the military—and he noticed the difference when he moved to a position in the private sector. He was frustrated when he'd say to his new secretary, for example, "Do we have a list of invitees?" and be told, "I don't know; we probably do" rather than "I'll get it for you." Indeed, he explained, at the Pentagon, such a question would likely be heard as a reproach that the list was not already on his desk.

19   The suggestion that indirectness is associated with the military must come as a surprise to many. But everyone is indirect, meaning more than is put into words and deriving meaning from words that are never actually said. It's a matter of where, when and how we each tend to be indirect and look for hidden meanings. But indirectness has a built-in liability. There is a risk that the other will either miss or choose to ignore your meaning.

20   On Jan. 13, 1982, a freezing cold, snowy day in Washington, Air Florida Flight 90 took off from National Airport, but could not get the lift it needed to keep climbing. It crashed into a bridge linking Washington to the state of Virginia and plunged into the Potomac. Of the 79 people on board, all but 5 perished, many floundering and drowning in the icy water while horror-stricken bystanders watched helplessly from the river's edge and millions more watched, aghast, on their television screens. Experts later concluded that the plane had waited too long after de-icing to take off. Fresh buildup of ice on the wings and engine brought the plane down. How could the pilot and co-pilot have made such a blunder? Didn't at least one of them realize it was dangerous to take off under these conditions?

21   Charlotte Linde, a linguist at the Institute for Research on Learning in Palo Alto, Calif., has studied the "black box" recordings of cockpit conversations that preceded crashes as well as tape recordings of conversations that took place among crews during flight simulations in which problems were presented. Among the black box conversations she studied was the one between the pilot and co-pilot just before the Air Florida crash. The pilot, it turned out, had little experience flying in icy weather. The co-pilot had a bit more, and it became heartbreakingly clear on analysis that he had tried to warn the pilot, but he did so indirectly.

22   The co-pilot repeatedly called attention to the bad weather and to ice building up on the other planes:

23   *Co-pilot: Look how the ice is just hanging on his, ah, back, back there, see that?*
      . . .

Co-pilot: See all those icicles on the back there and everything?   24
Captain: Yeah.   25

He expressed concern early on about the long waiting time   26
between de-icing:

Co-pilot: Boy, this is a, this is a losing battle here on trying to de-   27
ice those things, it [gives] you a false feeling of security, that's all that
does.

Shortly after they were given clearance to take off, he again   28
expressed concern:

Co-pilot: Let's check these tops again since we been setting here   29
awhile.

Captain: I think we get to go here in a minute.   30

When they were about to take off, the co-pilot called atten-   31
tion to the engine instrument readings, which were not normal:

Co-pilot: That don't seem right, does it? [three-second pause] Ah,   32
that's not right. . . .

Captain: Yes, it is, there's 80.   33

Co-pilot: Naw, I don't think that's right. [seven-second pause]   34
Ah, maybe it is.

Captain: Hundred and twenty.   35

Co-pilot: I don't know.   36

The takeoff proceeded, and 37 seconds later the pilot and co-   37
pilot exchanged their last words.

The co-pilot had repeatedly called the pilot's attention to   38
dangerous conditions but did not directly suggest they abort
the takeoff. In Linde's judgment, he was expressing his concern
indirectly, and the captain didn't pick up on it—with tragic
results.

That the co-pilot was trying to warn the captain indirectly is   39
supported by evidence from another airline accident—a relatively minor one—investigated by Linde that also involved the
unsuccessful use of indirectness.

On July 9, 1978, Allegheny Airlines Flight 453 was landing   40
at Monroe County Airport in Rochester, when it overran the
runway by 728 feet. Everyone survived. This meant that the
captain and co-pilot could be interviewed. It turned out that
the plane had been flying too fast for a safe landing. The captain should have realized this and flown around a second time,
decreasing his speed before trying to land. The captain said he
simply had not been aware that he was going too fast. But the

co-pilot told interviewers that he "tried to warn the captain in subtle ways, like mentioning the possibility of a tail wind and the slowness of flap extension." His exact words were recorded in the black box. The crosshatches indicate words deleted by the National Transportation Safety Board and were probably expletives:

41   *Co-pilot: Yeah, it looks like you got a tail wind here.*
42   *Captain: Yeah.*
43   *[?]: Yeah [it] moves awfully # slow.*
44   *Co-pilot: Yeah the # flaps are slower than a #.*
45   *Captain: We'll make it, gonna have to add power.*
46   *Co-pilot: I know.*

47   The co-pilot thought the captain would understand that if there was a tail wind, it would result in the plane going too fast, and if the flaps were slow, they would be inadequate to break the speed sufficiently for a safe landing. He thought the captain would then correct for the error by not trying to land. But the captain said he didn't interpret the co-pilot's remarks to mean they were going too fast.

48   Linde believes it is not a coincidence that the people being indirect in these conversations were the co-pilots. In her analyses of flight-crew conversations she found it was typical for the speech of subordinates to be more mitigated—polite, tentative or indirect. She also found that topics broached in a mitigated way were more likely to fail, and that captains were more likely to ignore hints from their crew members than the other way around. These findings are evidence that not only can indirectness and other forms of mitigation be misunderstood, but they are also easier to ignore.

49   In the Air Florida case, it is doubtful that the captain did not realize what the co-pilot was suggesting when he said, "Let's check these tops again since we been setting here awhile" (though it seems safe to assume he did not realize the gravity of the co-pilot's concern). But the indirectness of the co-pilot's phrasing certainly made it easier for the pilot to ignore it. In this sense, the captain's response, "I think we get to go here in a minute," was an indirect way of saying, "I'd rather not." In view of these patterns, the flight crews of some airlines are now given training to express their concerns, even to superiors, in more direct ways.

The conclusion that people should learn to express them- 50
selves more directly has a ring of truth to it—especially for
Americans. But direct communication is not necessarily always
preferable. If more direct expression is better communication,
then the most direct-speaking crews should be the best ones.
Linde was surprised to find in her research that crews that used
the most mitigated speech were often judged the best crews. As
part of the study of talk among cockpit crews in flight simulations, the trainers observed and rated the performances of the
simulation crews. The crews they rated top in performance had
higher rate of mitigation than crews they judged to be poor.

This finding seems at odds with the role played by indirect- 51
ness in the examples of crashes that we just saw. Linde concluded that since every utterance functions on two levels—the
referential (what it says) and the relational (what it implies
about the speaker's relationships), crews that attend to the relational level will be better crews. A similar explanation was
suggested by Kunihiko Harada. He believes that the secret of
successful communication lies not in teaching subordinates to
be more direct, but in teaching higher-ups to be more sensitive
to indirect meaning. In other words, the crashes resulted not
only because the co-pilots tried to alert the captains to danger
indirectly but also because the captains were not attuned to the
co-pilots' hints. What made for successful performance among
the best crews might have been the ability—or willingness—of
listeners to pick up on hints, just as members of families or
longstanding couples come to understand each other's meaning without being particularly explicit.

It is not surprising that a Japanese sociolinguist came up with 52
this explanation; what he described is the Japanese system, by
which good communication is believed to take place when
meaning is gleaned without being stated directly—or at all.

While Americans believe that "the squeaky wheel gets the 53
grease" (so it's best to speak up), the Japanese say, "The nail
that sticks out gets hammered back in" (so it's best to remain
silent if you don't want to be hit on the head). Many Japanese
scholars writing in English have tried to explain to bewildered
Americans the ethics of a culture in which silence is often given
greater value than speech, and ideas are believed to be best
communicated without being explicitly stated. Key concepts in

Japanese give a flavor of the attitudes toward language that they reveal—and set in relief the strategies that Americans encounter at work when talking to other Americans.

54   Takie Sugiyama Lebra, a Japanese-born anthropologist, explains that one of the most basic values in Japanese culture is *omoiyari,* which she translates as "empathy." Because of *omoiyari,* it should not be necessary to state one's meaning explicitly; people should be able to sense each other's meaning intuitively. Lebra explains that it is typical for a Japanese speaker to let sentences trail off rather than complete them because expressing ideas before knowing how they will be received seems intrusive. "Only an insensitive, uncouth person needs a direct, verbal, complete message," Lebra says.

55   *Sasshi,* the anticipation of another's message through insightful guesswork, is considered an indication of maturity.

56   Considering the value placed on direct communication by Americans in general, and especially by American business people, it is easy to imagine that many American readers may scoff at such conversational habits. But the success of Japanese businesses makes it impossible to continue to maintain that there is anything inherently inefficient about such conversation conventions. With indirectness, as with all aspects of conversational style, our own habitual style seems to make sense—seems polite, right and good. The light cast by the habits and assumptions of another culture can help us see our way to the flexibility and respect for other styles that is the only best way of speaking.

Expanding Vocabulary

Match each word in column A with its definition in column B. When in doubt, first find the word in the essay and look for context clues to aid your understanding of the word's meaning. Then, if necessary, use your dictionary to complete the matching exercise.

Column A	*Column B*
admonishing (3)	plain, blunt
self-deprecating (3)	relationship of mutual
bolstering (3)	understanding
bald (5)	a ranking of persons
orneriness (6)	exclusive right or privilege
prerogative (7)	arrogantly overbearing

subservience (8)
rapport (11)
deferential (12)
imperious (14)
hierarchy (17)
liability (19)
aghast (20)
simulations (21)
mitigated (48)
explicit (51)
gleaned (52)
empathy (54)
intrusive (54)
uncouth (54)
scoff (56)

courteous yielding to another
moderated or eased the
   force of
supporting, holding up
ability to identify with another's feelings or situation
struck by amazement, horror
clearly expressed
express scorn
warning, reproving gently
barging in without being invited
meanness, stubbornness
crude, unrefined
acknowledging another's
   superiority
modelings of real situations
putting oneself down
gathered bit by bit
obligation or debt

Understanding Content

1. In the workplace, requests can range from commands to what?
2. How do some people view indirect requests? Why does Tannen disagree with their attitude?
3. What is the view of many Americans about direct versus indirect speech? What does direct speech seem to indicate about a person?
4. In fact, how widely used—in terms of cultures and positions or ranking—is indirect speech?
5. In Tannen's view, does the way one makes requests necessarily reveal personality states? Why?
6. How common are indirect requests in the military? In other work situations with a clear ranking of leaders and subordinates?
7. When requests or information or concerns are expressed indirectly, whose task is it to understand what is being said? When misunderstandings occur between superiors and subordinates who are indirect, who needs to improve communication skills?
8. On what two levels does speech always function?

Drawing Inferences about Thesis and Purpose

1. Tannen's title suggests that she will contrast men's and women's ways of speaking, but her title may be somewhat misleading. What, actually, is her subject?

2. What is Tannen's thesis? Examine paragraph 4. Is it appropriate to say that she has several interconnected main ideas?

Analyzing Strategies and Style

1. What kind of attention-getting opening does Tannen use? What makes it effective?
2. Tannen provides many examples, including several lengthy ones. Why does she use such long examples? What do they provide for readers?
3. Which example do you think best shows the process of indirect speech? Why?
4. What does Tannen accomplish with her cross-cultural analysis, particularly with her concluding contrast with Japanese views of indirect speech?

Thinking Critically

1. How would you describe your way of making requests? Are you more direct or more indirect? Is there anything you might change about the way you speak? About the way you listen to others?
2. Were you surprised at the amount of indirect speech in the military? Does Tannen's explanation for this make sense?
3. Tannen reminds readers that all speech is both "referential (what it says)" and "relational (what it implies about the speaker's relationship)." Is this a new idea for you? Does it make sense? How would you explain the concept to someone else?
4. Do Americans, in particular, have some trouble dealing with differences in the positions of people? Can holding the idea that "everyone is equal" interfere with the understanding of indirect speech?
5. Can Americans learn something about communication from the Japanese? Is it important to understand the role of the listener, to develop greater empathy? Explain.

"Improving Your Body Language Skills"

SUZETTE H. ELGIN

A professor emeritus in linguistics from San Diego State University, Suzette Elgin (b. 1936) is the author of several books on language use, including *Try to Feel It My Way* (1996) and *How to*

Disagree without Being Disagreeable (1997). She has also written several science fiction novels. "Improving Your Body Language Skills" is a section from Elgin's book *Genderspeak* (1997). Here Elgin offers guidelines for finding the most respected way of speaking American English and for understanding the messages in body language.

Body language problems between men and women who are   1
speakers of American Mainstream English today begin at the most basic of nonverbal levels: with the *pitch* of the voice. The admired voice for the AME culture is the adult male voice; the deeper and richer it is, and the less nasal it is, the more it is admired. Women tend to pitch their voices higher than men do, and this is a strike against them in almost every language interaction. Not because there is anything inherently wrong with high-pitched voices, but because AME speakers associate them with children. A high-pitched voice that's also nasal is heard as the voice of a *whiny* child. People know, of course, that they're hearing an adult woman (or, for the occasional man with a high-pitched voice, an adult male). But at a level below conscious awareness they tend to perceive the voice as the voice of a child. This perception, however much it is in conflict with reality, affects their response to and their behavior toward the speaker.

The contrast in voice pitch isn't really a *physiological* matter;   2
the difference between adult male and female vocal tracts is too minor to account for it in the majority of people. In many other cultures, male voices are higher than those of AME-speaking men, although the physical characteristics of the males are the same. When American adults speak to infants, they pitch their voices lower as they talk to boys, and the infants respond in the same way. Females learn, literally in the bassinet and playpen, that they are expected to make higher-pitched sounds than males are.

In addition to the difference in baseline pitch, AME-speak-   3
ing women's voices have more of the quality called *dynamism:* They use more varied pitch levels, they move from one pitch to another more frequently, and they are more likely than men's voices are to move from one pitch to another that's quite a bit higher or lower. In other situations the term "dynamic" is a compliment, while "monotonous," its opposite, is a negative label. But not in language; not in the AME culture. The less

monotonous a woman's voice is, the more likely it is that her speech will be described by others as "emotional" or "melodramatic." Monotony in the male voice, however, is ordinarily perceived as evidence of strength and stability. (For a detailed discussion of these differences, see McConnell-Ginet 1983.)

4   Certainly male/female body language differences go beyond the voice. There are positions and gestures and facial expressions that are more typical of one gender than of the other. But the effect one gender achieves by learning to use such items of body language from the other gender is rarely positive. A woman who hooks her thumbs into her belt, spreads her feet wide, and juts out her chin usually looks foolish, as does a man who carefully crosses his legs at the ankles. There are a few stereotypically feminine items that reinforce the "childish" perception which a woman can be careful *not* to use, such as giggling behind her hand or batting her eyelashes. But the most useful thing any woman—or man—can do to get rid of the perceptually filtered "I'm listening to a child" effect is to make the voice lower, and less nasal, and more resonant, so that it will be perceived as an *adult* voice.

5   This is something that anyone not handicapped by a physical disability that interferes with voice quality can do. One way to do it is to put yourself in the hands of a competent voice *coach*. If you have the time and money to do that, and you live where such experts are available, that's an excellent idea. On the other hand, it's also something you can do by yourself, using an ancient technique that in the *Gentle Art* system is called *simultaneous modeling*. . . .

6   Let me make one thing clear, however, before we go on. I'm not suggesting that anyone, of either gender, "should" try to change the quality of their voice. As is true for many linguistic questions, this is not a moral issue but an issue of cultural fashion. Low voices are not "better" than high voices. In the same way that some people insist on their right to wear jeans in an office where everyone else dresses more formally, people have every right to take the position that the voice they have is the voice they prefer to have. I approve of that, one hundred percent. However, because that decision can have grave consequences, people need to be aware that the consequences exist and that the choice is theirs to make.

It's unacceptable for someone to be unaware that the pri-   7
mary reason for his or her communication problems is a high-
pitched voice, and to assume that the problems are caused by
the lack of a "powerful vocabulary," or a thin enough body, or
a sufficiently expensive blazer, or some such thing. It's also unacceptable for those who do realize what the problem is to believe they're helpless to do anything about it. Except in cases
requiring medical attention, *anyone,* working alone, can change
his or her voice to make it closer to what our culture perceives
as the ideal and adult voice. When a medical condition complicates the issue, the potential for improvement may be less,
but even limited change toward the ideal can bring about significant positive effects.

The facts about body language and its critical importance to   8
communication can be frightening. We don't study body language in school, and few of us are given formal training in the
subject. We read everywhere that "a more powerful vocabulary" is our ticket to communication success, and that seems
easy—just buy a book or a software program and learn some
new words. Improving our body language skills seems mysterious and difficult by contrast. But there's no need to be intimidated; it's simpler than you think.

Your internal grammar, the same one that you use to put the   9
right endings on your words and arrange your words in the
proper order in your sentences, contains all the rules for body
language in your culture. You just haven't had convenient *access* to that information that would let you use it consciously
and strategically. The sections that follow will help you establish that access.

Developing Your Observational Skills

The first step in developing observational skills for nonverbal   10
communication is simply learning to PAY ATTENTION to the
speaker's body and voice. Men in the AME culture tend not to
do this, and to be unaware that it matters; when they do pay
attention they usually follow a rule that tells them to pay attention only to the speaker's face. Women do somewhat better,
not because they have any built-in biological advantage, but
because it is universally true that those having less power pay

more attention to the body language of those having more power. (In the most primitive situations, this means being alert to the movements of the powerful person so that you will be able to get out of the way before the powerful person grabs or hits you.)

11   This gender difference is well known. In 1975 a footnote in the *Virginia Law Review* suggested that perhaps women should be excluded from jury duty, because their skill at observing and interpreting nonverbal communication might make them excessively vulnerable to body language effects, interfering with the defendant's right to an independent and unbiased jury. ("Notes: Judges' Nonverbal Behavior in Jury Trials: A Threat to Judicial Impartiality," *Virginia Law Review*, 1975, 61:1266–1298. For a review of research and an account of experiments proving that the body language of trial judges has a significant impact on jury decisions, see Blanck et al. 1985.)

12   Sometimes this language skill is an advantage for women; sometimes it's not. Like any other skill, it depends on how it is used. Nobody likes the idea that another person is able to read his or her mind. The woman who expresses in words what a man's body language tells her—with claims such as "I can tell by the look on your face that you don't want to go to St. Louis" or "Don't try to tell me you want to go to St. Louis; the way you keep wiggling your index fingers gives you away every time"—is almost sure to provoke hostility. Such remarks are equally counterproductive coming from men who have well-developed body language reading skills.

13   The only way to learn to pay attention to body language is to *practice*. You have to work at it consciously until you become so skilled that you do it automatically, just as you would work at your tennis or your golf or a favorite handicraft. If you're not accustomed to body language observation, you'll find it extremely difficult at first. You'll keep *forgetting* to do it.

14   You've probably had the experience of "coming to" as you take the last highway exit on your drive home and realizing that you have no memory of your previous ten minutes on the road. In the same way, you'll start out carefully observing someone's body language and then suddenly realize that it's been five minutes since you were consciously aware of anything but the words, and perhaps the facial expression, of the

speaker. If you continue to work at it, however, you'll get past this stage. As a first practice partner, I strongly recommend your television set. Unlike living persons, the tv set doesn't get tired, doesn't wonder why you're staring at it, is always available at your convenience, and—best of all—never gets its feelings hurt.

Establishing Baseline Values—and Spotting Deviations from Them—in Body Language

Body language baselines are profiles of people's speech when 15 they're relaxed, as in casual conversations with close friends. Baselines include such information as the typical pitch of the voice, rate of speed for speech, frequency of eyeblink, body posture, number of hand gestures, etc., for the individual you're interacting with, during *relaxed communication*. This information is important because a *deviation* from the baseline— a move away from these typical values—is a signal to be alert. It indicates some sort of emotional involvement, positive or negative; it indicates that something is happening; sometimes it indicates an attempt to deceive or mislead you.

You will have read books or listened to tapes telling you that 16 when you see a person cross his arms or scratch her nose it *means* a particular thing. You'll read that crossed arms signal defensiveness and disagreement with what you're saying; you'll hear that scratching the nose signals anxiety. Sometimes that's true, of course; but much of the time it means the person you're observing is cold or has a nose that itches. When such items *are* reliable, they hold for a restricted population in specific circumstances—usually for the middle class or upper class dominant white male in a business situation. Learning to establish baseline values for the other person and spotting deviations from that baseline is a great deal more reliable, and will be useful to you in every communication situation, including interactions with people from outside your own culture.

For example, one of the most reliable clues to anxiety, a lack 17 of sincere commitment to what's being said, and a possible intention to deceive is a change to a higher voice pitch. But you won't know there's been a change unless you have first learned what pitch the speaker uses in normal everyday conversation.

The same thing is true for other deviations from baseline values. Here are two simple and practical ways to get the necessary information:

❏ Make a phone call to the individual in advance of your meeting and discuss something entirely neutral, like how to get to the meeting site.

❏ When you're with the other person, don't begin by talking about anything important. Instead, spend five minutes—or as long as it takes—-making small talk on neutral subjects.

18   Now we can move on to improving your body language *performance* skills, as opposed to observation alone.

Simultaneous Modeling

19 When students learn t'ai chi, they learn not by watching the teacher and then trying out the posture or movement by themselves but by watching and then moving *with* the teacher. This technique has been successful for thousands of years. If you've studied a foreign language, you're familiar with the traditional procedure: Listen to a sequence of the foreign language, and then, during the pause provided, repeat what you've just heard. At the University of California San Diego, instead of repeating the foreign language sequence *after* the recorded model, students listen to it several times to become familiar with the content and then speak simultaneously *with* the model. This technique (developed at UCSD by linguist Leonard Newmark) consistently produces results far superior to the traditional method. And there are many cultures in which people learn to do things (weaving, for example) by first watching someone who already knows how and then sitting down beside that person and working along with her or him.

20 These are all examples of *simultaneous modeling*. They take *advantage* of the way human brains work instead of fighting against it. When you change your behavior to make it like someone else's you have to make many small adjustments all over your body, all at once. You can't do that very well *consciously*. But your brain can do it competently and successfully, if you just stay out of its way. You can use this information and your brain's built-in skills to improve the quality of your voice, by adapting Newmark's foreign language teaching method.

Changing voice quality requires an array of small but cru-   21
cial adjustments. You have to change the tension of the muscles
of your tongue and throat and chest, you have to move the
parts of your vocal tract in ways that you're not used to, and so
on. When you listen to a foreign language sequence and try to
repeat it afterward, you not only have to make all those adjustments but you have to *remember* the sequence. The final result is that you change your speech to match the sequence you
remember instead of the one you actually heard. When you
speak *with* the model voice instead of repeating on your own,
this doesn't happen. Your brain takes over and does all the adjustments, matching your voice to the model.

Working with the Tape Recorder

You need a tape recorder (an inexpensive one will do), a few   22
blank tapes, and a tape about thirty minutes long by someone
of your own gender whose voice sounds the way you'd like to
sound. For men, I recommend television anchorman Peter Jennings, or one of the male announcers on National Public
Radio's regular news programs ("Morning Edition" or "All
Things Considered," for example). For women I recommend a
tape of Diane Sawyer or one of the female NPR newscasters. If
you prefer someone else, either a public figure or someone in
your own circle, that's fine. Just be sure the voice you choose
as your model is one that you and others perceive as strong,
resonant, pleasant, compelling, and—above all—-the voice of a
mature adult. Then follow the steps below, at your own convenience, at your own speed, and in privacy.

1. Make a twenty- to thirty-minute *baseline* tape of your own   23
   speech, write down the date on which it was made, and
   keep it for comparison with tapes you make later on. Don't
   read aloud, and don't say something memorized—just *talk.*
   Talk about your childhood, or why you have trouble communicating with people of the opposite sex, or anything else
   you can talk about easily and naturally.
2. Listen to the tape you've chosen as a model, all the way   24
   through, to get a general idea of its content. Don't write it
   down, and don't try to memorize it—doing either of those
   things just gets in the way and keeps you from succeeding.

25 3. Choose a sentence of average length to work with, from any point on the tape. Listen to it a couple of times, to become familiar with it. Then repeat it, SPEAKING ALONG WITH THE TAPE, SIMULTANEOUSLY. Rewind the tape and do it again, as many times as you feel are necessary—ten times is not in any way unusual. Your goal is to be able to speak smoothly and easily with the model. Don't *struggle.* Trust your brain and let it carry out its functions without interference.

26 4. When you're bored with the sentence you chose, pick another sentence and repeat Step #3. You should also move on whenever you realize that you know a sentence so well that you've stopped needing the model voice; you aren't interested in learning to *recite* the tape. Continue in this way until you've finished the tape or achieved your goal, whichever happens first. (And go on to another model tape if you find that you need one.)

27 5. After about ten hours of practice (and after every additional five or six hours), make a new baseline tape of your own speech. Listen to it, and compare it with the earlier ones. When you're satisfied with the change you hear, STOP. The point of this technique is to improve your *own* voice. You don't want people to think you're doing Peter Jennings or Diane Sawyer imitations when you talk; if you go on too long, that's exactly what will happen.

28   How long this will take will depend on the amount of time you have for practice, how tired you are, whether you are a person who learns well by listening, and other individual factors. Try to make each practice session at least fifteen minutes long; thirty minutes is even better. Try to practice every other day, roughly. If all you can manage is ten minutes once a week, put in those ten minutes—just be prepared for it to take you much longer to achieve results on that basis. Remember: It doesn't make any *difference* how long it takes. You're not paying by the hour when you use this technique, and there won't be a final exam. Relax and let it take as long as it takes. Some of my clients have noticed substantial improvement in six weeks; others have needed six months or more for the same results.

29   The fact that you can't just take a Voice Quality Pill and change instantly is actually a good thing. The people you in-

teract with regularly (and especially the person or persons you live with) need to be able to get used to the change in your voice gradually. You don't want your partner to leave in the morning, accustomed to the voice you've always had, and come home that night to someone who sounds like an entirely different person. A pleasant adult voice is a powerful tool for improving your relationships, but it shouldn't come as a *shock* to those around you.

Note: You can also use this procedure to learn to speak other 30 varieties of English—other dialects or other registers—at will. If you feel that your native accent sometimes holds you back in the American Mainstream English environment, simultaneous modeling is a good way to learn a variety of English that's more helpful. Moving back and forth among varieties—called *codeswitching*—is a valuable skill.

Working with the Television Set

A voice coach (or an "image" coach) may be beyond the finan- 31 cial limits for many of us. It's fortunate that we have our television sets available to use as free coaches. In exactly the same way that you can improve your voice quality by speaking along with a tape recorded model, you can improve the rest of your body language by *moving* simultaneously with a model on videotape. Ideally, you will also have a VCR, so that you can work with a single tape over a period of time. If you have a video camera (or can rent one), to let you make a baseline video of your body language, that's also a plus. But if those items aren't available to you, choose as a model someone of your own gender that you can see on television several times a week, and practice moving simultaneously with that person at those times. As with voice quality, stop *before* you find yourself doing impersonations of your model.

I don't recommend that women try to learn "male body lan- 32 guage" by working with a videotape of a male speaker, or that men work with a videotape of a woman to learn "female body language." (The fact that the latter alternative is wildly unlikely outside the entertainment field is consistent with the power relationships in our society.) Cross-gender modeling is a bad idea, full of hidden hazards and boobytraps, and it almost always backfires. If you're gifted with the sort of superb

244 Using Process Analysis

acting ability that would let you do this *well*, like Dustin Hoffman playing the heroine in the movie *Tootsie*, you're not someone who needs improved body language anyway. You will be far more successful with the body language of a strong and competent adult of your own gender.

33   If you believe you have a long way to go in acquiring satisfactory body language skills, if you feel self-conscious trying to acquire them, if your opportunities to practice them are few and far between, by all means rely on the tv set. You can move on to practice with live partners when you feel more at ease.

Expanding Vocabulary

Study the definitions of any of the following words that are unfamiliar to you. Then use each of the words in a separate sentence.

perceptually (4)   vulnerable (11)
resonant (4)   boobytraps (31)
intimidated (8)

Understanding Content

1. What are the characteristics of a "whiny child's" voice?
2. What are the characteristics of the ideal adult voice for American speakers of English?
3. What do people "hear" when they listen to speakers whose voices lack these characteristics?
4. How hard is it to improve body language skills?
5. What is the first step to improving body language skills? What is a good way to practice?
6. What are body language baseline profiles? Why are they useful to establish?
7. How do you establish baseline profiles?
8. What is meant by simultaneous modeling? Why does it work well?
9. What can you change using simultaneous modeling?
10. Summarize the process of using a tape recorder to change your voice quality.
11. Summarize the process of working with a TV to improve your body language. What should be your standard to work with?

Drawing Inferences about Thesis and Purpose

1. What is Elgin's position on changing one's voice quality? Should the typical male voice be set as a standard for everyone?

2. What is Elgin's purpose in writing?
3. What is her thesis?

Analyzing Strategies and Style

1. What tone of voice do you "hear" in this essay? Do you respond to the author as a sympathetic teacher? Support your response.
2. Elgin uses italics and even all caps for some words. Why? What do they contribute?

Thinking Critically

1. Have you thought about the idea that the typical male voice is considered standard and that many women are perceived as talking like children? Does the idea make sense to you? Why or why not?
2. Does simultaneous modeling seem like a useful strategy for changing voice quality and body language? Why or why not?
3. Why is it important to develop sensitivity to body-language messages?
4. Do you agree that women tend to be better at this sensitivity than men? Does Elgin's explanation for this tendency make sense? Why or why not?
5. Are you going to tape yourself and examine your voice quality and body language? Why or why not?

"Restoring Recess"

CAROL KRUCOFF

A journalist, Carol Krucoff (b. 1954) is a freelance writer on health and exercise topics, a syndicated health columnist, and the author of a book on health and exercise to be published in 2000. Her health column, "Bodyworks," is also available on the Internet. Krucoff runs and holds a black belt in karate. In "Restoring Recess," which appeared in the *Washington Post*'s Health Section on January 12, 1999, Krucoff encourages readers to treat daily exercise not as work but as play.

So here we are, just a few weeks into the new year, and if 1 you're like most Americans you're already struggling to keep your resolution to shape up. Despite good intentions, the sad fact is that half of all adults who start a new exercise program drop out within six months.

2 Adopting a new habit isn't easy. As Sir Isaac Newton pointed out, a body at rest will tend to remain at rest. Even the promise of better health and improved appearance won't get most people to exercise regularly.

3 But there is one motivator that can pry even the most confirmed "potato" off the couch. Freud called it the pleasure principle: People do things that feel good and avoid things that feel bad. Most American adults get little or no exercise and more than half are overweight because many of them consider exercise to be hard, painful work—a distasteful chore they must force themselves to endure.

4 Yet as children we didn't feel this way about moving our bodies. Most kids see physical pursuits, like skipping and running, as exciting play to be enjoyed.

5 So this year, meet your fitness goals by turning exercise into child's play. Scratch the resolution to work out. Instead, vow to play actively for 30 minutes most days. Think of it as recess, and try to recapture the feeling you had as a child of being released onto the playground to swing, play ball or do whatever your little heart—and body—desired. Don't worry about flattening your abs or losing weight. Just enjoy the sensations of moving your body, breathing deeply and experiencing the moment.

6 This is your personalized playtime, so pick any form of movement that you like—a solitary walk, shooting hoops with a friend, a dance class, gardening, ping-pong, cycling. The options are vast, and nearly anything that gets you moving is fine, since even light-to-moderate exercise can yield significant health benefits.

7 The point is to stop thinking of your workout as one more demanding task you must cram into your busy day and start viewing it as a welcome recess that frees you from the confines of your chair. Most regular exercisers will tell you that this is the reason they remain active. Yes, they exercise to lose weight, build strong bones and all those other healthy reasons. But scratch deeper and most will admit that a central reason they're out there day after day is that it's fun—their exercise satisfies body and soul, and is a cherished highlight of their lives.

If you think this attitude adjustment is merely a mind game, 8
you're right. Getting in shape is, after all, a matter of mind over
body. But it's also a healthy way of approaching fitness, to enjoy
the journey as much as reaching the destination. Goals can be
helpful motivators to shape up. But once you drop a clothing
size, then what?

So instead of being caught up in reaching a certain scale 9
weight, view taking care of your physical self—which can play
a key role in boosting your emotional self—as an opportunity
for active play. This may be difficult in our culture, which considers play a frivolous time-waster. Yet "the ability to play is
one of the principal criteria of mental health," wrote anthropologist Ashley Montague in his book, *Growing Young.*

Just as kids need the release of recess to get the "wiggles" 10
out of the bodies, adults also need relief from the stiffness
caused by sitting and the chance to oxygenate sluggish brains.

Next time a problem has you stumped, take it out on a walk 11
in the fresh air—and bring along a pencil and paper. Solutions
will appear on the move that eluded you at your desk.

To make your play breaks happen, schedule them into your 12
life. Lack of time is the main reason people say they don't exercise, and it's true that most of us lead very busy lives. But it's
also true that we find time for things that are important to us.
It's a matter of making choices.

You may need to get up a half hour earlier—and go to bed a 13
half hour earlier—to make your play break happen. You might
have to turn off the TV, cut short a phone call or eat lunch at
your desk to squeeze in recess. But if it's fun, it won't be a terrible sacrifice—it'll be a willing trade-off. Besides, as a wise
person once said, "If you don't make time to exercise, you'll
have to take time to be sick."

To keep your break fun, remember to: 14

1. Start slowly and progress gradually. If you've been inactive, 15
   begin with as little as five minutes of your chosen activity.
   Add on five more minutes each week with the goal of playing actively for 30 minutes on most days.
2. Avoid negative talk about yourself. Instead of obsessing 16
   about your thunder thighs, have an attitude of gratitude
   about your body and all that it does for you.

17 3. Choose a positive exercise environment. Just as fresh air and music may enhance your recess, mirrors may detract from your experience if you're self-critical. If so, play outdoors or in a mirror-free room.

18 4. Consider a few sessions with a personal trainer if you need help getting started. For a referral, call the American Council on Exercise's consumer hot line at 1-800-529-8227.

19 5. Vary your activity. If you like doing the same thing, day after day, great. But it's fine to move in different ways on different days, depending on your mood, the weather and other factors you find relevant.

20 6. Focus on behaviors, not on outcomes. If you consistently exercise and eat right, results will come.

21 7. Avoid rushing back to routine. Take a few minutes to breathe deeply and bring the refreshing spirit of playfulness back to your grown-up world.

Expanding Vocabulary

Study the definitions of any of the following words that are unfamiliar to you. Then use each of the words in a separate sentence.

pry (3)	oxygenate (10)
confines (7)	sluggish (10)
frivolous (9)	eluded (11)

Understanding Content

1. How many adults drop out of an exercise program within six months?
2. How many Americans are overweight?
3. How did most of us feel about movement and play when we were children?
4. How much exercise and what kinds of exercise does the author recommend?
5. How do adults who exercise regularly usually feel about it?
6. What steps should we take to get back to "recess"?

Drawing Inferences about Thesis and Purpose

1. What are the advantages of exercise suggested throughout Krucoff's essay?
2. What is Krucoff's purpose in writing? What does she want to accomplish?

3. What is her thesis?

Analyzing Strategies and Style

1. How does the author use New Year's resolutions as an opening strategy? How does she use the idea of resolutions to develop her essay?
2. Krucoff writes with brief paragraphs and ends with a list. What is the effect of these strategies? How does her style connect to audience and purpose?

Thinking Critically

1. Do you make New Year's resolutions to exercise more? If so, do you keep them? If not, why not?
2. Do you exercise regularly? If not, why not? How would you defend your inactivity to Krucoff?
3. Do you agree that we choose to do what is important to us? Do you think that most of us could find thirty minutes most days for exercise if we really wanted to? Explain your response.
4. Has Krucoff convinced you to treat exercise as play and to start playing more? Why or why not?

"Camping Out"

ERNEST HEMINGWAY

One of the most popular of twentieth-century fiction writers, Ernest Hemingway (1899–1961) is best known for his short stories and novels, especially *A Farewell to Arms, The Sun Also Rises,* and *The Old Man and the Sea.* Hemingway, winner of the Nobel Prize for Literature, began his writing career as a journalist and returned to journalism from time to time, most notably as a correspondent during the Spanish Civil War and World War II. His guidelines for a successful camping trip, first published in the *Toronto Star Weekly* in 1920, continue to provide good advice for today's campers.

Thousands of people will go into the bush this summer to   1
cut the high cost of living. A man who gets his two weeks' salary while he is on vacation should be able to put those two

weeks in fishing and camping and be able to save one week's salary clear. He ought to be able to sleep comfortably every night, to eat well every day and to return to the city rested and in good condition.

2   But if he goes into the woods with a frying pan, an ignorance of black flies and mosquitoes, and a great and abiding lack of knowledge about cookery, the chances are that his return will be very different. He will come back with enough mosquito bites to make the back of his neck look like a relief map of the Caucasus. His digestion will be wrecked after a valiant battle to assimilate half-cooked or charred grub. And he won't have had a decent night's sleep while he has been gone.

3   He will solemnly raise his right hand and inform you that he has joined the grand army of never-agains. The call of the wild may be all right, but it's a dog's life. He's heard the call of the tame with both ears. Waiter, bring him an order of milk toast.

4   In the first place he overlooked the insects. Black flies, no-see-ums, deer flies, gnats and mosquitoes were instituted by the devil to force people to live in cities where he could get at them better. If it weren't for them everybody would live in the bush and he would be out of work. It was a rather successful invention.

5   But there are lots of dopes that will counteract the pests. The simplest perhaps is oil of citronella. Two bits' worth of this purchased at any pharmacist's will be enough to last for two weeks in the worst fly- and mosquito-ridden country.

6   Rub a little on the back of your neck, your forehead and your wrists before you start fishing, and the blacks and skeeters will shun you. The odor of citronella is not offensive to people. It smells like gun oil. But the bugs do hate it.

7   Oil of pennyroyal and eucalyptol are also much hated by mosquitoes, and with citronella they form the basis for many proprietary preparations. But it is cheaper and better to buy the straight citronella. Put a little on the mosquito netting that covers the front of your pup tent or canoe tent at night, and you won't be bothered.

8   To be really rested and get any benefit out of a vacation a man must get a good night's sleep every night. The first requi-

site for this is to have plenty of cover. It is twice as cold as you expect it will be in the bush four nights out of five, and a good plan is to take just double the bedding that you think you will need. An old quilt that you can wrap up in is as warm as two blankets.

Nearly all outdoor writers rhapsodize over the browse bed. 9 It is all right for the man who knows how to make one and has plenty of time. But in a succession of one-night camps on a canoe trip all you need is level ground for your tent floor and you will sleep all right if you have plenty of covers under you. Take twice as much cover as you think that you will need, and then put two-thirds of it under you. You will sleep warm and get your rest.

When it is clear weather you don't need to pitch your tent if 10 you are only stopping for the night. Drive four stakes at the head of your made-up bed and drape your mosquito bar over that, then you can sleep like a log and laugh at the mosquitoes.

Outside of insects and bum sleeping, the rock that wrecks 11 most camping trips is cooking. The average tyro's idea of cooking is to fry everything and fry it good and plenty. Now, a frying pan is a most necessary thing to any trip, but you also need the old stew kettle and the folding reflector baker.

A pan of fried trout can't be bettered and they don't cost any 12 more than ever. But there is a good and bad way of frying them.

The beginner puts his trout and his bacon in and over a 13 brightly burning fire the bacon curls up and dries into a dry tasteless cinder and the trout is burned outside while it is still raw inside. He eats them and it is all right if he is only out for the day and going home to a good meal at night. But if he is going to face more trout and bacon the next morning and other equally well-cooked dishes for the remainder of two weeks, he is on the pathway to nervous dyspepsia.

The proper way is to cook over coals. Have several cans of 14 Crisco or Cotosuet or one of the vegetable shortenings along that are as good as lard and excellent for all kinds of shortening. Put the bacon in and when it is about half cooked lay the trout in the hot grease, dipping them in cornmeal first. Then put the bacon on top of the trout and it will baste them as it slowly cooks.

15   The coffee can be boiling at the same time and in a smaller skillet pancakes being made that are satisfying the other campers while they are waiting for the trout.

16   With the prepared pancake flours you take a cupful of pancake flour and add a cup of water. Mix the water and flour and as soon as the lumps are out it is ready for cooking. Have the skillet hot and keep it well greased. Drop the batter in and as soon as it is done on one side loosen it in the skillet and flip it over. Apple butter, syrup or cinnamon and sugar go well with the cakes.

17   While the crowd have taken the edge from their appetites with flapjacks, the trout have been cooked and they and the bacon are ready to serve. The trout are crisp outside and firm and pink inside and the bacon is well done—but not too done. If there is anything better than that combination the writer has yet to taste it in a lifetime devoted largely and studiously to eating.

18   The stew kettle will cook you dried apricots when they have resumed their predried plumpness after a night of soaking, it will serve to concoct a mulligan in, and it will cook macaroni. When you are not using it, it should be boiling water for the dishes.

19   In the baker, mere man comes into his own, for he can make a pie that to his bush appetite will have it all over the product that mother used to make, like a tent. Men have always believed that there was something mysterious and difficult about making a pie. Here is a great secret. There is nothing to it. We've been kidded for years. Any man of average office intelligence can make at least as good a pie as his wife.

20   All there is to a pie is a cup and a half of flour, one-half teaspoonful of salt, one-half cup of lard and cold water. That will make piecrust that will bring tears of joy into your camping partner's eyes.

21   Mix the salt with the flour, work the lard into the flour, make it up into a good workmanlike dough with cold water. Spread some flour on the back of a box or something flat, and pat the dough around a while. Then roll it out with whatever kind of round bottle you prefer. Put a little more lard on the surface of the sheet of dough and then slosh a little flour on and roll it up and then roll it out again with the bottle.

Cut out a piece of the rolled-out dough big enough to line a 22
pie tin. I like the kind with holes in the bottom. Then put in
your dried apples that have soaked all night and been sweet-
ened, or your apricots, or your blueberries, and then take another sheet of the dough and drape it gracefully over the top,
soldering it down at the edges with your fingers. Cut a couple
of slits in the top dough sheet and prick it a few times with a
fork in an artistic manner.

Put it in the baker with a good slow fire for forty-five min- 23
utes and then take it out, and if your pals are Frenchmen they
will kiss you. The penalty for knowing how to cook is that the
others will make you do all the cooking.

It is all right to talk about roughing it in the woods. But the 24
real woodsman is the man who can be really comfortable in the
bush.

Expanding Vocabulary

Examine the following words in their contexts in the essay and then
write a definition for each one. (Do not use a dictionary; try to guess
the word's meaning from its context.)

relief map (2)	requisite (8)
Caucasus (2)	rhapsodize (9)
valiant (2)	browse bed (9)
assimilate (2)	tyro (11)
grub (2)	dyspepsia (13)
dopes (5)	concoct (18)
skeeters (6)	mulligan (18)
proprietary (7)	

Understanding Content

1. What are the three problems of camping for which Hemingway
   provides guidelines?
2. Explain the processes for coping with each of the first two problems.
3. Hemingway devotes most of his article to the third problem. Why?
4. How does he organize his guidelines for cooking?
5. When explaining pie making, what misconception does Hemingway clear up?
6. What will happen to the reader who follows Hemingway's guidelines and becomes a good cook?

Drawing Inferences about Thesis and Purpose

1. Hemingway's title announces the broad subject of camping but not his specific subject. State his subject by completing the phrase: "how to _____."
2. What is Hemingway's purpose in writing about camping? What does he want to accomplish?
3. State a thesis for the essay.

Analyzing Strategies and Style

1. Examine Hemingway's opening paragraphs. He begins by establishing what two ways of camping out?
2. How does Hemingway use this pattern as an organizing principle for his instructions on bugs, sleeping, and cooking?
3. Hemingway has written a lively and entertaining essay, not a list of impersonal instructions. How did he make his process essay interesting? Discuss specific passages that you think are effective.
4. When Hemingway writes, in paragraph 4, "It was a rather successful invention," what writing technique is he using? What tone do we hear in the line?
5. Who is Hemingway's anticipated audience? Who does he think are potential campers among the newspaper's readers? What passages reveal his assumption?
6. Camping out has changed since the 1920s. Writers on this topic today would not assume a male audience, and they would be careful not to write in a sexist manner. How would this essay have to be edited to eliminate sexist writing? What specific changes would you make?
7. The essay's conclusion is brief—only two sentences. Why is it effective in spite of its brevity? How does it connect to the essay's thesis?

Thinking Critically

1. What reasons for camping does Hemingway suggest? Are these still the reasons most people camp out today?
2. Are the problems Hemingway addresses—bugs, uncomfortable sleeping, bad food—still the basic problems to be solved to enjoy a camping trip? What modern equipment can help campers with these problems?
3. Many people today go "camping" in well-equipped RVs. Is this really camping? What would Hemingway say? What do you say? Why?

"The Day That I Sensed a New Kind of Intelligence"

GARRY KASPAROV

Garry Kasparov was born in 1963 in Baku, Azerbaijan. When he won the world title in chess in 1985, he was the youngest winner ever. He remains the highest-ranked active player in the world. In 1987 his autobiography, *Child of Change,* was published. The following column, published in *Time* in 1996, was part of a *Time* cover story on artificial intelligence.

I got my first glimpse of artificial intelligence on Feb. 10, 1996, at 4:45 P.M. EST, when in the first game of my match with Deep Blue, the computer nudged a pawn forward to a square where it could easily be captured. It was a wonderful and extremely human move. If I had been playing White, I might have offered this pawn sacrifice. It fractured Black's pawn structure and opened up the board. Although there did not appear to be a forced line of play that would allow recovery of the pawn, my instincts told me that with so many "loose" Black pawns and a somewhat exposed Black king, White could probably recover the material, with a better overall position to boot.

But a computer, I thought, would never make such a move. A computer can't "see" the long-term consequences of structural changes in the position or understand how changes in pawn formations may be good or bad.

Humans do this sort of thing all the time. But computers generally calculate each line of play so far as possible within the time allotted. Because chess is a game of virtually limitless possibilities, even a beast like Deep Blue, which can look at more than 100 million positions a second, can go only so deep. When computers reach that point, they evaluate the various resulting positions and select the move leading to the best one. And because computers' primary way of evaluating chess positions is by measuring material superiority, they are notoriously materialistic. If they "understood" the game, they might act differently, but they don't understand.

4 So I was stunned by this pawn sacrifice. What could it mean? I had played a lot of computers but had never experienced anything like this. I could feel—I could *smell*—a new kind of intelligence across the table. While I played through the rest of the game as best I could, I was lost; it played beautiful, flawless chess the rest of the way and won easily.

5 Later I discovered the truth. Deep Blue's computational powers were so great that it did in fact calculate every possible move all the way to the actual recovery of the pawn six moves later. The computer didn't view the pawn sacrifice as a sacrifice at all. So the question is, If the computer makes the same move that I would make for completely different reasons, has it made an "intelligent" move? Is the intelligence of an action dependent on who (or what) takes it?

6 This is a philosophical question I did not have time to answer. When I understood what had happened, however, I was reassured. In fact, I was able to exploit the traditional shortcomings of computers throughout the rest of the match. At one point, for example, I changed slightly the order of a well-known opening sequence. Because it was unable to compare this new position meaningfully with similar ones in its database, it had to start calculating away and was unable to find a good plan. A human would have simply wondered, "What's Garry up to?," judged the change to be meaningless and moved on.

7 Indeed, my overall thrust in the last five games was to avoid giving the computer any concrete goal to calculate toward; if it can't find a way to win material, attack the king or fulfill one of its other programmed priorities, the computer drifts planlessly and gets into trouble. In the end, that may have been my biggest advantage: I could figure out its priorities and adjust my play. It couldn't do the same to me. So although I think I did see some signs of intelligence, it's a weird kind, an inefficient, inflexible kind that makes me think I have a few years left.

Expanding Vocabulary

Examine the following words in their contexts in the essay and then write a brief definition or synonym for each one. (Do not use the dictionary; try to guess the word's meaning from its context.)

nudged (1)   exploit (6)

Understanding Content

1. Explain the process by which Deep Blue won its match.
2. How did Kasparov win the succeeding matches with Deep Blue? How did he take advantage of Deep Blue's limitations? What primarily "motivates" Deep Blue's chess playing?
3. Do computers have intelligence? How does the author answer this question?

Drawing Inferences about Thesis and Purpose

1. What is Kasparov's subject? To what particular event is he referring?
2. What is Kasparov's thesis?

Analyzing Strategies and Style

1. Examine Kasparov's opening. What is the effect of beginning with the exact time and date of Deep Blue's move? How does the second sentence contrast with the first?
2. The author places several words in quotation marks: "loose," "see," "understood," and "intelligent." Why? How are we to understand these words when they are placed in quotations?
3. A quick reading of this essay might result in some confusion. Is Kasparov saying that computers have intelligence, or not? Look carefully at his wording and then explain how he balances his position.

Thinking Critically

1. Have you played chess—or checkers? Can you visualize the game moves that Kasparov describes? If not, are you now interested in learning the game? Why or why not? (Many people find both chess and checkers to be quite fascinating games.)
2. Have you had an experience similar to Kasparov's while playing a game or sport? Has an opponent constructed a strategy that surprised you and left you confused in response? Think of the games and sports that you know. In what kinds of games or sports might a surprise tactic, or some unusual strategy, be successful?
3. Do computers have intelligence? Part of the problem we have in answering this question comes from confusion over the word *intelligence.* How should the word be defined? Are there differences in degrees of intelligence, or are there differences in kinds as well?

"Plus C'est La Même Chose"

KATHERINE McALPINE

Katherine McAlpine (b.1948) is co-editor of *The Muse Strikes Back* (1997), a collection of poems by women in response to poems by men, and is author of a book of sonnets *Gaelic and Saphires* (1999). The following poem appeared in *The Nation* in 1994.

When did these little girls turn into women?
Lip-glossed and groomed, alarmingly possessed
of polish, poise and, in some cases, breasts,
they're clustered at one corner of the gym in
elaborate indifference to the boys,   5
who, at the other end, convene with cables,
adjusting speakers, tuners and turntables
to make the optimum amount of noise.
If nobody plans to dance, what's this dance for?
Finally the boys all gather in formation,   10
tentatively begin a group migration
across the fearsome distance of the floor—
and then retreat, noticing no one's there.
The girls have gone, en masse, to fix their hair.

Understanding Content and Strategies

1. What do we learn about the girls? How have they "grown up"? What do they end up doing?
2. What do we learn about the boys? What do they focus on initially? When they finally venture toward the girls, how do they move?
3. Look at the poem's shape and pattern: number of lines, meter, rhyme. What kind of poem is this?
4. What words are connected by rhyme or sound similarities? How do the sound connections affect the poem's tone? How would you describe the poem's tone?

Drawing Inferences about Theme

1. If no one is dancing, are we to conclude that no one is having fun? Why or why not?

2. What seems to be the poet's attitude toward the boys and girls? Is she appalled, delighted, amused, angry, something else?
3. What process does the poem capture?
4. What observations about this process does the poem make—or imply?

Thinking Critically

1. Has McAlpine captured a typical scene of teenage dances? If not, what is wrong with her scene? If yes, what makes it typical?
2. Do we grow up "in a straight line"? Do we grow up all at once?

MAKING CONNECTIONS

---

1. Both Deborah Tannen and Suzette Elgin examine the communication habits of women. After studying these writers, make a list of some typical "female" speech habits. Then consider which of these patterns may be sound, even good, and which may need changing.

2. John Aigner encourages interviewees to develop a power vocabulary. Deborah Tannen suggests that indirectness in speech may be a virtue. Can these two points of view be reconciled?

3. Select a sport, game, or recreational activity that may interest you and read about it in at least one encyclopedia or other appropriate reference book. Write a two-page account of the basic process of the activity for someone unfamiliar with it. Alternatively, write a two-page explanation of the process of completing one complex part of the activity.

4. Take an informal survey of those with whom you work or those you know at school to analyze their conversational styles. Are most direct or indirect in their speech? Are there other observations about conversational styles that are useful to note?

5. Deborah Tannen in this chapter and Nancy Sakamoto in Chapter 4, present elements of Japanese language use, values, and cultural styles. Compare the writers and then draw

some general points about Japanese culture from their works. Summarize your findings in one or two pages.

TOPICS AND GUIDELINES FOR WRITING

---

1. In an essay examine some process of change that has taken place in your life. Consider physical, emotional, intellectual, or occupational changes. Although you will use chronological order, make certain that you focus on specific *stages* or *steps* that led to the change so that you write a process analysis, not a narrative. Possible topics include: how you grew (or shrank) to the size you are now, how you developed your skill in some sport or hobby, how you changed your taste in music, how you decided on a career. Analyze the change into at least three separate stages. Explain and illustrate each stage. Remember that your essay needs a thesis. Why do you want to share this process of change with readers? You may want to show, for example, that change, although painful, is ultimately rewarding, or perhaps that some changes are just painful. Reflect on *your* reason for writing about the change in your life. Then state your thesis in your first paragraph and restate it, enlarging on it, in your concluding paragraph.

2. Select a change in human society that has occurred in stages over time and that has had a significant effect on the way we live. Your thesis is the significance of the development— significance for good or ill. Develop that thesis by analyzing the process of change, the stages in development. Be sure to analyze the change into several distinct stages of development. Possible topics include technological changes (e.g., the generations of computers), changes in the classroom or school buildings, changes in recreation, and changes in dress.

3. Do you have advice to give someone preparing for a job interview, advice that is different from or in addition to the advice given by John Aigner in "Putting Your Job Interview into Rehearsal"? If so, organize your advice into a series of specific steps and write your guide to the successful interview. Your thesis, stated or implied, is that following these

steps will improve one's chances of obtaining the desired position.

4. Have you taken the same type of vacation (camping, renting a beach house, sightseeing by car, traveling abroad) several times? If so, you may have learned the hard way what to do and what not to do to have a successful vacation. In an essay, pass your knowledge along to readers. Organize your essay into a process—a series of steps or directions—but also approach your analysis by explaining both the wrong way and the right way to complete each step. Avoid writing about your last vacation. Keep your focus on general guidelines for readers. Ernest Hemingway's "Camping Out" is your model for this topic. Your thesis is that preparing the right way will ensure a pleasant vacation.

5. Many people have misconceptions about processes or tasks they are unfamiliar with, particularly if those activities are a part of a different culture. Do you understand how to do something that others might have misconceptions about? If so, prepare a process analysis that will explain the activity and thereby clear up the reader's misconceptions. In your opening paragraph you might refer to the typical misconceptions that people have and then move on to explain how the task or activity is actually done. If your activity is part of a particular culture (how to cook with a wok, how to prepare pita bread, how to serve a Japanese dinner, how to wrap a sari), enrich your process analysis with appropriate details about that culture.

6. Some social situations can be difficult to handle successfully. If you have had success in one of them (such as asking someone for a date, meeting a close friend's or a fiancé's family, attending a large family reunion, attending the office Christmas party), then explain how to handle the situation with ease and charm. Select either a chronological ordering of steps or a list of specific instructions, including dos and don'ts. Humorous examples can be used with this topic to produce lively writing.

7. Prepare a detailed, knowledgeable explanation of a particular activity or task from your work or play for interested

nonspecialists. You are the expert carefully explaining the process of, for example, bunting down the third-base line, booting up the computer, tuning an engine, building a deck, sewing a dress, or whatever you know well. Be sure to give encouragement as you give directions. Make certain that you have included all the steps, in the right order, and that you have your audience clearly in mind.

7

Using Division and Classification

Examining Human Connections

You have probably discovered by now that your college library organizes its book collection not by the Dewey decimal system but by the Library of Congress *Classification* system. And you are probably taking courses offered by several different departments. Those departments, English for example, may be further *classified* by colleges—the college of arts of sciences. If you needed to find an apartment near campus or a part-time job, you may have looked in the newspaper's *classified* section. We *divide* or separate individual items and then group or *classify* them into logical categories because order is more convenient than disorder and because the process helps us make sense of a complex world. Just think how frustrated you would be if you had to search through a random listing of want ads rather than being able to look under several headings for specific jobs, or if you had to search up and down shelves of books because they were not grouped by any system.

When to Use Division and Classification

Division and classification are not similar but distinct strategies, as are comparison and contrast. Rather, division and classification work together; they are part of the same thinking process that brings order to a mass of items, data, ideas, forms of behavior, groups of people, or whatever else someone chooses to organize. Division is another term for analysis, the breaking down of something into its parts. Division, or analysis, provides the plan or pattern of grouping. To devise a classification system for books, books have to be divided by type: books on history, or art, or botany. Then large categories need to be subdivided: U.S. history, British history, Russian history. Then each individual book can be given a number that is its very own but also shows into what categories it has been classified, twentieth-century U.S. history, for example. The categories have been developed after thoughtful analysis; each book can be placed in one of the established categories.

A thinking process that has served us so well solving organizational problems from the biologist's classification of the animal kingdom to the phone company's classification of businesses in the Yellow Pages must surely be a useful strategy for writers. And indeed it is. If you have written essays using examples and have sought to group examples to support different parts of your topic, you have already started working with the process of division and classification. The difference between the essays in Chapter 5 ("Explaining and Illustrating") and those in this chapter lies in the rigor of the classification system. To use classification effectively, you need a logical, consistent principle of division, and your classification needs to be complete. So, when thinking about possible topics for an essay and when thinking about purpose in writing, ask yourself: Am I interested in giving some specific examples to develop an idea, or am I interested in analyzing a topic, dividing it logically into its parts? For example, Peter Drucker does not support the idea that many companies use a team concept by using Procter & Gamble and General Motors as examples. Rather, he asserts that there are three kinds of teams used in companies, analyzes the characteristics of each type of team, and then gives examples to further explain the idea of three *categories* of teams.

How to Use Division and Classification

Thinking and Organizing

Suppose that you are asked to write about some element of campus life. Reflecting on the fun you have had getting acquainted with classmates over meals in nearby restaurants, you decide to write about the various restaurants available to college students. How many and how varied are the restaurants within walking distance of the campus? To be thorough, you may not want to trust your memory; better to walk around, making a complete list of the area restaurants. Next, analyze your list to see the possible categories into which the restaurants can be grouped. You may see more than one way to classify them, perhaps by type of food (French, Chinese, Italian) and by cost (cheap, moderate, expensive). You need to avoid overlapping categories and to classify examples according to the division you select. The following chart illustrates the general principle:

TOPIC

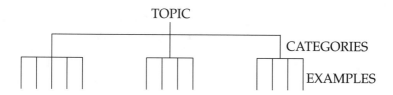

CATEGORIES

EXAMPLES

Thesis

The divisions and classifications you create must also support a thesis. What do you want to explain to your readers? This is the key question to answer in deciding on a classification pattern. If you decide to stress the variety of food available to students, for example, then you will want to classify your examples of restaurants by food type, not by cost.

In your essay on restaurants, division and classification provide an effective strategy for developing your thesis. Sometimes, though, a writer's thesis *is* the classification pattern. Put another way, what the writer has learned is that the subject can best be grasped by understanding the author's classification of that subject. Ralph Whitehead, writing about American class structure, asserts that the old categories are no longer accurate and that his new categories give us more insight into American society. Similarly, Peter Drucker wants business leaders to understand that there isn't *one* team model but *three*.

Much of what is important in your division and classification essay lies in your analysis, in the logical and perhaps new way you ask readers to examine your topic. This means that you may need to explain your categories to readers, to explain how and why you have divided your subject in your particular way and to show, if necessary, why the categories do not overlap, or how they are sometimes modified. In "The Science and Secrets of Personal Space," Curt Suplee defines the required distances for each category or zone—intimate, personal, social, and public—but then explains how various cultures modify their space requirements. Remember, too, that you need to illustrate each of your divisions. In the essay on restaurants, the student needs to name and describe sample restaurants in each of the categories.

Getting Started: Classifying Recent Reading or Viewing

Make a list of all the works (books, magazines, newspapers, texts, etc.) you have read in the past three months. Study your list, thinking of several classifying principles you could use to organize your reading. Consider: Which pattern seems the most logical and complete? Could several patterns work, depending on your purpose in classifying? Alternately, complete the same exercise for all the movies or all the television shows you have seen in the past three months.

"Friends, Good Friends— and Such Good Friends"

JUDITH VIORST

Judith Viorst (b. 1931) is a poet, journalist, and author of books for both adults and children. She has published several volumes of poetry and more than a dozen books, both fiction and nonfiction. *Necessary Losses* (1986) is an important book for adults about coping with change. Viorst is probably best known as a contributing editor to *Redbook* magazine, and she has received several awards for her *Redbook* columns. Her classification of the kinds of friends women have was published in *Redbook* in 1977.

Women are friends, I once would have said, when they to- 1
tally love and support and trust each other, and bare to each
other the secrets of their souls, and run—no questions asked—
to help each other, and tell harsh truths to each other (no, you
can't wear that dress unless you lose ten pounds first) when
harsh truths must be told.

Women are friends, I once would have said, when they share 2
the same affection for Ingmar Bergman,[1] plus train rides, cats,
warm rain, charades, Camus,[2] and hate with equal ardor New-
ark[3] and Brussels sprouts and Lawrence Welk[4] and camping.

In other words, I once would have said that a friend is a 3
friend all the way, but now I believe that's a narrow point of
view. For the friendships I have and the friendships I see are
conducted at many levels of intensity, serve many different
functions, meet different needs and range from those as all-the-
way as the friendships of the soul sisters mentioned above to
that of the most nonchalant and casual playmates.

Consider these varieties of friendship: 4

1. Convenience friends. These are women with whom, if our 5
paths weren't crossing all the time, we'd have no particular
reason to be friends: a next-door neighbor, a woman in our car
pool, the mother of one of our children's closest friends or
maybe some mommy with whom we serve juice and cookies
each week at the Glenwood Co-op Nursery.

Convenience friends are convenient indeed. They'll lend us 6
their cups and silverware for a party. They'll drive our kids to
soccer when we're sick. They'll take us to pick up our car when
we need a lift to the garage. They'll even take our cats when we
go on vacation. As we will for them.

But we don't, with convenience friends, ever come too close 7
or tell too much; we maintain our public face and emotional
distance. "Which means," says Elaine, "that I'll talk about
being overweight but not about being depressed. Which means

[1]Swedish filmmaker very popular among those enjoying thoughtful, psychological films.—Ed.
[2]French novelist and political activist noted for his existentialist philosophy.—Ed.
[3]City in New Jersey that many find unattractive.—Ed.
[4]Big band leader whose music would be called "square" by many.—Ed.

I'll admit being mad but not blind with rage. Which means that I might say that we're pinched this month but never that I'm worried sick over money."

8   But which doesn't mean that there isn't sufficient value to be found in these friendships of mutual aid, in convenience friends.

9   2. Special-interest friends. These friendships aren't intimate, and they needn't involve kids or silverware or cats. Their value lies in some interest jointly shared. And so we may have an office friend or a yoga friend or a tennis friend or a friend from the Women's Democratic Club.

10   "I've got one woman friend," says Joyce, "who likes, as I do, to take psychology courses. Which makes it nice for me—and nice for her. It's fun to go with someone you know and it's fun to discuss what you've learned, driving back from the classes." And for the most part, she says, that's all they discuss.

11   "I'd say that what we're doing is *doing* together, not being together," Suzanne says of her Tuesday-doubles friends. "It's mainly a tennis relationship, but we play together well. And I guess we all need to have a couple of playmates."

12   I agree.

13   My playmate is a shopping friend, a woman of marvelous taste, a woman who knows exactly *where* to buy *what*, and furthermore is a woman who always knows beyond a shadow of a doubt what one ought to be buying. I don't have the time to keep up with what's new in eyeshadow, hemlines and shoes and whether the smock look is in or finished already. But since (oh, shame!) I care a lot about eyeshadow, hemlines and shoes, and since I don't *want* to wear smocks if the smock look is finished, I'm very glad to have a shopping friend.

14   3. Historical friends. We all have a friend who knew us when . . . maybe way back in Miss Meltzer's second grade, when our family lived in that three-room flat in Brooklyn, when our dad was out of work for seven months, when our brother Allie got in that fight where they had to call the police, when our sister married the endodontist from Yonkers and when, the morning after we lost our virginity, she was the first, the only, friend we told.

15   The years have gone by and we've gone separate ways and we've little in common now, but we're still an intimate part of each other's past. And so whenever we go to Detroit we always

go to visit this friend of our girlhood. Who knows how we looked before our teeth were straightened. Who knows how we talked before our voice got un-Brooklyned. Who knows what we ate before we learned about artichokes. And who, by her presence, puts us in touch with an earlier part of ourself, a part of ourself it's important never to lose.   16

"What this friend means to me and what I mean to her," says Grace, "is having a sister without sibling rivalry. We know the texture of each other's lives. She remembers my grandmother's cabbage soup. I remember the way her uncle played the piano. There's simply no other friend who remembers those things."

4. Crossroads friends. Like historical friends, our crossroads   17 friends are important for *what was*—for the friendship we shared at a crucial, now past, time of life. A time, perhaps, when we roomed in college together; or worked as eager young singles in the Big City together; or went together, as my friend Elizabeth and I did, through pregnancy, birth and that scary first year of new motherhood.

Crossroads friends forge powerful links, links strong enough   18 to endure with not much more contact than once-a-year letters at Christmas. And out of respect for those crossroads years, for those dramas and dreams we once shared, we will always be friends.

5. Cross-generational friends. Historical friends and cross-   19 roads friends seem to maintain a special kind of intimacy— dormant but always ready to be revived—and though we may rarely meet, whenever we do connect, it's personal and intense. Another kind of intimacy exists in the friendships that form across generations in what one woman calls her daughter-mother and her mother-daughter relationships.

Evelyn's friend is her mother's age—"but I share so much   20 more than I ever could with my mother"—a woman she talks to of music, of books and of life. "What I get from her is the benefit of her experience. What she gets—and enjoys—from me is a youthful perspective. It's a pleasure for both of us."

I have in my own life a precious friend, a woman of 65 who   21 has lived very hard, who is wise, who listens well; who has been where I am and can help me understand it; and who represents not only an ultimate ideal mother to me but also the person I'd like to be when I grow up.

22   In our daughter role we tend to do more than our share of self-revelation; in our mother role we tend to receive what's revealed. It's another kind of pleasure—playing wise mother to a questing younger person. It's another very lovely kind of friendship.

23   6. Part-of-a-couple friends. Some of the women we call our friends we never see alone—we see them as part of a couple at couples' parties. And though we share interests in many things and respect each other's views, we aren't moved to deepen the relationship. Whatever the reason, a lack of time or—and this is more likely—a lack of chemistry, our friendship remains in the context of a group. But the fact that our feeling on seeing each other is always, "I'm *so* glad she's here" and the fact that we spend half the evening talking together says that this too, in its own way, counts as a friendship.

24   (Other part-of-a-couple friends are the friends that came with the marriage, and some of these are friends we could live without. But sometimes, alas, she married our husband's best friend; and sometimes, alas, she *is* our husband's best friend. And so we find ourself dealing with her, somewhat against our will, in a spirit of what I'll call *reluctant* friendship.)

25   7. Men who are friends. I wanted to write just of women friends, but the women I've talked to won't let me—they say I must mention man–woman friendships too. For these friendships can be just as close and as dear as those that we form with women. Listen to Lucy's description of one such friendship:

26   "We've found we have things to talk about that are different from what he talks about with my husband and different from what I talk about with his wife. So sometimes we call on the phone or meet for lunch. There are similar intellectual interests—we always pass on to each other the books that we love—but there's also something tender and caring too."

27   In a couple of crises, Lucy says, "he offered himself for talking and for helping. And when someone died in his family he wanted me there. The sexual, flirty part of our friendship is very small, but *some*—just enough to make it fun and different." She thinks—and I agree—that the sexual part, though small, is always *some*, is always there when a man and a woman are friends.

It's only in the past few years that I've made friends with 28 men, in the sense of a friendship that's *mine*, not just part of two couples. And achieving with them the ease and the trust I've found with women friends has value indeed. Under the dryer at home last week, putting on mascara and rouge, I comfortably sat and talked with a fellow named Peter. Peter, I finally decided, could handle the shock of me minus mascara under the dryer. Because we care for each other. Because we're friends.

8. There are medium friends, and pretty good friends, and 29 very good friends indeed, and these friendships are defined by their level of intimacy. And what we'll reveal at each of these levels of intimacy is calibrated with care. We might tell a medium friend, for example, that yesterday we had a fight with our husband. And we might tell a pretty good friend that this fight with our husband made us so mad that we slept on the couch. And we might tell a very good friend that the reason we got so mad in that fight that we slept on the couch had something to do with that girl who works in his office. But it's only to our very best friends that we're willing to tell all, to tell what's going on with that girl in his office.

The best of friends, I still believe, totally love and support 30 and trust each other, and bare to each other the secrets of their souls, and run—no questions asked—to help each other, and tell harsh truths to each other when they must be told.

But we needn't agree about everything (only 12-year-old 31 girl friends agree about *everything*) to tolerate each other's point of view. To accept without judgment. To give and to take without ever keeping score. And to *be* there, as I am for them and as they are for me, to comfort our sorrows, to celebrate our joys.

Expanding Vocabulary

Study the definitions for any of the following words you do not know. Then use each of the words in a separate sentence.

nonchalant (3)   dormant (19)
endodontist (14)   questing (22)
sibling (16)   calibrated (29)
forge (18)

Understanding Content

1. List the author's main divisions, the primary categories of friendships, according to Viorst.
2. What is the main characteristic of a convenience friend? What will we do for these friends? What will we not share with them?
3. What describes a relationship with a special-interest friend?
4. What is important about historical friends? What do they give to us?
5. Why will we always be friends with crossroads friends?
6. What makes cross-generational friends so special?
7. Part-of-a-couple friends are not always chosen. What are the various ways we can feel about them?
8. What makes friendships with men different?
9. What are the marks of best-friend relationships?

Drawing Inferences about Thesis and Purpose

1. What is Viorst's subject?
2. What is her thesis? Where is it stated?
3. Find evidence in the essay that Viorst expects her readers to be women.

Analyzing Strategies and Style

1. Examine Viorst's opening. With what assertion does she begin? How does she qualify her assertions to lead to her thesis statement? What writing strategy shapes the style of the opening sentences? What is effective about her opening?
2. The author usually illustrates a category of friendship by quoting the views of one of her friends. What does she gain by using direct quotations and the names of the women she's quoting?
3. How does Viorst end her essay? (Compare it to her opening. How are the opening and close alike? How do they differ?) Why is this an effective strategy?

Thinking Critically

1. Which of the types of friendships described by Viorst have you experienced? Have they been pretty much as Viorst characterizes them? Would you like to experience some of the other types of friendships described here? Why or why not?
2. Viorst is writing to a female readership. Which of the friends described by her do men normally have as well? If you exclude any from Viorst's classification, explain why.

3. Are there types of friends that men have that are not included in Viorst's list? If you think so, describe them.
4. Viorst distinguishes among casual and close friends in large part by how much of ourselves we share or reveal to these friends. Do you agree that how much is shared is a chief indicator of the closeness of the friendship? Are there other indicators you would include? If so, explain them.
5. Viorst includes friendship with men in her list of possibilities. Do you agree that women can be friends with men? Will there always be some flirting? Explain.
6. How important is it to have friends? To have different kinds of friends? To have many friends? Do we use the term *friend* too casually in this culture? Reflect on these questions.

"The Roles of Manners"

JUDITH MARTIN

Judith Martin (b. 1938) is "Miss Manners." After graduating from Wellesley College, Martin began her career as a reporter for the *Washington Post*. She is best known now for her syndicated column, "Miss Manners." She has also published a novel, *Gilbert* (1982), *Miss Manners' Guide to Rearing Perfect Children* (1984), and *Common Courtesy* (1985). In the following, a slightly shortened version of an article that appeared in the Spring 1996 issue of *The Responsive Community*, Martin analyzes the several roles of manners.

Ritual serves one of three major functions of manners. 1 Oddly enough, the greatest scoffers at the traditions of American etiquette, who scorn the rituals of their own society as stupid and stultifying, voice respect for the custom and folklore of Native Americans, less industrialized peoples, and other societies they find more "authentic" than their own.

Americans who disdain etiquette in everyday life often go 2 into an etiquette tailspin in connection with marriage. Although the premise on which the 20th-century American wedding forms were based—that a young girl is given by the father whose protection she leaves to a husband who will perform the same function—has changed, the forms retain their emotional value. If it happens that the bride has been supporting the bridegroom for years in their own household, she may well ask their own toddler age son to "give her away" just to preserve the ritual.

3   Ritual provides a reassuring sense of social belonging far more satisfying than behavior improvised under emotionally complicated circumstances. Rituals of mourning other than funerals have been nearly abandoned, but at a great emotional cost. Not only are the bereaved unprotected from normal social demands by customs of seclusion and symbols of vulnerability, but they are encouraged to act as if nothing had happened—only to be deemed heartless if they actually succeed.

4   A second function of manners is the symbolic one. It is the symbolic function that confuses and upsets people who claim that etiquette is "simply a matter of common sense" when actually the symbols cannot be deduced from first principles, but must be learned in each society, and, within that society, for different times, places, ages, and social classes.

5   Because symbols are arbitrary, it can happen that opposite forms of behavior may symbolize the same idea, as when a man takes off his hat to show respect in a church, but puts on his hat to show respect in a synagogue. But once these rules are learned, they provide people with a tremendous fund of non-verbal knowledge about one another, helping them to deal appropriately with a wide range of social situations and relationships. Forms of greeting, dressing, eating, and restraining bodily functions can all be read as symbols of degrees of friendliness or hostility, respect or contempt, solidarity with the community or alienation from it. It is safe to assume that a person who advances on you with an outstretched hand is symbolizing an intent to treat you better than one who spits on the ground at the sight of you.

6   The law, the military, diplomacy, the church, and athletics have particularly strict codes of etiquette, compliance with which is taken to symbolize adherence to the particular values that these professions require: fairness, obedience, respect, piety, or valor. And following the conventions of the society is taken as a measure of respect for it—which is why people who are facing juries are advised by their own lawyers to dress and behave with the utmost convention.

It does not matter how arbitrary any of the violated rules   7
may be—ignoring them is interpreted as defiance of, or indifference to, or antagonism toward, the interests of the person or community whose standard is being ignored. The person who wears blue jeans to a formal wedding, or a three-piece suit at a beach party, may protest all he likes that his choice had only to do with a clothing preference, but it is hard to imagine anyone so naive as to believe that the people whose standards he is violating will not interpret the choice as disdain. In New York, a 15-year-old was shot on the street in a gang fight started over his refusal to return another teenager's high five sign of greeting. "Dissin'," the current term for showing disrespect, is cited as a leading provocation for modern murder.

The third function of etiquette is the regulative function,   8
which is less troublesome to the literal-minded, because those rules can be understood functionally. Between them, etiquette and law divide the task of regulating social conduct in the interest of community harmony, with the law addressing grave conflicts, such as those threatening life or property, and administering serious punishments, while etiquette seeks to forestall such conflicts, relying on voluntary compliance with its restraints.

This is why etiquette restricts freedom of self-expression   9
more than the law does (and why etiquette rejects encounter group theories of achieving harmony through total communication). It is within my legal right to tell you that you are ugly, or that your baby is, but this is likely to lead to ugly—which is to say dangerous—behavior, which it will require the law to address, no longer as a mere insult, but as a more serious charge of slander, libel, or mental cruelty.

But the danger of attempting to expand the dominion of the   10
law to take over the function of etiquette—to deal with such violations as students calling one another nasty names, or protesters doing provocative things with flags—is that it may compromise our constitutional rights. For all its strictness, a generally understood community standard of etiquette is more flexible than the law and, because it depends on voluntary compliance, less threatening.

Jurisprudence itself cannot function without etiquette. In en-   11
forcing standards of dress, rules about when to sit and when to

stand, restricting offensive language and requiring people to speak only in proper turn, courtroom etiquette overrides many of the very rights it may protect. So does the etiquette of legislatures, such as that specified in *Robert's Rules of Order.* This is necessary because the more orderly is the form of a social structure, the more conflict it can support. Etiquette requires participants in adversarial proceedings to present their opposing views in a restrained manner, to provide a disciplined and respectful ambience in which to settle conflicts peacefully.

Responding to Changing Times

12 That we cannot live peacefully in communities without etiquette, using only the law to prevent or resolve conflicts in everyday life, has become increasingly obvious to the public. And so there has been, in the last few years, a "return to etiquette," a movement for which I am not totally blameless. It has been hampered by the idea that etiquette need not involve self-restriction. Those who must decry rudeness in others are full of schemes to punish those transgressors by treating them even more rudely in return. But the well-meaning are also sometimes stymied, because they understand "etiquette" to consist of the social rules that were in effect approximately a generation ago, when women rarely held significant jobs, and answering machines and Call Waiting had not yet been invented. As the same social conditions do not apply, they assume that there can be no etiquette system, or that each individual may make up his or her own rules.

13 One often hears that etiquette is "only a matter of being considerate of others," and that is certainly a good basis for good behavior. Obviously, however, it does not guide one in the realms of symbolic or ritual etiquette. And if each individual improvises, the variety of resulting actions would be open to misinterpretations and conflicts, which a mutually intelligible code of behavior seeks to prevent.

14 Yet many of the surface etiquette issues of today were addressed under the codes of earlier times, which need only be adapted for the present. . . . [A] system of precedence must exist, although it need not be "ladies first." One must regulate the access of others to one's attention—if not with a butler an-

nouncing the conventional fiction that "Madam is not at home," then by a machine that says, "If you leave a message after the beep. . . ." But dropping one unfinished conversation to begin another has always been rude, and that applies to Call Waiting. Usually, changes happen gradually, as, for example, most people have come to accept the unmarried couple socially, or to issue their wedding invitations in time for guests to take advantage of bargain travel prices.

There is, of course, ideologically motivated civil disobedience of etiquette, just as there is of law. But people who mean to change the behavior of the community for its own supposed benefit by such acts must be prepared to accept the punitive consequences of their defiance. They would be well advised to disobey only the rule that offends them, carefully adhering to other conventions, if they do not wish to have their protests perceived as a general contempt for other people. Thanks to her symbolic meaning, the well-dressed, soft-spoken grandmother is a more effective agitator than the unkempt, obscenity-spouting youth. 15

Ignorance of etiquette rules is not an easily accepted excuse, except on behalf of small children or strangers to the community. An incapacity to comply is acceptable, but only if convincingly explained. To refuse to shake someone's hand will be interpreted as an insult, unless an explanation, such as that one has crippling arthritis, is provided. 16

Such excuses as "Oh, I never write letters" or "I just wasn't in the mood" or "I'm not comfortable with that" are classified as insolence and disallowed. Etiquette cannot be universally abandoned in the name of individual freedom, honesty, creativity, or comfort, without social consequences. 17

In 1978, when I began chronicling and guiding the legitimate changes in etiquette, and applying the rules in specific cases, where there may be extenuating circumstances or conflicting rules—as a judge does in considering a case—it was difficult to get people to agree that etiquette was needed. Now it is only difficult to get people to comply with its rules. 18

Expanding Vocabulary

Match each word in column A with its definition in column B. When in doubt, first find the word in the essay and look for context clues to aid your understanding of the word's meaning. Then, if necessary, use your dictionary to complete the matching exercise.

Column A	Column B
scoffers (1)	inflicting punishment
stultifying (1)	thwarted
tailspin (2)	left desolate, especially by death
bereaved (3)	unity of sympathies or interest within a group
arbitrary (5)	state of estrangement, feeling of separation from others
solidarity (5)	sudden deep decline or slump
alienation (5)	simple, lacking worldliness
adherence (6)	act of inciting anger or stirring action
naive (7)	special atmosphere of a particular place
provocative (10)	those expressing scorn
adversarial (11)	openly condemn
ambiance (11)	antagonistic, behaving as an opponent
decry (12)	determined by chance or whim
stymied (12)	devotion to or commitment to
punitive (15)	providing partial excuses
extenuating (18)	limiting or stifling

Understanding Content

1. What are the three functions or roles of manners?
2. What is often illogical about marriage rituals today? Why do we continue with these rituals anyway?
3. Why is it incorrect to insist that manners are simply common sense?
4. When you follow the codes of etiquette, diplomacy, or athletics, what does your behavior symbolize?
5. When you do not follow expected codes in society, how are you perceived? What do you appear to be doing?
6. What is the relationship between the law and etiquette? What may happen if we try to get the law to take over the role of etiquette?
7. Since times have changed, does this mean that manners can be ignored or individuals can make up their own rules?
8. If you want to change particular etiquette, what should you do to be most successful?
9. Why is ignorance not usually accepted as an excuse for being unmannerly?

Drawing Inferences about Thesis and Purpose

1. What is Martin's purpose in writing? Does she have more than one? Explain.
2. What is Martin's thesis? Try to write a thesis that makes her purpose clear.
3. Does Martin think that people today are more—or less—likely to follow codes of etiquette? How do you know?
4. What is the author's attitude toward Call Waiting? How do you know?

Analyzing Strategies and Style

1. Think about the ordering of the three roles of manners. What does the author gain by her choice of order?
2. Examine her choice of examples. What makes them effective?
3. Why does the author put *authentic* in quotation marks in paragraph 1? What do they signify to the reader?

Thinking Critically

1. Have you thought before about the ritual and symbolic roles of manners? If not, does Martin's explanation make sense to you?
2. Why are rituals helpful? Think of ways that the rituals of etiquette can aid us—and think of specific examples to illustrate your points.
3. Do you agree that etiquette can be a better choice than laws in controlling some kinds of behavior and that we should not turn to the law as a way to make people behave? Look specifically at Martin's examples and see whether you agree or disagree with her. Explain your position.
4. Has there been a loss of manners in our time? If so, what do you suggest that we do about the loss?

"Hot Boxes for Ex-Smokers"

FRANKLIN E. ZIMRING

Franklin Zimring (b. 1942) completed his law degree at the University of Chicago in 1967 and taught there until 1985. He now teaches at the University of California at Berkeley's School of Law and directs the Earl Warren Legal Institute. Zimring has published extensively, both articles and books, usually on such legal issues as capital punishment, youth crime, the criminal justice system, and violence in society. An important recent book is *The Search for Rational Drug Control* (1992). The following article, appearing in *Newsweek* on April 20, 1987, departs from legal issues to draw on the writer's experience as an ex-smoker.

1   Americans can be divided into three groups—smokers, nonsmokers, and that expanding pack of us who have quit. Those who have never smoked don't know what they're missing, but former smokers, ex-smokers, reformed smokers can never forget. We are veterans of a personal war, linked by that watershed experience of ceasing to smoke and by the temptation to have just one more cigarette. For almost all of us ex-smokers, smoking continues to play an important part in our lives. And now that it is being restricted in restaurants around the country and will be banned in almost all indoor public places in New York state starting next month, it is vital that everyone understand the different emotional states cessation of smoking can cause. I have observed four of them; and in the interest of science I have classified them as those of the zealot, the evangelist, the elect, and the serene. Each day, each category gains new recruits.

2   Not all antitobacco zealots are former smokers, but a substantial number of fire-and-brimstone opponents do come from the ranks of the reformed. Zealots believe that those who continue to smoke are degenerates who deserve scorn, not pity, and the penalties that will deter offensive behavior in public as well. Relations between these people and those who continue to smoke are strained.

3   One explanation for the zealot's fervor in seeking to outlaw tobacco consumption is his own tenuous hold on abstaining from smoking. But I think part of the emotional force arises from sheer envy as he watches and identifies with each lung-filling puff. By making smoking in public a crime, the zealot seeks reassurance that he will not revert to bad habits; give him strong social penalties and he won't become a recidivist.

4   No systematic survey has been done yet, but anecdotal evidence suggests that a disproportionate number of doctors who have quit smoking can be found among the fanatics. Just as the most enthusiastic revolutionary tends to make the most enthusiastic counterrevolutionary, many of today's vitriolic zealots

include those who had been deeply committed to tobacco habits.

By contrast, the antismoking evangelist does not condemn smokers. Unlike the zealot, he regards smoking as an easily curable condition, as a social disease, and not a sin. The evangelist spends an enormous amount of time seeking and preaching to the unconverted. He argues that kicking the habit is not *that* difficult. After all, *he* did it; moreover, as he describes it, the benefits of quitting are beyond measure and the disadvantages are nil.

The hallmark of the evangelist is his insistence that he never misses tobacco. Though he is less hostile to smokers than the zealot, he is resented more. Friends and loved ones who have been the targets of his preachments frequently greet the resumption of smoking by the evangelist as an occasion for unmitigated glee.

Among former smokers, the distinctions between the evangelist and the elect are much the same as the differences between proselytizing and nonproselytizing religious sects. While the evangelists preach the ease and desirability of abstinence, the elect do not attempt to convert their friends. They think that virtue is its own reward and subscribe to the Puritan theory of predestination.[1] Since they have proved themselves capable of abstaining from tobacco, they are therefore different from friends and relatives who continue to smoke. They feel superior, secure that their salvation was foreordained. These ex-smokers rarely give personal testimony on their conversion. They rarely speak about their tobacco habits, while evangelists talk about little else. Of course, active smokers find such bluenosed[2] behavior far less offensive than that of the evangelist or the zealot, yet they resent the elect simply because they are smug. Their air of self-satisfaction rarely escapes the notice of those lighting up. For active smokers, life with a member of the ex-smoking elect is less stormy than with a zealot or evangelist, but it is subtly oppressive nonetheless.

I have labeled my final category of former smokers the serene. This classification is meant to encourage those who find

---

[1]Puritans believed that those of the elect, those saved, have been chosen by God.—Ed.

[2]Puritanical.—Ed.

the other psychic styles of ex-smokers disagreeable. Serenity is quieter than zealotry and evangelism, and those who qualify are not as self-righteous as the elect. The serene ex-smoker accepts himself and also accepts those around him who continue to smoke. This kind of serenity does not come easily, nor does it seem to be an immediate option for those who have stopped. Rather it is a goal, an end stage in a process of development during which some former smokers progress through one or more of the less-than-positive psychological points en route. For former smokers, serenity is thus a positive possibility that exists at the end of the rainbow. But all former smokers cannot reach that promised land.

9   What is it that permits some former smokers to become serene? I think the key is self-acceptance and gratitude. The fully mature former smoker knows he has the soul of an addict and is grateful for the knowledge. He may sit up front in an airplane, but he knows he belongs in the smoking section in back. He doesn't regret that he quit smoking, nor any of his previous adventures with tobacco. As a former smoker, he is grateful for the experience and memory of craving a cigarette.

10   Serenity comes from accepting the lessons of one's life. And ex-smokers who have reached this point in their worldview have much to be grateful for. They have learned about the potential and limits of change. In becoming the right kind of former smoker, they developed a healthy sense of self. This former smoker, for one, believes that it is better to crave (one hopes only occasionally) and not to smoke than never to have craved at all. And by accepting that fact, the reformed smoker does not need to excoriate, envy, or dissociate himself from those who continue to smoke.

Expanding Vocabulary

Match each word in column A with its definition in column B. When in doubt, first find the word in the essay and look for context clues to aid your understanding of the word's meaning. Then, if necessary, use your dictionary to complete the matching exercise.

Column A	*Column B*
watershed (1)	flimsy, uncertain
cessation (1)	deliberate self-restraint

zealot (1)
degenerates (2)
tenuous (3)
recidivist (3)
anecdotal (4)
vitriolic (4)
proselytizing (7)
sects (7)
abstinence (7)
foreordained (7)
smug (7)
psychic (8)
excoriate (10)

based on casual accounts
   rather than strong evidence
one fanatically devoted to a
   cause
seeking to convert others from
   one belief to another
self-satisfied
turning point
scathing, caustic, sarcastic
mental, behavioral
declines in quality
denounce strongly
ceasing, halt
narrowly defined religious
   groups
predestined
one who lapses into previous
   behavior

Understanding Content

1. How does the zealot feel about smokers? What motivates the zealot? What group of ex-smokers can often be found among the zealots?
2. What is the evangelist's attitude toward quitting? How do smokers feel about the evangelist?
3. How do the elect differ from evangelists? What attitude of the elect bothers smokers?
4. How do the serene differ from the other ex-smokers? How should ex-smokers view this category? What is the psychological state of the serene ex-smoker?

Drawing Inferences about Thesis and Purpose

1. What is Zimring's subject?
2. What are his four categories of Americans exsmokers? Into which category does the author fit?
3. What is Zimring's thesis, his classification of ex-smokers?

Analyzing Strategies and Style

1. Zimring draws one word (*recidivist*) from his field, the law, but many of his words come from what other field or subject area? What does he gain from using so many words from this field or subject?

2. Zimring announces early in his essay that he is an ex-smoker. Why is it important for him to tell this to readers?
3. How would you describe the author's tone? Is he deadly serious, or poking some fun at ex-smokers? How do you know?

Thinking Critically

1. Are you an ex-smoker? If so, do you see yourself in one of Zimring's categories? Are there other categories that he should add?
2. Are you a smoker? If so, do you recognize Zimring's classification of ex-smokers? Which type bothers you the most? (Why are you still smoking?)
3. What is the best approach to take to smokers? Why?
4. Is it always best to serenely accept what others do—their habits, their speech, their lifestyles? Or, is there a role for zealots or evangelists? Support your position.

"The Science and Secrets of Personal Space"

CURT SUPLEE

Curt Suplee (b. 1945) is a science writer and editor for the *Washington Post.* He has written *Everyday Science Explained* (1996) and *Physics in the 20th Century* (1999). His analysis of personal to public spaces appeared in the *Post*'s Horizon Section on June 9, 1999.

1   It's a free country, right? Well, not exactly. Every day, all day long, the specific position of your body and the state of your mind are under the control of a powerful and authoritative force of which you are almost entirely unaware.

2   It's the system of personal space. Every culture has its own, and some are so drastically different that they can cause friction—or at least extreme unease—when groups such as Arabs and northern Europeans get together.

3   Individual idiosyncracies and social context can modify the rules slightly, as we shall see. But within a culture, the code usually is firmly imprinted by age 12 and remains surprisingly constant from town to town and region to region.

For the average American, according to anthropologist Ed- 4
ward T. Hall, there are four distinctive spacial zones, each with
a well-understood spectrum of appropriate behavior.

The nearest Hall calls the "intimate" zone, which extends 5
outward from the skin about 18 inches. This is the range within
which lovers touch and parents communicate with infants. At
that distance, it is difficult to focus on another person's face,
which appears larger than your entire field of vision. That is
one reason why people often kiss with their eyes closed.

Within this zone, the sense of smell is important; and body 6
heat is felt immediately. For example, sexual arousal customarily floods the abdomen with blood. Many people say they
can sense the condition of a partner, even during cocktail
conversation or formal ballroom dancing, by feeling the radi-
ated heat.

The next, or "personal," zone, extends from 18 inches to 7
about 4 feet. Within this range, you discuss private or serious
matters and confer with literally "close" friends. Touch is easy
throughout the nearest part of this space, up to about 30 inches.
Alternatively, you can keep someone "at arm's length."

(Although you may be unaware of the rules of personal 8
space, your language is not. Many of our familiar phrases reflect our cultural code and what happens when somebody is
too close for comfort.)

Within the personal zone, you can focus sharply on another 9
person's face and read very subtle details of expression. But
you'll probably move your eyes a lot to focus on various parts
of the other person's face. Watch somebody else talking at this
distance, and you'll see his or her gaze flick rapidly from one
spot to another.

You'll also notice that personal groups larger than two or 10
three are very rare, because it becomes difficult to maintain appropriate spacing with more people.

Casual acquaintances or people who just want to tell you 11
something relatively unimportant had better stay well outside
the 30-inch inner personal zone. If they don't, they'll make you
very uncomfortable, and you may find yourself inadvertently
backing up until you're trapped against a wall.

One reason that economy-class air travel frequently is so 12
ghastly is that the strangers who are your seatmates are way

inside the close personal zone. Worse yet, side-by-side seating is widely felt to be the most intimate arrangement. Men will not voluntarily choose it unless the alternative is sitting too far apart to talk.

13 In one study, American, English, Dutch, Swedish and Pakistani subjects all ranked side-by-side position as psychologically closest, followed by corner seating, face-to-face, and various diagonal arrangements.

14 The "social-consultive" zone, in which most day-to-day work and ordinary conversation occurs, starts at 4 feet and goes to about 10 feet. In American culture, eight feet is the point at which you pretty much have to acknowledge another person's presence. Beyond that, you can ignore someone without giving obvious offense.

15 Usually, there are no smell or heat sensations at 4 to 10 feet, and much nonverbal information is conveyed by large-scale body language. The whole body is visible as a unit at about seven feet, although you can only focus on part because the clearest vision occurs in a cone of about 15 degrees from the eyeball.

16 Finally, there is an all-purpose "public" zone that begins at about 10 feet and extends to 25 feet. Thirty feet is the customary nearest distance for addresses by public officials or celebrities.

17 Studies have shown that people are more likely to interact with somebody who looks weird if that person stays well outside the personal zone. In one experiment, a researcher dressed as a punk rocker pretended to be looking for help from people sitting at tables in a shopping mall food court.

18 "Although only one in 15 people consented to help the punker when she sat right next to them, and 40 percent agreed to help when she sat at a medium distance," the researchers found. But "80 percent of the people agreed to help her when she took the seat farthest away."

Over The Line

19 When someone does something that violates the tacit rules of the zone system, we are perplexed, annoyed or both. For example, if a person wanted a date with you and asked you out

from 10 feet away—two feet beyond the farthest range of business conversation—you'd certainly think twice about agreeing, even if you were initially inclined to go.

On the other hand, a Latin American or French person, from 20 a culture with a much closer personal interaction distance, could seem to be too "forward" or "coming on too strong" if he or she made the request from two feet away.

Sometimes, the resulting discomfort is intentional. Psychol- 21 ogist Robert Sommer notes in his book *Personal Space* that police interrogators are taught to intrude well inside the personal zone when questioning suspects.

Similarly, we often decide that someone is wearing "too 22 much" perfume or cologne if the scent extends past the distance of personal space. So if you can smell a woman's perfume 8 feet away, you may find it irritating—not just because of the odor itself but because she is making what should be an intimate olfactory statement in public space. . . .

Size Does Matter

Variations abound. In much of India, there are only two zones: 23 intimate and public. Some Mediterranean cultures have personal zones that begin much closer than those typical of Americans or northern Europeans. That's why Americans sometimes feel crowded or stressed in France or Italy.

And, of course, some cultures simply build things differ- 24 ently. Japanese rooms seem too small by Western standards, and the furniture tends to be placed in the center rather than along the walls. What we don't know is that the traditional Japanese room configuration can be changed by moving the lightweight walls.

Thus, what we perceive as a permanent space is merely a 25 temporary arrangement from another perspective. Conversely, our fondness for big spaces with furniture at the edges can make Western rooms look barren to the Japanese eye.

In 1967, Hong Kong's housing authority was constructing 26 apartments with 35 square feet per occupant. That's 5-by-7, about the size of a modern work "cubicle." When a westerner asked why the design was so stingy, a construction supervisor replied, "With 60 square feet per person, the tenants would sublet."

Birth and Turf

27 But each culture's rules arise from the same fundamental biological impetus, which extends throughout the animal kingdom—the tendency to mark and defend one's own territory or to avoid intruding on someone else's.

28   Think about that next time you sit down in a cafeteria or library. If you find an empty table that can seat six or eight, you're probably going to sit at one of the corner chairs—an "avoidance" position, according to psychologists—and you'll most likely face the door because some ancestral instinct says you might have to flee.

29   Dogs mark their territory by urinating at the boundaries. Happily, human civilization has not evolved this trait. But we're constantly doing the equivalent.

30   Everyone has been vaguely irritated by the person in a movie theater who spreads coats and bags across six seats and then goes off for popcorn. Nonetheless, we'll bypass any space that faintly appears to be "marked" by an absentee squatter. One study showed that, even in a busy and crowded library, a simple stack of magazines in front of a chair kept that seat open for more than an hour.

31   Analogously, you may find that when you enter someone's home, you carefully avoid sitting in what seems to be the father's "personal" chair. Or you may notice how some passengers in the Metro system claim two spaces—an "aggressive" position—by putting a briefcase next to them or taking the outermost of the two side-by-side seats. . . .

Eyes Right

32 Space can be invaded by vision as well as another's presence, and visual territories also differ from culture to culture. Unlike, say, the French, whose "frank" stares can be intimidating to outsiders, Americans rarely look directly at each other for very long, even during intense conversation.

33   In the animal kingdom, an averted gaze often indicates a passive stance. But in America, it is merely polite. We consider

it an invasion of personal space to "stare" at someone, even briefly, and sensitivity varies by distance.

Thus, when the door closes on a crowded elevator, you'll 34 usually notice two behaviors. First, the occupants automatically adjust their positions to create the same amount of space between each. Then most people either look down at their feet or up at the floor indicator rather at at one another.

In fact, one experiment showed that people will sit closer to 35 a picture of a person with the eyes closed than to an otherwise identical image with the eyes open.

The English, on the other hand, regard it as rude not to look 36 directly at the other person during conversation. To do otherwise makes it appear that you're not paying attention.

But in order to hold the head still and the gaze steady while 37 listening to someone, one has to be far enough away so the eyes aren't constantly shifting around the other person's face. Thus the English tend to stand near the outer limits of American personal space, making them seem aloof, reserved or literally "stand-offish."

Expanding Vocabulary

Examine the following words in their contexts in the essay and then write a brief definition or synonym of each one. Do not use a dictionary; try to guess each word's meaning from the context.

idiosyncracies (3)	interrogators (21)
spectrum (11)	olfactory (22)
inadvertently (11)	impetus (27)
tacit (19)	Analogously (31)

Understanding Content

1. How many separate spatial zones do Americans have?
2. What are the characteristics of the intimate zone?
3. What are the dimensions and uses of the personal zone?
4. What terms have evolved from the dynamics of the personal zone?
5. How do most people view sitting next to strangers?
6. What are the dimensions and characteristics of the third zone? At what distance do we usually have to acknowledge another person?
7. What are the dimensions of the public zone?
8. How can the police use knowledge of personal space to aid their work?

9. What are some cultures that tolerate closer personal zones and smaller living spaces than Americans?
10. What are some of the ways we "mark" our personal space?
11. How do American and British and French patterns differ regarding looking directly at someone?

Drawing Inferences about Thesis and Purpose

1. Why are we irritated by people who spread out their things over several chairs?
2. What is Suplee's purpose in writing?
3. What is his thesis?

Analyzing Strategies and Style

1. What are the sources of the author's information? How does he provide this information for readers?
2. Describe the strategies Suplee uses to introduce each of his four space zones.
3. What *type* of information does the author provide for each of the zones?

Thinking Critically

1. Are you familiar with this information about personal space? If not, does Suplee's analysis make sense to you? Think about your own experiences on elevators and in movie theaters.
2. What information about zones is most helpful for our personal relationships? Explain your response.
3. What information is most helpful for our dealings with people we don't know? Explain your response.

"There's Three Kinds of Teams"

PETER DRUCKER

Probably the most recognized name in business and management theory, Peter Drucker (b. 1909) has taught at the Claremont Graduate School since 1971 and is the author of more than twenty books on management, business organization, and economics. The following discussion of team models for companies is from a section of his book *Managing in a Time of Great Change* (1995).

"Team-building" has become a buzzword in American busi- 1
ness. The results are not overly impressive.

Ford Motor Company began more than ten years ago to 2
build teams to design its new models. It now reports "serious
problems," and the gap in development time between Ford
and its Japanese competitors has hardly narrowed. General
Motors' Saturn Division was going to replace the traditional assembly line with teamwork in its "factory of the future." But
the plant has been steadily moving back toward the Detroit-
style assembly line. Procter and Gamble launched a team-
building campaign with great fanfare several years ago. Now
P&G is moving back to individual accountability for developing and marketing new products.

One reason—perhaps the major one—for these near-failures 3
is the all-but-universal belief among executives that there is
just one kind of team. There actually are three—each different
in its structure, in the behavior it demands from its members,
in its strengths, its vulnerabilities, its limitations, its requirements, but above all, in what it can do and should be used for.

The first kind of team is the baseball team. The surgical team 4
that performs an open-heart operation and Henry Ford's assembly line are both "baseball teams." So is the team Detroit
traditionally sets up to design a new car.

The players play *on* the team; they do not play *as* a team. 5
They have fixed positions they never leave. The second base-
man never runs to assist the pitcher; the anesthesiologist never
comes to the aid of the surgical nurse. "Up at bat, you are totally alone," is an old baseball saying. In the traditional Detroit
design team, marketing people rarely saw designers and were
never consulted by them. Designers did their work and passed
it on to the development engineers, who in turn did their work
and passed it on to manufacturing, which in turn did its work
and passed it on to marketing.

The second kind of team is the football team. The hospital 6
unit that rallies around a patient who goes into shock at three
a.m. is a "football team," as are Japanese automakers' design
teams. The players on the football team, like those on the baseball team, have fixed positions. But on the football team players play as a team. The Japanese automakers' design teams,
which Detroit and P&G rushed to imitate, are football-type

teams. To use engineering terms, the designers, engineers, manufacturing people, and marketing people work "in parallel." The traditional Detroit team worked "in series."

7   Third, there is the tennis doubles team—the kind Saturn management hoped would replace the traditional assembly line. It is also the sort of team that plays in a jazz combo, the team of senior executives who form the "president's office" in big companies, or the team that is most likely to produce a genuine innovation like the personal computer fifteen years ago.

8   On the doubles team, players have a primary rather than a fixed position. They are supposed to "cover" their teammates, adjusting to their teammates' strengths and weaknesses and to the changing demands of the "game."

9   Business executives and the management literature have little good to say these days about the baseball-style team, whether in the office or on the factory floor. There is even a failure to recognize such teams as teams at all. But this kind of team has enormous strengths. Each member can be evaluated separately, can have clear and specific goals, can be held accountable, can be measured—as witness the statistics a true aficionado reels off about every major-leaguer in baseball history. Each member can be trained and developed to the fullest extent of the individual's strengths. And because the members do not have to adjust to anybody else on the team, every position can be staffed with a "star," no matter how temperamental, jealous, or limelight-hogging each of them might be.

10   But the baseball team is inflexible. It works well when the game has been played many times and when the sequence of its actions is thoroughly understood by everyone. That is what made this kind of team right for Detroit in the past.

11   As recently as twenty years ago, to be fast and flexible in automotive design was the last thing Detroit needed or wanted. Traditional mass production required long runs with minimum changes. And since the resale value of the "good used car"—one less than three years old—was a key factor for the new-car buyer, it was a serious mistake to bring out a new design (which would depreciate the old car) more than every five years. Sales and market share took a dip on several occasions when Chrysler prematurely introduced a new, brilliant design.

12   The Japanese did not invent "flexible mass production"; IBM was probably the first to use it, around 1960. But when the

Japanese auto industry adopted it, it made possible the introduction of a new car model in parallel with a successful old one. And then the baseball team did indeed become the wrong team for Detroit, and for mass-production industry as a whole. The design process then had to be restructured as a football team.

The football team does have the flexibility Detroit now 13 needs. But it has far more stringent requirements than the baseball team. It needs a "score"—such as the play the coach signals to the huddle on the field. The specifications with which the Japanese begin their design of a new car model—or a new consumer-electronics product—are far more stringent and detailed than anything Detroit is used to in respect to style, technology, performance, weight, price and so on. And they are far more closely adhered to.

In the traditional "baseball" design team, every position— 14 engineering, manufacturing, marketing—does its job its own way. In the football team there is no such permissiveness. The word of the coach is law. Players are beholden to this one boss alone for their orders, their rewards, their appraisals, their promotions.

The individual engineer on the Japanese design team is a 15 member of his company's engineering department. But he is on the design team because the team's leader has asked for him—not because the chief engineer sent him there. He can consult engineering and get advice. But his orders come from the design-team chief, who also appraises his performance. If there are stars on these teams, they are featured only if the team leader entrusts them with a "solo." Otherwise they subordinate themselves to the team.

Even more stringent are the requirements of the doubles 16 team—the kind that GM's Saturn Division hoped to develop in its "flexible-manufacturing" plant and a flexible plant does indeed need such a team. The team must be quite small, with five to seven members at most. The members have to be trained together and must work together for quite some time before they fully function as a team. There must be one clear goal for the entire team yet considerable flexibility with respect to the individual member's work and performance. And in this kind of team only the team "performs"; individual members "contribute."

17   All three of these kinds of teams are true teams. But they are so different—in the behavior they require, in what they do best, and in what they cannot do at all—that they cannot be hybrids. One kind of team can play only one way. And it is very difficult to change from one kind of team to another.

18   Gradual change cannot work. There has to be a total break with the past, however traumatic it may be. This means that people cannot report to both their old boss and to the new coach, or team leader. And their rewards, their compensation, their appraisals, and their promotions must be totally dependent on their performance in their new roles on their new teams. But this is so unpopular that the temptation to compromise is always great.

19   At Ford, for instance, the financial people have been left under the control of the financial staff and report to it rather than to the new design teams. GM's Saturn Division has tried to maintain the authority of the traditional bosses—the first-line supervisors and the shop stewards—rather than hand decision-making power over to the work teams. This, however, is like playing baseball and a tennis doubles match with the same people, on the same field, and at the same time. It can only result in frustration and nonperformance. And a similar confusion seems to have prevailed at P&G.

20   Teams, in other words, are tools. As such, each team design has its own uses, its own characteristics, its own requirements, its own limitations. Teamwork is neither "good" nor "desirable"—it is a fact. Wherever people work together or play together they do so as a team. Which team to use for what purpose is a crucial, difficult, and risky decision that is even harder to unmake. Managements have yet to learn how to make it.

Expanding Vocabulary

Examine the following words in their contexts in the essay and then write a brief definition or synonym for each one. Do not use a dictionary; try to guess the word's meaning from its context.

aficionado (9)	appraisals (14)
depreciate (11)	hybrids (17)
stringent (13)	traumatic (18)

Understanding Content

1. Why has the idea of creating teams in business and industry not always worked well?
2. What are the characteristics of the "baseball" team?
3. What are the characteristics of the "football" team? How does it differ from the "baseball" team?
4. What are the characteristics of the "tennis doubles" team?
5. What are the strengths of the baseball team? What is its primary weakness? Why was it a good model for car manufacture in the past?
6. Why has Detroit switched to a football-team model? What does it gain?
7. Why does General Motors want to switch to a tennis team model? What will it gain?
8. Why must change from one team model to another be total, not gradual? What are companies tempted to do?

Drawing Inferences about Thesis and Purpose

1. Drucker says that teams are tools. What does he mean by this statement?
2. Who is Drucker's primary audience?
3. What are his purposes in writing?
4. What is Drucker's thesis?

Analyzing Strategies and Style

1. What primary strategy does Drucker use to explain three ways in which workers can do their work together? What makes his strategy effective?
2. What other strategy does the author use to develop and explain his classification? How are his particular choices effective, given his primary audience?

Thinking Critically

1. What are the goals of people, like Drucker, who analyze behavior on the job and try to determine how to organize workers? What do they want to accomplish?
2. Would you rather be on a baseball, football, or tennis team at work? Why?
3. Can the three team models be applied to the classroom? If so, how would each type of classroom be run? If not, explain why.

"Class Acts: America's Changing Middle Class"

RALPH WHITEHEAD, JR.

Beginning his career as a journalist in Chicago, Ralph White-head (b. 1943) became a professor of journalism at the University of Massachusetts in 1973. He is the author of many articles on social structures and public opinion and has been a consultant to political and labor groups and to the Department of Labor. His study of the changing social/economic hierarchy in American society was first published in the Jan./Feb. 1990 issue of the *Utne Reader.*

1   As we enter the 1990s, American society exhibits a vastly different social and economic makeup from the one that we grew accustomed to in the thirty years that followed World War II. The gap between the top and bottom is far greater now, of course, but the economic position of people in the middle is changing, too. This new social ladder is seen most vividly in the lives of our younger generations, the baby boom and the later baby bust. Because the new ladder is so much steeper than the old one, it's creating an alarming new degree of polarization in American life.

2   As it held sway for roughly the first three decades after World War II, the old social ladder was shaped largely by the continuing expansion of the middle class. For the first time, many people could afford to buy a house, a car (or two), a washer and dryer, an outdoor grill, adequate health coverage, maybe a motor boat, and possibly college for the kids. And for the first time, a growing number of blacks and Hispanics could enter the middle class.

3   Within this expanding middle class, there were a couple of fairly well-defined ways of life: white-collar life and blue-collar life. White-collar life was typified by TV characters like Ward and June Cleaver and later Mike and Carol Brady. Blue-collar life was typified by characters like Ralph and Alice Kramden and later Archie and Edith Bunker.

At the top of the old social ladder stood a small number of 4
rich people. A larger but declining number of poor people
stood at the bottom, and the rest of the ladder was taken up
by the middle-class. The old social ladder looked roughly like
this:

THE RICH

THE EXPANDING MIDDLE CLASS:
White collar
Blue collar

THE POOR

The new social ladder is markedly different. Within the baby 5
boom and baby bust generations, the middle class is no longer
expanding. Therefore the new social ladder is shaped by—and
at the same time is helping to shape—a new polarization between the haves and the have-nots. The social ladder of the
1990s looks roughly like this:

UPSCALE AMERICA:
The Rich
The Overclass

THE DIVERGING MIDDLE CLASS:
Bright collar
New collar
Blue collar

DOWNSCALE AMERICA:
The Poor
The Underclass

The rich are still on top, of course. But the new generation of
rich people is typified by Donald Trump, the billionaire developer of luxury buildings for the newly rich, rather than by
someone like his father, Fred Trump, a developer who made
millions building modestly priced postwar homes and apartments for the expanding middle class—the kinds of homes in
which the Kramdens and Bunkers lived.

298 Using Division and Classification

6   The poor are still with us, of course, but they're no longer at the bottom. It's not because they've risen to the middle class but rather because some of them have fallen into the underclass. Because definitions of the underclass vary, so do estimates of its size. However, it does include at least two million people who lead lives that aren't typified in America's popular culture. To belong to the underclass is to be without a face and without a voice.

7   Just as an underclass has emerged, so has an overclass, which occupies the rung just below the rich. Located chiefly in a dozen metropolises and heavily concentrated in lucrative management and professional jobs, the overclass is roughly the same size as the underclass. Its significance lies not in its numbers, however, but in its immense power throughout American society. The overclass holds the highest level positions in the fields of entertainment, media, marketing, advertising, real estate, finance, and politics. It's pursued for its consumption dollars and cajoled for its investment dollars. It is crudely typified by the media stereotype of the yuppie.

8   What clearly stood out on the old social ladder that shaped American society during the fifties and sixties was the dominant presence of an expanding middle class. What is noticeable about the new social ladder is the unmistakable emergence of distinct upper and lower rungs, and the vast social, economic, and psychological distance between them. Together, the rich and the overclass form Upscale America. Together, the underclass and the poor form Downscale America.

9   The expanding middle class, with its white and blue collars, has given way in the baby boom and baby bust generations to a diverging middle class. It consists largely of three kinds of workers:

❑ **Bright collars.** Within the ranks of managerial and professional workers a new category of job has emerged. The white-collar worker is receding and the bright-collar worker is advancing. The bright collars are the 20 million knowledge workers born since 1945: lawyers and teachers, architects and social workers, accountants and budget analysts, engineers and consultants, rising executives and midlevel administrators. They earn their living by taking intellectual initiatives. They face the luxury and the necessity of making their own decisions on the job and in their personal lives.

Bright-collar people lack the touchstones that guided white-col- 10
lar workers like Ward Cleaver in the 1950s and 1960s. The white
collars believed in institutions; bright collars are skeptical of them.
The corporate chain of command, a strong force in white-collar life
then, is far weaker for bright collars today. They place a premium
on individuality, on standing out rather than fitting in. Although
the older white collars knew the rules and played by them, bright
collars can't be sure what the rules are and must think up their
own. The white collars were organization men and women (mostly
men); bright collars are entrepreneurs interested in building careers for themselves outside big corporations.

Three quarters of the managers and professionals of the 1950s 11
were men. Today half are women. Seven percent are black or Hispanic or Asian. Bright collars make up a third of the baby boom
work force. They're typified by figures like *L.A. Law's* attorneys.

❑ **Blue Collars.** Within the manufacturing workplace, blue-collar
work endures, but on a much smaller scale. Thirty years ago almost
40 percent of the adult work force did blue-collar work. Today, after
the relative decline of American heavy industry, it's done by less
than 25 percent of baby boom workers. During the fifties and sixties, blue-collar wages rose steadily, thus helping fuel the expansion of the middle class. In the past 15 years these wages have been
relatively flat. Young blue collars often must live near the economic
margins.

The blue-collar world is still a man's world. Roughly three quar- 12
ters of today's younger blue collars are men—the same percentage
as in the 1950s. Twelve percent are black, Hispanic, or Asian. Within
a growing number of innovative manufacturing workplaces, new
models of blue-collar work have begun to emerge, but they haven't
yet advanced enough to trigger a new category of American worker.
In the popular culture the new generation of blue collars finds a
voice in Bruce Springsteen, but it still hasn't found a face.

❑ **New Collars.** These people aren't managers and professionals,
and they don't do physical labor. Their jobs fall between those two
worlds. They're secretaries, clerks, telephone operators, key-punch
operators, inside salespeople, police officers. They often avoid the
grime and regimentation of blue-collar work. Two thirds of the
new collars are women. More than 15 percent are black, Hispanic,
or Asian. The new collars make up at least 35 percent of the baby
boom work force.

Federal Express truck drivers are typical new-collar workers. 13
They design pickup and delivery routes, explain the company's ser-

vices and fees, provide mailing supplies, and handle relatively so-phisticated information technology in their trucks. They aren't tra-ditional truck drivers so much as sales clerks in offices on wheels.

14   The rise of the new social ladder has helped to drive a num-ber of changes in American life, but one of them, already evi-dent, should be underscored: the dramatic shift of power within both the middle class and the society as a whole.

15   As members of the expanding middle class of the postwar years, blue collars once held considerable leverage. In the elec-torate, for every vote cast by the white collars in 1960, the blue collars cast two. In the workplace, they acted through power-ful unions. In the marketplace, they were valued as consumers. As a result, blue collars dealt with white collars as equals. In the fifties and sixties, whatever class lines still divided the two groups seemed to be dissolving.

16   Within the diverging middle class today, the balance of power is much different. In the electorate, for every vote cast by younger blue collars in 1988, bright collars cast two. In the workplace, younger blue-collar workers are losing union power, while bright collars exert the power of their knowledge and privilege of their status. In the marketplace, blue-collar consumers are written off as too downscale, while the bright-collar consumer is courted as an aspiring member of the over-class. Deep divisions have sprung up between bright collars and blue collars. They look a lot like class lines.

17   The rise of an overclass throws the decline of blue-collar life into sharper relief, and vice versa. Upscale yuppie haunts spring up: the health club, the gourmet takeout shop, the pricy boutique, the atrium building. Downscale blue-collar haunts wither: the union hall, the lodge, the beauty parlor, the mill. The guys with red suspenders began showing up in the beer commercials right about the time the loggers and guys with air hammers began to disappear. The overclass's stock portfolios began to get fat just as blue-collar families were losing their pensions and health insurance. Condo prices were climbing in Atlanta just as bungalow prices fell in Buffalo. It seems that there's a battle here, a zero-sum game, whereby the rise of one comes at the expense of the other.

18   The contrast between the rich and the underclass is sharper than ever. If you look at the new social ladder in New York, you

see Donald Trump in his penthouse and the homeless people
in the subways.

This situation intensifies the shift of power in society as a   19
whole. With the middle class divided, the center cannot hold.
The dominant forces in society become Upscale America and
Downscale America—or, more precisely, Upscale America *versus* Downscale America. Upscale America uses its power to secure privileges such as proposed cuts in the capital gains tax.
Downscale America strikes back blindly through rising rates of
crime. Through the old social ladder, the expanding middle
class acted as the nation's glue. With the new social ladder, the
diverging middle class is merely caught in the crossfire.

Expanding Vocabulary

Study the definitions for any of the following words that you do not
know. Then select five words and use each one in a separate sentence.

polarization (1)   innovative (11)
lucrative (7)   sophisticated (13)
cajoled (7)   leverage (15)
yuppie (7)   zero-sum (17)
entrepreneurs (10)

Understanding Content

1. In the social ladder for thirty years after World War II, what was
   happening to the middle class?
2. What were the four categories on the older social ladder?
3. The social ladder of the 1990s has what three major categories?
   What is happening between the rich and poor?
4. What two important changes are taking place in the middle class?
5. What are the characteristics of the underclass?
6. What makes up the new overclass?
7. What are the characteristics of the three new categories of workers
   in the new middle class?
8. How has power changed in the new bright collar and blue collar
   classes?

Drawing Inferences about Thesis and Purpose

1. What is Whitehead's purpose in writing? Does he have more than
   one?
2. What is his thesis? Where is it stated?

3. What does Whitehead mean when he writes of a "zero-sum game" played between upscale and downscale America (paragraph 17)?
4. What implications for America do we find in the final paragraph?

Analyzing Strategies and Style

1. What does the author gain by the visual presentation of both the former and the current class categories?
2. Whitehead uses several TV characters as examples. How are they effective? What do they imply about his expected audience?
3. What does Whitehead mean by his use of "collar," as in "bright collar" and "new collar"? What does "collar" stand for?
4. The author uses contrast within his classification structure. Find several nicely balanced contrast sentences and consider why they are effective.

Thinking Critically

1. Does Whitehead's classification of contemporary American class structure seem on target? Why or why not?
2. Many Americans like to believe that we are a "classless" society; everybody is the same. Whitehead doesn't do anything to address, or counter, this attitude. What might this tell us about his expected audience?
3. Do you agree with Whitehead that the diverging middle class and the conflict between upscale and downscale America pose serious social problems for the United States? Why or why not?

"The Secret Life of Walter Mitty"

JAMES THURBER

A native of Columbus, Ohio, and graduate of Ohio State University, James Thurber (1894–1962) established himself as a humorist and cartoonist during his many years on the staff of *The New Yorker* magazine. Thurber is best known for the following story, first published in *The New Yorker* in 1939, made into a movie in 1947, and now reprinted in numerous collections the world over. Although stories are not structured in the same way that essays are, still you can see a "division" in Mitty and a "classification" of traits within the categories established by Thurber. Approaching the story in this way may help you understand better the character that Thurber has created, a character who has become a part of American culture.

"We're going through!" The Commander's voice was like 1
thin ice breaking. He wore his full-dress uniform, with the heavily braided white cap pulled down rakishly over one cold gray eye. "We can't make it, sir. It's spoiling for a hurricane, if you ask me." "I'm not asking you, Lieutenant Berg," said the Commander. "Throw on the power lights! Rev her up to 8,500! We're going through!" The pounding of the cylinders increased: ta-pocketa-pocketa-pocketa-*pocketa-pocketa.* The Commander stared at the ice forming on the pilot window. He walked over and twisted a row of complicated dials. "Switch on No. 8 auxiliary!" he shouted. "Switch on No. 8 auxiliary!" repeated Lieutenant Berg. "Full strength in No. 3 turret!" shouted the Commander. "Full strength in No. 3 turret!" The crew, bending to their various tasks in the huge, hurtling eight-engined Navy hydroplane, looked at each other and grinned. "The Old Man'll get us through," they said to one another. "The Old Man ain't afraid of Hell!" . . .

"Not so fast! You're driving too fast!" said Mrs. Mitty. "What 2
are you driving so fast for?"

"Hmm?" said Walter Mitty. He looked at his wife, in the seat 3
beside him, with shocked astonishment. She seemed grossly unfamiliar, like a strange woman who had yelled at him in a crowd. "You were up to fifty-five," she said. "You know I don't like to go more than forty. You were up to fifty-five." Walter Mitty drove on toward Waterbury in silence, the roaring of the SN202 through the worst storm in twenty years of Navy flying fading in the remote, intimate airways of his mind. "You're tensed up again," said Mrs. Mitty. "It's one of your days. I wish you'd let Dr. Renshaw look you over."

Walter Mitty stopped the car in front of the building where 4
his wife went to have her hair done. "Remember to get those overshoes while I'm having my hair done," she said. "I don't need overshoes," said Mitty. She put her mirror back into her bag. "We've been all through that," she said, getting out of the car. "You're not a young man any longer." He raced the engine a little. "Why don't you wear your gloves? Have you lost your gloves?" Walter Mitty reached in a pocket and brought out the gloves. He put them on, but after she had turned and gone into

the building and he had driven on to a red light, he took them off again. "Pick it up, brother!" snapped a cop as the light changed, and Mitty hastily pulled on his gloves and lurched ahead. He drove around the streets aimlessly for a time, and then he drove past the hospital on his way to the parking lot.

5 . . . "It's the millionaire banker, Wellington McMillan," said the pretty nurse. "Yes?" said Walter Mitty, removing his gloves slowly. "Who has the case?" "Dr. Renshaw and Dr. Benbow, but there are two specialists here, Dr. Remington from New York and Mr. Pritchard-Mitford from London. He flew over." A door opened down a long, cool corridor and Dr. Renshaw came out. He looked distraught and haggard. "Hello, Mitty," he said. "We're having the devil's own time with McMillan, the millionaire banker and close personal friend of Roosevelt. Obstreosis of the ductal tract. Tertiary. Wish you'd take a look at him." "Glad to," said Mitty.

6 In the operating room there were whispered introductions: "Dr. Remington, Dr. Mitty. Mr. Pritchard-Mitford, Dr. Mitty." "I've read your book on streptothricosis," said Pritchard-Mitford, shaking hands. "A brilliant performance, sir." "Thank you," said Walter Mitty. "Didn't know you were in the States, Mitty," grumbled Remington. "Coals to Newcastle, bringing Mitford and me up here for a tertiary." "You are very kind," said Mitty. A huge, complicated machine, connected to the operating table, with many tubes and wires, began at this moment to go pocketa-pocketa-pocketa. "The new anesthetizer is giving way!" shouted an interne. "There is no one in the East who knows how to fix it!" "Quiet, man!" said Mitty, in a low, cool voice. He sprang to the machine, which was now going pocketa-pocketa-queep-pocketa-queep. He began fingering delicately a row of glistening dials. "Give me a fountain pen!" he snapped. Someone handed him a fountain pen. He pulled a faulty piston out of the machine and inserted the pen in its place. "That will hold for ten minutes," he said. "Get on with the operation." A nurse hurried over and whispered to Renshaw, and Mitty saw the man turn pale. "Coreopsis has set in," said Renshaw nervously. "If you would take over, Mitty?" Mitty looked at him and at the craven figure of Benbow, who drank, and at the grave, uncertain faces of the two great specialists. "If you wish," he said. They slipped a white gown on

him; he adjusted a mask and drew on thin gloves; nurses handed him shining . . .

"Back it up, Mac! Look out for that Buick!" Walter Mitty 7 jammed on the brakes. "Wrong lane, Mac," said the parking-lot attendant, looking at Mitty closely. "Gee. Yeh," muttered Mitty. He began cautiously to back out of the lane marked "Exit Only." "Leave her sit there," said the attendant. "I'll put her away." Mitty got out of the car. "Hey, better leave the key." "Oh," said Mitty, handing the man the ignition key. The attendant vaulted into the car, backed it up with insolent skill, and put it where it belonged.

They're so damn cocky, thought Walter Mitty, walking along 8 Main Street; they think they know everything. Once he had tried to take his chains off, outside New Milford, and he had got them wound around the axles. A man had had to come out in a wrecking car and unwind them, a young, grinning garage-man. Since then Mrs. Mitty always made him drive to a garage to have the chains taken off. The next time, he thought, I'll wear my right arm in a sling; they won't grin at me then. I'll have my right arm in a sling and they'll see I couldn't possibly take the chains off myself. He kicked at the slush on the sidewalk. "Overshoes," he said to himself, and he began looking for a shoe store.

When he came out into the street again, with the overshoes 9 in a box under his arm, Walter Mitty began to wonder what the other thing was his wife had told him to get. She had told him, twice, before they set out from their house for Waterbury. In a way he hated these weekly trips to town—he was always getting something wrong. Kleenex, he thought, Squibb's, razor blades? No. Toothpaste, toothbrush, bicarbonate, carborundum, initiative and referendum? He gave it up. But she would remember it. "Where's the what's-its-name?" she would ask. "Don't tell me you forgot the what's-its-name." A newsboy went by shouting something about the Waterbury trial.

. . . "Perhaps this will refresh your memory." The District 10 Attorney suddenly thrust a heavy automatic at the quiet figure on the witness stand. "Have you ever seen this before?" Walter Mitty took the gun and examined it expertly. "This is my Webley-Vickers 50.80," he said calmly. An excited buzz ran around the courtroom. The Judge rapped for order. "You are a crack shot with any sort of firearms, I believe?" said the District Attorney, insinuatingly. "Objection!" shouted Mitty's attorney. "We have shown that the defendant could not have fired the shot. We have shown that he wore his right arm in a sling on the night of the fourteenth of July." Walter Mitty raised his hand briefly and the bickering attorneys were stilled. "With any known make of gun," he said evenly, "I could have killed Gregory Fitzhurst at three hundred feet *with my left hand*." Pandemonium broke loose in the courtroom. A woman's scream rose above the bedlam and suddenly a lovely, dark-haired girl was in Walter Mitty's arms. The District Attorney struck at her savagely. Without rising from his chair, Mitty let the man have it on the point of the chin. "You miserable cur!" . . .

11   "Puppy biscuit," said Walter Mitty. He stopped walking and the buildings of Waterbury rose up out of the misty courtroom and surrounded him again. A woman who was passing laughed. "He said 'Puppy biscuit,' " she said to her companion. "That man said 'Puppy biscuit' to himself." Walter Mitty hurried on. He went into an A. & P., not the first one he came to but a smaller one farther up the street. "I want some biscuit for small, young dogs," he said to the clerk. "Any special brand, sir?" The greatest pistol shot in the world thought a moment. "It says 'Puppies Bark for It' on the box," said Walter Mitty.

12   His wife would be through at the hairdresser's in fifteen minutes, Mitty saw in looking at his watch, unless they had trouble drying it; sometimes they had trouble drying it. She didn't like to get to the hotel first; she would want him to be there waiting for her as usual. He found a big leather chair in the lobby, facing a window, and he put the overshoes and the puppy biscuit on the floor beside it. He picked up an old copy of *Liberty* and sank down into the chair. "Can Germany Conquer the World Through the Air?" Walter Mitty looked at the pictures of bombing planes and of ruined streets.

13   . . . "The cannonading has got the wind up in young Raleigh, sir," said the sergeant. Captain Mitty looked up at him through tousled hair. "Get him to bed," he said wearily. "With the others. I'll fly alone." "But you can't, sir," said the sergeant anxiously. "It takes two men to handle that bomber and the Archies are pounding the hell out of the air. Von Richtman's circus is between here and Saulier." "Somebody's got to get

that ammunition dump," said Mitty. "I'm going over. Spot of Brandy?" He poured a drink for the sergeant and one for himself. War thundered and whined around the dugout and battered at the door. There was a rending of wood and splinters flew through the room. "A bit of a near thing," said Captain Mitty carelessly. "The box barrage is closing in," said the sergeant. "We only live once, Sergeant," said Mitty, with his faint, fleeting smile. "Or do we?" He poured another brandy and tossed it off. "I never see a man could hold his brandy like you, sir," said the sergeant. "Begging your pardon, sir." Captain Mitty stood up and strapped on his huge Webley-Vickers automatic. "It's forty kilometers through hell, sir," said the sergeant. Mitty finished one last brandy. "After all," he said softly, "what isn't?" The pounding of the cannon increased; there was the rat-rat-tatting of machine guns, and from somewhere came the menacing pocketa-pocketa-pocketa of the new flame-throwers. Walter Mitty walked to the door of the dugout humming "Auprés de Ma Blonde." He turned and waved to the sergeant. "Cheerio!" he said. . . .

Something struck his shoulder. "I've been looking all over 14 this hotel for you," said Mrs. Mitty. "Why do you have to hide in this old chair? How did you expect me to find you?" "Things close in," said Walter Mitty vaguely. "What?" Mrs. Mitty said. "Did you get the what's-its-name? The puppy biscuit? What's in that box?" "Overshoes," said Mitty. "Couldn't you have put them on in the store?" "I was thinking," said Walter Mitty. "Does it ever occur to you that I am sometimes thinking?" She looked at him. "I'm going to take your temperature when I get you home," she said.

They went out through the revolving doors that made a 15 faintly derisive whistling sound when you pushed them. It was two blocks to the parking lot. At the drugstore on the corner she said, "Wait here for me. I forgot something. I won't be a minute." She was more than a minute. Walter Mitty lighted a cigarette. It began to rain, rain with sleet in it. He stood up against the wall of the drugstore, smoking. . . . He put his shoulders back and his heels together. "To hell with the handkerchief," said Walter Mitty scornfully. He took one last drag on his cigarette and snapped it away. Then, with that faint, fleeting smile playing about his lips, he faced the firing squad;

erect and motionless, proud and disdainful, Walter Mitty the Undefeated, inscrutable to the last.

Expanding Vocabulary

After studying definitions of the following words, use each one in a separate sentence.

rakishly (1)   insinuatingly (10)
hydroplane (1)   pandemonium (10)
distraught (5)   bedlam (10)
anesthetizer (6)   derisive (15)
craven (6)   inscrutable (15)
insolent (7)

Understanding Content

1. What is the situation of the story? Where does the story take place? What do Walter Mitty and his wife do in the course of the story?
2. Since Mitty is not a commander or surgeon or on trial for murder, what is happening in the passages that do not take place in Waterbury?
3. What do the dream passages have in common? What do they tell us about the person Mitty would like to be?
4. How do the details of his real life help to reveal Mitty's character? What kinds of problems does he have?

Drawing Inferences about Theme

1. What are Mitty's dominant traits? Describe the personality or character of Walter Mitty.
2. How does Thurber want us to respond to his character? Are we to relate to him? Laugh at him? Feel sorry for him? To what extent is Mitty like most people?

Analyzing Strategies and Style

1. What is the major structural technique by which Thurber develops Mitty's character?
2. Examine each of Mitty's daydreams. What in Mitty's real world triggers each dream? That is, how do the details of his real life get incorporated into each particular dream?
3. Consider Mitty's two purchases; how does Thurber use them to comment on Mitty's character?

4. Look again at the dream of "Mitty the famous surgeon." Do you recognize any of the medical terms? What is the point of having Mitty talk about "obstreosis" and "streptothricosis"?
5. What details or situations of the story are humorous? Should these same passages also be viewed as serious or sad? Why or why not?
6. Using the chart in the chapter's introduction (page 265) illustrating division and classification, diagram Thurber's presentation of Walter Mitty. Consider: What are the "two" Walter Mittys? Next, what are the dominant characteristics of each one? Then, what are the specific details in the story that illustrate the characteristics?

Thinking Critically

1. Walter Mitty has particular problems with the modern marvel of his time: the car. If you were to update Thurber's story, how might you show Mitty's clumsiness or incompetence in the 1990s?
2. Can you relate to Mitty's feelings of incompetence? If so, in what situations? How do you try to cope with these situations? What advice would you give to Mitty?
3. Mitty has become our representative dreamer. When you dream about a different life, what do you imagine yourself doing or becoming? How does your dream life differ from your actual life? Is your dream world possibly attainable or wildly improbable as Mitty's is? What can you learn about yourself by analyzing your dreams?

MAKING CONNECTIONS

1. The writers in this chapter have examined many ways in which humans connect to one another. Sometimes the connections are good ones (using manners, serene ex-smokers); sometimes the connections are less than ideal (selecting the wrong team). What can you learn from these writers about human needs in relationships? What do we need to feel good? What missing needs lead to conflicts in human relationships?
2. Review the questions about advertising at the beginning of Chapter 4. Then think about what human needs are appealed to in the advertising of various products. How, for example, are perfumes (or cars) sold to us? To what specific needs do

perfume (or car) ads appeal? You may want to do some reading on this subject, either in articles on advertising or in psychology texts, to review a list of basic human needs.

3. Which writer in this chapter offers the greatest insight into human connections? To answer this question, you will need to define *greatest*. The term could mean most profound, or most useful to readers, or most original or startling. You may want to classify the writers into these three categories—or others of your own—before deciding whom to select as having the greatest insight. Your initial analysis then becomes the basis for the defense of your choice.

TOPICS AND GUIDELINES FOR WRITING

---

1. Look over your Getting Started exercise—your classification of recent reading, movies, or television shows. Do you think your reading (or viewing) habits are fairly typical of someone in your situation? Or are your reading (or viewing) habits unusual, reflecting, perhaps, a hobby or special interest? If you see some point—a thesis—that your classification of reading (or viewing) can support, then you have an essay topic. (Remember that division and classification is a strategy, not a purpose in writing.)

2. Reflect on the parents, teachers, or coaches you have known. Can they be divided into categories based on their ways of using discipline? Select one group (parents, teachers, or coaches), and then classify that group according to their strategies for disciplining. Be sure to have a thesis and to illustrate each division of the group with examples from your experience. (You might want to give each type or category a label, as Zimring labels ex-smokers.)

3. Along the same lines as in topic 2, reflect on a particular group of people you know well—teachers, students, dates, workers in a particular field, athletes, and so on. Select one group and classify it according to the different types within that group. Try to make your classification complete. You are saying to your reader that these are the types of dates—or

teachers—that one could conceivably know. Make your divisions clear by labeling each type, and then define and illustrate each type. Be sure to have a thesis. One possible thesis could be your view of the best and worst types in the group you are writing about.

4. Watch (and perhaps tape so that you can review) at least six evenings of the ABC, NBC, or CBS evening news. Analyze the news programs according to the types of news stories and determine the amount of time given to each type of story, to commercials, and to "what's coming" segments. What have you learned? How much serious news do we get in a half hour? How much time (in minutes or seconds) is devoted to each type of story? Report the results of your study in an essay. Introduce your topic in paragraph 1, explain how you conducted your analysis in paragraph 2, and then report on the results of your study. Illustrate your categories with specific examples from the programs you watched. (For example, if one type of story that appears regularly is what can be called "national news," then what news stories from the shows you watched fit into that category? You might explain and illustrate the category with several stories about the president or Congress.)

5. What are some of the "games" that people play in their relationships with one another? That is, what strategies are used by people to get along or get ahead? In what situations are they likely to use particular games? If you have been a careful observer of human behavior or if you have watched people behaving in one particular situation, you potentially have an essay on this topic. Take one of two approaches. (1) Write on the games people play, classifying game playing as fully as you can. Explain and illustrate each game with examples. Remember that you can use hypothetical (made-up) examples as well as those drawn from your experience. (2) Write on the ways that people behave in a particular situation you know well. That is, how can people be classified by their behavior in a particular situation? Possible situations include the classroom, at the doctor's (or dentist's) office, in the library, at the beach, while driving, or at the movies. This second approach can be serious or humorous.

6. Think of one job category you know well (such as small business, farming, the medical profession, teaching, or banking). Then, within that one category, think of all the various workers and classify them according to Whitehead's new class divisions. Your point will be to show that not everyone in a job category is in the same class, although you may discover that not all categories are represented. For example, would anyone in teaching be placed in the underclass?

8

Using Definition

Understanding Ideas and Values

"Define your terms!" someone shouts in the middle of a heated debate. Although yelling may not be the best strategy, the advice is sound. Quite frequently the basis for a disagreement turns out to be a key word used differently by those whose discussion can now best be defined as an argument. We cannot let words mean whatever we want them to and still communicate, but, as you know from your study of vocabulary, many words have more than one dictionary definition (*denotation*). If we add to those meanings a word's *connotation* (associations and emotional suggestions), it is no wonder that we disagree over a word's meaning. To some, civil disobedience is illegal behavior; to others it is an example of patriotism. When we don't disagree over a word's generally understood meaning, we can still disagree over its connotation.

When to Use Definition

When do you need to define terms to avoid confusion? First, define words that most readers are not likely to know. If you need to use a technical term in an essay directed to nonspecialists, then you should provide a brief definition. Textbooks are, as you know, filled with definitions as the authors guide students through the vocabulary of a new subject. Second, define any word that you are using in a special way or in one of its special meanings. If you were to write: "We need to teach discrimination at an early age," you probably should add: "By discrimination I do not mean prejudice; I mean discernment, the ability to see differences." (*Sesame Street* has been teaching children this good kind of discrimination for years.)

A third occasion for using definition occurs when a writer chooses to develop a detailed explanation of the meaning of a complex, abstract, frequently debated, or emotion-laden term. Words such as *freedom, happiness, wisdom,* and *honesty* need to be reexamined, debated, and clarified in discussions that go beyond a dictionary's brief entry. We use the term *extended definition* to refer to the essay that has, as its primary purpose, the examination of a word's meaning. Sometimes the writer's purpose is to clarify our thinking: what does it mean to be *happy*? Sometimes a writer wants to reclaim a word from its current negative (or positive) connotations. This is what Robert Miller does when he argues that *discrimination* can have—and should be used with—a positive connotation.

How to Develop an Extended Definition

Extended definition describes a writing purpose. It does not suggest a particular organizational strategy. To develop an extended definition, you need to use some of the writing strategies that you have already been practicing. Suppose three Martians landed in your backyard, saw your Burmese cat, and asked, "What is that?" They are curious to know more than just the name of your pet. You could begin to answer their question with a dictionary-styled definition: a cat is a domesticated mammal (placing the object in a class) with retractable claws (distinguishing it from other members of the class—such as dogs). Your Martian friends, possibly interested in taking some cats home, want more information, so you continue with *descriptive details:* soft fur, usually long tails, padded feet, agile climbers (onto furniture, trees, and rooftops), rumbling sounds when contented. Developing your definition further, you can *contrast* cats with dogs: cats are more independent, can be trained to a box, will clean themselves. You can continue by providing *examples:* there are Siamese cats, Persian cats, tabby cats, and so on.

"This is all very interesting," the Martians respond, "but what do cats do, what are cats for?" You answer by explaining *use* or *function:* cats are pets, friends and companions, fun to play with and cuddle. Some people have even worshipped cats as gods, you add, providing *history.* A variation of providing history is to explain *word origin* or *etymology*. Often we get clues about a word's meaning by studying its origin and the changes in meaning over time. This information can be found in dictionaries that specialize in etymology, the *Oxford English Dictionary (OED)*, for example. (Your library will have the *OED*, probably both in a print format and online.)

The previous two paragraphs list and illustrate a number of strategies for developing an extended definition:

descriptive details   comparison/contrast
examples   use or function
etymology

To write a definition essay, you need to select those strategies that best suit your word and your particular purpose in defining that word. Remembering that effective writing is concrete writing, you want to include plenty of details and examples. Also give thought to the most effective organization of specifics so that the result is a unified essay, not a vocabulary exercise. Keep in mind that one of the most important strategies is contrast, for your purpose in defining is to discriminate, to explain subtle differences among words. (For example, what is the difference between wisdom and knowledge? Can one be wise without having knowledge? Or, how do self-esteem and self-respect differ? Is one better than the other?) Keep in mind that one kind of contrast, the metaphor, is especially useful because metaphors help make the abstract concrete. The Getting Started exercise below shows you how one writer used metaphors to define the concept *democracy*.

Getting Started: Reflections on E. B. White's Ideas of Democracy

E. B. White, author of "Education" (see pp. 130–34), once defined democracy largely through a series of metaphors. Three of his metaphors are

1. Democracy is "the line that forms on the right"
2. Democracy is "the hole in the stuffed shirt through which the sawdust slowly trickles"
3. Democracy is "the score at the beginning of the ninth"

First, analyze each metaphor. For each one, explain what the concrete situation is to which democracy is being compared. Ask yourself, how is that situation democratic? That is, what is White saying about democracy through the comparison? Then select the metaphor you like best and expand the idea that it suggests into a paragraph of your own on democracy. Try to include at least one metaphor of your own in your paragraph.

"On Friendship"

MARGARET MEAD AND RHODA METRAUX

Margaret Mead (1901–1978) may be the most famous anthropologist of our time. She revolutionized the field with the publication of her field work: *Coming of Age in Samoa* and *Growing Up in New Guinea*. Curator at the American Museum of Natural History and adjunct professor at Columbia University for many years, in later life, Mead wrote and spoke often on issues in modern culture. Rhoda Metraux (b. 1914), also an anthropologist attached to the American Museum in New York City and coauthor with Mead of *Themes in French Culture*, did her field work in several Caribbean and South American countries. Mead and Metraux wrote a series of articles for *Redbook* magazine that were collected in *A Way of Seeing* in 1970. Their definition of friendship, from the *Redbook* series, reveals the cross-cultural approach of anthropology.

1   Few Americans stay put for a lifetime. We move from town to city to suburb, from high school to college in a different state, from a job in one region to a better job elsewhere, from the home where we raise our children to the home where we plan to live in retirement. With each move we are forever making new friends, who become part of our new life at that time.

2   For many of us the summer is a special time for forming new friendships. Today millions of Americans vacation abroad, and they go not only to see new sights but also—in those places where they do not feel too strange—with the hope of meeting new people. No one really expects a vacation trip to produce a close friend. But surely the beginning of a friendship is possible? Surely in every country people value friendship?

They do. The difficulty when strangers from two countries 3
meet is not a lack of appreciation of friendship, but different expectations about what constitutes friendship and how it comes
into being. In those European countries that Americans are
most likely to visit, friendship is quite sharply distinguished
from other, more casual relations, and is differently related to
family life. For a Frenchman, a German or an Englishman
friendship is usually more particularized and carries a heavier
burden of commitment.

But as we use the word, "friend" can be applied to a wide 4
range of relationships—to someone one has known for a few
weeks in a new place, to a close business associate, to a childhood playmate, to a man or woman, to a trusted confidant.
There are real differences among these relations for Americans—a friendship may be superficial, casual, situational or
deep and enduring. But to a European, who sees only our surface behavior, the differences are not clear.

As they see it, people known and accepted temporarily, ca- 5
sually, flow in and out of Americans' homes with little ceremony and often with little personal commitment. They may be
parents of the children's friends, house guests of neighbors,
members of a committee, business associates from another
town or even another country. Coming as a guest into an American home, the European visitor finds no visible landmarks.
The atmosphere is relaxed. Most people, old and young, are
called by first names.

Who, then, is a friend? 6

Even simple translation from one language to another is dif- 7
ficult. "You see," a Frenchman explains, "if I were to say to you
in France, 'This is my good friend,' that person would not be
as close to me as someone about whom I said only, 'This is my
friend.' Anyone about whom I have to say *more* is really less."

In France, as in many European countries, friends generally 8
are of the same sex, and friendship is seen as basically a relationship between men. Frenchwomen laugh at the idea that
"women can't be friends," but they also admit sometimes that
for women "it's a different thing." And many French people
doubt the possibility of a friendship between a man and a
woman. There is also the kind of relationship within a group—
men and women who have worked together for a long time,
who may be very close, sharing great loyalty and warmth of

feeling. They may call one another *copains*—a word that in English becomes "friends" but has more the feeling of "pals" or "buddies." In French eyes this is not friendship, although two members of such a group may well be friends.

9   For the French, friendship is a one-to-one relationship that demands a keen awareness of the other person's intellect, temperament and particular interests. A friend is someone who draws out your own best qualities, with whom you sparkle and become more of whatever the friendship draws upon. Your political philosophy assumes more depth, appreciation of a play becomes sharper, taste in food or wine is accentuated, enjoyment of a sport is intensified.

10   And French friendships are compartmentalized. A man may play chess with a friend for thirty years without knowing his political opinion, or he may talk politics with him for as long a time without knowing about his personal life. Different friends fill different niches in each person's life. These friendships are not made part of family life. A friend is not expected to spend evenings being nice to children or courteous to a deaf grandmother. These duties, also serious and enjoined, are primarily for relatives. Men who are friends may meet in a café. Intellectual friends may meet in larger groups for evenings of conversation. Working people may meet in the little *bistro* where they drink and talk, far from the family. Marriage does not affect such friendships; wives do not have to be taken into account.

11   In the past in France, friendships of this kind seldom were open to any but intellectual women. Since most women's lives centered on their homes, their warmest relations with other women often went back to their girlhood. The special relationship of friendship is based on what the French value most—on the mind, on compatibility of outlook, on vivid awareness of some chosen area of life.

12   Friendship heightens the sense of each person's individuality. Other relationships commanding as great loyalty and devotion have a different meaning. In World War II the first resistance groups formed in Paris were built on the foundation of *les copains*. But significantly, as time went on these little groups, whose lives rested in one another's hands, called themselves "families." Where each had a total responsibility for all, it was kinship ties that provided the model. And even today

such ties, crossing every line of class and personal interest, remain binding on the survivors of these small, secret bands.

In Germany, in contrast with France, friendship is much 13 more articulately a matter of feeling. Adolescents, boys and girls, form deeply sentimental attachments, walk and talk together—not so much to polish their wits as to share their hopes and fears and dreams, to form a common front against the world of schools and family and to join in a kind of mutual discovery of each other's and their own inner life. Within the family, the closest relationship over a lifetime is between brothers and sisters. Outside the family, men and women find in their closest friends of the same sex the devotion of a sister, the loyalty of a brother. Appropriately, in Germany friends usually are brought into the family. Children call their father's and their mother's friends "uncle" and "aunt." Between French friends, who have chosen each other for the congeniality of their point of view, lively disagreement and sharpness of argument are the breath of life. But for Germans, whose friendships are based on mutuality of feeling, deep disagreement on any subject that matters to both is regarded as a tragedy. Like ties of kinship, ties of friendship are meant to be irrevocably binding. Young Germans who come to the United States have a great difficulty in establishing such friendships with Americans. We view friendship more tentatively, subject to changes in intensity as people move, change their jobs, marry, or discover new interests.

English friendships follow still a different pattern. Their 14 basis is shared activity. Activities at different stages of life may be of very different kinds—discovering a common interest in school, serving together in the armed forces, taking part in a foreign mission, staying in the same country house during a crisis. In the midst of the activity, whatever it may be, people fall into step—sometimes two men or two women, sometimes two couples, sometimes three people—and find that they walk or play a game or tell stories or serve on a tiresome and exacting committee with the same easy anticipation of what each will do day by day or in some critical situation. Americans who have made English friends comment that, even years later, "you can take up just where you left off." Meeting after a long interval, friends are like a couple who begin to dance again when the orchestra strikes up after a pause. English friendships are formed outside the family circle, but they are not, as in Germany, contrapuntal to the family nor are they, as in France, separated from the family. And a break in an English friendship comes not necessarily as a result of some irreconcilable difference of viewpoint or feeling but instead as a result of misjudgment, where one friend seriously misjudges how the other will think or feel or act, so that suddenly they are out of step.

15   What, then, is friendship? Looking at these different styles, including our own, each of which is related to a whole way of life, are there common elements? There is the recognition that friendship, in contrast with kinship, invokes freedom of choice. A friend is someone who chooses and is chosen. Related to this is the sense each friend gives the other of being a special individual, on whatever grounds this recognition is based. And between friends there is inevitably a kind of equality of give and take. These similarities make the bridge between societies possible, and the American's characteristic openness to different styles of relationships makes it possible for him to find new friends abroad with whom he feels at home.

Expanding Vocabulary

Mead and Metraux do not use complex terms from the social sciences, but they do use words that frequently appear in discussions of human relationships. Thus the following words are ones you want to know and use. Study their use in the essay, look up their definitions if necessary, and then use eight of the words in separate sentences of your own.

particularized (3)	mutuality (13)
commitment (3)	irrevocably (13)
confidant (4)	exacting (14)
superficial (4)	kinship (12)
landmarks (5)	articulately (13)
accentuated (9)	congeniality (13)
compartmentalized (10)	contrapuntal (14)
niches (10)	invokes (15)
enjoined (10)	

Understanding Content

1. How do Americans use the word *friend*?
2. Why do American friendships confuse many Europeans?
3. In general, how do the friendships of French, German, and English people differ from many American friendships?

4. What are the specific characteristics of friendship for the French? What sort of friendship do they think unlikely? What other term do the French use for people whom they would not consider close friends?
5. How do friendships often differ for women and men in France?
6. What lies at the core of friendships for Germans? How are friendships related to families? What can destroy a German friendship?
7. What is the basis for English friendships? What image best characterizes English friendships? How does this make possible a renewal of friendship after a time? What will lead to a break in friendships among the English?
8. After examining American and some European concepts of friendship, what do the authors conclude about the characteristics of friendship that extend over cultural differences?

Drawing Inferences about Thesis and Purpose

1. What is the authors' primary purpose in writing? Does their discussion of cultural differences play a major or supporting role in the essay? Do the authors make any judgments about friendships in the four countries?
2. What is their thesis? Is it stated or implied?

Analyzing Strategies and Style

1. Analyze the essay's organization. What paragraphs compose the introduction? The body of the essay? The conclusion?
2. What question indicates the shift from introduction to body? From body to conclusion?
3. Look at the use of transitions. What phrases guide readers through the paragraphs on French friendships? How is the shift to German friendship indicated? How is the shift to English friendship indicated?
4. Examine the authors' lengthy introduction. How do paragraphs 1 and 2 provide an attention-getter? How does the attention-getter lead into the authors' cross-cultural approach?
5. What is the authors' primary technique for achieving paragraph coherence? Look especially at paragraphs 8, 13, and 15.

Thinking Critically

1. Do you think that the authors accurately describe American attitudes toward friendship? Why or why not?
2. Had it occurred to you that friendship might be understood somewhat differently in different cultures? Does it make sense? Do you know of other lifestyle differences between Americans and the

French, Germans, English, or those of another culture? If so, be prepared to discuss these differences in class.

3. Do you think American friendships are significantly different from those described in France, Germany, or England? Do you have some friends who match the descriptions of those in France, Germany, or England?

4. Is at least part of the difference a carelessness with words on the part of Americans? That is, do we use the word *friend* to refer to relationships that could be more accurately described by a different word? What are some other words that we could use? Should we use these more often than we do? Why or why not?

5. Do you agree with the key definition of friendship offered in the essay's final paragraph? If not, why not? Are there points you would add? If so, what?

"Is Everybody Happy?"

JOHN CIARDI

A graduate of Tufts and the University of Michigan, John Ciardi (1916–1986) was a lecturer, critic, and, primarily, a poet. Ciardi had many collections of poetry published, including some delightful poems for children. His major critical study is *On Poetry and the Poetic Process* (1971). Ciardi was also for many years poetry editor of *Saturday Review*. In the following essay, from *Saturday Review* (May 14, 1964), Ciardi defines happiness as never perfectly attainable and requiring effort.

1   The right to pursue happiness is issued to Americans with their birth certificates, but no one seems quite sure which way it ran. It may be we are issued a hunting license but offered no game. Jonathan Swift[1] seemed to think so when he attacked the idea of happiness as "the possession of being well-deceived," the felicity of being "a fool among knaves." For Swift saw society as Vanity Fair, the land of false goals.

2   It is, of course, un-American to think in terms of fools and knaves. We do, however, seem to be dedicated to the idea of

---

[1]Irish-born English clergyman and satiric writer, 1667–1745.—Ed.

buying our way to happiness. We shall all have made it to Heaven when we possess enough.

And at the same time the forces of American commercialism 3 are hugely dedicated to making us deliberately unhappy. Advertising is one of our major industries, and advertising exists not to satisfy desires but to create them—and to create them faster than any man's budget can satisfy them. For that matter, our whole economy is based on a dedicated insatiability. We are taught that to possess is to be happy, and then we are made to want. We are even told it is our duty to want. It was only a few years ago, to cite a single example, that car dealers across the country were flying banners that read "You Auto Buy Now." They were calling upon Americans, as an act approaching patriotism, to buy at once, with money they did not have, automobiles they did not really need, and which they would be required to grow tired of by the time next year's models were released.

Or look at any of the women's magazines. There, as Bernard 4 DeVoto[2] once pointed out, advertising begins as poetry in the front pages and ends as pharmacopoeia and therapy in the back pages. The poetry of the front matter is the dream of perfect beauty. This is the baby skin that must be hers. These, the flawless teeth. This, the perfumed breath she must exhale. This, the sixteen-year-old figure she must display at forty, at fifty, at sixty, and forever.

Once past the vaguely uplifting fiction and feature articles, 5 the reader finds the other face of the dream in the back matter. This is the harness into which Mother must strap herself in order to display that perfect figure. These, the chin straps she must sleep in. This is the salve that restores all, this is her laxative, these are the tablets that melt away fat, these are the hormones of perpetual youth, these are the stockings that hide varicose veins.

Obviously no half-sane person can be completely persuaded 6 either by such poetry or by such pharmacopoeia and orthopedics. Yet someone is obviously trying to buy the dream as offered and spending billions every year in the attempt. Clearly the happiness-market is not running out of customers, but what is it trying to buy?

[2]American novelist and critic, 1897–1955.—Ed.

7   The idea "happiness," to be sure, will not sit still for easy definition: the best one can do is try to set some extremes to the idea and then work in toward the middle. To think of happiness as acquisitive and competitive will do to set the materialistic extreme. To think of it as the idea one senses in, say, a holy man of India will do to set the spiritual extreme. That holy man's idea of happiness is in needing nothing from outside himself. In wanting nothing, he lacks nothing. He sits immobile, rapt in contemplation, free even of his own body. Or nearly free of it. If devout admirers bring him food he eats it; if not, he starves indifferently. Why be concerned? What is physical is an illusion to him. Contemplation is his joy and he achieves it through a fantastically demanding discipline, the accomplishment of which is itself a joy within him.

8   Is he a happy man? Perhaps his happiness is only another sort of illusion. But who can take it from him? And who will dare say it is more illusory than happiness on the installment plan?

9   But, perhaps because I am Western, I doubt such catatonic happiness, as I doubt the dreams of the happiness-market. What is certain is that his way of happiness would be torture to almost any Western man. Yet these extremes will still serve to frame the area within which all of us must find some sort of balance. Thoreau[3]—a creature of both Eastern and Western thought—had his own firm sense of that balance. His aim was to save on the low levels in order to spend on the high.

10   Possession for its own sake or in competition with the rest of the neighborhood would have been Thoreau's idea of the low levels. The active discipline of heightening one's perception of what is enduring in nature would have been his idea of the high. What he saved from the low was time and effort he could spend on the high. Thoreau certainly disapproved of starvation, but he would put into feeding himself only as much effort as would keep him functioning for more important efforts.

11   Effort is the gist of it. There is no happiness except as we take on life-engaging difficulties. Short of the impossible, as Yeats[4]

[3]American author and naturalist, 1817–62.—Ed.
[4]Irish essayist, dramatist, and poet, 1865–1939.—Ed.

put it, the satisfactions we get from a lifetime depend on how high we choose our difficulties. Robert Frost[5] was thinking in something like the same terms when he spoke of "The pleasure of taking pains." The mortal flaw in the advertised version of happiness is in the fact that it purports to be effortless.

We demand difficulty even in our games. We demand it be- 12 cause without difficulty there can be no game. A game is a way of making something hard for the fun of it. The rules of the game are an arbitrary imposition of difficulty. When the spoil-sport ruins the fun, he always does so by refusing to play by the rules. It is easier to win at chess if you are free, at your pleasure, to change the wholly arbitrary rules, but the fun is in winning within the rules. No difficulty, no fun.

The buyers and sellers at the happiness-market seem too 13 often to have lost their sense of pleasure of difficulty. Heaven knows what they are playing, but it seems a dull game. And the Indian holy man seems dull to us, I suppose, because he seems to be refusing to play anything at all. The Western weakness may be in the illusion that happiness can be bought. Perhaps the Eastern weakness is in the idea that there is such a thing as perfect (and therefore static) happiness.

Happiness is never more than partial. There are no pure 14 states of mankind. Whatever else happiness may be, it is neither in having nor in being, but in becoming. What the Founding Fathers declared for us as an inherent right, we should do well to remember, was not happiness but the *pursuit* of happiness. What they might have underlined, could they have foreseen the happiness-market, is the cardinal fact that happiness is in the pursuit itself, in the meaningful pursuit of what is life-engaging and life-revealing, which is to say, in the idea of *becoming*. A nation is not measured by what it possesses or wants to possess, but by what it wants to become.

By all means let the happiness-market sell us minor satis- 15 factions and even minor follies so long as we keep them in scale and buy them out of spiritual change. I am no customer for either puritanism or asceticism. But drop any real spiritual capital at those bazaars, and what you come home to will be your own poorhouse.

[5]U.S. poet, 1874–1963.—Ed.

Expanding Vocabulary

Match each word in column A with its definition in column B. When in doubt, first find the word in the essay and look for context clues to aid your understanding of the word's meaning. Then, if necessary, use your dictionary to complete the matching exercise.

Column A	*Column B*
insatiability (3)	ointment that soothes or heals
pharmacopoeia (4)	beliefs of Puritans who regarded
therapy (4)	pleasure as sinful
salve (5)	medical specialty dealing with injuries
varicose (5)	to the skeleton
orthopedics (6)	in a stupor, with rigid body
acquisitive (7)	stock of drugs
catatonic (9)	professes to be
purports (11)	treatment of illness
inherent (14)	intrinsic, essential characteristic
puritanism (15)	belief in life of austerity
asceticism (15)	eager to possess, grasping
	abnormally swollen or knotted
	state of not being satisfied

Understanding Content

1. Did Jonathan Swift believe that real happiness is possible? How would Swift have described people who thought they were happy?
2. What seems to be the American concept of happiness? What role does advertising play in shaping that happiness?
3. What are the two extremes of happiness? What are Ciardi's examples of each extreme?
4. Why does Ciardi reject both extremes?
5. How do the extremes help to define happiness? What must we find to begin to achieve happiness?
6. What else is essential to happiness? What role does this ingredient play in our games? Why is the advertised version of happiness flawed? Why is the Eastern version flawed?
7. Ciardi says that "happiness is never more than partial." What is another characteristic of happiness?

Drawing Inferences about Thesis and Purpose

1. What are the ingredients for happiness that Ciardi presents? State, in your own words, the key elements of his definition.

Analyzing Strategies and Style

1. In developing his definition, Ciardi refers to five writers. What do these references tell you about the author? What do they suggest about Ciardi's anticipated audience?
2. Examine Ciardi's discussion of American advertising in paragraphs 3 through 5. What is his attitude toward advertising? What elements of style (word choice, sentence structure, examples) in these paragraphs develop and make clear his attitude?
3. Ciardi begins and ends his essay with metaphors. Explain the metaphor in his first two sentences and the metaphor in his last two sentences. What points about happiness does each metaphor suggest?
4. List all the strategies that Ciardi uses to develop his definition; then give an example of each one.

Thinking Critically

1. Ciardi thinks that happiness is a difficult term to define. Do you agree? Would you agree that it is the sort of concept that we think we understand until we are pressed to define it?
2. Ciardi asserts that "there is no happiness except as we take on life-engaging difficulties." Do you agree? Why or why not?
3. Do you agree with Ciardi's definition of happiness? If not, what would you add? What would you change?
4. Ciardi does not think that happiness can be found in "getting the most toys," to use a modern expression. What is the relationship between money and happiness? Can some money help? Does having money make happiness more difficult to obtain? Be prepared to explain and defend your views.

"Entropy"

K. C. COLE

K. C. Cole (b. 1946), a graduate of Barnard College, is a journalist and freelance writer. She began her writing career focusing on Eastern European affairs but is best known for her writing about science and health issues. She has written several books about scientific subjects as a result of her work with Exploratorium, a San Francisco science museum, including *Vision: In the*

Eye of the Beholder (1978) and *Order in the Universe* (1982). Currently, Cole writes a regular column for *Discover* magazine. Her ability to make scientific concepts both clear and interesting for nonspecialists is evident in the following article, which appeared in the *New York Times* in 1982.

1   It was about two months ago when I realized that entropy was getting the better of me. On the same day my car broke down (again), my refrigerator conked out and I learned that I needed root-canal work in my right rear tooth. The windows in the bedroom were still leaking every time it rained and my son's baby sitter was still failing to show up every time I really needed her. My hair was turning gray and my typewriter was wearing out. The house needed paint and I needed glasses. My son's sneakers were developing holes and I was developing a deep sense of futility.

2   After all, what was the point of spending half of Saturday at the Laundromat if the clothes were dirty all over again the following Friday?

3   Disorder, alas, is the natural order of things in the universe. There is even a precise measure of the amount of disorder, called entropy. Unlike almost every other physical property (motion, gravity, energy), entropy does not work both ways. It can only increase. Once it's created it can never be destroyed. The road to disorder is a oneway street.

4   Because of its unnerving irreversibility, entropy has been called the arrow of time. We all understand this instinctively. Children's rooms, left on their own, tend to get messy, not neat. Wood rots, metal rusts, people wrinkle and flowers wither. Even mountains wear down; even the nuclei of atoms decay. In the city we see entropy in the rundown subways and worn-out sidewalks and torn-down buildings, in the increasing disorder of our lives. We know, without asking, what is old. If we were suddenly to see the paint jump back on an old building, we would know that something was wrong. If we saw an egg unscramble itself and jump back into its shell, we would laugh in the same way we laugh at a movie run backward.

5   Entropy is no laughing matter, however, because with every increase in entropy energy is wasted and opportunity is lost. Water flowing down a mountainside can be made to do some

useful work on its way. But once all the water is at the same level it can work no more. That is entropy. When my refrigerator was working, it kept all the cold air ordered in one part of the kitchen and warmer air in another. Once it broke down the warm and cold mixed into a lukewarm mess that allowed my butter to melt, my milk to rot and my frozen vegetables to decay.

Of course the energy is not really lost, but it has diffused and 6 dissipated into a chaotic caldron of randomness that can do us no possible good. Entropy is chaos. It is loss of purpose.

People are often upset by the entropy they seem to see in the 7 haphazardness of their own lives. Buffeted about like so many molecules in my tepid kitchen, they feel that they have lost their sense of direction, that they are wasting youth and opportunity at every turn. It is easy to see entropy in marriages, when the partners are too preoccupied to patch small things up, almost guaranteeing that they will fall apart. There is much entropy in the state of our country, in the relationships between nations—lost opportunities to stop the avalanche of disorders that seems ready to swallow us all.

Entropy is not inevitable everywhere, however. Crystals and 8 snowflakes and galaxies are islands of incredibly ordered beauty in the midst of random events. If it was not for exceptions to entropy, the sky would be black and we would be able to see where the stars spend their days; it is only because air molecules in the atmosphere cluster in ordered groups that the sky is blue.

The most profound exception to entropy is the creation of 9 life. A seed soaks up some soil and some carbon and some sunshine and some water and arranges it into a rose. A seed in the womb takes some oxygen and pizza and milk and transforms it into a baby.

The catch is that it takes a lot of energy to produce a baby. It 10 also takes energy to make a tree. The road to disorder is all downhill but the road to creation takes work. Though combating entropy is possible, it also has its price. That's why it seems so hard to get ourselves together, so easy to let ourselves fall apart.

Worse, creating order in one corner of the universe always 11 creates more disorder somewhere else. We create ordered energy from oil and coal at the price of the entropy of smog.

12   I recently took up playing the flute again after an absence of several months. As the uneven vibrations screeched through the house, my son covered his ears and said, "Mom, what's wrong with your flute?" Nothing was wrong with my flute, of course. It was my ability to play it that had atrophied, or entropied, as the case may be. The only way to stop that process was to practice every day, and sure enough my tone improved, though only at the price of constant work. Like anything else, abilities deteriorate when we stop applying our energies to them.

13   That's why entropy is depressing. It seems as if just breaking even is an uphill fight. There's a good reason that this should be so. The mechanics of entropy are a matter of chance. Take any ice-cold air molecule milling around my kitchen. The chances that it will wander in the direction of my refrigerator at any point are exactly 50–50. The chances that it will wander away from my refrigerator are also 50–50. But take billions of warm and cold molecules mixed together, and the chances that all the cold ones will wander toward the refrigerator and all the warm ones will wander away from it are virtually nil.

14   Entropy wins not because order is impossible but because there are always so many more paths toward disorder than toward order. There are so many more different ways to do a sloppy job than a good one, so many more ways to make a mess than to clean it up. The obstacles and accidents in our lives almost guarantee that constant collisions will bounce us on to random paths, get us off the track. Disorder is the path of least resistance, the easy but not the inevitable road.

15   Like so many others, I am distressed by the entropy I see around me today. I am afraid of the randomness of international events, of the lack of common purpose in the world; I am terrified that it will lead into the ultimate entropy of nuclear war. I am upset that I could not in the city where I live send my child to a public school; that people are unemployed and inflation is out of control; that tensions between the sexes and races seem to be increasing again; that relationships everywhere seem to be falling apart.

16   Social institutions—like atoms and stars—decay if energy is not added to keep them ordered. Friendships and families and

economies fall apart unless we constantly make an effort to keep them working and well oiled. And far too few people, it seems to me, are willing to contribute to those efforts. Of course, the more complex things are, the harder it is. If there were only a dozen or so air molecules in my kitchen, it would be likely—if I waited a year or so—that at some point the six coldest ones would congregate inside the freezer. But the more factors in the equation—the more players in the game—the less likely it is that their paths will coincide in an orderly way. The more pieces in the puzzle, the harder it is to put back together once order is disturbed. "Irreversibility," said a physicist, "is the price we pay for complexity."

Expanding Vocabulary

Examine the following words in their contexts in the essay and then write a brief definition or synonym for each one. (Do not use a dictionary; try to guess the word's meanings from its context.)

conked (1)
futility (1)
nuclei (4)
diffused (6)
dissipated (6)

caldron (6)
buffeted (7)
tepid (7)
atrophied (12)

Understanding Content

1. How does entropy differ from all other physical properties?
2. When entropy increases, what is wasted?
3. Since energy cannot be lost, what is a better way to describe what happens to it?
4. As we observe entropy in our lives, how does it make us feel?
5. What are some examples of exceptions to entropy? What is the most profound exception?
6. Which is harder to create: order or disorder? Which is the path of least resistance?
7. Does complexity make order or entropy easier? Why?

Drawing Inferences about Thesis and Purpose

1. According to Cole, what are the chief characteristics of entropy? Write a brief definition in your own words.

Analyzing Strategies and Style

1. What opening strategy does Cole use? What author voice or tone does her opening set for the rest of the essay?
2. Examine Cole's examples. What kind of range do they provide for the reader? What does Cole accomplish by using her range of examples?
3. When Cole writes about "the arrow of time" and a "caldron of randomness," what writing strategy is she using? Explain each expression.
4. Find some examples of Cole's humor. In what paragraphs does she seem particularly serious? What is her subject when she is most serious?
5. List the various strategies the author uses to define entropy.

Thinking Critically

1. Is Cole's definition of entropy your first introduction to the term? If so, have you found her definition clear and helpful? If you are familiar with the term, would you judge Cole's definition to be helpful to nonspecialist readers? Why or why not?
2. Cole seeks not just to give a "scientific" definition but to explain how the principle of *entropy* connects to our lives. What, for you, is the most telling example that makes the connection to ordinary lives? Why?
3. Select one of the other physical properties mentioned in paragraph 3, read about it in a science reference book, and then think of some examples from ordinary life that would illustrate the property.
4. Cole relates entropy not only to ordinary life but also to social institutions (see paragraph 16). There she asserts that too few of us are willing to make the effort to work at maintaining order. Do you agree with her assessment? Do you agree that this is a problem? If not, why not? If so, what can be done to withstand entropy in friendships? In families? In economies?

"Discrimination Is a Virtue"

ROBERT KEITH MILLER

Holding a Ph.D. from Columbia University, Robert Keith Miller (b. 1949) is a professor of English at St. Thomas University. He has published scholarly articles and books on such writers as Mark Twain, Oscar Wilde, and Willa Cather and has written for popular magazines and newspapers as well. In the following essay, which appeared in *Newsweek*'s "My Turn" column in 1980, Miller seeks to rescue the word *discrimination* from its misuse in our time.

When I was a child, my grandmother used to tell me a story 1 about a king who had three daughters and decided to test their love. He asked each of them "How much do you love me?" The first replied that she loved him as much as all the diamonds and pearls in the world. The second said that she loved him more than life itself. The third replied "I love you as fresh meat loves salt."

This answer enraged the king; he was convinced that his 2 youngest daughter was making fun of him. So he banished her from his realm and left all of his property to her elder sisters.

As the story unfolded it became clear, even to a 6-year-old, 3 that the king had made a terrible mistake. The two older girls were hypocrites, and as soon as they had profited from their father's generosity, they began to treat him very badly. A wiser man would have realized that the youngest daughter was the truest. Without attempting to flatter, she had said, in effect, "We go together naturally; we are a perfect team."

Years later, when I came to read Shakespeare, I realized that 4 my grandmother's story was loosely based upon the story of King Lear, who put his daughters to a similar test and did not know how to judge the results. Attempting to save the king from the consequences of his foolishness, a loyal friend pleads, "Come sir, arise, away! I'll teach you differences." Unfortunately, the lesson comes too late. Because Lear could not tell the difference between true love and false, he loses his kingdom and eventually his life.

We have a word in English which means "the ability to tell 5 differences." That word is *discrimination*. But within the last twenty years, this word has been so frequently misused that an entire generation has grown up believing that "discrimination" means "racism." People are always proclaiming that "discrimination" is something that should be done away with. Should that ever happen, it would prove to be our undoing.

6   Discrimination means discernment; it means the ability to perceive the truth, to use good judgment and to profit accordingly. The *Oxford English Dictionary* traces this understanding of the word back to 1648 and demonstrates that, for the next 300 years, "discrimination" was a virtue, not a vice. Thus, when a character in a nineteenth-century novel makes a happy marriage, Dickens has another character remark, "It does credit to your discrimination that you should have found such a very excellent young woman."

7   Of course, "the ability to tell differences" assumes that differences exist, and this is unsettling for a culture obsessed with the notion of equality. The contemporary belief that discrimination is a vice stems from the compound "discriminate against." What we need to remember, however, is that some things deserve to be judged harshly: we should not leave our kingdoms to the selfish and the wicked.

8   Discrimination is wrong only when someone or something is discriminated against because of prejudice. But to use the word in this sense, as so many people do, is to destroy its true meaning. If you discriminate against something because of general preconceptions rather than particular insights, then you are not discriminating—bias has clouded the clarity of vision which discrimination demands.

9   One of the great ironies of American life is that we manage to discriminate in the practical decisions of daily life, but usually fail to discriminate when we make public policies. Most people are very discriminating when it comes to buying a car, for example, because they realize that cars have differences. Similarly, an increasing number of people have learned to discriminate in what they eat. Some foods are better than others—and indiscriminate eating can undermine one's health.

10   Yet in public affairs, good judgment is depressingly rare. In many areas which involve the common good, we see a failure to tell differences.

11   Consider, for example, some of the thinking behind modern education. On the one hand, there is a refreshing realization that there are differences among children, and some children—be they gifted or handicapped—require special education. On the other hand, we are politically unable to accept the consequences of this perception. The trend in recent years has been

to group together students of radically different ability. We call this process "mainstreaming," and it strikes me as a characteristically American response to the discovery of differences: we try to pretend that differences do not matter.

Similarly, we try to pretend that there is little difference be- 12 tween the sane and the insane. A fashionable line of argument has it that "everybody is a little mad" and that few mental patients deserve long-term hospitalization. As a consequence of such reasoning, thousands of seriously ill men and women have been evicted from their hospital beds and returned to what is euphemistically called "the community"—which often means being left to sleep on city streets, where confused and helpless people now live out of paper bags as the direct result of our refusal to discriminate.

Or to choose a final example from a different area: how 13 many recent elections reflect thoughtful consideration of the genuine differences among candidates? Benumbed by television commercials that market aspiring officeholders as if they were a new brand of toothpaste or hair spray, too many Americans vote with only a fuzzy understanding of the issues in question. Like Lear, we seem too eager to leave the responsibility of government to others and too ready to trust those who tell us whatever we want to hear.

So as we look around us, we should recognize that "discrim- 14 ination" is a virtue which we desperately need. We must try to avoid making unfair and arbitrary distinctions, but we must not go to the other extreme and pretend that there are no distinctions to be made. The ability to make intelligent judgments is essential both for the success of one's personal life and for the functioning of society as a whole. Let us be open-minded by all means, but not so open-minded that our brains fall out.

Expanding Vocabulary

Examine the following words in their contexts in the essay and then write a brief definition or synonym for each one. (Do not use a dictionary; try to guess the word's meanings from its context.)

banished (2)	undermine (9)
realm (2)	evicted (12)
hypocrites (3)	euphemistically (12)

discernment (6)   benumbed (13)
preconceptions (8)

Understanding Content

1. What does *discrimination* mean, as Miller defines it?
2. Currently, how is the word being used? How does the current use of the word change its connotation? (See the Glossary, if necessary, for the definition of *connotation*.)
3. Why do Americans have trouble with discrimination as Miller would define it?
4. When is discrimination wrong? When it is wrong, what should it be called? What has actually happened to one's ability to discriminate?
5. Under what circumstances do people usually discriminate? In what area of life do we often fail to discriminate?

Drawing Inferences about Thesis and Purpose

1. What is Miller's purpose in defining *discrimination*? What point does he want to make about the word?
2. State Miller's thesis.

Analyzing Strategies and Style

1. What opening strategy does Miller use? How does it lead into his subject?
2. What are Miller's examples of public policy failures in discrimination? Are they effective examples, showing a range of public policy problems?
3. Examine Miller's closing paragraph. Is it effective in its balanced language? What makes the final sentence clever?

Thinking Critically

1. Is the definition of *discrimination* that Miller wants to highlight familiar to you, or do you know the word only as it means to show prejudice? Do you see how the two meanings could develop in the same word?
2. Do you agree with Miller that we are "benumbed by television commercials" and "vote with only a fuzzy understanding of the issues"? Have you voted with a good knowledge of the candidates and the issues? (Have you voted? If not, why not?)
3. Is the American focus on equality keeping us from learning discrimination, from learning to discern differences? Explain.
4. Should differences in ability be ignored in education in favor of "mainstreaming"? Why or why not?

"Personal Worth"

E. J. DIONNE, JR.

A syndicated columnist for the *Washington Post* and Senior Fellow at Brookings Institution, E. J. Dionne, Jr., (b. 1952) holds degrees from Harvard and Oxford Universities. He is the author of several books, including *Why Americans Hate Politics* (1981) and *They Only Look Dead* (1996). "Personal Worth" appeared in the *Post* Sunday Magazine on October 18, 1998. In this column Dionne both defines and contrasts self-esteem and self-respect.

1   Which would you prefer kids to learn: **self-respect or self-esteem?**

2   I'd make a case that this is not an interesting question only about words but also about philosophy—and perhaps even psychology. The evidence is that self-esteem now far outstrips self-respect in the public discourse—by a huge margin, if my Internet and newspaper searches are any indication. But is self-esteem's apparent victory over self-respect in the conceptual wars a good thing? I'd claim that it's not, though I'd welcome arguments to the contrary.

3   The word "esteem" does have a noble sound to it, and in the dictionaries, its meaning overlaps with that of the word "respect." The *New College Edition of the American Heritage Dictionary*, for instance, defines esteem as "to regard as of a high order; think of with respect; prize." Respect, in turn, is defined as "to feel or show esteem for; to honor."

4   But Ronald Thiemann, dean of Harvard University's Divinity School, notes that the ancient meanings of the two words suggest a difference in emphasis.

5   In the old "cultures of honor," he said, esteem usually attached to rank. "The king deserved esteem no matter what he did," Dr. Thiemann said. The implication for self-esteem is that "I deserve esteem no matter what I do." Respect on the other hand, was earned by behaving in a certain way, and, he argues, also by accepting limits on one's behavior. Nobody out there needs to be convinced of how big the idea of self-esteem has become. But if you surf the Net, you might be astonished

nonetheless at the range of books, activities and organizations that promise to help you raise your self-esteem—or somebody else's.

6   This being America, there's a National Association for Self-Esteem whose purpose is "to fully integrate self-esteem into the fabric of American society so that every individual, no matter what their age or background, experiences personal worth and happiness." There's the Self-Esteem Shop Online (*www. selfesteemshop.com*), which offers titles such as *Parents as Therapeutic Partners, 101 Ways to Be a Special Mom* and *Cutting Loose: Why Women Who End Their Marriages Do So Well.*

7   Self-esteem has entered the vocabulary in part as a response by members of groups that have suffered oppression or discrimination to what they see as society's effort to keep them down, and diminish their sense of self-worth. To the extent that the self-esteem movement is about the insistence that all human beings are worthy of respect—from themselves and others—the movement can be seen as a positive force.

8   My crankiness on the relative merit of self-respect over self-esteem is rooted in something else—the arrogance that can go along with too much self-esteem. As Martha Minow, a Harvard law professor and author of *Not Only for Myself*, explains it, the first definition of esteem "is about ranking, and if you add the 'self' to esteem, it's how you rank yourself." High self-esteem, in other words, can mean ranking yourself above everybody else. That breeds arrogance. Respect, on the other hand, carries a notion of dignity in relationship to others. Can you ever have too much self-respect?

9   Elisabeth Lasch-Quinn, a historian at Syracuse University, points to another aspect of self-esteem—it reflects the triumph of our therapeutic era.

10   Therapy is aimed at making people "feel good, feel comfortable." That's why you want self-esteem. "But the drive for self-respect is completely opposite in every way," she says. "It means being uncomfortable because you're in struggle, trying to live up to a standard of excellence or remaining true to your most deeply held moral beliefs."

11   Following from this, there is a vigorous debate among educators over whether teaching self-esteem helps kids learn by making them believe they can and are personally worthy or

whether, on the contrary, the process of learning, performing tasks well and treating others decently must come prior to self-esteem (or, as I'd prefer, self-respect).

Lasch-Quinn suggests that if you want to trace the trajectory 12 of ideas in American education, you could contrast the 19th century's emphasis on "character building" with the late-20th-century focus on self-esteem.

Minow's interest in this subject was inspired by the much- 13 cited thought of the first-century sage Hillel: "If I am not for myself, who will be? If I am only for myself, who am I? If not now, when?" Of course we should have respect and, if you must, some esteem for ourselves. But in my gut, I fear that if we spend a few more decades promoting self-esteem, we might convince ourselves to forget that there's anyone of value out there—other than ourselves. "We can't have respect for ourselves if we're only for ourselves," Minow says. "We become egotistical selfish beasts." To feel that way would lower our self-esteem—and our self-respect, too.

Expanding Vocabulary

Examine the following words in their contexts in the essay and then write a brief definition or synonym for each one. Do not use a dictionary; try to guess the word's meaning from its context.

discourse (2)	crankiness (8)
conceptual (2)	arrogance (8)
astonished (5)	therapeutic (9)
diminish (7)	trajectory (12)

Understanding Content

1. Which word, *self-esteem* or *self-respect,* is most commonly used today?
2. What is the emphasis of the older meaning of *esteem?*
3. What is the emphasis of the older meaning of *respect?*
4. Why has the concept of self-esteem become so important in American society?
5. What, according to Dionne, is the danger in emphasizing self-esteem?
6. To what in our culture does Lasch-Quinn connect the emphasis on self-esteem?

Drawing Inferences about Thesis and Purpose

1. Dionne writes: "This being America, there's a National Association for Self-Esteem." Explain his meaning.
2. What is Dionne's purpose in writing? Does he have more than one purpose?
3. What is his thesis?

Analyzing Strategies and Style

1. Dionne begins with a question. How does he expect many readers to answer this question? What makes this an effective opening?
2. Dionne uses several sources to develop his definition. How do they aid his purpose?
3. Find specific ways that Dionne makes his preference for *respect* clear.

Thinking Critically

1. Is Dionne the first person in your experience to question the value of self-esteem? Are you surprised? Does his argument make sense to you? Why or why not?
2. Which needs to come first: a belief in one's worth or building self-respect through positive actions? Should educators have the role of building self-esteem, or should self-respect be viewed as what will come when students learn and get along with classmates? Explain your views.
3. Would you rather be esteemed or respected? Explain your position.

"Curiosity"

ALASTAIR REID

A Scotsman who prefers to live in Spain, Alastair Reid (b. 1926) is a poet, translator, essayist, writer of children's books, and lecturer. Holding a master's degree from Scotland's St. Andrews University, Reid has lectured at schools in England, Spain, and the United States. He has had several books of poems published, has translated much of the poetry of Latin American poet Pablo Neruda, and has been a staff writer for the *New Yorker* since 1959. "Curiosity" appeared first in the *New Yorker* and was then included in the collection *Weathering* (1959).

Curiosity

may have killed the cat. More likely,
the cat was just unlucky, or else curious
to see what death was like, having no cause
to go on licking paws, or fathering
litter on litter of kittens, predictably.   5

Nevertheless, to be curious
is dangerous enough. To distrust
what is always said, what seems,
to ask odd questions, interfere in dreams,
smell rats, leave home, have hunches,   10
does not endear cats to those doggy circles
where well-smelt baskets, suitable wives, good lunches
are the order of things, and where prevails
much wagging of incurious heads and tails.

Face it. Curiosity   15
will not cause us to die—
only lack of it will.
Never to want to see
the other side of the hill
or that improbable country   20
where living is an idyll
(although a probable hell)
would kill us all.
Only the curious
have if they live a tale   25
worth telling at all.
Dogs say cats love too much, are irresponsible,
are dangerous, marry too many wives,
desert their children, chill all dinner tables
with tales of their nine lives.   30

Well, they are lucky. Let them be
nine-lived and contradictory,
curious enough to change, prepared to pay
the cat-price, which is to die
and die again and again,   35

each time with no less pain.
A cat-minority of one
is all that can be counted on
to tell the truth; and what cats have to tell
on each return from hell   40
is this: that dying is what the living do,
that dying is what the loving do,
and that dead dogs are those who never know
that dying is what, to live, each has to do.

Understanding Content and Strategies

1. What is more likely than curiosity to have killed the cat?
2. Why is being curious "dangerous enough"?
3. What kind of people belong to "doggy circles"?
4. What do dogs say about cats? What traits do they ascribe to them? Are we to agree with the dogs' view of cats? How do you know?
5. What are the characteristics of the curious life? Given the rather negative-sounding elements of this life, why should we be like the curious cat rather than the incurious dog?
6. Notice that the title runs into the first line. How does Reid's use of punctuation (to stop us) or no punctuation (to keep us reading) parallel what he is observing about curiosity or the lack of it?
7. What is the term for poems that have the pattern—or lack of pattern—that you find in "Curiosity"?

Drawing Inferences about Theme

1. When the poet writes that "dying is what, to live, each has to do," what does he mean? The statement seems contradictory. What is the term for this strategy for gaining emphasis? For the statement to make sense, how do you have to take the word *dying?*
2. State the poem's meaning or theme. What does Reid want us to understand about the role of curiosity in life?

Thinking Critically

1. Do you find the use of cats and dogs an effective one? For the most part, do the personalities of cats and dogs seem to fit the distinction Reid wants to make?
2. Is curiosity an important trait? Why or why not? What are its virtues? What are its dangers?
3. Are most children more like cats or dogs? If they are like cats, then why are some adults so incurious? If they are like dogs, what are some ways they can be encouraged to develop curiosity?

STUDENT ESSAY: DEFINITION

"EVERYDAY HEROES"
Kiki Sorovacu

Arachne was a skillful weaver from Lydia, according to Greek mythology. Confident of her skill, the daring maiden challenged the goddess Athena to a weaving contest. When the contest ended in a tie, Athena in her wrath destroyed Arachne's tapestry and turned her into a spider. Fearless Arachne, who had the courage to challenge the gods, spent the rest of her life weaving menial webs.

Attention-getting introduction

Arachne, like Rambo or John Wayne, brings the word hero to mind. The epitome of courage, heroes perform superhuman deeds, often putting their lives in jeopardy to save others. But there are other kinds of heroes, everyday heroes, who show "ordinary" courage.

Introduction connected to student's subject

Thesis

Every morning, your alarm clock goes off. To get up or not to get up; that is the question. Maybe you have a midterm in biology today. You didn't study. Maybe you have to give an oral presentation in class. You're deathly shy. Maybe today's the day to visit your grandmother in the hospital, where she is dying. Maybe today is Christmas. Maybe while everybody is celebrating love and brotherhood you are

Examples of situations requiring courage

visiting your parent's grave. In our age of freeways, high-rises, assignments, deadlines, competition, AIDS, drugs, disappearing ozone, and nuclear missiles, it takes courage to get up and face the world. Imagine waking up to find yourself still in the hospital after a third operation to remove a cancerous tumor. And what about the growing number of people stricken with AIDS? They must find the exceptional courage within themselves to face each new day, watching their bodies dwindle away, knowing their time is soon to come.

Standing up for what you believe in takes courage, especially when your beliefs are not widely held or are oppressed by a higher authority. No one will argue that it takes courage to introduce your "stone-age" father to your views on sex and marriage or, rather, sex but no marriage. You will probably be on restriction until you are eighteen. If you lived in a society where people who did not engage in homosexuality were considered deviant, would you stand up for the rights of heterosexuals and be shunned by society? Or would you put your beliefs on the back burner along with your pride and conform to society's ways?

Change takes courage. I don't mean changing the way you part your hair or the color of your lipstick. Although if you dyed your hair purple and wore only black, even lipstick, I would say you have courage to be seen in public, unless, of course, you live where purple and black are the "in" colors.

You have seen the movies before. A battered wife with two children finally finds the courage within herself to strike out on her own, leaving her abusive husband behind. Although daily life isn't so dramatic, I can name, and I'm sure you can, too, at least ten couples who aren't happy with their relationship, be it marriage or going steady. Bickering constantly, bringing out the worst in one another, making themselves number one rather than their partner, these people do not love each other. What they are getting out of the relationship is security. Sameness brings security. A family pet, for example, will come home from its roaming for food and shelter. Even the mistreated pet will come back because it achieves a security in belonging. A cat or dog cannot imagine a better life, but a human can. A cat or dog cannot have courage to move on from a bad situation;

Contrast between humans and animals to illustrate courage

a human can. People can bravely venture
into the unknown, into new experiences,
relying on themselves, or they can be a
grain of sand in the vast ocean of life,
passive to the endless tide of destiny.

Metaphor used to help define courage

Does it take courage to hunt? If the
deer all had guns it would. The man with
the eight-foot bear in his living room
boasts of his prowess and gloats with
pride as he tells his exaggerated tale
of the kill. The once mighty bear stands
rigidly in its fierce pose. It doesn't
look anything like the peaceable bear
frolicking in the forest when a bullet
from a nearby treetop pierced its brain.
Nevertheless, the hunter enjoys his feelings of false courage, his bravado. The
teenager recklessly zipping down the
freeway in and out of cars with seconds
to spare is no better than the hunter.
There is a thin but important line between bravery and stupidity, courage and
bravado.

Contrast between bravado and courage

Courage is too often thought of in
terms of great deeds and great people.
Martin Luther King, Jr., was a bold man
whose wisdom and determination inspired
millions of black citizens to demand
their rights without using force. An
American soldier going into hostile ter-

Conclusion: cleverly restates thesis by contrasting famous heroes with ordinary heroes

ritory to uphold democratic ideals is
brave. The astronauts on the Apollo mission who were the first to leave earth
and explore the unknown of space certainly had courage. But, what about you?
You got up this morning, didn't you?

MAKING CONNECTIONS

1. John Ciardi says that happiness is difficult to define—and to obtain. Is happiness possible without the ability to discriminate, as Robert Miller defines the term? How would each author answer this question? How would you answer the question?

2. Is happiness possible without curiosity? How would Ciardi and Alastair Reid each answer the question? How would Liane Ellison Norman (see Chapter 4) answer the question? How would you answer the question?

3. K. C. Cole asserts that we are unwilling to work hard enough to keep disorder from displacing order. E. J. Dionne suggests that we prefer self-esteem to self-respect because it is easier. Are we getting tired? Or lazy? As a group? Individually? Examine Cole's and Dionne's essays and then prepare your answer to these questions.

4. E. J. Dionne suggests that self-esteem is designed to make us feel good, but seeking self-respect requires effort and accomplishment. Would Ciardi embrace self-esteem or self-respect as a part of happiness? How do you know?

TOPICS AND GUIDELINES FOR WRITING

1. In this chapter you can find definitions of *friendship, happiness, entropy, intensity,* even *curiosity.* If you have disagreed at least in part with one of the definitions presented here,

write your own definition of that term. Include in your essay at least one reference to the writer with whom you disagree, discussing his or her views and contrasting them with your own. Make your purpose your own definition, but use the ideas with which you disagree as one way to develop your definition.

2. In an essay develop a definition of one of the terms below. Use at least three of the specific strategies for developing a definition discussed in the chapter's introduction. Try to make one of those strategies the metaphor, including several in your essay. And use contrast as one of your strategies, contrasting the word you select with its contrasting term in parentheses.

patriotism (chauvinism)	wisdom (knowledge)
courtesy (manners)	ghetto (neighborhood)
liberty (freedom)	hero (star)
community (subdivision)	gossip (conversation)

3. In "Curiosity," Alastair Reid plays paradoxically with the terms *living* and *dying*. In an essay, define either *work* or *play*, developing your definition in part by reflecting on the word's relationship with its apparent opposite. In what situations, under what conditions, can play become work? Or, in what situations, under what conditions, can work be play? We use these terms frequently to suggest opposite activities. In your definition of one of these words, show that there are some contexts in which its "opposite" is not really opposite.

4. Define a term that is currently used to label people with particular traits and values. Possibilities include: *nerd, yuppie, freak, jock, redneck, bimbo, wimp*. Reflect, before selecting this topic, on why you want to explain the meaning of the word you have chosen. One purpose might be to explain the term to someone from a different culture. Another purpose might be to defend people who are labeled negatively by one of these terms; that is, your goal is to show why the term should not have a negative connotation.

5. Select a word that you believe is currently misused. The word can be misused because it has taken on a negative (or

positive) connotation that it did not once have, or because it has changed meaning and has lost something in the change. A few suggestions include *awful, fabulous, exceptional* (in education), *awesome, propaganda*. Be sure to begin with a clear understanding of the word's definitions provided by a good dictionary. You might also want to consult a dictionary of word origins.

9

Using Causal Analysis

Examining Social and Political Issues

You may know the old—and very bad—joke that asks why the chicken crossed the road. When we give up and ask for the answer, the jokester, laughing merrily at trapping us in such silliness, says: "to get to the other side." The joke isn't in the answer but on us because we expect a more profound explanation of cause. Human beings characteristically ask why things happen. The four-year-old who asks her mother why there are stars in the sky may grow up to be the astrophysicist who continues, in a more sophisticated manner, to probe the same question.

When to Use Causal Analysis

We want to know what produced past events (why did the Roman Empire collapse?), what is causing current situations (why is there an increased fear of violence in our society?), and what will happen if we act in a particular way (will inflation be avoided if the Federal Reserve lowers interest rates?). Whether the questions are about the past, the present, or the future, we are seeking a causal explanation. We usually make a distinction between a study of *causes* (what produced A) and a study of *effects* (what has happened or will happen as a result of B), but actually the distinction is more one of wording than of approach or way of thinking. If, for example, we think that inflation can be avoided (effect) by raising interest rates (cause), we are saying that low interest can cause inflation. So, when we want to know why, we need to explore cause, whether we approach the "connection" from the causal end or the effects end.

How to Use Causal Analysis

In the study of causes and effects, we need to stress the key word *analysis*. In Chapter 6, you learned that process analysis answers the question *how* something is done or was accomplished by determining the steps, in proper time sequence, to completing the activity. When we examine cause, we also need to analyze the situation, both present and past, to make certain that we recognize all contributing elements and that we sort out the more important from the less important. Fortunately, there are some terms for distinguishing among different kinds of causes that can help us examine cause in a thoughtful and thorough way.

Thinking about Cause

First, events do not occur in a vacuum. There are *conditions* that surround an event, making the finding of only one cause unlikely. Suppose you have decided to become a veterinarian, and you want to understand why you have made that career choice. The conditions of your family life and upbringing probably affected your decision. You grew up with a dog that you loved and cared for; your parents tolerated all the frogs and wounded birds you brought home and taught you to value living things. Second, there are more specific *influences* that contribute to an event. Perhaps the family vet let you help when your dog needed shots or bandaging and by examples influenced your career plans.

In addition to conditions and influences, there are the more *immediate causes* that shape an event, leading up to the *precipitating cause*, the triggering event. In your choice to become a veterinarian, these events may include your good grades in and enjoyment of high school chemistry and biology, a recognition that you like working with your hands and that you want to be your own boss, and two summers of working at an animal hospital. In short, going off to college and having to declare a major did not cause you to choose veterinary medicine. The search for cause is a search for deeper, more fundamental answers than the college's requirement that you state a major field of study.

In our need, as humans, to have explanations for what happens, we can sometimes fool ourselves into thinking that we understand events, and we can be comforted by "finding" simple explanations for complex situations. But the desire to settle for simplistic explanations or for explanations for which there is no clear evidence of a causal connection must be resisted, both in thinking about life and in writing about cause. Two all-too-common ways of generating illogical causal explanations are to mistake a *time relationship* for a causal one and a *correlation* between two events for a causal relationship. For example, you went out to dinner last night and awoke with an upset stomach this morning. Can you conclude that something you ate last night caused the stomach upset? Certainly not without further evidence. Perhaps you already had a stomach virus before you went to dinner. To understand the difference between a correlation and a cause, consider the relationship between IQ scores and college grades. Students who have high IQ scores generally get good grades in college, but scores on an IQ test do not *cause* the good grades. (Whatever skills or knowledge produce high IQ scores are certainly one cause, though, of good grades. On the other hand, IQ tests do not measure motivation or good study habits.)

Evidence and Thesis

Writing a causal analysis challenges both thinking and writing skills. Remember that readers will evaluate your logic and evidence. After all, your purpose in writing is to show readers that your analysis of cause is sound and therefore useful to them. So, resist simplistic thinking and consider the kinds of evidence needed to illustrate and support your analysis. In addition to drawing on your own experience, you may need, depending on your topic, to obtain some evidence from reading. You will discover, for example, that many writers in this chapter include statistical evidence drawn from their reading. If you plan to emphasize one cause of a situation because you believe others have overlooked that cause or have failed to understand its importance, be certain that readers understand this limited and focused purpose. Stephen King mentions several reasons why people are drawn to horror movies, but he devotes most of his essay to examining only one of the causes, the psychological.

Organization

Several organizational strategies are appropriate, depending on your topic and purpose. If you are examining a series of causes, beginning with background conditions and early influences, then your basic plan will be time sequence. Use appropriate terms for types of causes you discuss and transitional words to guide your reader through the sequence of events. If you want to examine an overlooked cause, you could begin by briefly discussing the causes that are usually stressed and then go on to introduce and explain the cause you want to emphasize. If your goal is to demonstrate that the same cause has operated in several different circumstances, then you need to show how that cause is the single common denominator in each circumstance. Whatever your overall strategy, remember to illustrate your points and to explain how your examples serve as evidence in support of your thesis.

Getting Started: Reflections on Why You Are in College

Why are you in college? List the main reasons for your decision to attend college. Then reflect on some of the sources of those reasons. What people (parents, teachers, friends) and what experiences helped shape your decision? What, in other words, were the conditions and influences, as well as the more immediate causes, that led to your decision? Write in your journal on these questions or prepare responses for class discussion.

"Why We Crave Horror Movies"

STEPHEN KING

One of the best-known novelists today, Stephen King (b. 1947), famous for his horror books and the films made from them, graduated from the University of Maine and taught high school

English before making his name with the novel *Carrie* in 1974. Just two of his many works include *The Shining* (1977) and *Pet Sematary* (1983). One of his short stories was made into the film *Stand by Me.* In the following essay, published in *Playboy* in 1982, King examines some of the reasons why so many people like to go to horror movies.

1   I think that we're all mentally ill; those of us outside the asylums only hide it a little better—and maybe not all that much better, after all. We've all known people who talk to themselves, people who sometimes squinch their faces into horrible grimaces when they believe no one is watching, people who have some hysterical fear—of snakes, the dark, the tight place, the long drop . . . and, of course, those final worms and grubs that are waiting so patiently underground.

2   When we pay our four or five bucks and seat ourselves at tenth-row center in a theater showing a horror movie, we are daring the nightmare.

3   Why? Some of the reasons are simple and obvious. To show that we can, that we are not afraid, that we can ride this roller coaster. Which is not to say that a really good horror movie may not surprise a scream out of us at some point, the way we may scream when the roller coaster twists through a complete 360 or plows through a lake at the bottom of the drop. And horror movies, like roller coasters, have always been the special province of the young; by the time one turns 40 or 50, one's appetite for double twists or 360-degree loops may be considerably depleted.

4   We also go to re-establish our feelings of essential normality; the horror movie is innately conservative, even reactionary. Freda Jackson as the horrible melting woman in *Die, Monster, Die!* confirms for us that no matter how far we may be removed from the beauty of a Robert Redford or a Diana Ross, we are still light-years from true ugliness.

5   And we go to have fun.

6   Ah, but this is where the ground starts to slope away, isn't it? Because this is a very peculiar sort of fun indeed. The fun comes from seeing others menaced—sometimes killed. One critic has suggested that if pro football has become the voyeur's version of combat, then the horror film has become the modern version of the public lynching.

It is true that the mythic, "fairytale" horror film intends to   7
take away the shades of gray. . . . It urges us to put away our
more civilized and adult penchant for analysis and to become
children again, seeing things in pure blacks and whites. It may
be that horror movies provide psychic relief on this level because this invitation to lapse into simplicity, irrationality and
even outright madness is extended so rarely. We are told we
may allow our emotions a free rein . . . or no rein at all.

If we are all insane, then sanity becomes a matter of degree.   8
If your insanity leads you to carve up women like Jack the Rip-
per or the Cleveland Torso Murderer, we clap you away in the
funny farm (but neither of those two amateur-night surgeons
was ever caught, heh, heh, heh); if, on the other hand your insanity leads you only to talk to yourself when you're under
stress or to pick your nose on your morning bus, then you are
left alone to go about your business . . . though it is doubtful
that you will ever be invited to the best parties.

The potential lyncher is in almost all of us (excluding saints,   9
past and present; but then, most saints have been crazy in their
own ways), and every now and then, he has to be let loose to
scream and roll around in the grass. Our emotions and our
fears form their own body, and we recognize that it demands
its own exercise to maintain proper muscle tone. Certain of
these emotional muscles are accepted—even exalted—in civilized society; they are, of course, the emotions that tend to
maintain the status quo of civilization itself. Love, friendship,
loyalty, kindness—these are all the emotions that we applaud,
emotions that have been immortalized in the couplets of Hallmark cards and in the verses (I don't dare call it poetry) of
Leonard Nimoy.

When we exhibit these emotions, society showers us with   10
positive reinforcement; we learn this even before we get out of
diapers. When, as children, we hug our rotten little puke of a
sister and give her a kiss, all the aunts and uncles smile and
twit and cry, "Isn't he the sweetest little thing?" Such coveted
treats as chocolate-covered graham crackers often follow. But
if we deliberately slam the rotten little puke of a sister's fingers in the door, sanctions follow—angry remonstrance from
parents, aunts and uncles; instead of a chocolate-covered graham cracker, a spanking.

11   But anticivilization emotions don't go away, and they demand periodic exercise. We have such "sick" jokes as, "What's
the difference between a truckload of bowling balls and a
truckload of dead babies?" (You can't unload a truckload of
bowling balls with a pitchfork . . . a joke, by the way, that I originally heard from a ten-year-old.) Such a joke may surprise a
laugh or a grin out of us even as we recoil, a possibility that
confirms the thesis: If we share a brotherhood of man, then we
also share an insanity of man. None of which is intended as a
defense of either the sick joke or insanity but merely as an explanation of why the best horror films, like the best fairy tales,
manage to be reactionary, anarchistic, and revolutionary all at
the same time.

12   The mythic horror movie, like the sick joke, has a dirty job
to do. It deliberately appeals to all that is worst in us. It is morbidity unchained, our most base instincts let free, our nastiest
fantasies realized . . . and it all happens, fittingly enough, in the
dark. For those reasons, good liberals often shy away from horror films. For myself, I like to see the most aggressive of them—
Dawn of the Dead, for instance—as lifting a trap door in the
civilized forebrain and throwing a basket of raw meat to the
hungry alligators swimming around in that subterranean river
beneath.

13   Why bother? Because it keeps them from getting out, man.
It keeps them down there and me up here. It was Lennon and
McCartney who said that all you need is love, and I would
agree with that.

14   As long as you keep the gators fed.

Expanding Vocabulary

Match each word in column A with its definition in column B. When
in doubt, first find the word in the essay and look for context clues to
aid your understanding of the word's meaning. Then, if necessary, use
your dictionary to complete the matching exercise.

Column A	Column B
grubs (1)	gruesomeness
depleted (3)	threatened by
innately (4)	strong inclination
menaced (6)	mental

voyeurs (6)
penchant (7)
psychic (7)
exalted (9)
twit (10)
recoil (11)
morbidity (12)

glorified, praised
annoying person
possessing at birth
shrink back
worm-like larvae of some insects
those who find gratification
    from observing others—
    usually having sex
used up

Understanding Content

1. According to King, what are moviegoers doing when they go to horror movies?
2. What age group particularly enjoys horror movies?
3. What three reasons do we have for going to horror movies?
4. Which one of the three is the difficult one to understand?
5. Why do we enjoy seeing others threatened or destroyed in a horror film?
6. How is a horror film similar to a sick joke? What does each "do" for us?

Drawing Inferences about Thesis and Purpose

1. King says that perhaps love is all we need—so long as we feed the alligators within us. What does he mean by this? What do the alligators represent in us?
2. What is King's primary purpose in writing? Given who he is, could he have an additional purpose? Explain.
3. What is the author's thesis?

Analyzing Strategies and Style

1. King certainly has a striking opening. Explain how he uses the idea that we are all somewhat insane throughout the essay—including in the final sentence.
2. The author makes an interesting comparison in paragraph 3. How does he use this analogy to develop his idea in the paragraph?
3. In paragraph 10 King uses an example of sibling rivalry. How does his word choice make his writing especially clever in this paragraph?

Thinking Critically

1. What has surprised you the most in this essay? Why?

2. Do you think there are other reasons why people go to horror movies? If so, what are they?
3. Do you agree with King that we are all insane? Why or why not? (Don't settle for a simplistic answer here.)

"Duty: The Forgotten Virtue"

AMITAI ETZIONI

Amitai Etzioni (b. 1929) is an internationally renowned sociologist. He was born in Germany and earned his Ph.D. at the University of California. He is now University Professor at George Washington University and director of the Center for Policy Research. He is also the author of many books, including *An Immodest Agenda: Rebuilding America Before the Twenty-First Century* (1983) in which he calls for an increased sense of community and decreased focus on the self. Similar ideas are expressed in his article on duty, published in 1986 in the *Washington Post*.

1   Air accidents can be viewed as random tests of the extent to which those responsible for keeping airplanes flying are doing their duty.

2   For example, the crew of an American Airlines plane recently tried to land it three times, in low visibility, with 124 people aboard, in Harlingen, Texas. On the third pass, they hit two sets of runway approach lights four feet off the ground. The collision was severe enough to deploy some oxygen masks in the passenger cabin and knock ceiling panels loose. Yet after the plane regained altitude and landed safely in San Antonio, other crews took it to Dallas-Fort Worth and then on to Denver where damage to the exterior of the plane was discovered and the plane taken out of service.

3   One may view this as nothing more than an isolated incidence of questionable judgment, but there is some evidence to suggest that Americans—always ambivalent about their duties—have been particularly loath to live up to their responsibilities in recent years.

4   A survey of young Americans found that most rank trial by jury high among their rights. However, few indicated a willingness to serve on a jury.

Patriotism is reported to be in vogue. However, Americans 5
would rather pay volunteers to serve in the military than support a draft in which all would share the burden.

A survey conducted by H & R Block shows that Americans 6
favor a flat tax. However, that support is offered on one troubling condition: that the respondent's favorite loophole not be closed.

These observations led me to ask my class at The George 7
Washington University what the term "duty" brought to their mind. They responded uneasily. They felt that people ought to be free to do what *they* believe in. Duties are imposed, alien, authoritarian—what the principal, the curriculum committee, the society, "they," want you to do.

I responded with a little impassioned address about the 8
common good: If everyone goes to the forest and fells a tree, soon the hillsides will be denuded. We cannot rely on the fact that once we are out of trees, people will recognize the need to plant new ones; it takes years for trees to grow. Hence, we must, I explained, expect members of society to plant some trees now, invest in the infrastructure, trim the deficit, etc., so that the next generation will have a forest, a thriving economy, a future. We must balance the desire to focus on one's own interests with some obligation to the commons. True, duties are not fun, *otherwise there would be no need to impose them.* But a civil society cannot do without them.

Well, the students reflected aloud; they understood where I 9
was coming from. Okay, they said, maybe there was room for duty, but—compliance ought to be voluntary, they insisted. I felt I had failed them; I never got the point across.

Americans have never been very duty-bound. The country 10
was created by people who escaped duties imposed by authoritarian monarchies and dogmatic churches. And the ethos of the pioneers was of striking out on one's own—even if, as a matter of fact, settlement was carried out by groups very much dependent on one another.

But over the last decades the need for duty to the commons 11
has grown as the supply diminished. Consider:

Demand Side. Practically no one expects that America can do 12
without *some* defense. The problem is that defense requires a *continuous* willingness to dedicate resources to national security that might otherwise be used to enhance one's standard of

living. As obvious as this may seem, the fact is that Americans have found it very difficult to sustain such a commitment. The defense budget typically reflects cycles of neglect followed by hysterical reactions to some real or alleged crisis. There is no well-grounded commitment.

13 On the domestic front, voluntarism is now supposed to replace many government services. Anyone who points to the limits of such an approach is immediately suspect of being an old-time liberal, a champion of big government. But this simple-minded dichotomy—do things privately *or* via the government—conceals the real issue: What duties to the commons *should* the government impose?

14 Most would include, aside from defense, support for basic and medical research, some environmental protection, public education and services for the deserving poor. But today these obligations to the commons are left without a moral underpinning. Most do not subscribe to a social philosophy which endorses these commitments. Instead, we celebrate *laissez faire* and a generation rich in Me-ism.

15 *Supply Side.* Americans are hardly enamored with the notion that they have duties to the social weal. They find escape in an odd concoction: a misapplication of Adam Smith mixed with surging libertarianism, pop psychology and a dash of liberation theory.

16 Americans have been brought up on a highly simplified notion of the invisible hand: Everybody goes out and tries to "maximize" himself—and the economy thrives for all. There is no need to curb self-interest, even greed; it is the propellant that fires up economies.

17 Now the reach of the invisible hand has been extended to wholly new spheres. Antismoking campaigns, pro-seatbelt moves, Social Security, environmental protection and employee safety are said to work best without "coercion"—if people are left to their own devices.

18 In this rejection of any sense that we have duties to each other, we gloss over the consequences to innocent bystanders of such a free-for-all, it's-up-to-you-Jack attitude. These range from the effect on children of those who choose not to buy insurance, to the neglect of "public goods"—goods we all need but no one is individually entrusted with procuring (e.g., highways).

Pop psychology is still with us. It argues that everyone 19 ought to focus on his or her own growth. Society and its duties are viewed as standing in the way of self-fulfillment.

Pollster Daniel Yankelovich estimated that in the late 1970s, 20 17 percent of Americans were deeply committed to a philosophy of self-fulfillment and another 63 percent subscribed to it in varying degrees. These people said they "spend a great deal of time thinking about myself" and "satisfactions come from shaping oneself rather than from home and family life." They had a strong need for excitement and sensation and tended to feel free to look, live and act however they wanted, even if this violated others' concepts of what is proper.

The significance of this is that the escape from duty reaches 21 beyond neglect of the community's needs to the neglect of one's immediate family.

Last but not least are the interest groups which elevate Me- 22 ism to a group level. True, lobbies have been around since the founding of the Republic. But in recent years their power has increased sharply. And the consequence is that service to each interest group is easily put above a concern for the general welfare.

How do we redress the balance between the "I" and the 23 "We"—so that we enhance the sense of duty?

There obviously are no simple solutions, but schools could 24 help. They could change their civics courses from teaching that the government has three branches and the Supreme Court nine members (and so on), and instead promote civility. However, since most schools are overworked and underfunded, they are unlikely to do much.

More may be achieved if the issue is put on the agenda of 25 the nationwide town-hall meetings we are, in effect, constantly conducting. The subjects vary, from civil rights to environmental protection to deficit reduction. However, the process is the same: triggered by a leading book (such as *Silent Spring*), a series of reports in leading newspapers or on television (e.g., on Vietnam), or by commissions (on education), we turn our collective attention to an issue. We debate it at length.

At first it seems nothing happens, but gradually a new con- 26 sensus arises that affects people's behavior. We agree to pollute less or drink less; we exercise more; we become more sensitive to the rights of minorities or women.

27   The issue of our social obligations as Americans—our duties—is overdue for such a treatment. Meanwhile, we each ought to examine ourselves: What have you done for your community lately?

Expanding Vocabulary

Etzioni's essay provides a good opportunity for expanding your knowledge of terms and concepts used in discussing social and political issues.

1. In a sentence or two, explain each of the following terms or references.

loophole (6)	libertarianism (15)
infrastructure (8)	pop psychology (15)
deficit (8)	liberation theory (15)
ethos (10)	invisible hand (16)
laissez faire (14)	civics (24)
Me-ism (14)	civility (24)
Adam Smith (15)	*Silent Spring* (25)

2. Be able to define each of the following words. Then, select five words and use each one in a separate sentence.

deploy (2)	alleged (12)
ambivalent (3)	dichotomy (13)
loath (3)	enamored (15)
denuded (8)	concoction (15)
dogmatic (10)	consensus (26)

Understanding Content

1. When Etzioni asked his students about the concept of duty, what was their response? Where does duty come from? Should it be imposed or voluntary?
2. Etzioni says that Americans have never had a strong sense of duty. In your own words, state several examples Etzioni gives to show that we have little sense of duty today.
3. What are the contemporary causes for the American's escape from a sense of duty? That is, what are the current ideas and values used to justify a lack of duty to society?
4. In the author's view, what is the dominant value affecting the behavior of Americans?
5. What three solutions does Etzioni offer to "enhance the sense of duty"?

Drawing Inferences about Thesis and Purpose

1. The author uses two economic terms—*Demand Side* and *Supply Side*—as subheadings. How is he using these terms in this essay? What is being "demanded"? What is being "supplied"?
2. How did Etzioni feel about his students' views on duty?
3. What is Etzioni's attitude toward duty? What is his thesis?
4. Etzioni offers three solutions. How have his own actions shown his attempt to act on each one of them—to take his own advice?
5. What does Etzioni hope to gain by taking his own advice?

Analyzing Strategies and Style

1. Look at the first six paragraphs. What do they provide?
2. One could say that paragraphs 7 through 9 are also part of the introduction. What does the author present in these paragraphs?
3. What is effective about Etzioni's use of specifics and his own students as an introductory strategy? Why might long introductions filled with specifics be effective openings for controversial topics?
4. The author uses a popular three-part organization for discussing a problem: (1) statement of the problem, (2) causes of the problem, (3) solutions to the problem. Analyze the essay according to this pattern, indicating the paragraphs that make up each of the three parts.
5. Now that you have marked the essay's parts, can you find sentences that signal the beginning of the second and third parts? Which sentence sums up the point of the first part?

Thinking Critically

1. If you had been in Etzioni's class, would you have responded much as his students did? If not, how would your response have been different?
2. Do you agree that most Americans are motived by the desire for self-fulfillment? Why or why not? What evidence can you offer to support your view?
3. Etzioni suggests that special-interest groups are really a form of "Me-ism." Is this a helpful way to understand these groups?
4. Is Etzioni suggesting that participating in groups is only a self-centered act, not a sign of commitment to others? What are the characteristics of the politically active groups Etzioni has in mind? Can you give some specific examples?
5. What kinds of groups might Etzioni approve of?
6. What is your answer to the essay's final question? Are you satisfied with your answer? Why or why not?

"To Lift All Boats"

ROBERT B. REICH

Economist Robert B. Reich, Labor Secretary during President
Clinton's first term, is University Professor of social and economic policy at Brandeis University and senior editor of the
American Prospect. He is the author of many articles and books,
including *Tales of a New America* (1987) and *The Work of Nations*
(1991). "To Lift All Boats" appeared in the Outlook Section of the
Washington Post on May 16, 1999. In this article, Reich explores
the effects of some of the new ideas for income redistribution,
and the effects of not making any changes.

1   Suddenly, there's a new conversation among the country's
movers and shakers, and several ambitious plans for helping the
bottom half share in the nation's prosperity: Give them, literally,
a share in America. Spread capitalism by spreading capital.

2   Consider President Clinton's proposed "Universal Savings
Accounts." Families earning less than $40,000 would get an an-
nual $600 tax credit deposited directly into their USA account,
plus another $700 if they deposited $700 of their own money
into the account. That adds up to an annual nest egg of $2,000.
If they continue doing the same thing for 40 years, assuming a
modest 5 percent rate of return on their savings, their nest egg
would grow into a brontosaurus egg of more than $250,000.
That would give most families a big boost for retirement.

3   Make no mistake. The effect of this plan would be to redistribute capital assets to lower-income families. Higher-income
families would get a much smaller federal contribution. Cost to
taxpayers: Roughly $30 billion annually.

4   Or consider Sen. Bob Kerrey's "Kid Save." Under this plan,
the government would provide every newborn with a $1,000
savings account, and would add another $500 a year until the
child's fifth birthday. The money accumulates and the interest
compounds until the child reaches 21, and—presto—the kid
has $20,000 to start his or her adult life. The taxpayers' tab:
About $15 billion a year.

If neither of these is ambitious enough for you, here's an- 5
other idea, proposed by Bruce Ackerman and Anne Alstott,
both professors at Yale Law School, in a slim volume called *The
Stakeholder Society* (Yale University Press): Every 21-year-old
American gets $80,000, to do with as he or she sees fit. The cost
is a whopping $255 billion a year—borne either through
mandatory payback of the original stake (plus interest) at
death, or an annual 2 percent wealth tax on the wealthiest 40
percent of Americans.

I know what you're thinking. It can't happen. Even Kerrey's 6
idea is too expensive. This Congress would never go for any of
this. Besides, we're likely to have political gridlock between
now and 2000.

But don't get hung up on the politics right now, or on the de- 7
tails of these plans. What's important here is the big idea common to all of them: Rather than just redistributing income to
people after they've become poor, give them capital upfront to
build their fortunes. Give a young family a starter nest egg.
Give a young adult a capital stake.

This way, we get the benefits of a market economy: We en- 8
courage saving, rely on private ownership and depend on de-
centralized, personal choices about how to invest money. But
we also get the social benefits of a more egalitarian society. It's
a twofer.

A big idea like this is significant because it can reframe the 9
public debate. It can change the prevailing assumptions. Eventually, it can change the course of the nation.

Actually, it's not as novel as it may seem. After all, the 10
Homestead Act of 1862 gave 160 acres of Western land to anyone willing to settle there for five years. In the 1980s, Prime
Minister Margaret Thatcher invited residents of Britain's pub-
licly owned housing (then almost a third of the country's housing stock) to purchase their homes at bargain-basement rates.
More recently, Vaclav Klaus, as Czech prime minister, auc-
tioned off shares of state-owned companies to Czech citizens
holding redeemable vouchers.

So why the buzz here and now? Three reasons. First, it is 11
dawning on many people that the old ways of trying to
broaden prosperity aren't working nearly as well or as fast as

we'd like. Not even the buoyant expansion of the 1990s has done much to reverse the long-term decline in real incomes of those in the bottom third. Those just above them haven't gained any ground. The median American family's income is about where it was a decade ago in real terms, and its members are now working a total of six more weeks a year than they did then. To be sure, the incomes of the very poor have bounced up a bit since 1996, both because the minimum wage was raised and because the labor market became so tight that they've had an easier time finding jobs. But that bounce was from a long way down, so they're still very poor. And when the economy cools—as it will, eventually—the slide will likely resume.

12   Most of the people who have been losing out don't have an adequate education—the first prerequisite in this global, digital economy. So obviously, the best investment in their future prosperity is to improve their store of "human capital." But this takes considerable time, and it's far from a sure bet. Even if the half-trillion dollars we spend every year on public schools were perfectly utilized, and children from poorer homes were learning like mad, they'd still start off their adult lives at a severe financial disadvantage. Many will have a hard time financing a college education or a first home.

13   Meanwhile, it has also become clear that we can't rely on direct handouts to do the job. They have all sorts of negative side effects, like dependency, and there's no political will to carry them out on a large scale. Trying to redistribute income from those relatively rich to those relatively poor through specific federal programs, funded by annual appropriations, has become next to impossible, as evidenced by the difficulties of funding everything from Head Start to housing subsidies.

14   The second reason for the new conversation is that capital assets—rather than income—is now where the action is. The story of the 1990s, if you hadn't noticed, is the extraordinary boom in the market valuations of companies, followed by that of homes and even American dollars. The boom may end tomorrow, of course. But it's been an amazing ride, and it can't help but affect how people think about the public interest, as well as their own personal gain. The debate over privatizing Social Security was not galvanized by the program's projected

insolvency some 30 years hence. It was spurred by the prospect of cashing in on Wall Street's effervescence. Does anybody seriously believe we'd be talking about privatization if the stock market were in the doldrums?

To date, most Americans haven't gotten much out of this 15 capital boom, however, because most don't have much capital. Without money to invest, it's of no consequence to you whether the Dow is at 11,000 or 1,100. While almost half of American families own some shares of stock nowadays, most of those holdings are valued under $5,000. Young families are even less likely to own capital. The average young family has a net worth of only about $11,400, including the value of the family car. Fewer than half own a home, which is usually heavily mortgaged. The typical young family in the bottom half of the income distribution has a net worth of $2,000 or less.

On the other hand, people at the top have never had it so 16 good. The biggest single consequence of the Clinton bull market (or, if you prefer, the Greenspan bull market) has been to make those who were already rich before 1991 fabulously richer. The wealthiest 10 percent of Americans have received 85 percent of Wall Street's gains since then. The wealthiest 1 percent have gotten 40 percent of them. Even before the run-up in stock prices, America's wealth gap had already turned into a chasm—wider and more permanent than the income gap. It's now a canyon. Bill Gates's net worth exceeds the combined net worth of the bottom 45 percent of American households.

Even if—or more likely, when—the stock market sags, the 17 wealth gap is likely to endure. When the parents of today's baby boomers leave this world, the wealthier of them will also leave behind a collection of assets worth hundreds of billions of dollars more than they paid for them. Their boomer offspring will inherit the largest inter-generational windfall in the history of modern civilization. And thanks to the "stepped-up-basis-at-death" tax rule, these assets will arrive free of capital-gains taxes. (When I once had the temerity to suggest to then-Treasury Secretary Lloyd Bentsen that the rule be modified, he scolded that death is an "involuntary conversion.")

The tax favors don't end there. Those people who have 18 earned enough to be able to invest in this buoyant capital market are also advantaged by rules allowing them to defer taxes on that portion of their incomes. The resulting benefits are wildly tilted toward the very people who are already gaining the most from the surge in capital values. Two-thirds of all the tax benefits for pensions and retirement savings now go to families earning more than $100,000 a year. Only 7 percent of these benefits go to families earnings $50,000 or less.

19   The asset elevator has been lifting America's wealthy to ever-higher vistas, without their moving a muscle (except, perhaps, to speed-dial their brokers). Current tax law is lifting them, and their children, even higher. Hence the case for allowing the rest of America on the elevator, too. Whether it's government-subsidized universal savings accounts for Americans of modest means, or schemes to give every young adult a certain amount of capital, the goal is to let everyone in on the ride.

20   The third reason for the new conversation is that, hey, we can afford to do something like this. Budget surpluses now extend as far as the eye can see. The president wants to fund his plan out of them. Sen. Kerrey's Kid Save would cost half as much. The price tag on the Ackerman-Alstott proposal is a lot higher—but with the value of stocks, real estate and other assets heading into the stratosphere, their notion of funding it out of a 2 percent tax on the wealthiest doesn't seem quite as far-fetched as it might in more normal eras.

21   To be sure, even asset-poor Americans are better off than most people around the world. Still, this new conversation is important. Vast inequalities of wealth and income can strain the social fabric of a nation. They make collective decisions more difficult—whether about trade, immigration, labor or the environment—because citizens in sharply different economic positions are likely to be affected by these sorts of decisions in very different ways. Politics can only become more fractious.

22   Were inequality to grow too wide, we would risk an erosion of Americans' sense of common purpose and identity. Those who already worry about the fragmenting of our culture and the fading of civility will have far greater cause for concern. A polarized society is also less stable than one with a large and strong middle. Such a society offers fertile ground for demagogues

eager to exploit the politics of resentment. No less an oracle than Federal Reserve Board Chairman Alan Greenspan has warned that inequality is potentially a "major threat to our security."

Will any of this new conversation be part of the upcoming 23 presidential election? Don't hold your breath. Candidates watch the polls, and the polls don't yet reflect the new conversation. But there's at least an outside chance that during the dreary days next winter, after the early primaries have worn down the aspirants, exhausted the press and numbed the public, there will be an opening for some bold ideas about something truly important.

Expanding Vocabulary

Match each word in column A with its definition in column B. When in doubt, first find the word in the essay and look for context clues to aid your understanding of the word's meaning. Then, if necessary, use your dictionary to complete the matching exercise.

Column A	*Column B*
brontosaurus (2)	getting two things for the price of one
gridlock (6)	spirited
egalitarian (8)	a great disparity or gap
twofer (8)	nerve
buoyant (11)	process of wearing away, destroying
effervescence (14)	leaders who get power by appealing to emotions and prejudices
doldrums (14)	
chasm (16)	
temerity (17)	unruly, inclined to conflict
fractious (21)	wise person
erosion (22)	one of the largest dinosaurs
demagogues (22)	period of stagnation or slump
exploit (22)	equal
oracle (22)	people desiring, seeking advancement
aspirants (23)	jam in which no movement is possible
	take advantage of
	upward force

Understanding Content

1. Explain each of the three plans Reich discusses: "Universal Savings Accounts," "Kid Save," and the idea of Ackerman and Alstott.
2. What do the three plans have in common that interests Reich?
3. How do these plans apply "the benefits of a market economy"?
4. What are the three reasons why these plans are exciting to think about at this time?
5. What do people need to take advantage of a strong stock market? What is the net worth of a "typical young family in the bottom half of the income distribution"?
6. Who has benefited the most from the strong stock market?
7. Which group of people benefit the most from tax laws?
8. What is the potential negative effect if the country continues to have "vast inequalities of wealth and income"?

Drawing Inferences about Thesis and Purpose

1. Does Reich expect politicians to participate in a conversation about income redistribution during the 2000 campaign? Does he hope that they will? How do you know?
2. What is Reich's purpose in writing? What does he want to accomplish?
3. What is the author's thesis?

Analyzing Strategies and Style

1. Reich begins by describing three specific proposals for spreading capital. What does he gain by the specifics he provides?
2. In paragraph 10 Reich explains how other programs have been devised to redistribute wealth. Why does he include this information?

Thinking Critically

1. Which of the three specific plans do you like the most? Why?
2. Reich says there are three good reasons to have a conversation about these ideas. Which of the three is the most convincing reason in your view? Why?
3. Reich is quick to stress that he is more interested in the big idea than in the specifics. What do you think of the big idea? Has Reich convinced you that we need to do something to give those in the bottom half a chance to benefit from our current expanding economy? Why or why not?
4. Examine Reich's analysis of the effects on society of a disparity of wealth. Which of his points is the most sobering or distressing to you? Why?

"Enough Blame to Go Around"

ROBERT J. SAMUELSON

Journalist Robert Samuelson (b. 1945) began his career as a *Washington Post* reporter after earning a B.A. degree in government from Harvard University. He is now a syndicated columnist whose columns are printed weekly in many papers and bi-weekly in *Newsweek* magazine. Samuelson usually writes about economics, but also, as in the following article (published May 3, 1999), he examines the effects of cultural changes and the sometimes faulty logic we use to explain social problems.

Americans like to believe that all problems are solvable and all tragedies preventable. The mass murder at Columbine High teaches us otherwise. But even so, we go through the process of assessing blame and seeking solutions, because anything else would seem un-American and because this tragedy (like many others) quickly becomes a political vehicle for agendas and ambitions. Our search for scapegoats, though, promises to disappoint.

The usual suspects have emerged. Guns, of course, top the list. I don't own guns, dislike them and believe that, in an ideal world, they would be illegal. But let's get real. The federal government reckons there are 230 million handguns, rifles, shotguns and machine guns in America. Perhaps 40 percent or slightly fewer of households have a gun. Does anyone truly think that all these people are social misfits and that, as a practical matter, even handguns can be outlawed? Suppose they were. Would the existing supply vanish? Not likely. Black markets would flourish.

Someone determined and intelligent will get guns—or something. Timothy McVeigh used fertilizer to craft his bomb that killed 168 in Oklahoma City. One paradox of the Columbine tragedy is that it occurred when guns are becoming harder to get and sales seem to be declining. The Brady bill, passed in 1993, required law enforcement agencies to check buyers' backgrounds. Between 1993 and 1997, annual purchases of new guns dropped from 7.8 million to 4.3 million, according to government figures.

4   Parents also rank high as scapegoats. These parents (it's said or implied) must have raised their children poorly. Or they ignored danger signals. In one boy's room, said the Jefferson County sheriff, a sawed-off shotgun barrel was visible. The parents should have suspected. Maybe. But candid parents will admit to doubts. There are limits to child control.

5   Last year, the psychologist Judith Rich Harris published a book, *The Nurture Assumption,* that challenged the American faith that parents can shape their children as they please. Although she went too far (denying most parental influence), her central point was correct. Heredity—the innate differences among people—and peer influences play a huge role. Every child is different, and children conceal their lives from parents.

6   A lot of this is inevitable, and much of it is harmless. Some of it, though, leads to tragedies. Even "good" parents are only human. They practice denial and hope. Perhaps Eric Harris's and Dylan Klebold's parents should have known that their sons' weird behavior marked them as mass murderers. But parents regularly miss, or can't alter, signs of trouble in their children. In 1995 there were 2,227 suicides among those under 20 (about half the number of homicides).

7   America has long suffered from acts of mass violence. In 1927 Andrew Kehoe, angry over a school tax, set off bombs—including one at a school—that killed 38 children, five adults and himself. In 1949 Howard Unruh, a World War II veteran, shot 13 people to death. In 1966, Charles Whitman set himself up in a tower at the University of Texas with a rifle and killed 16. What's distinctive now is that students have become shooters.

8   The other day, the First Lady criticized a media culture that "glorifies violence on TV, in the movies, on the Internet, in songs" and features video games where winning is "based on how many people you kill." The effect, she said, is that "our children become desensitized to violence."

9   There is probably some truth to this, but it overlooks larger, harder truths. High schools have become more chaotic because we have made them that way. We have wanted everyone to graduate. In 1950 only about half of young adults had completed high school. Even in 1960 the dropout rate was 27 percent. It's now about 11 percent. Students who might have once

left because they felt angry or inadequate now stay. Schools
have grown bigger and more impersonal. In 1950 almost 25,000
public high schools had 5.7 million students. In 1995 fewer
than 24,000 schools had 12.5 million students. Columbine has
about 1,800.

There has been a loss of control—and it's not just size. In a   10
superb book (*The World We Created at Hamilton High*), sociologist Gerald Grant of Syracuse University described how one
high school changed. In the 1950s it was white and middle
class. There was a dress code. The principal's authority was un-
questioned. Discipline problems were few. By the 1970s the
school was racially and economically integrated. Electives had
diluted the basic curriculum. Students' "rights" to due process
had burgeoned. There was no dress code.

Teachers went on the defensive. "Many began to look the   11
other way, to shrink from a challenge and to avoid bringing a
charge because they might not only lose the legal battle, but
wind up having to defend themselves," wrote Grant. This
legacy endures.

Even if a return to the 1950s were possible—and it isn't—it   12
wouldn't be desirable. The principal at Hamilton High was a
petty tyrant. Education was exclusionary, conformity widespread. But the change reflects a wider upheaval. It's not just
media fare where boundaries between childhood and adulthood have eroded. Teenagers expect many adult freedoms
with few adult burdens. They have jobs, cars, income. By and
large, society accepts this, gives teens "space" and respects
their individuality.

Schools are less protective and more open. They are more   13
mixed economically, racially and ethnically. Our culture cele-
brates "diversity" and urges people to feel proud of their differences. But in teenagers—who often are struggling to
discover who they are—this may be a formula for tension as
well as tolerance. People may exaggerate differences or feel
them more acutely.

We search for meaning. But the explanation, if any, of the   14
Columbine slaughter lies at the juncture of the dark side of
human nature and the drift of our culture. As adolescence and
adulthood blend, so do the problems and tragedies. This is a
condition that, though it may be influenced, can't be ended.

Expanding Vocabulary

Select the six words you are least familiar with, study their definitions, and then use each one in a separate sentence.

scapegoats (1)	burgeoned (10)
candid (4)	legacy (11)
innate (5)	petty (12)
desensitized (8)	exclusionary (12)
chaotic (9)	eroded (12)

Understanding Content

1. What do Americans like to do when problems arise?
2. What are the first two sources of blame for the Columbine shootings?
3. How many guns are owned by what percent of Americans? What has happened to gun sales since 1993?
4. What reasons does Samuelson give for not blaming parents too much?
5. What does Mrs. Clinton blame? How does Samuelson respond to her charge?
6. How have many schools changed since the 1950s?
7. How have teens changed?

Drawing Inferences about Thesis and Purpose

1. Samuelson writes that the cause of the Columbine tragedy "lies at the juncture of the dark side of human nature and the drift of our culture." Explain his meaning.
2. What is the author's thesis? Where is it stated?

Analyzing Strategies and Style

1. When discussing guns, Samuelson asserts that he doesn't own or like guns. Why does he make that point in paragraph 2?
2. In paragraph 9 the author provides interesting statistics about schools. How do they contribute to his analysis?
3. Samuelson discusses a number of possible causes. What does he gain by exploring several, even ones he rejects in whole or in part?

Thinking Critically

1. Samuelson has some interesting observations about children and parents. Do you disagree with any of his points? If so, which ones and why? If not, why do you think his analysis of parents and children is sound?

2. How much influence do parents have over their children? Do you know any "good" parents with troubled or difficult teens? How do we explain this phenomenon?
3. Which cause do you think is most influential in tragedies such as Columbine? Why?
4. Samuelson does not offer much hope for solving the problems—eliminating the conditions—that lead to teen violence. Are you as pessimistic? If not, how do you think we can change the conditions leading to teen violence?

"Family Values Go to Work"

ROSALIND C. BARNETT AND CARYL RIVERS

Rosalind C. Barnett (b. 1937) is senior scientist in the women's studies program at Brandeis University and senior scholar at the Murray Research Center at Radcliffe College. A graduate of Trinity College and Columbia University, Caryl Rivers (b. 1937) is a professor of journalism at Boston University and a freelance writer. Both are authors of several books, and together they have written *Beyond Sugar and Spice* (1981) and *She Works He Works* (1996), the latter a study of how two-income families are better off. The following report of research on families, jobs, and stress—and proposals for ways to reduce the stress—appeared in the *Washington Post* on May 10, 1999.

Nearly 80 percent of couples are now working couples. 1
Fifty-five percent of mothers of toddlers are working, and some 70 percent of all women are in the work force. Men's incomes have been flat or declining for the past decade. We are seeing the end of the era of the male breadwinner. The two-income family is now the norm, and all indications are that it will continue to be. Women now outnumber men in most college classrooms, as they prepare for a lifelong commitment to the work force.

Jobs that offer flexibility so that workers can meet their fam- 2
ily needs are the top priority for men and women. Our major study of full-time-employed, two-earner couples, funded by the National Institute of Mental Health, found that the healthiest couples were those with reliable child care and flexibility

in their jobs to meet family needs—such as a child's illness or an important school event. The lack of flexibility to deal with family issues was linked to stress, depression and anxiety—for men and women. And more than half the men in major surveys say they would forgo raises and advancement for more time to spend with their families.

3   In light of these facts, we would propose a "family impact initiative" as a tool to help companies deal with the family issues confronted by their workers. The concept of the Environmental Impact Statement grew out of a national concern for the health of the planet, as pollution and other hazards took their toll. We believe the time has come for an initiative to guard the health of America's working families.

4   A family impact initiative would not be a program mandated by government but one that companies could adapt in their own self-interest. Flexibility is good for the bottom line. Research shows that "family-friendly" corporate policies reduce burnout, absenteeism and turnover while increasing employee loyalty. Employees—men as well as women—desperately want more flexibility to deal with family and community issues. A Du Pont survey showed that 56 percent of male employees favored flexible schedules that allow more family time.

5   These employee concerns are backed up by our study, which found that a major source of illness-producing stress for couples was not having the flexibility to deal with family issues. This stress was shared by men and women alike; there were no gender differences. Men in our study spent as many hours parenting as did their wives when the children reached school age, and men were as stressed by family problems as were women.

6   With a family impact initiative in place, managers would consider the effects of decisions and policies on the families of employees. Travel policies, meeting plans, relocation plans, job assignments, work hours and leave and vacation policies would be viewed in the light of family impact.

7   Of course, not all decisions would be made on this lone criterion, but it would be part of the mix—and a big step forward in protecting employee health and productivity. This initiative wouldn't mean that companies would have to be turned upside down. In many cases, small changes can have major effects. Ending "meeting macho" policies that make employees get to the office at 7 a.m., when parents are trying to get kids

off to school, can be a big help. Giving employees enough lead time to blend travel schedules with family plans can strengthen father-child and mother-child bonds. Adequate vacation time, encouragement of parental leave and a sick-leave policy that includes fatherhood in the equation can ease stress. Maximum possible use of teleconferencing, faxes and other technology can avoid keeping employees constantly on the road. Dismantling a corporate culture that decrees that the best employee is the one who is first in the door in the morning and the last to leave at night can not only ease stress but help the bottom line. Research shows that employees with more flexibility are more productive than those who lack it.

In an era of downsizing, fewer employees are having to do 8 more work, and our study found that in the new leaner workplace, employees are at increased health risk because of growing job demands over time. Short-term savings gained by downsizing can turn into long-term costs. Chronic exposure of workers to increasing job demands may rack up huge costs in turnover, absenteeism and workers' compensation claims. And our study showed that when one member of the dual-earner couple was experiencing high stress, so was his or her spouse.

Trying to anticipate such problems makes good sense for 9 everyone. A family impact initiative could be such a forward-looking tool. It would move family concerns from the peripheral vision of business—where they too often languish—nearer to center stage. In this scenario everybody wins—workers and managers and the ever-important bottom line is enhanced in the process.

Expanding Vocabulary

Examine the following words in their contexts in the essay and then write a brief definition or synonym for each one. Do not use a dictionary; try to guess the word's meaning from its context.

initiative (3)	peripheral (9)
burnout (4)	languish (9)
criterion (7)	scenario (9)
dismantling (7)	enhanced (9)
downsizing (8)	

Understanding Content

1. What is now the norm for families and the workplace?

2. According to the authors' study, what produced the healthiest working couples?
3. What was the effect of lack of flexibility?
4. What do the authors propose to reduce stress for working families?
5. What are the effects of flexibility for employers?
6. How would companies be affected by adopting the authors' proposal? What are some changes that can be made? How will changes affect workers and the company?
7. What happens when one worker in a two-worker family feels stress over work and family conflicts?

Drawing Inferences about Thesis and Purpose

1. What is the essay's thesis?
2. What is the authors' purpose in writing? What do they want to accomplish?

Analyzing Strategies and Style

1. The authors open with several statistics. How does this make an effective opening?
2. The writing in this article seems almost "without style"—that is, simple, direct, uncomplicated. How can such writing be an effective strategy? (What have the authors avoided with their choice of style?)

Thinking Critically

1. Which statistic in the essay is the most surprising to you? Why?
2. Are you currently one member of a two-worker family? If so, do you get stressed out trying to meet all commitments? Alternatively, do you anticipate becoming part of a two-worker family? If so, how do you expect to handle the situation?
3. Do you think the authors have a good idea for making the workplace more friendly to families? Why or why not?
4. If you do not like their proposals, what would you propose?

"When Parents Are Toxic to Children"

KEITH ABLOW

Keith Ablow (b. 1961), a graduate of the Johns Hopkins University Medical School, is a writer and psychiatrist who practices in the Boston area. He has published two nonfiction books, *To Wrestle with Demons* (1995) and *With Mercy* (1996), and is working on a novel. In the following article, which appeared in the *Washington Post*'s Health Section in May 1996, Ablow examines the effects of bad parenting and argues for change.

I sat with a 15-year-old girl in the interview room where I   1
meet psychiatric inpatients for the first time, watching her as she gazed through her long black hair at her forearm. She gingerly traced the superficial cuts she had made with a razor the night before when she had flirted with suicide.

Her chart indicated that since the age of 11 she had suffered   2
repeated bouts of severe depression that antidepressant medication didn't touch. At times she was intermittently paranoid, believing that someone was out to steal her mind or even to take her life.

"I'm not going back there," she finally said, looking up at   3
me. "I'll kill myself, if they make me live with my parents."

"What happens there?" I asked.   4

"Constant fighting. Screaming. Swearing. Hitting. It's been   5
like that my whole life."

"Do they hit you?" I asked.   6

"They used to. A lot. They don't anymore. They hit my   7
brothers, though. And they keep telling me I'm ugly . . . and stupid. Worthless." She looked at her arm. "I don't care where I get sent. I'll go anywhere but home."

I was certain she would return home. Social service agencies   8
had been involved in her case for years. No doubt there would be another family meeting during her hospitalization, perhaps more frequent home visits by a social worker afterward. But the mental health system's prejudice in favor of keeping families intact, as well as a perennial shortage of acceptable foster parents, would likely keep my young patient with her own parents and in peril.

I have repeatedly treated teenagers like this girl whose biological parents have inflicted irreparable psychological harm   9
on their children. Some are the victims of sexual abuse, others of pervasive neglect. They end up in my office with symptoms that include panic attacks, severe depression and psychosis. Many are addicted to drugs before they even begin high

school. Some see suicide as a reasonable way to end their pain. I prescribe them a variety of antidepressant, anti-anxiety and sometimes antipsychotic medications, hoping that their symptoms of mental illness are temporary, but worried that the damage they have suffered may be permanent. Worst of all I know that these are preventable illnesses.

10   Nor does the damage end with them. These teenage patients are tomorrow's parents. And experience has repeatedly demonstrated that many of them are likely to reenact the same destructive scenarios with their own children. Most people who harbor rage from their childhood don't expect it to surface after they become parents. Many fail to see the traumas they survived as sources of great risk for a new generation.

11   If we are to make a serious attempt to prevent some forms of serious mental illness, parenting must no longer be seen as an inalienable right, but as a privilege that can—and will—be revoked for abuse or neglect. Society must be much less tolerant of harm to children and also must be willing to devote considerably more resources to providing alternative living situations for children and adolescents who are in danger.

12   Only in the most egregious cases of physical violence or emotional neglect have I seen the state terminate parental rights. It seems that damage to children must reach the level of near catastrophe to justify cleaving a parent-child relationship that has been anything but loving.

13   Parents need to get a new message. If you do a lousy job parenting, you lose your job. In cases involving child custody, blood ties must be given less weight not only by the mental health system, but by the government and the court system. At the federal, state and local levels, keeping children with their parents can no longer be considered more important than keeping them safe.

14   Another young woman I treated had been repeatedly beaten by her older brothers for years. As a girl she had been raped by her mother's boyfriend. Her moods had become erratic, and her temper unpredictable. She had turned to marijuana for relief and had been expelled from school for fighting. Yet she continued to live at home, with the blessing of the state Department of Social Services.

"She's got to get off these damn drugs," her mother com- 15
plained in my office. "That [stuff] has got her all screwed . . . "

"I'm not gonna listen to you," the girl interrupted. She 16
turned to me. "This is the woman who let me get beat on for
about 10 years and let her boyfriend sneak into my bedroom,
without her saying two words. How am I supposed to live as
a normal human being with a mother like her?"

Privately I agreed with her. I felt hopeless about the situation 17
myself. I could see that this girl was trapped in a family that was
eroding her emotional resiliency, leaving her increasingly vulnerable to severe psychiatric illness. And society had no plan to
rescue her from this situation. In fact, it tacitly endorsed it.

One of the difficulties of working as a therapist with ado- 18
lescents is that they often clearly perceive the psychological
dangers confronting them, but are powerless to deal with
them. It's no wonder then that such experiences lay the
groundwork for panic attacks, post-traumatic stress disorder,
depression and paranoia that seem to come "out of the blue"
later in life. The coping mechanisms of some of the teenagers I
treat have short-circuited already. These patients "dissociate":
They unpredictably enter altered states of consciousness in
which they lose touch with reality.

One 17-year-old whom I treated for depression asked me 19
plainly: "If you were me, what would you do to make sure
your parents didn't get you even sicker during the next year? I
mean, if I can get to 18, I can leave home, maybe join the Army
or something, and they won't be able to do anything about it."

I told him that he needed to be less confrontational in the 20
face of his parents' unreasonable demands for strict obedience,
if only to conserve his emotional energy, not to mention avoid
his father's belt. "Prisoners of war don't get in beefs every day
with their captors," I told him. "They lay low until they can
escape."

Like most of the abusive parents I have met, this young 21
man's father, for example, made it clear to me that he too had
faced traumas as a young person, including horrific beatings.
He tried to do his best for his son despite severe depression and
alcoholism that limited his ability to function. Doing his best,
however, was not nearly good enough.

22   This is why a social policy that would raise expectations for healthy parenting and more frequently and quickly impose the loss of parental rights should include a vigorous attempt to educate parents on how to avoid harming their children. The loss of parental rights is a tragedy we should attempt to avoid.

23   Another key requirement is to recruit good foster families. Too often such families have not proven to be much better for kids than the homes they have left; sometimes they are even worse. It makes no sense to take the admittedly drastic step of removing children from bad biological parents only to place them with bad foster parents.

24   One 19-year-old woman I met recently had spent a decade living in a foster family. She had been beaten and neglected for the years prior to her placement and, even with obviously concerned and empathic foster parents, had required years of psychotherapy to cope with her traumatic past.

25   With the support of a new family, however, she had achieved in school, shunned drugs and made close and lasting friendships. She hoped to save money to attend college. While she considered leaving her biological parents as one of the major stresses in her life, she made it clear that she would have been much worse staying with them. "I'm one of the lucky ones," she said. "I got out."

26   The tragedy is that too few children do.

Expanding Vocabulary

Match each word in column A with its definition in column B. When in doubt, first find the word in the essay and look for context clues to aid your understanding of the word's meaning. Then, if necessary, use your dictionary to complete the matching exercise.

Column A	Column B
bouts (2)	dividing, separating
paranoid (2)	impossible to repair or fix
perennial (8)	quietly, implied rather than
irreparable (9)	stated
psychosis (9)	outlines of possible future
scenarios (10)	events
traumas (10)	serious emotional shocks that
inalienable (11)	may result in lasting damage

egregious (12)
cleaving (12)
eroding (17)
resiliency (17)
tacitly (17)

notably offensive
contests, matches
destroying, eating away at
one with a disorder
   characterized by delusions
   of persecution or grandeur
ability to recover from serious
   problems
lasting through many years
what cannot be transferred to
   another
mental disorder marked by
   disconnection with reality
   and social dysfunction

Understanding Content

1. For what two reasons are abused children kept with the parents who are abusing them?
2. What problems do the abused teenagers experience; what are the effects of their situation? How does Ablow treat them?
3. What are long-term effects of abusing children?
4. How do abused adolescents view their situation?

Drawing Inferences about Thesis and Purpose

1. What is Ablow's subject?
2. What is Ablow's thesis? What change in policy does he want to see? Where does he state his thesis?
3. What specific actions are needed to improve the health of abused children?

Analyzing Strategies and Style

1. Reflect on Ablow's title. What is the key word in his title? What point is he making about physical and psychological abuse of children?
2. The author provides several examples of abused teenagers; how do the examples help to advance his argument? Ablow begins and ends with extended examples that include dialogue. What makes these effective ways to begin and end?
3. What, in your view, is the most telling example, detail, or argument in the essay? Why?

Thinking Critically

1. Have you known any abused teens? If so, have you seen any good solutions to their problems, such as foster care or therapy? Do you know adolescents who need help? If so, what can you do?
2. Should bad parents lose their children? Why or why not?
3. Would you favor more resources to help abused children? Why or why not?
4. How can we improve education for prospective parents so that they will be prepared for good parenting? What suggestions do you have?

"Social Science Finds: 'Marriage Matters' "

LINDA J. WAITE

A former senior sociologist at the Rand Corporation, Linda Waite (b. 1947) is currently a professor at the University of Chicago. She has several books—with co-authors—including Teenage Motherhood *(1979) and* New Families, No Families? *(1991). In this article, published in* The Responsive Community *in 1996, Waite examines various studies of marriage to determine the effects that marriage has on those who are married.*

1   As we are all too aware, the last few decades have witnessed a decline in the popularity of marriage. This trend has not escaped the notice of politicians and pundits. But when critics point to the high social costs and taxpayer burden imposed by disintegrating "family values," they overlook the fact that individuals do not simply make the decisions that lead to unwed parenthood, marriage, or divorce on the basis of what is good for society. Individuals weigh the costs and benefits of each of these choices to themselves—and sometimes their children. But how much is truly known about these costs and benefits, either by the individuals making the choices or demographers like myself who study them? Put differently, what are the implications, for individuals, of the current increases in nonmarriage? If we think of marriage as an insurance policy—which it

is, in some respects—does it matter if more people are uninsured, or are insured with a term rather than a whole-life policy? I shall argue that it does matter, because marriage typically provides important and substantial benefits, benefits not enjoyed by those who live alone or cohabit.

A quick look at marriage patterns today compared to, say, 2 1950 shows the extent of recent changes. Figures from the Census Bureau show that in 1950, at the height of the baby boom, about a third of white men and women were not married. Some were waiting to marry for the first time, some were divorced or widowed and not remarried. But virtually everyone married at least once at some point in their lives, generally in their early twenties.

In 1950 the proportion of black men and women not married 3 was approximately equal to the proportion unmarried among whites, but since that time the marriage behavior of blacks and whites has diverged dramatically. By 1993, 61 percent of black women and 58 percent of black men were not married, compared to 38 percent of white men and 41 percent of white women. So, in contrast to 1950 when only a little over one black adult in three was not married, now a majority of black adults are unmarried. Insofar as marriage "matters," black men and women are much less likely than whites to share in the benefits, and much less likely today than they were a generation ago.

The decline in marriage is directly connected to the rise in 4 cohabitation—living with someone in a sexual relationship without being married. Although Americans are less likely to be married today than they were several decades ago, if we count both marriage and cohabitation, they are about as likely to be "coupled." If cohabitation provides the same benefits to individuals as marriage does, then we do not need to be concerned about this shift. But we may be replacing a valuable social institution with one that demands and offers less.

Perhaps the most disturbing change in marriage appears in 5 its relationship to parenthood. Today a third of all births occur to women who are not married, with huge but shrinking differences between blacks and whites in this behavior. One in five births to white mothers and two-thirds of births to black mothers currently take place outside marriage. Although about a quarter of the white unmarried mothers are living with someone when they give birth, so that their children are born into two-parent—if unmarried—families, very few black children born to unmarried mothers live with fathers too.

6   I believe that these changes in marriage behavior are a cause for concern, because in a number of important ways married men and women do better than those who are unmarried. And I believe that the evidence suggests that they do better because they are married.

Marriage and Health

7   The case for marriage is quite strong. Consider the issues of longevity and health. With economist Lee Lillard, I used a large national survey to follow men and women over a 20-year period. We watched them get married, get divorced, and remarry. We observed the death of spouses and of the individuals themselves. And we compared deaths of married men and women to those who were not married. We found that once we took other factors into account, married men and women faced lower risks of dying at any point than those who have never married or whose previous marriage has ended. Widowed women were much better off than divorced women or those who had never married, although they were still disadvantaged when compared with married women. But all men who were not currently married faced significantly higher risks of dying than married men, regardless of their marital history. Other scholars have found disadvantages in death rates for unmarried adults in a number of countries besides the United States.

8   How does marriage lengthen life? First, marriage appears to reduce risky and unhealthy behaviors. For example, according to University of Texas sociologist Debra Umberson, married men show much lower rates of problem drinking than unmarried men. Umberson also found that both married men and women are less likely to take risks that could lead to injury than are the unmarried. Second, as we will see below, marriage increases material well-being—income, assets, and wealth. These can be used to purchase better medical care, better diet, and safer surroundings, which lengthen life. This material improvement seems to be especially important for women.

9   Third, marriage provides individuals—especially men—with someone who monitors their health and health-related be-

haviors and who encourages them to drink and smoke less, to eat a healthier diet, to get enough sleep and to generally take care of their health. In addition, husbands and wives offer each other moral support that helps in dealing with stressful situations. Married men especially seem to be motivated to avoid risky behaviors and to take care of their health by the sense of meaning that marriage gives to their lives and the sense of obligation to others that it brings.

More Wealth, Better Wages—For Most

Married individuals also seem to fare better when it comes to   10
wealth. One comprehensive measure of financial well-being—household wealth—includes pension and Social Security wealth, real and financial assets, and the value of the primary residence. According to economist James Smith, in 1992 married men and women ages 51–60 had median wealth of about $66,000 per spouse, compared to $42,000 for the widowed, $35,000 for those who had never married, $34,000 among those who were divorced, and only $7,600 for those who were separated. Although married couples have higher incomes than others, this fact accounts for only about a quarter of their greater wealth.

How does marriage increase wealth? Married couples can   11
share many household goods and services, such as a TV and heat, so the cost to each individual is lower than if each one purchased and used the same items individually. So the married spend less than the same individuals would for the same style of life if they lived separately. Second, married people produce more than the same individuals would if single. Each spouse can develop some skills and neglect others, because each can count on the other to take responsibility for some of the household work. The resulting specialization increases efficiency. We see below that this specialization leads to higher wages for men. Married couples also seem to save more at the same level of income than do single people.

The impact of marriage is again beneficial—although in this   12
case not for all involved—when one looks at labor market outcomes. According to recent research by economist Kermit Daniel, both black and white men receive a wage premium if they are married: 4.5 percent for black men and 6.3 percent for

white men. Black women receive a marriage premium of almost 3 percent. White women, however, pay a marriage penalty, in hourly wages, of over 4 percent. In addition, men appear to receive some of the benefit of marriage if they cohabit, but women do not.

13   Why should marriage increase men's wages? Some researchers think that marriage makes men more productive at work, leading to higher wages. Wives may assist husbands directly with their work, offer advice or support, or take over household tasks, freeing husbands' time and energy for work. Also, as I mentioned earlier, being married reduces drinking, substance abuse, and other unhealthy behaviors that may affect men's job performance. Finally, marriage increases men's incentives to perform well at work, in order to meet obligations to family members.

14   For women, Daniel finds that marriage and presence of children together seem to affect wages, and the effects depend on the woman's race. Childless black women earn substantially more money if they are married but the "marriage premium" drops with each child they have. Among white women only the childless receive a marriage premium. Once white women become mothers, marriage decreases their earnings compared to remaining single (with children), with very large negative effects of marriage on women's earnings for those with two children or more. White married women often choose to reduce hours of work when they have children. They also make less per hour than either unmarried mothers or childless wives.

15   Up to this point, all the consequences of marriage for the individuals involved have been unambiguously positive—better health, longer life, more wealth, and higher earnings. But the effects of marriage and children on white women's wages are mixed, at best. Marriage and cohabitation increase women's time spent on housework; married motherhood reduces their time in the labor force and lowers their wages. Although the family as a whole might be better off with this allocation of women's time, women generally share their husbands' market earnings only when they are married. Financial well-being declines dramatically for women and their children after divorce and widowhood; women whose marriages have ended are often quite disadvantaged financially by their investment in

their husbands and children rather than in their own earning power. Recent changes in divorce law—the rise in no-fault divorce and the move away from alimony—seem to have exacerbated this situation, even while increases in women's education and work experience have moderated it.

Improved Intimacy

Another benefit of married life is an improved sex life. Married 16 men and women report very active sex lives—as do those who are cohabiting. But the married appear to be more satisfied with sex than others. More married men say that they find sex with their wives to be extremely physically pleasurable than do cohabiting men or single men say the same about sex with their partners. The high levels of married men's physical satisfaction with their sex lives contradicts the popular view that sexual novelty or variety improves sex for men. Physical satisfaction with sex is about the same for married women, cohabiting women, and single women with sex partners.

In addition to reporting more active and more physically 17 fulfilling sex lives than the unmarried, married men and women say that they are more emotionally satisfied with their sex lives than do those who are single or cohabiting. Although cohabitants report levels of sexual activity as high as the married, both cohabiting men and women report lower levels of emotional satisfaction with their sex lives. And those who are sexually active but single report the lowest emotional satisfaction with it.

How does marriage improve one's sex life? Marriage and co- 18 habitation provide individuals with a readily available sexual partner with whom they have an established, ongoing sexual relationship. This reduces the costs—in some sense—of any particular sexual contact, and leads to higher levels of sexual activity. Since married couples expect to carry on their sex lives for many years, and since the vast majority of married couples are monogamous, husbands and wives have strong incentives to learn what pleases their partner in bed and to become good at it. But I would argue that more than "skills" are at issue here. The long-term contract implicit in marriage—which is not implicit in cohabitation—facilitates emotional investment in the relationship, which should affect both frequency of and satisfaction with sex. So the wife or husband who knows what the spouse wants is also highly motivated to provide it, both because sexual satisfaction in one's partner brings similar rewards to oneself and because the emotional commitment to the partner makes satisfying him or her important in itself.

19   To this point we have focused on the consequences of marriage for adults—the men and women who choose to marry (and stay married) or not. But such choices have consequences for the children born to these adults. Sociologists Sara McLanahan and Gary Sandefur compare children raised in intact, two-parent families with those raised in one-parent families, which could result either from disruption of a marriage or from unmarried childbearing. They find that approximately twice as many children raised in one-parent families than children from two-parent families drop out of high school without finishing. Children raised in one-parent families are also more likely to have a birth themselves while teenagers, and to be "idle"—both out of school and out of the labor force—as young adults.

20   Not surprisingly, children living outside an intact marriage are also more likely to be poor. McLanahan and Sandefur calculated poverty rates for children in two-parent families—including stepfamilies—and for single-parent families. They found very high rates of poverty for single-parent families, especially among blacks. Donald Hernandez, chief of marriage and family statistics at the Census Bureau, claims that the rise in mother-only families since 1959 is an important cause of increases in poverty among children.

21   Clearly poverty, in and of itself, is a bad outcome for children. In addition, however, McLanahan and Sandefur estimate that the lower incomes of single-parent families account for only half of the negative impact for children in these families. The other half comes from children's access—or lack of access—to the time and attention of two adults in two-parent families. Children in one-parent families spend less time with their fathers (this is not surprising given that they do not live with them), but they also spend less time with their mothers than children in two-parent families. Single-parent families and step-

families also move much more frequently than two-parent families, disrupting children's social and academic environments. Finally, children who spend part of their childhood in a single-parent family report substantially lower quality relationships with their parents as adults and have less frequent contact with them, according to demographer Diane Lye.

Correlation versus Causality

The obvious question, when one looks at all these "benefits" of 22 marriage, is whether marriage is responsible for these differences. If all, or almost all, of the benefits of marriage arise because those who enjoy better health, live longer lives, or earn higher wages anyway are more likely to marry, then marriage is not "causing" any changes in these outcomes. In such a case, we as a society and we as individuals could remain neutral about each person's decision to marry or not, to divorce or remain married. But scholars from many fields who have examined the issues have come to the opposite conclusion. Daniel found that only half of the higher wages that married men enjoy could be explained by selectivity; he thus concluded that the other half is causal. In the area of mental health, social psychologist Catherine Ross—summarizing her own research and that of other social scientists—wrote, "The positive effect of marriage on well-being is strong and consistent, and the selection of the psychologically healthy into marriage or the psychologically unhealthy out of marriage cannot explain the effect." Thus marriage itself can be assumed to have independent positive effects on its participants.

So, we must ask, what is it about marriage that causes these 23 benefits? I think that four factors are key. First, the institution of marriage involves a long-term contract—" 'til death do us part." This contract allows the partners to make choices that carry immediate costs but eventually bring benefits. The time horizon implied by marriage makes it sensible—a rational choice is at work here—for individuals to develop some skills and to neglect others because they count on their spouse to fill in where they are weak. The institution of marriage helps individuals honor this long-term contract by providing social support for the couple as a couple and by imposing social and economic costs on those who dissolve their union.

24   Second, marriage assumes a sharing of economic and social resources and what we can think of as co-insurance. Spouses act as a sort of small insurance pool against life's uncertainties, reducing their need to protect themselves—by themselves— from unexpected events.

25   Third, married couples benefit—as do cohabiting couples— from economies of scale.

26   Fourth, marriage connects people to other individuals, to their social groups (such as in-laws), and to other social institutions (such as churches and synagogues) which are themselves a source of benefits. These connections provide individuals with a sense of obligation to others, which gives life meaning beyond oneself.

27   Cohabitation has some but not all of the characteristics of marriage and so carries some but not all of the benefits. Cohabitation does not generally imply a lifetime commitment to stay together; a significant number of cohabiting couples disagree on the future of their relationship. Frances Goldscheider and Gail Kaufman believe that the shift to cohabitation from marriage signals "declining commitment within unions, of men and women to each other and to their relationship as an enduring unit, in exchange for more freedom, primarily for men." Perhaps, as a result, many view cohabitation as an especially poor bargain for women.

28   The uncertainty that accompanies cohabitation makes both investment in the relationship and specialization with this partner much riskier than in marriage and so reduces them. Cohabitants are much less likely than married couples to pool financial resources and more likely to assume that each partner is responsible for supporting himself or herself financially. And whereas marriage connects individuals to other important social institutions, cohabitation seems to distance them from these institutions.

29   Of course, all these observations concern only the average benefits of marriage. Clearly, some marriages produce substantially higher benefits for those involved. Some marriages produce no benefits and even cause harm to the men, women, and children involved. That fact needs to be recognized.

Reversing the Trend

Having stated this qualification, we must still ask, if the aver- 30
age marriage produces all of these benefits for individuals,
why has it declined? Although this issue remains a subject of
much research and speculation, a number of factors have been
mentioned as contributing. For one, because of increases in
women's employment, there is less specialization by spouses
now than in the past; this reduces the benefits of marriage.
Clearly, employed wives have less time and energy to focus on
their husbands, and are less financially and emotionally dependent on marriage than wives who work only in the home.
In addition, high divorce rates decrease people's certainty
about the long-run stability of their marriage, and this may reduce their willingness to invest in it, which in turn increases
the chance they divorce—a sort of self-fulfilling prophecy.
Also, changes in divorce laws have shifted much of the financial burden for the breakup of the marriage to women, making
investment within the marriage (such as supporting a husband
in medical school) a riskier proposition for them.

Men, in turn, may find marriage and parenthood a less at- 31
tractive option when they know that divorce is common, because they may face the loss of contact with their children if
their marriage dissolves. Further, women's increased earnings
and young men's declining financial well-being may have
made women less dependent on men's financial support and
made young men less able to provide it. Finally, public policies
that support single mothers and changing attitudes toward sex
outside of marriage, toward unmarried childbearing, and toward divorce have all been implicated in the decline in marriage. This brief list does not exhaust the possibilities, but
merely mentions some of them.

So how can this trend be reversed? First, as evidence accu- 32
mulates and is communicated to individuals, some people will
change their behavior as a result. Some will do so simply because of their new understanding of the costs and benefits, to
them, of the choices involved. In addition, we have seen that
attitudes frequently change toward behaviors that have been
shown to have negative consequences. The attitude change
then raises the social cost of the newly stigmatized behavior.

33   In addition, though, we as a society can pull some policy
levers to encourage or discourage behaviors. Public policies
that include asset tests (Medicaid is a good example) act to exclude the married, as do AFDC programs and most states. The
"marriage penalty" in the tax code is another example. These
and other policies reinforce or undermine the institution of
marriage. If, as I have argued, marriage produces individuals
who drink less, smoke less, abuse substances less, live longer,
earn more, are wealthier, and have children who do better, we
need to give more thought and effort to supporting this valuable social institution.

Expanding Vocabulary

After studying definitions of the following words, select five and use
each one in a separate sentence.

pundits (1)	exacerbated (15)
demographers (1)	monogamous (18)
cohabit (1)	implicit (18)
diverged (3)	disruption (19)
unambiguously (15)	stigmatized (32)

Understanding Content

1. Waite argues that most people weigh the advantages and disadvantages of marriage based on what?
2. How have marriage statistics changed for blacks since 1950?
3. Although marriage has declined, what has taken its place?
4. What percentage of births occur to women who are not married?
What percentage of white mothers are living with someone?
What percentage of black mothers are living with someone?
5. What groups are healthiest and live the longest? What three reasons does Waite list to explain these health facts?
6. Which arrangement type has the greatest income? Which type has
the least?
7. In what ways can marriage increase wealth? Who, when married,
loses in hourly wages?
8. What may be causes for increased productivity for married men?
9. Which living arrangement reports having the most physical and
emotional satisfaction from sex?
10. What situations increase poverty for children?
11. What are some effects of single-parent families on children?

12. Does Waite conclude that marriage itself is a cause of the improved lives of most married people? In general, who benefits the least from marriage?

Drawing Inferences about Thesis and Purpose

1. What does Waite assert about marriage; that is, what is her thesis?
2. Why, if marriage has benefits, are fewer people getting married and more getting divorced?
3. What does Waite think should be done to change the movement away from marriage?

Analyzing Strategies and Style

1. This is a longish essay. What does Waite do to help readers follow her discussion?
2. What kind of evidence, primarily, does the author provide? How is this consistent with your expectations, based on your knowledge of the author?

Thinking Critically

1. Which statistic most surprises you? Why?
2. Do you think that the evidence Waite provides should encourage people to choose marriage over divorce, cohabitation, or the single life? If so, why? If not, why not?
3. What can be done to increase marriage benefits for women, the ones who have least benefited by marriage?

"Dream Deferred"

LANGSTON HUGHES

Like many American writers, Langston Hughes (1902–1967) came from the Middle West to New York City, lived in Europe, and then returned to the United States to a career of writing. He was a journalist, fiction writer, and poet, and author of more than sixty books. Hughes was also the first African American to support himself as a professional writer. Known as "the bard of Harlem," Hughes became an important public figure and voice for black writers. "Dream Deferred," one of Hughes's best-loved poems, which comes from *The Panther and the Lash: Poems of Our Time* (1951), illustrates the effective use of metaphor to convey the poet's attitudes and emotions.

What happens to a dream deferred?

Does it dry up
like a raisin in the sun?
Or fester like a sore—
And then run?   5
Does it stink like rotten meat?
Or crust and sugar over—
like a syrupy sweet?

Maybe it just sags
like a heavy load.   10

Or does it explode?

Understanding Content and Strategies

1. How is the poem structured; that is, what is it a series of?
2. The "answers" to the poem's first question are all similes except one. Which line is a metaphor? Explain the metaphor. Why is the one metaphor an effective strategy?
3. What does Hughes mean by a "deferred" dream?
4. Explain each simile. How does each one present a response to, or the effect of, a deferred dream?
5. What do the similes and metaphor have in common?

Drawing Inferences about Theme

1. What, then, is Hughes's attitude toward his subject? What does he want us to understand about deferred dreams?
2. Might the poem also be making a social comment? If so, what?

Thinking Critically

1. Which simile do you find most effective? Why?
2. Has Hughes included most of the responses to deferred dreams? Is there any response you would add? If so, can you state it as a simile?

3. Is there a dream that you have not been able to fulfill? If so, has Hughes aptly described the effect of that experience on you? What advice would you give to someone to help that person cope with the effects of deferred dreams?

MAKING CONNECTIONS

1. Amatai Etzioni sees today's obsession with self-fulfillment as a major cause of social problems. Could one describe the breakdown of family as a loss of a sense of duty? Compare Etzioni's views with Robert Samuelson's and Linda Waite's. Will an obsession with the self bring happiness? Consider what Ciardi (see Chapter 8) has to say about happiness.

2. Linda Waite thinks that, generally, people's lives are improved by marriage. Keith Ablow is concerned with the deviance of parents that leads to abused children. Apparently not all marriages result in happier adults and children. Should we encourage marriage for everyone? Should there be testing of some kind leading to a marriage license? A parenting license?

3. Robert Reich raises issues about a divided America—divided by income. Have we, in this society, chosen the search for affluence over family commitments and family joys? Does this search divide us by gender and by class? Does it affect our compassion for those less fortunate? If the answer is yes to these questions, should we be concerned? Are these problems for society? If so, what can we do to change?

TOPICS AND GUIDELINES FOR WRITING

1. Do you like horror movies? If so, why? Has Stephen King explained your reasons, or are there other reasons that motivate you, and perhaps others you know? If you have other causes to add to King's analysis, write an essay explaining them. Begin with credit to King for his discussion of the topic and then add your insights.

2. In your prereading exercise, you reflected on your decision to attend college. Now reflect on your reasons for selecting the particular college you are attending. In an essay, explain the causes for your choice of school. You can organize according to the decision process you went through, or you can organize from least important to most important causes. You might think of writing this essay as a feature article in your college newspaper.

3. Have you ever done something that you did not think you ought to do? If so, why did you do it? And what were the consequences of your actions? In an essay, examine the causes and effects of your action. Be sure that you have a point to make. You might want to show that you should have listened to the warning voice inside you, or you might want to show that one effect of such a situation is that we do learn something about ourselves.

4. Are you "addicted" to something? To chocolate or beer or cigarettes? To television soaps, video games, bridge, or something else? If so, reflect on why you and others like you are addicted to whatever it is that absorbs you. Drawing on your personal experience, your knowledge of others, and perhaps some reading on the topic, develop an analysis of the causes of your addiction. Organize your causes from least to most important and illustrate each one. If you use ideas from your reading, give proper credit by stating author and title.

5. Do you get along well (or poorly) with a parent? If so, reflect on why you have a good (or bad) relationship with that parent. What are the causes? Are your experiences similar to those of friends? What do some of the experts say about parent/children relationships? Drawing on your personal situation, your knowledge of others, and perhaps some reading, develop an analysis of the causes for good (or bad) parent/child relationships. Organize causes from least to most important and illustrate each one. If you use ideas from your reading, give proper credit.

6. Have you experienced divorce either as a once-married person or as a child of divorced parents? If so, reflect on the ef-

fects of divorce. Drawing on your own experience, your knowledge of the experiences of others, and perhaps some reading, develop an analysis of the effects of divorce on divorced persons or their children. Follow the guidelines for organization and crediting your reading given in topic 4.

7. Amitai Etzioni feels strongly about the decline of a sense of duty in our society, and this has led him to write on the subject. Is there a current social or political problem that you are especially interested in? If so, think about the causes and effects of this problem. Then write an essay on the problem. Focus on the causes of the problem, the effects of the problem, or both causes and effects. You might want to conclude with one or more proposed solutions to the problem.

10

Using Argument and Persuasion

Preserving the Health of Our World

Losing patience with two friends, you finally moan, "Will you two *please* stop arguing! You've been bickering all evening; you're ruining the party." How often many of us have said, or wanted to say, something similar to parents, children, colleagues, or friends who seem unable to stop yelling or name calling, or quibbling over some insignificant point. In this context, the term *argument* has a negative connotation. In a classroom debate, a courtroom, a business conference, or writing, however, a sound argument is highly valued.

The Characteristics of Argument

Understanding the characteristics of good argument will help you to think critically about the arguments of others and to write better arguments of your own. Some of these characteristics may surprise you, so read thoughtfully and reflect on the following points.

❑ An argument makes a point. Sound reasons and relevant evidence are presented to support a claim, a main idea that the arguer keeps in focus. Collecting data on a particular topic may produce an interesting report, but unless the specifics support a point, there is no argument.

❑ Argument assumes an audience. The purpose of argument is not just to provide information but to change the way listeners or readers think about an issue, to move them to agree with you. Once you accept that argument implies an audience, you have to accept the possibility of counterarguments, of listeners or readers who will not agree with you and will challenge your thinking. You have not defended your argument by simply asserting that it is *your opinion.* If you have not based your opinion on good evidence and reasons, your opinion will be challenged, and you will lose the respect of your audience.

❏ Good argument is based on a recognition of the complexities of most issues and the reality of opposing views. One of the greatest dangers to good argument lies in oversimplifying complex issues, or in oversimplifying reality by assuming that our claim is "clearly right" and that therefore everyone agrees with us.

❏ Good argument makes clear the values and beliefs that we consider relevant to the issue. Argument is not just an intellectual game. We need to recognize the values that are a part of our reasoning, our way of approaching a particular issue. For example, if you argue that abortion is wrong because it is murder, you *believe* that the fetus is a human being at the moment of conception. Your argument is convincing only to those who share your *belief.* Wanting no uncertainty about the values upon which his claim was founded, Thomas Jefferson wrote: "We hold these truths to be self-evident" and then listed such values as "all men are created equal" and "governments are instituted among men."

❏ In argument, we present evidence to support a claim on the *assumption* that there is a valid or logical connection between evidence and claim, what British philosopher Stephen Toulmin calls a *warrant.* When you argue that abortion is wrong because it is murder, you assume or warrant that the fetus is a human being who can be murdered. Arguments can be challenged not only on the evidence or stated reasons but also on the assumptions or warrants that support the argument's structure. Therefore, you must know what your assumptions or warrants are because you may need to defend them as part of the support for your argument.

❏ Argument includes the use of persuasive strategies. When you write an argumentative essay, you want to convince readers to share your views, or at least to reconsider theirs in the light of your discussion. Of course you are involved in your topic and want to affect readers. Indeed, you will write more persuasively if you write about issues that concern you. In good argument, however, emotions are tempered by logic and channeled into the energy needed to think through the topic, to gather evidence, to consider audience, and to plan the paper. Remember that one of the best *persuasive* strategies is to present yourself to readers as a reasonable person who has done your homework on the topic and who wants to find some common ground with those who disagree.

Causes of Bad Argument: Logical Fallacies

When you ignore the complexities of issues or choose emotional appeals over logic, you risk producing an essay filled with *logical fallacies.* Many arguments that could be won are ruined by those who leave reasoned debate for emotional appeals or who oversimplify the issues. Here are some frequent fallacies to avoid in your writing and to watch out for in the arguments of others.

❑ *ad hominem*   Attacking the opponents instead of defending your position is not an effective strategy with intelligent readers. You have not supported an anti-abortion position, for example, by calling pro-choice advocates "murderers" or labeling them "pro-abortion."

❑ **Straw Man**   The straw man fallacy seeks to defend one position by accusing opponents of holding a position that is easier to attack but is not actually what the opponents believe. To "argue" that those seeking gun registration just want to take guns away from good people and leave them in the hands of criminals is a good example. Those who want gun registration certainly do not want criminals to have guns.

❑ **Bandwagon**   Another substitute for good argument is the appeal to join in, or join the majority, often without providing evidence that a majority holds the view of the arguer or, even more important, that the view is a sound one. Appeals to national interest or the good of the country often contain the bandwagon fallacy. For example: All good Americans want respect shown for the flag, so we need a law banning flag burning. Some "good Americans" also value free speech and see flag burning as an example of free speech.

❑ **Common Practice**   Similar to the bandwagon fallacy, the appeal to common practice is the false logic that "everyone is doing it, so it must be a good thing." However, cheating on tests or on one's income taxes, for example, cannot be logically defended by "arguing" that everybody does it. First, it is not true that everybody does it, and second, even if that were true, it would not make cheating right.

❑ **Hasty Generalization or Overstatement**   When drawing on your own experiences for evidence, you need to judge if your experiences are representative. For example, you may be having difficulty in calculus, but it would be illogical to conclude that the instructor is inept or that the course is too hard. These could be explanations, but they are not the only possible ones. How are other students doing in the course is a key question to ask. Even when you gather extensive evidence from reading, be cautious about generalizing. It is not true that all people on welfare are lazy or that lawyers only want to make piles of money. Qualify assertions; avoid such words as *always, never, everybody,* and *none.* (These words entice readers to find the one exception that will disprove your sweeping generalization.)

❑ **False Dilemma**   The false dilemma is often called either/or thinking. It is the illogic of asserting that only two possibilities are available when there may be several. The effectiveness of this strategy (if you have readers who are not thinking critically) is that you can make one possibility seem a terrible choice, thereby making your choice sound good by contrast. For example: Either we pay more taxes or we will have to cut educational programs. Now these are clearly not the only two possibilities. First, there are other programs that could be cut. Second, we could find ways to save money in the running of government. Third, we can have a growing economy that brings in more government revenues without increasing taxes. Those are just three additional possibilities; there are probably others.

❑ **Slippery Slope**   The slippery slope fallacy makes the argument that we cannot allow A to take place because if we do, then we will head down a slope all the way to Z, a place where no one wants to be. The strategy here is to make Z so awful that readers will agree with you that we should not do A. The error in logic is the unsupported assumption that if A takes place, Z will follow. For example: If the government is allowed to register guns, then before you know it they will ban handguns and then take away all guns, even hunting rifles. Unfortunately, for those who want to scare people with this illogic, there is no evidence that registration will lead to confiscation. We register cars and planes and boats; the government has not confiscated any of these items.

How to Use Argument and Persuasion

How can you put together a good argumentative essay? Accepting that writing an effective argument is a challenging task, you may want to give appropriate time and thought to *preparing to write* before you actually draft your essay. Use the following guidelines to aid your writing.

1. **Think about audience and purpose.** Unless you are writing about a most unusual topic, expect your readers to be aware of the issue. This does not mean that you can skip an

appropriate introduction or necessary background information. It does mean that you can expect readers to know (and perhaps be a part of) the opposition, so be prepared to challenge counterarguments and consider the advantages of pointing out common ground. Also define your purpose in writing; that is, recognize the *type* of argument you are planning. Are you presenting the results of a study, perhaps the results of a questionnaire you prepared? (For example, you could do a survey of attitudes toward campus security, or proposals to eliminate the school newspaper.) Are you writing to state your position on a value-laden issue, such as euthanasia or capital punishment? Are you writing on a public-policy issue, such as whether to restrict smoking in all public buildings? Each of these types of arguments needs somewhat different support and development, so as you work on your argument's thesis or claim, think about the type of argument as well.

2. **Brainstorm about your topic to develop a tentative thesis and think about the kinds of support your thesis (claim) will need.** If you have done an investigation, you need to study your evidence to see what appropriate conclusions can be drawn. (For example, if 51 percent of the students you polled want more security on campus at night, you could say that a majority of students think that increased security is needed. But, it is more accurate to say that about half of the students polled expressed that view.) If you are writing an argument based primarily on values rather than facts, decide on your position and then begin to list your reasons. Suppose you support euthanasia. What, exactly, are you in favor of? Physician-assisted suicide? A patient's right to refuse all life-support systems? A family-member's right to make that decision? Be sure that you state your claim so that it clearly represents your position, a position you believe you can support. Then consider why: to eliminate unnecessary suffering? To give individuals control over their deaths? If you are examining a problem in education or arguing for restricting smoking in public buildings, you may need to do some reading to locate appropriate facts and statistics. You may also need to consider the feasibility of putting your proposal into place. Will it cost money? Where

will the money come from? Who may be hurt or inconvenienced? How can you bring these people to your side?
3. **Plan the organization of your essay.** Remember that any plan is just a guide so that you can get started. As you draft or when you revise, you may find that you want to switch parts around or add new ideas and examples that have come to you while writing. But remember as well that usually some plan is better than no plan. If you are writing an argument based on values, consider these steps:

   a. **Begin with an introduction to get your reader's attention.** If you are writing on euthanasia, you can mention the news coverage of Dr. Kevorkian.

   b. **Decide where to place your thesis.** Although typically a thesis or claim comes early in the essay, you may want to experiment with placing it at the end, after you have presented support for that claim.

   c. **Organize reasons in a purposeful way.** One strategy is to move from less important to most important reasons. Another approach is to organize around counterarguments, explaining why each of the opposition's arguments does not hold up. (In this chapter, Molly Ivins uses the arguments of the gun lobby as an organizing strategy in her argument for gun control.) Consider using some of the methods of development discussed throughout this text. Draw on your reading for statistical details, on your own experience for examples.

   d. **Provide support for each reason.** You have not written an effective argument just by stating your reasons. You need to argue for them, to show why they are reasonable, or better than the opposition's reasons, or have the support of good evidence.

   e. **Conclude by effectively stating or restating your claim.** As a part of your conclusion, you may want to explain to readers how this issue affects them, how they could benefit from embracing your position or your proposal for change.

4. **Revise, revise, revise.** After completing a first draft based on your tentative plan, study the draft carefully both for readability and effective argument. Examine reasons and support to be sure you have avoided logical fallacies. See

where you may need to qualify statements or control your language. Be certain that you have maintained an appropriate level of seriousness so that you retain the respect of readers. As the writers in this chapter illustrate, you want to write movingly about issues that concern you without forsaking good sense and relevant evidence.

Getting Started: Reflections on the Challenges Facing Ourselves, Our Society, Our World

What do you consider the greatest challenge facing you in your personal life? Is it completing school? Giving up cigarettes or junk food? Reestablishing a relationship with a parent or friend? What do you consider the greatest challenge facing society? Is it reestablishing a sense of community? Improving schools? Improving race relations? Finding deterrents to crime? What do you consider the greatest challenge facing the world? Is it saving the environment? Establishing world peace? Eliminating hunger and injustice? Decide on the challenge, in one of the categories, that most troubles you and brainstorm about the reasons for the problem and possible solutions to the problem. Be prepared to discuss your reasons and proposed solutions with classmates.

"Border Hazards: An Obsession to Become Unhealthy"

RICHARD RODRIGUEZ

Richard Rodriguez (b. 1944) holds degrees in literature from Stanford and Columbia Universities and has studied at Berkeley and the Warburg Institute in London. He is an editor of Pacific News Service and an author of both articles and books, including *Days of Obligation: An Argument with My Mexican Father* (1992). He has won awards for his writing, and excerpts from his autobiography *Hunger of Memory* (1982) are frequently anthologized. In the following article, published September 20, 1998, Rodriguez examines the effects of migration to the United States and the changes in lifestyles occurring around the world.

Maybe we need to put a sign at the border and in our inter- 1
national airports. WARNING: AMERICA MAY BE DANGER-
OUS TO YOUR HEALTH.

It has never been easy to be an immigrant. Imagine what 2
those 19th-century immigrants knew, leaving certainty behind,
abandoning Ireland and Italy and Russia, to travel to America.
(In those days, an ocean's separation from loved ones was permanent as death.) What bravery, what recklessness the journey
to Ellis Island required. What a price there was to pay for leaving certain poverty.

A study, headed by Professor William Vega of UC Berkeley 3
and published last week, has found that Mexican immigrants
suffer increased mental stress the longer they stay in this country. Rates of mental illness and other social disorders, like drug
use and divorce, rise after immigration. Vega's team of researchers observed the breakdown of immigrant families
within a generation, on a scale comparable to other Americans.

These findings are, at least, ironic. For generations, Ameri- 4
cans have assumed moral superiority toward Latin America.
Early this century, for example, citizens of San Diego traveled
south, into Tijuana, whenever they wanted to sin. Just as today,
Americans like to imagine that Mexican drug lords are contaminating our "innocent" youth.

The tables have turned. Four years ago, the Center for Sci- 5
ence in the Public Interest in Washington warned Americans
away from Mexican food. Eating a chile relleno is the equivalent of devouring a cube of butter! Now, U.S. professors warn
immigrants away from burgers and fries.

A week before Vega's report, a panel of the National Research 6
Council and the Institute of Medicine found that the longer an
immigrant child lives in this country, the greater the chance of
physical and psychological deterioration. The panel's chairman, Dr. Evan Charney of the University of Massachusetts
Medical School, warned, "The longer you're in this country, the
more you want to eat at McDonald's."

Immigrants. I see them all the time in California, their eyes 7
filled with terror and wonder. Their jogging shoes have transported them from villages in Mexico or Central America into
the postmodern city of freeways and peroxide and neon. How
will they find their way?

8   Vega and his team of researchers studied the problems of Mexican immigrants in Fresno County. But the researchers would, I suspect, have come up with similar findings of social breakdown had they talked with young Mexicans in Tijuana. The poor are in movement, all over the world, from village to city, from tradition toward change.

9   Recently, in the boomtown of Monterrey, Mexico, I met teenagers, poor alongside rich, who were busy consuming drugs. Cocaine was evidence of their modernity, a habit that made them just like the Americans on TV and the movies. Monterrey has not yet turned as violent as Mexico City. But the women in the new factories, on the outskirts of town, know divorce.

10   All over the world, from Andean villages to Southeast Asia, America advertises the "I." You can drink America from a Coke bottle; you can dance America. America is seducing the young all over the world with the idea of individual freedom. Change. Movement. Dollars.

11   On the line between Tijuana and San Diego tonight, you can meet kids waiting for dark to run into the United States. They say they do not want to become Americans. They do not speak of Thomas Jefferson or the Bill of Rights. There is, they say, a job waiting for them in Glendale or Fresno. A job in a pizza parlor or a job as a roofer that will keep them and their families from going hungry.

12   The U.S. professors fret. The panelists for the National Research Council advise against attempts "to push immigrant youth toward assimilation." But they might as well bemoan the jet engine or the bicycle.

13   Movement. America is not an easy country for either the native-born or the immigrant. Everything keeps changing. In small towns in Arkansas today, Mexican immigrants arrive to pluck dead chickens because no one else will do it. They paint their houses gaudy colors, speak Spanish at the post office. Native-born Americans bemoan the change. They become foreigners in their own town.

14   The kid from Oaxaca ends up making pizzas in Santa Monica. He learns English by hearing "Hold the pepperoni!" Day after day, he breathes America. America flows into his ears—California slang, the thump of rap. There is no resisting it.

Assimilation is more a biological process than a matter of 15 choice. Immigrant kids end up breathing America, swallowing America. When you approach the counter at McDonald's, you buy more than a burger: You buy an American spirit of impatience. Immigrants end up walking like the native-born, assuming the same nervous slouch.

Drugs. Divorce. Anonymity. The religions of the world that 16 are growing today are those religions that address the sadness of the migrating poor and their longing for the abandoned, lost village. Islam spreads through U.S. prisons. Evangelical Protestantism teaches children in Lima or in Los Angeles to be reborn and cleansed of the terrible city.

Immigrant parents turn pro-choice. They chose to leave Mex- 17 ico, so they imagine their U.S.-born kids can choose to absent themselves from Los Angeles, "remain" Mexican despite the heaving and throbbing city around them. Papa is always grumbling that the kids are becoming disrespectful U.S. teenagers. Mama is always saying that everyone was happier—poorer, yes, but happier—in the Mexican village.

America is a most remarkable country, the model of moder- 18 nity for people all over the world. It offers the world the possibility of individual life: the freeway onramp, the separate bedroom, the terrible loneliness, the range of choices on a TV remote.

The Mexican kid from Oaxaca will not go back. His dollars, 19 and maybe something more he cannot describe, will keep him making pizzas in Santa Monica. Yes, he will regret the disrespect of his U.S.-born children. Perhaps he will even send them back to Mexico during—that most American of seasons— adolescence.

But the village of Mexico is not, in truth, what it used to be. 20 It has changed. There are blond soap operas blaring from the television in the old family kitchen. Everyone in the village talks of jobs in Dallas and Guadalajara.

The guilt. The terrible guilt of becoming an American re- 21 mains. Every child of immigrant parents knows it. It is as old as America. The scorn of a grandmother: her black dress and her face at the window. Her mutterings in Yiddish or Chinese or Swedish. Her complaint: You are turning into a gringo, goy, a stranger to her.

22   Dear Nana. Forgive us! Forgive us our love of America, this very strange country, the envy of the world. Look! Look at the fresh fruits at Ralphs. The meats and the cheeses, dear abuelita. Forgive us for transporting the 18th-century pronoun, the "I," all the way to Fresno. It has driven us mad. But it has gotten us a washer and dryer.

23   It has made your grandchildren so tall and so straight, like movie stars. Look! Who would have guessed, dear Nana, you would have grandchildren so beautiful!

Expanding Vocabulary

Examine the following words in their contexts in the essay and then write a brief definition or synonym for each one. Do not use a dictionary; try to guess the word's meaning from its context.

contaminating (4)   bemoan (12)
deterioration (6)   slouch (15)
boomtown (9)   anonymity (16)
assimilation (12)

Understanding Content

1. According to a study by William Vega, what happens to Mexican immigrants to the United States?
2. What is ironic about these findings, according to Rodriguez?
3. What happens to immigrant children, according to the National Research Council?
4. What is happening to the poor all over the world?
5. What ideas does America "sell," especially to young people?
6. What happens to those who settle here? What do they gain? What do they lose?

Drawing Inference about Thesis and Purpose

1. Rodriguez calls adolescence "that most American of seasons." What does he mean by this?
2. What is Rodriguez's subject?
3. What is his thesis? (You may need more than one sentence to combine Rodriguez's several related ideas.)

Analyzing Strategies and Style

1. Look at paragraphs 7, 12, 13, 16, 21, and 22. What kind of sentence is an important part of Rodriguez's style? What makes it effective?

2. In paragraph 18, the author lists specifics that life in America offers. What is startling about this list? How is it effective?
3. Rodriguez begins with the results of studies, but his essay rather quickly moves away from being a report of research findings. How would you describe his style of writing and the tone of the essay?

Thinking Critically

1. Have you or your parents experienced the wonder and terror that Rodriguez describes as part of the immigrant experience? Do you think this is a fairly common experience for immigrants? Why or why not?
2. Have you seen an American town change as a result of immigrants moving in? If so, what was the general reaction in the town? What was your reaction? Have attitudes changed at all over time?
3. Do you agree with Rodriguez that what America offers is a mixed blessing? Why or why not?
4. Is this mixed blessing experienced by everyone, not just immigrants? Is America hazardous to our health—physical and psychological? Why or why not? If yes, what suggestions do you have for making it less hazardous?

"*SUVs: Killer Cars*"

ELLEN GOODMAN

After beginning her journalism career as a researcher at *Newsweek*, Ellen Goodman (b. 1941) became a feature writer at the Boston *Globe* and then a syndicated columnist in 1976. Her columns appear in over 250 newspapers, and many have been reprinted in collections. A winner of a Pulitzer Prize for distinguished commentary, Goodman examines social problems as frequently as political issues, as the following column, printed May 15, 1999, demonstrates. Here she expresses strong feelings about sport utility vehicles.

For my second career, I want to write car ads. Or better yet, 1
I want to live in a car ad.

In the real world, you and I creep and beep on some mis- 2
nomered expressway, but in the commercial fantasy land, drivers cruise along deserted, tree-lined roads.

3   We stall and crawl on city streets, but the man in the Lexus races "in the fast lane"—on an elevated road that curves around skyscrapers. We circle the block, looking for a place to park, but the owner of a Toyota RAV4 pulls up onto the sandy beach. We get stuck in the tunnel, but the Escalade man navigates down empty streets because "there are no roadblocks."

4   The world of the car ads bears about as much resemblance to commuter life as the Marlboro ads bear to the cancer ward.

5   All of this is a prelude to a full-boil rant against the archenemy of commuters everywhere: sport utility vehicles. Yes, those gas-guzzling, parking space-hogging bullies of the highway.

6   These sport utility vehicles are bought primarily by people whose favorite sport is shopping and whose most rugged athletic event is hauling the kids to soccer practice.

7   The sales and the size of the larger SUVs have grown at a speed that reminds me of the defense budget. In the escalating highway arms race, SUVs are sold for self-defense. Against what? Other SUVs.

8   As someone who has spent many a traffic-jammed day in the shadow of a behemoth, I am not surprised that the high and weighty are responsible for some 2,000 additional deaths a year. If a 6,000-pound Suburban hits an 1,800-pound Metro, it's going to be bad for the Metro. For that matter, if the Metro hits the Suburban, it's still going to be bad for the Metro.

9   The problem with SUVs is that you can't see over them, you can't see around them and you have to watch out for them. I am by no means the only driver of a small car who has felt intimidated by the big wheels barreling past me. Their macho reputation prompted even the Automobile Club of Southern California to issue an SUV driver tip: "Avoid a 'road warrior' mentality. Some SUV drivers operate under the false illusion that they can ignore common rules of caution."

10   But the biggest and burliest of the pack aren't just safety hazards; they're environmental hazards. Until now, SUVs have been allowed to legally pollute two or three times as much as automobiles. All over suburbia there are people who conscientiously drive their empty bottles to the suburban recycling center in vehicles that get 15 miles to the gallon. There are parents putting big bucks down for a big car so the kids can be safe while the air they breathe is being polluted.

At long last some small controls are being promoted. The 11 EPA has proposed for the first time that SUVs be treated like cars. If the agency, and the administration, has its way, a Suburban won't be allowed to emit more than a Taurus. That's an important beginning, but not the whole story.

Consider Ford, for example. The automaker produces rela- 12 tively clean-burning engines. But this fall it will introduce the humongous Excursion. It's 7 feet tall, 80 inches wide, weighs four tons and gets 10 miles to the gallon in the city. No wonder the Sierra Club calls it "the Ford Valdez." This is a nice car for taking the kids to school—if you're afraid you'll run into a tank.

Do I sound hostile? Last week a would-be SUV owner com- 13 plained to the *New York Times'* ethics critic that his friends were treating him as if he were "some kind of a criminal." The ethicist wrote back: "If you're planning to drive that SUV in New York, pack a suitcase into your roomy cargo area, because you're driving straight to hell."

I wouldn't go that far, though I have wished that hot trip on 14 at least one SUV whose bumper came to eye level with my windshield. Still, the SUV backlash is growing so strong that today's status symbol may become the first socially unacceptable vehicle since cars lost their fins.

It's one thing to have an SUV in the outback and quite an- 15 other to drive it around town. In the end, the right place for the big guy is in an ad. There, the skies are always clean, the drivers are always relaxed and there's never, ever another car in sight.

Expanding Vocabulary

Examine the following words in their contexts in the essay and then write a brief definition or synonym for each one. Do not use a dictionary; try to guess the word's meaning from its context.

prelude (5)	burliest (10)
escalating (7)	conscientiously (10)
behemoth (8)	emit (11)
macho (9)	humongous (12)

Understanding Content

1. Who, according to Goodman, are buying SUVs?
2. Why are people buying them?

3. SUVs account for how many additional deaths a year? Why?
4. According to Goodman, how many miles to the gallon do SUVs get?
5. What is ironic about some suburban owners of SUVs?
6. How does the EPA want to restrict SUVs?
7. What does the author predict may happen to SUVs?

Drawing Inferences about Thesis and Purpose

1. What is Goodman's subject? Is it appropriate to say that she has two subjects?
2. What is the author's thesis, the claim of her argument?
3. What would Goodman like to see happen regarding SUVs?

Analyzing Strategies and Style

1. Goodman begins and ends with a discussion of car ads. Why? How does this topic connect to her subject and purpose?
2. Explain the author's meaning in paragraph 4.
3. Look at the author's word choice in paragraphs 2 and 3. What makes her writing clever here?

Thinking Critically

1. Do you drive an SUV or wish you did? If so, why? How would you respond to Goodman's argument?
2. Have you had experiences with SUVs on the road similar to those Goodman describes? Can you understand her concern that they are dangerous to others on the road? Why or why not?
3. Have you thought about Goodman's second point—that SUVs are polluters? Has the author convinced you that they should be held to the same emissions standards as cars?
4. Should SUVs be restricted from urban areas? Why or why not?

"Save the Kids, Fight Tobacco"

DAVID SATCHER

David Satcher (b. 1941) is the Surgeon-General of the United States and Assistant Secretary of Health and Human Services. A graduate of Case Western Reserve University with both an M.D. and Ph.D., Satcher is the author of *Tobacco Use among U.S.*

Racial/Ethnic Minority Groups (1998), a detailed study published
by HHS. In *"Save the Kids,"* published in the *Washington Post* in
1999, Satcher argues for more programs to help keep young
people from starting to smoke.

The single most promising public health intervention today   1
is not the development of a new drug but the opportunity to
invest part of the recent $246 billion settlement with the to-
bacco companies into public health and proven programs that
would prevent our nation's children from smoking.

Those lawsuits were about health—the health of genera-   2
tions of Americans, living and dead, young and old. The success of the tobacco settlement should be measured by how it
improves the public health. I believe a great achievement is
possible if Congress and the states work together to commit
some of these resources to effective programs that will help
prevent millions of our children from becoming victims of
tobacco-related diseases.

The money from the settlement offers our country an op-   3
portunity similar in some respects to that of the polio vaccine
in the 1950s. While polio was for decades the silent killer of
children, today tobacco quietly addicts thousands of children
each day to a drug that will frequently lead to awful health
consequences later in life.

The polio vaccine saved thousands of lives because as a na-   4
tion we invested in its discovery and ensured that Americans
would benefit from its use. We have now reached a point in our
knowledge of public health where an investment in comprehensive state tobacco control programs could achieve similar
results.

The facts speak for themselves. Tobacco represents the sin-   5
gle most preventable cause of premature death and preventable illness. More than 425,000 people die each year from
smoking-related illnesses. Each day, 3,000 young people become regular smokers. One-half of them will be addicted to tobacco before they are legally old enough to buy cigarettes, and
one-third will eventually die from smoking-related illness.
More than 45 million Americans already are addicted, and the
industry continues to spend billions of dollars each year promoting the sale of tobacco.

6　　These facts reveal nothing less than a public health care crisis, which requires a focused public health effort to reduce youth smoking. Last year's settlement between the states and the tobacco industry was a step in the right direction, but clearly more needs to be done. With money in hand, states now have the necessary resources to launch a comprehensive, effective public health program against tobacco. Successful models of statewide programs exist in Massachusetts, California and other states; we know what programs work. Effective tobacco control programs require:

(1) Public education. Messages that promote smoking must be countered with creative ads that run in prime time and are designed to educate as well as motivate.

(2) Community-based programs. Community involvement is essential to reducing tobacco use. Public-private partnerships can be quite effective.

(3) Treatment for tobacco addiction. Effective cessation services should be available to anyone who needs help quitting. These programs can help millions of tobacco users quit for the rest of their lives.

(4) School-based programs. Our schools need programs that teach children the dangers of tobacco but also impart the life skills, refusal skills and media literacy that help them resist peer pressure and powerful tobacco advertising.

(5) Enforcement, evaluation, surveillance. State laws prohibiting tobacco sales to children need to be taken seriously and vigorously enforced. Kids should not have access to cigarettes. Evaluation and surveillance are essential to monitor and improve program effectiveness.

7　　In addition, experts agree that the single most important step we can take to reduce youth smoking is to significantly raise the price of cigarettes. The president has proposed doing so by 55 cents per pack. States should also recognize the powerful effect that price has on our children's health.

8　　There are a number of deserving programs that seek a portion of the settlement funds. But I would suggest that there can be no greater priority to public health, community health or family health in this country than ensuring a robust and comprehensive tobacco control program in every state.

We have not had a case of Y-virus polio in the United States 9
since 1979, and we are moving rapidly toward global eradica-
tion. If we work together and make a commitment to tobacco
control, one day we will be able to say the same thing about
smoking-related diseases.

Expanding Vocabulary

Examine the following words in their contexts in the essay and then
write a brief definition or synonym for each one. Do not use a dictionary; try to guess the word's meaning from its context.

ensured (4)	cessation (9)
launch (6)	surveillance (11)
comprehensive (6)	eradication (14)

Understanding Content

1. How much money has been obtained from state lawsuits against
   tobacco companies?
2. Satcher compares investing in public health programs to keep children from smoking to what other public health program?
3. How many people die each year from smoking-related illnesses?
4. How many young people become smokers every day?
5. How many Americans are currently addicted?
6. What are the necessary specifics of effective tobacco-control programs?
7. What two purposes should anti-smoking ads have?
8. What should programs in schools provide youngsters?
9. In addition to programs, what else is effective in reducing youth
   smoking?

Drawing Inferences about Thesis and Purpose

1. Examine Satcher's use of a comparison with the discovery and use
   of the polio vaccine. What makes this comparison effective?
2. The author presents statistics. How do they support his argument?

Thinking Critically

1. Are you prepared to accept the evidence that smoking is a major
   health hazard? Why or why not? Is your answer influenced by
   whether you smoke?

2. Do you agree that smoking represents a public health crisis? Why or why not?
3. What evidence or reasoning do you think is most effective in this argument? Why?
4. If you were an elected official in a state government, would you vote for a tax increase on cigarettes? If so, how much? If not, why not?

"Ban the Things. Ban Them All"

MOLLY IVINS

Molly Ivins (b. 1944), a graduate of Smith College and Columbia University, began her career as a reporter. She has been a columnist since 1980 and is currently with the *Fort Worth Star-Telegram*. Ivins is also a contributor to magazines such as the *Nation* and *Ms.*, and she has a collection of essays published under the title *Molly Ivins Can't Say That, Can She?* An insightful political commentator, Ivins is also known for her wit and irreverent style, traits shown in the following column published March 16, 1993.

1   AUSTIN—Guns. Everywhere guns.

2   Let me start this discussion by pointing out that I am not anti-gun. I'm pro-knife. Consider the merits of the knife.

3   In the first place, you have to catch up with someone to stab him. A general substitution of knives for guns would promote physical fitness. We'd turn into a whole nation of great runners. Plus, knives don't ricochet. And people are seldom killed while cleaning their knives.

4   As a civil libertarian, I of course support the Second Amendment. And I believe it means exactly what it says: "A well-regulated militia being necessary to the security of a free state, the right of the people to keep and bear arms shall not be infringed." Fourteen-year-old boys are not part of a well-regulated militia. Members of wacky religious cults are not part of a well-regulated militia. Permitting unregulated citizens to have guns is destroying the security of this free state.

I am intrigued by the arguments of those who claim to fol- 5
low the judicial doctrine of original intent. How do they know
it was the dearest wish of Thomas Jefferson's heart that teenage
drug dealers should cruise the cities of this nation perforating
their fellow citizens with assault rifles? Channeling?
There is more hooey spread about the Second Amendment. 6
It says quite clearly that guns are for those who form part of a
well-regulated militia, i.e., the armed forces including the National Guard. The reasons for keeping them away from everyone else get clearer by the day.

The comparison most often used is that of the automobile, 7
another lethal object that is regularly used to wreak great carnage. Obviously, this society is full of people who haven't got
enough common sense to use an automobile properly. But we
haven't outlawed cars yet.

We do, however, license them and their owners, restrict their 8
use to presumably sane and sober adults and keep track of who
sells them to whom. At a minimum, we should do the same
with guns.

In truth, there is no rational argument for guns in this soci- 9
ety. This is no longer a frontier nation in which people hunt
their own food. It is a crowded, overwhelmingly urban country in which letting people have access to guns is a continuing
disaster. Those who want guns—whether for target shooting,
hunting or potting rattlesnakes (get a hoe)—should be subject
to the same restrictions placed on gun owners in England—a
nation in which liberty has survived nicely without an armed
populace.

The argument that "guns don't kill people" is patent non- 10
sense. Anyone who has ever worked in a cop shop knows how
many family arguments end in murder because there was a gun
in the house. Did the gun kill someone? No. But if there had
been no gun, no one would have died. At least not without a
good footrace first. Guns do kill. Unlike cars, that is all they do.

Michael Crichton makes an interesting argument about 11
technology in his thriller *Jurassic Park*. He points out that power
without discipline is making this society into a wreckage. By
the time someone who studies the martial arts becomes a
master—literally able to kill with bare hands—that person has

also undergone years of training and discipline. But any fool can pick up a gun and kill with it.

12   "A well-regulated militia" surely implies both long training and long discipline. That is the least, the very least, that should be required of those who are permitted to have guns, because a gun is literally the power to kill. For years, I used to enjoy taunting my gun-nut friends about their psychosexual hangups— always in a spirit of good cheer, you understand. But letting the noisy minority in the National Rifle Association force us to allow this carnage to continue is just plain insane.

13   I do think gun nuts have a power hangup. I don't know what is missing in their psyches that they need to feel they have the power to kill. But no sane society would allow this to continue.

14   Ban the damn things. Ban them all.

15   You want protection? Get a dog.

Expanding Vocabulary

Study definitions of the following words and then use each of them in separate sentences.

ricochet (3)	lethal (7)
wacky (4)	carnage (7)
intrigued (5)	taunting (12)
perforating (5)	psyches (13)
hooey (6)	

Understanding Content

1. What, according to Ivins, does the Second Amendment mean? How does she cleverly turn the pro-gun group's use of the Second Amendment to her advantage in this paragraph?
2. What is the point of her comparison of guns to cars?
3. What reason does Ivins give to support the assertion that "there is no rational argument for guns in this society"? What restrictions does she want this country to adopt?
4. Why, in the author's view, is the pro-gun argument that guns don't kill people "patent nonsense"?
5. What can be the difference between someone with a gun and someone trained in the martial arts?
6. What psychological explanation does Ivins offer to account for "gun nuts"?

Drawing Inferences about Thesis and Purpose

1. What is Ivins's thesis, the claim of her argument? Where does she state it?
2. When Ivins writes, in paragraph 2, that she is "not anti-gun," how do you know that she does not mean this?
3. When the author writes, in paragraph 2, "I'm pro-knife," she introduces an idea that she develops through an entire paragraph and returns to later in her essay. In what sense do knives have "merit"? In what way is she being serious? What else is she doing; that is, what does she accomplish through her discussion of the merits of the knife?

Analyzing Strategies and Style

1. Characterize Ivins's style. Consider her word choice and sentence patterns.
2. Look especially at her first two and last two paragraphs; what tone is created by her style?
3. Ivins is not timid about expressing her views. Find words that are clearly negative, that reveal her attitude through their negative meanings and connotations.
4. When Ivins writes that she used to taunt friends "in a spirit of good cheer," does she mean what she says? What technique does she use in this passage?
5. How does Ivins organize her discussion of gun control? To what points is she responding as a way to develop her argument? What type of argument is this?

Thinking Critically

1. Does the author effectively challenge the "Second Amendment argument" of the gun lobby? The argument that licensing will lead to outlawing guns? The "guns don't kill" argument? Do you think that her refutation of one argument is more convincing than another? Explain and defend your evaluation of her argument.
2. What audience is likely to be offended by this column? What does your answer tell you about the audience to which her essay is targeted? Which audience do you fit into? Does that explain, at least in part, the way you responded to the first set of questions?
3. How might Ivins justify her approach of "grabbing the reader by the shoulders and shaking him or her"? Why does she think this approach is necessary? Is handgun violence a serious problem in our society? If not, why not? If so, what are the solutions, the actions we need to take to stop the killings?

"Gun Registration: It's Common Sense"

SARAH BRADY

An advocate for gun control legislation since her husband was
shot and severely disabled when President Reagan was shot,
Sarah Brady (b. 1942), a graduate of William and Mary and a
former teacher, is chair of Handgun Control and the Center to
Prevent Handgun Violence. In her article, published June 11,
1999 (shortly after the student shootings in Colorado), Brady argues for gun registration.

1   In an interview on "Good Morning, America" last week, the
president said that we should consider registering guns just as
we register cars. He's right, of course. In the same way that we
require the registration of cars, we should require that the sale
or transfer of firearms—at least handguns—be reported to law
enforcement authorities.

2   Registration is a vital law enforcement tool. It's a crime-
solver. By permitting guns to be readily traced back to their last
lawful owner, police can more readily identify who pulled the
trigger and, if the shooter is a prohibited purchaser, who ille-
gally sold or transferred the gun to the shooter. When police
are unable to trace a gun, a criminal and his accomplice can,
quite literally, get away with murder. And that's what happens
all too often.

3   It took law enforcement officials two weeks to determine
who sold the TEC-9 assault pistol to the two shooters in Littleton, Colo. And if the seller hadn't identified himself, the police
might never have made the link. The police in Littleton were
not searching for the killers; the two killed themselves. But in
many criminal investigations, the shooters and their accom-
plices are not identified and, thanks in part to weak gun laws,
they may never be caught.

4   The gun lobby will insist that the president has made a critical miscalculation. No sitting president since Lyndon B. Johnson has dared suggest that firearms should be registered. The
NRA would like everyone to believe that gun registration, in
whatever form, is the third rail of American politics.

Some third rail. A public opinion survey conducted last year   5
by the National Opinion Research Center found that 85 percent
of Americans, including 75 percent of gun owners, support
mandatory registration of handguns.

It all comes down to common sense. Almost everywhere else   6
in the world, sales or transfers of firearms must be recorded.
Some countries, such as Japan and Great Britain, have banned
handguns altogether.

Meanwhile, in this country, it took a massacre the size of Lit-   7
tleton for congressional leaders to acknowledge that background checks should be conducted at gun shows. And it was
regarded as a giant step forward when the Senate a few weeks
ago voted to prohibit the sale of AK-47s and Uzis to children.
Requiring gun manufacturers to provide a simple safety lock
with every handgun they sell was, by American standards, a
major accomplishment.

So as the House of Representatives prepares to consider the   8
Senate-passed gun legislation, congressional leaders are urging
caution. Some on both sides are suggesting that going beyond
the Senate-passed bill may be going too far. Establishing a minimum 72-hour waiting period on handgun purchases so that
law enforcement can do a more thorough background check?
Not likely. Limiting handgun purchases to one handgun per
month so that professional gun traffickers cannot go around
buying 50 or 100 guns a month? Forget it, too controversial.

And while the House might consider prohibiting the sale of   9
handguns at gun shows to those between the ages of 18 and 21,
it might stop short of prohibiting 18-year-olds from actually
possessing handguns. It doesn't seem to matter that 18- and 19-
year-olds lead the nation in homicides. These youth shouldn't
be limited, so the argument goes, to possessing rifles and shotguns. They need handguns.

Is it any wonder that the president seemed upset the other   10
day when he was questioned about his commitment to tougher
gun laws? This president has done far more than any other
to advance our thinking about guns, and yet Congress is still
playing political games. When the Senate took up the issue of
guns a few weeks ago, the first amendment that passed was one
that would have gutted our gun laws, stopping Brady background checks on criminals reclaiming guns at pawn shops and

permitting federally licensed gun dealers to sell at gun shows in all 50 states. Now some in the House want to limit the time that can be taken for background checks at gun shows—even if the records are showing a problem, such as a felony arrest, that needs more investigation. Allowing felons to get guns in the interest of promoting quick gun sales makes no sense.

11   When is this insanity going to end? Anyone who bemoans the "inconvenience" that these new gun-show restrictions might impose on gun-show promoters should be required to talk to as many victims of gun violence as I have. Let them start with some of the 13 mothers who every day lose a child to gun violence. And then let them talk to some of the many children who have lost classmates.

12   The simple truth is that we don't need to ban guns in this country to reduce gun violence. All we need are common-sense gun laws. Since the Brady Law was passed in 1993, gun crimes have dropped sharply. But we still have so far to go. Common sense, when it comes to guns, remains in short supply. At least in Congress.

Expanding Vocabulary

Examine the following words in their contexts in the essay and then write a brief definition or synonym for each one. Do not use a dictionary; try to guess the word's meaning from its context.

mandatory (5)   bemoans (11)

Understanding Content

1. How can gun registration help police solve crime?
2. What percentage of Americans support handgun registration? What percent of gun owners support such registration?
3. What countries ban all handguns? How common are records of gun sales and transfers?
4. How many mothers lose a child to gun violence each day?

Drawing Inferences about Thesis and Purpose

1. When Brady writes, in paragraph 8, "Not likely" and "forget it, too controversial," what is she really saying? Does she agree with members of Congress who have doubts about passing gun legislation?
2. What is Brady's thesis, the claim of her argument? Where does she state it?

Analyzing Strategies and Style

1. How would you describe the author's style and tone? What can make her choice an effective strategy?
2. Brady is, of course, associated with lobbying for "gun control." What does she gain by asserting that "we don't need to ban guns in this country to reduce gun violence"?

Thinking Critically

1. Are you among the 85 percent who support gun registration? Why or why not?
2. Should sales of semi-automatics to children be banned? Should ownership be banned except for military personnel? Explain your position.
3. Should 18- or 19-year-olds be allowed to buy handguns? Why or why not?
4. Should those attending gun shows be limited to the purchase of one gun? Why or why not?
5. America is a violent country with a fascination for guns. How do you explain these characteristics of American society?

"As Temperatures Rise"

DAVID IGNATIUS

A former foreign correspondent with degrees from Harvard and Cambridge Universities, David Ignatius is currently assistant managing editor of the *Washington Post*. He is also a writer of espionage thrillers, including *A Firing Offense* (1977) and *The Sun King* (1999). Ignatius's article on global warming issues appeared in the *Post* on May 30, 1999.

In her 1962 book, *Silent Spring,* Rachel Carson described 1 some of the early warning signs that DDT and other pesticides were harming the environment.

A vivid example occurred at a vacation spot called Clear 2 Lake, near San Francisco, after pest-control officials started using insecticide in 1949 to eradicate gnats. Water birds began to die in large numbers during the 1950s, and scientists didn't understand why—until they realized that the poisons were being absorbed by plankton in the lake, which were being eaten by the fish, which were being eaten by the birds.

3   With dozens of examples like these, Carson's book helped launch the environmental movement, which among its many accomplishments stopped the indiscriminate use of deadly pesticides.

4   Today, there are similar early warning signs that global warming is starting to affect plants and animals around the world. Most of this evidence is not questioned by mainstream scientists. Yet nothing serious is being done about the problem—least of all in the United States.

5   Here's a sampler of evidence that even the most jaded among us (a club in which I'm normally happy to claim membership) shouldn't ignore. It was assembled by Adam Markham, the director of energy and climate policy for the World Wildlife Fund. Think of these examples as ecological alarm bells—the canaries in our global coal mine:

6   ❏ The Arctic region is taking the first blows, according to a recent study by the International Arctic Science Committee. In Fairbanks, the number of 40-below days is now half what it was in the 1950s. The permafrost is warming, by an estimated two to four degrees, centigrade. And sea ice is shrinking: In the Bering Sea, it has been reduced by about 5 percent over the past 40 years.

7   These climate changes appear to be harming wildlife, according to a paper presented last month in Norway by Gunter Weller and Manfred Lange. One species of sea lion declined by 50 percent to 80 percent over the past two years. The number of northern fur seal pups declined by half between the 1950s and '80s in the Pribilof Islands, the major breeding ground in the Bering Sea.

8   One haunting sign of change comes from Caleb Pungowiyi, an Inuk who works with the Eskimo Walrus Commission in Nome. He told colleagues last month that because of warming in the arctic, the traditional Inuk name for the month of October no longer is accurate. That name literally means "time of crossing" and referred to the hardening of the ice in Alaskan rivers. But in recent years, he says, the rivers haven't yet frozen in October.

9   ❏ Salmon are dying in the North Pacific. The World Wildlife Fund will present evidence next month of a massive threat to

salmon stocks, due to changing climate and ocean conditions. According to the Alaska Department of Fish and Game, last year's catch of sockeye salmon in Bristol Bay—the largest sockeye fishery in the world—was half what was expected and the lowest in more than 20 years.

David Welch, a scientist with the Canadian Department of 10 Fisheries and Oceans who has studied the issue carefully, warns that salmon may not be able to survive in the warmer ocean temperatures that have been measured recently in the North Pacific. Welch believes that if current trends continue, sockeye salmon could disappear from the Pacific by the middle of the next century.

❑ Coral reefs are dying. Last year, coral around the world 11 was devastated by "bleaching," which is caused by loss of the algae that give the coral its food and color. According to a report presented two months ago by the State Department, it was the most severe epidemic of bleaching ever recorded—in some parts of the Indian Ocean, up to 90 percent of the coral was affected.

Many scientists blame warmer tropical water temperatures, 12 which last year were the highest ever recorded. The State Department study noted: "Even under the best of conditions, many of these coral reef ecosystems will need decades to recover."

❑ Species are disappearing in the cloud forests of Costa Rica. 13 As sea-level temperatures have risen, the air in these highlands has become warmer and dryer—affecting the animals that live there. The golden toad appears to have become extinct, and 20 other species of toads and frogs have disappeared since 1987. Bird and lizard populations have also been affected.

What seems to be causing all these disparate effects is the 14 measurable global warming trend that has taken place over the past century—with an increase in the average surface temperature of about 0.5 degrees centigrade. Among scientists, there is a growing conviction that this global warming trend is directly linked to the increase in carbon dioxide and other greenhouse gases in the atmosphere over the past century—due to burning fossil fuel and other activities associated with industrialization.

And what does Congress do, in response to the evidence of 15 global warming? Because of pressure from business lobbyists, it refuses even to consider the issue. The Kyoto agreement, a fledging international pact hammered out last year, is deader than a Costa Rican golden toad.

16   Here's how bad it is: Rep. Joseph Knollenberg, a Republican from the Detroit area, sponsored a successful rider last year that effectively bans the federal government from spending any new money to curb greenhouse gas emissions.

17   Is there intelligent life on earth? You sometimes have to wonder.

Expanding Vocabulary

Study definitions of the following words and then use each one of them in a separate sentence.

eradicate (2)	ecological (5)
plankton (2)	permafrost (6)
indiscriminate (3)	devastated (11)
jaded (5)	disparate (14)

Understanding Content

1. What are today's "early warning signs" telling us?
2. How do most scientists view these signs?
3. What are the signs of warming in the Arctic and Alaska?
4. What signs can be found in the North Pacific?
5. Why is coral dying?
6. What signs can be found in Costa Rica? What is causing these problems?
7. What is producing global warming?
8. How is Congress responding to the problem?

Drawing Inferences about Thesis and Purpose

1. What is the author's topic? (Don't just write global warming; be more precise.)
2. What is Ignatius's thesis? Where is it stated?
3. Ignatius concludes with a brief paragraph. Explain his meaning in that paragraph.

Analyzing Strategies and Style

1. The author opens with three paragraphs about Rachel Carson's famous and important book *Silent Spring*. How does this provide an effective introduction to his topic?

2. The author uses four bulleted paragraphs. What does each one provide? Describe the author's organizational strategy. (You may want to make an outline.)

Thinking Critically

1. Another way to look at this essay's structure is to see it as a problem-solution essay. The author establishes a problem we should be concerned about, discusses causes of that problem, but—in this case—does not spell out specific solutions. What solution(s) does he imply? What does he want to see happen?
2. Has Ignatius convinced you that global warming is happening? That it is a problem we need to address? Why or why not?
3. If you do not agree that we face an environmental problem, how would you refute Ignatius's argument? (If you do not see any way to challenge his argument, but you don't want to agree that we face the problem of global warming, are you thinking critically?)

"Dolly's False Legacy"

IAN WILMUT

Ian Wilmut (b. 1944) is the Scottish embryologist who led the team of researchers at Roslin Institute that cloned the sheep Dolly from her mother in February 1997. A graduate of Cambridge University, Wilmut and colleagues Keith Campbell and Colin Tudge have written *Dolly and the Age of Biological Control* (1999). His article for *Time* magazine, published January 11, 1999, examines problems in cloning humans.

Overlooked in the arguments about the morality of artificially reproducing life is the fact that, at present, cloning is a very inefficient procedure. The incidence of death among fetuses and offspring produced by cloning is much higher than it is through natural reproduction—roughly 10 times as high as normal before birth and three times as high after birth in our studies at Roslin.[1] Distressing enough for those working with animals, these failure rates surely render unthinkable the notion of applying such treatment to humans.

[1]Institute in Scotland where Dolly the Sheep was cloned. —Ed.

2   Even if the technique were perfected, however, we must ask ourselves what practical value whole-being cloning might have. What exactly would be the difference between a "cloned" baby and a child born naturally—and why would we want one?

3   The cloned child would be a genetically identical twin of the original, and thus physically very similar—far more similar than a natural parent and child. Human personality, however, emerges from both the effects of the genes we inherit (nature) and environmental factors (nurture). The two clones would develop distinct personalities, just as twins develop unique identities. And because the copy would often be born in a different family, cloned twins would be less alike in personality than natural identical twins.

4   Why "copy" people in the first place? Couples unable to have children might choose to have a copy of one of them rather than accept the intrusion of genes from a donor. My wife and I have two children of our own and an adopted child, but I find it helpful to consider what might have happened in my own marriage if a copy of me had been made to overcome infertility. My wife and I met in high school. How would she react to a physical copy of the young man she fell in love with? How would any of us find living with ourselves? Surely the older clone—I, in this case—would believe that he understood how the copy should behave and so be even more likely than the average father to impose expectations upon his child. Above all, how would a teenager cope with looking at me, a balding, aging man, and seeing the physical future ahead of him?

5   Each of us can imagine hypothetical families created by the introduction of a cloned child—a copy of one partner in a homosexual relationship or of a single parent, for example. What is missing in all this is consideration of what's in the interests of the cloned child. Because there is no form of infertility that could be overcome only by cloning, I do not find these proposals acceptable. My concerns are not on religious grounds or on the basis of a perceived intrinsic ethical principle. Rather, my judgment is that it would be difficult for families created in this way to provide an appropriate environment for the child.

6   Cloning is also suggested as a means of bringing back a relative, usually a child, killed tragically. Any parent can understand that wish, but it must first be recognized that the copy would be a new baby and not the lost child. Herein lies the difficulty, for

the grieving parents are seeking not a new baby but a return of the dead one. Since the original would be fondly remembered as having particular talents and interests, would not the parent expect the copy to be the same? It is possible, however, that the copy would develop quite differently. Is it fair to the new child to place it in a family with such unnatural expectations?

What if the lost child was very young? The shorter the life, the fewer the expectations parents might place on the substitute, right? If a baby dies within a few days of birth and there is no reason to think that death was caused by an inherited defect, would it then be acceptable to make a copy? Is it practical to frame legislation that would prevent copying of adults or older children, but allow copying of infants? At what age would a child be too old to be copied in the event of death? 7

Copying is also suggested as a means by which parents can have the child of their dreams. Couples might choose to have a copy of a film star, baseball player or scientist, depending on their interests. But because personality is only partly the result of genetic inheritance, conflict would be sure to arise if the cloned child failed to develop the same interests as the original. What if the copy of Einstein shows no interest in science? Or the football player turns to acting? Success also depends upon fortune. What of the child who does not live up to the hopes and dreams of the parent simply because of bad luck? 8

Every child should be wanted for itself, as an individual. In making a copy of oneself or some famous person, a parent is deliberately specifying the way he or she wishes that child to develop. In recent years, particularly in the U.S., much importance has been placed on the right of individuals to reproduce in ways that they wish. I suggest that there is a greater need to consider the interests of the child and to reject these proposed uses of cloning. 9

By contrast, human cloning could, in theory, be used to obtain tissues needed to treat disorders such as Parkinson's disease and diabetes. These diseases are associated with cell types that do not repair or replace themselves, but suitable cells will one day be grown in culture. These uses cannot be justified now; nor are they likely to be in the near future. 10

Moreover, there is a lot we do not know about the effects of cloning, especially in terms of aging. As we grow older, changes occur in our cells that reduce the number of times they can 11 reproduce. The clock of age is reset by normal reproduction during the production of sperm and eggs; that is why children of each new generation have a full life span. It is not yet known whether aging is reversed during cloning or if the clone's natural life is shortened by the years its parent has already lived.[2] Then there is the problem of the genetic errors that accumulate in our cells. There are systems to seek out and correct such errors during normal reproduction; it is not known if that can occur during cloning. Research with animals is urgently required to measure the life span and determine the cause of death of animals produced by cloning.

12   Important questions also remain on the most appropriate means of controlling the development and use of these techniques. It is taken for granted that the production and sale of drugs will be regulated by governments, but this was not always the case. A hundred years ago, the production and sale of drugs in the U.S. was unregulated. Unscrupulous companies took the opportunity to include in their products substances, like cocaine, that were likely to make the patients feel better even if they offered no treatment for the original condition. After public protest, championed by publications such as the *Ladies' Home Journal,* a federal act was passed in 1906. An enforcement agency, known now as the FDA, was established in 1927. An independent body similar to the FDA is now required to assess all the research on cloning.

13   There is much still to be learned about the biology associated with cloning. The time required for this research, however, will also provide an opportunity for each society to decide how it wishes the technique to be used. At some point in the future, cloning will have much to contribute to human medicine, but we must use it cautiously.

Expanding Vocabulary

Examine the following words in their contexts in the essay and then write a brief definition or synonym for each one. Do not use a dictionary; try to guess the word's meaning from its context.

incidence (1)	hypothetical (5)
genetically (3)	intrinsic (5)
intrusion (4)	unscrupulous (12)

---

[2]New evidence suggests that these years do affect the youthful clone.

Understanding Content

1. Why does Wilmut say that cloning is inefficient?
2. How would a cloned child be similar to and how different from its original?
3. What difficulties may develop if an infertile couple cloned one of them to have a child?
4. What difficulties may develop if a dead child is "replaced" by a cloned version?
5. What problems may be associated with cloning someone famous because a couple wants "the child of their dreams"?
6. For what reason does Wilmut reject cloning to create a "specific" child?
7. What about cloning do we not know yet?
8. What questions do we still need to answer about regulating cloning?

Drawing Inferences about Thesis and Purpose

1. What is Wilmut's topic?
2. What is the claim of his argument?
3. What is Wilmut's primary reason for taking his position? What strategies for making decisions about what we should or should not do does the author choose not to use?

Analyzing Strategies and Style

1. How does the author's title announce both his subject and his attitude?
2. What does the author gain by using himself and his wife as an example?
3. Wilmut begins and ends with a discussion of what we do not know or cannot do well yet regarding cloning. Why? How does he use this discussion in his argument?

Thinking Critically

1. We know that Wilmut is at the forefront of scientific work on cloning. How does knowledge of the author's credentials affect your response to his argument?
2. Do you think we should push ahead to develop the capacity to clone humans? Why or why not?
3. Should we create a federal agency to review and control cloning research? If so, what powers should the agency have? If not, why not? Does this agency need to be international? If not, why not? If so, how would such an agency be created and what powers should it have?

"In the Death of a Friend, a Lesson for the Living"

PATTI DAVIS

Patti Davis (born in 1952 as Patricia Ann Reagan) is a freelance journalist living in California. She has had an acting and singing career and is also the author of several novels, including *Deadfall* (1989) and *A House of Secrets* (1991). In the following article, which appeared in the Health Section of the *Washington Post* on June 8, 1999, Davis reflects on the loss of so many young people to AIDS.

1   A friend of mine died today. I got the call at 6:30 in the morning, as I was lacing up my running shoes. It was simultaneously a surprise and an anticipated event. Maybe death is always like that, waiting in the wings, suddenly taking over the stage. Lewis Brownback was 35; he had been infected for 14 years with the virus that causes AIDS.

2   We never really talked about death, not at length anyway. But our conversations glanced off it occasionally; he was blunt about the impending brevity of his life. I think I saw the shadow of death in his eyes long before he told me he had AIDS.

3   We met a few years ago when I was living in New York and dropped by the small antique shop owned by a friend. I met Lewis' dog first, a tiny round tuft of black fur scurrying around the store, miraculously avoiding all the precious antiques that sat precariously in the way. In a whirlwind of efficiency, Lewis—also a friend of the store's owner—was rearranging the merchandise, periodically grumbling about so many things crammed into such a small space. After that day he was a dependable presence in my Upper West Side neighborhood. Especially when the weather got warmer, I could count on strolling down the street in the evening and finding him at one of the outdoor restaurants. I'll remember him for all the long cocktail conversations that stretched into the "maybe-we-should-eat" hour.

4   When someone we care about dies, other feelings mingle with the inevitable sadness; there is a reverence for each hour,

each shiver of wind, each splash of sunlight on wet leaves. The day is different and, if we're lucky, so are the ones that follow. We float, buoyed by something we can neither define nor ignore. There is a remove, a disconnectedness from people, from the ordinary "busyness" of daily life, but also an awareness of the thread that binds us to one another, fragile humans that we are. We're all going to die; it's such an obvious point, yet we don't linger on it until death floats in, reminding us that it's always around—patient, waiting.

We have said goodbye to so many because of AIDS. The 5 numbers resemble combat statistics. It is a war against a disease that keeps outsmarting us. We tend to use battle terms, words like "fight" and "conquer." Then, in the quietest hours of night, we wonder how we will fit in all the grieving. It is said that people who have lived in war-ravaged countries are unable to recall what life was like before. Was there a time when they weren't stumbling over death?

I don't want to forget the world that was before this disease 6 entered our lives and our lexicon, before it became so entrenched in our society that it's barely front-page news anymore. I don't want to forget, yet the years preceding AIDS often seem a fantasy.

The cause of Lewis' death was listed as "cardiac arrest." His 7 body was so riddled with infection that his heart just got tired. I think that happens to the rest of us, the survivors. Our hearts become weighed down by grief. Yet we seem to sense that pushing it away, denying its existence, accomplishes little. If we explore death, try to come to some understanding of it, we will move closer to what is essential about life.

When I was a child, I overheard my grandfather commenting on how difficult it was to get old and see more and more of his friends die. That's how I thought life unfolded: Death visited more often the older that one got. There was a sequence to it, an orderliness.

We are all too young, casualties and survivors of AIDS, to 9 have said so many goodbyes. By anyone's definition, 35 is too soon to die; some victims never reached puberty. The names will stretch for miles, even if we find a cure tomorrow.

Despite that, there is a sweetness threaded through the sad- 10 ness of this day. In the inevitable letting go, the loosening of our grip on memories and relationships, we must hold tighter to the mysterious interplay between life and death. If we don't, something in us dies prematurely; it is the sense of wonderment, of not knowing, a vague notion that there just might be something beyond this life.

11   It also could be that, if we are more accepting of death, we will in turn live our lives more gracefully. It might be the best way to honor all those we have lost.

Expanding Vocabulary

Study the context for each word's meaning and then use each word in a separate sentence of your own.

impending (2)	shiver (4)
brevity (2)	buoyed (4)
precariously (3)	lexicon (6)
reverence (4)	

Understanding Content

1. What is the occasion for this essay?
2. What thoughts and feelings are often triggered by the death of a friend?
3. How has AIDS made experiencing death around us different from the way death is supposed to be?
4. Why is there "sweetness threaded through the sadness" of the day the author learned of her friend's death? Why does there need to be?
5. What may be the best way to honor loved ones who have died?

Drawing Inferences about Thesis and Purpose

1. What is the author's topic? (Do not write AIDS or death; be more precise.)
2. What is Davis's thesis?
3. What is her purpose? Does she have more than one?

Analyzing Strategies and Style

1. Examine Davis's opening. What makes it effective?
2. What do the details in paragraph 3 contribute?
3. Examine paragraph 4. There is a lyrical quality to the writing here. How does the author achieve her lyricism?

Thinking Critically

1. Have you known any AIDS victims? If so, how did the death affect you? Alternatively, have you known someone who died young? How did you feel?
2. Do you agree with Davis that there can be a mix of sweetness with the sadness of loss? Why or why not?
3. How does one live life "more gracefully"? How would you advise someone to do this?

STUDENT ESSAY

"BLAME IT ON THE MEDIA AND OTHER WAYS TO DRESS A WOLF IN SHEEP'S CLOTHING"
David M. Ouellette

If an activity is legal, then people should be free to engage in that activity without fear of defamation. But smokers are being defamed, even persecuted, by a biased media bent on casting smoking as an unmitigated evil. This is Robert J. Samuelson's assertion in his September 24, 1997, <u>Newsweek</u> article "Do Smokers Have Rights." He says the media distort research on passive smoking's effects, demonize tobacco companies into teen-targeting drug pushers, and use these ill-founded claims as justification for punitive cigarette taxes. The result, Samuelson says, is that we "deny, ignore or minimize" the right of smokers

Introduction includes author, title, publication place, and date of work to be refuted.

Attention-getter

to do something that is perfectly legal.

He is mistaken on all counts.   *Thesis*

When it comes to the effects of passive smoking, Samuelson does not want to
accept what researchers have to say. He   *Student blends*
                                              summary and
cites a ten-year study of non-smoking   *direct quotation to*
                                              present author's
nurses that reported 25 to 30 percent of   *position.*
their heart attacks were caused by pas-
sive smoking. No matter how you look at
the figure, it clearly states that passive smoking is dangerous. He says, "the
practical significance of this is negligible." Ask any one of those people whose
heart attacks were caused by someone
else's smoking if what happened to them
was "negligible." The practical impact
is that if smoking were eliminated,
heart attacks among nonsmokers would
drop by 25 to 30 percent, according to
this study.

The media, contrary to Samuelson, are
not the ones who have painted tobacco
companies as purveyors of addiction to
teenagers. The tobacco industry has de-
monized itself. Samuelson himself admits   *Student analyzes*
                                            the author's logic.
that "the tobacco industry no doubt tar-
gets teens," but he excuses this by saying, "the ads may affect brand choices
more than the decision to smoke." However, advertising for a brand of ciga-

rettes is, necessarily, at the same time advertising for smoking. If a brand is made to look attractive, then that also means smoking itself is made to look attractive, for you cannot have one without the other.

Finally, Samuelson argues that heavy cigarette taxes actually hurt smokers more than help them. In reality, the taxes are intended to deter people from smoking by raising the price. The people who would most likely be deterred are teenagers and the poor, both of whom smoke more than any other age group or economic class. "Sin taxes," such as cigarette taxes, attempt to limit or discourage legal behavior. A high price is not tantamount to unlegislated prohibition; it is society's way of dissuading people from destructive behavior. Samuelson asks whether we have a right to limit legal behaviors, or is this infringing on individuals' rights. There is a middle ground between prohibition and unlimited right. Alcohol consumption is just such an example, a behavior so dangerous that its use is controlled yet still legal. Clearly, society has a right to prohibit or control dangerous behavior. Not only is it society's right to

Student uses a comparison with alcohol to challenge the author's argument.

control the danger to which its citizens
are exposed, it is its responsibility.

Samuelson's claim that the media are
besmirching smokers and tobacco companies
with misleading reports is false. It is
the media's responsibility to report
news, such as the health threat of passive smoking, and how tobacco companies
target teenagers. As for the right to
smoke, smoking's dangers--both to smokers and nonsmokers alike--demand its control. Conceding fist-pounding demands for
unlimited rights, regardless of who gets
hurt or what other rights get infringed,
would be an abdication of our responsibility to protect the health and welfare
of the nation.

*Student concludes
by resisting his
thesis and defend-
ing it as the
responsible one.*

MAKING CONNECTIONS

1. Examine the arguments in this chapter for the various strategies the authors use. Then decide: (a) What particular strategy works consistently well from one essay to another? And
   (b) which particular essay is the best argument, overall? Be
   prepared to defend your decisions.

2. Ian Wilmut raises the issue of cloning or, by extension, genetic engineering. Think about this issue. Consider: How serious a problem will this be for us individually, as a society,
   and as the human race? And, at what level will the problem
   be most serious? Why?

3. Ellen Goodman raises the issue of gas-guzzling, polluting
   SUVs. David Ignatius is concerned about the problem of
   global warming—and that political leaders seem uncon-

cerned about this problem. How can we balance a need to preserve the environment and other species with a need to foster business and industry? When do "advancements" run counter to human needs?

TOPICS AND GUIDELINES FOR WRITING

---

1. Select a personal problem that concerns you, perhaps because you have a friend or family member with that problem. In an essay, present and defend your view on this issue. You can write to a general audience or directly to the person involved in a letter format and tone. Possible topics include staying in school, quitting smoking or using drugs or abusing alcohol, controlling starving or binge eating, maintaining relationships with parents, selecting a career, eliminating abusive language, or other bad habits.

2. Select any writer in this chapter whose position you disagree with and prepare a refutation of the writer's argument. Do not assume that your reader has read the article you are refuting. As shown in the student essay, begin by giving author, title, publication information, and the author's position. Then present and support your position. Your argument may be developed in part by showing weaknesses in the opposing view.

3. Reflect on educational issues and problems to select a topic from this area that interests and concerns you. There are many possible topics, including censorship of books in high school libraries, control of high school and college newspapers, discrimination in sororities and fraternities, academic freedom, plagiarism, grading systems, admissions policies, and others. Definitions may play an important role in developing your argument. Be sure that you understand the arguments on both sides, acknowledge whatever common ground you share with opponents, and write in a restrained, conciliatory manner.

4. Many serious problems face our society—from drugs to taxes (and the deficit) to illegal aliens to homelessness to insider trading and other business and banking crimes to

AIDS to ethical concerns such as abortion, euthanasia, and genetic engineering. Select a problem that concerns you, and write an argumentative essay that presents and defends your proposed solutions to the problem. Part of your development will probably include challenging other proposed solutions with which you disagree. You may want to do some reading so that you have current facts about the problem. (If you use sources, be sure to credit them properly.) You may also need to consider causes of the problem, for solutions that do not take causes into account are rarely effective. You may want to organize your essay to present your thesis in your conclusion after presenting support for it.

5. Serious problems also face our world, for example, depletion of the ozone layer, acid rain, deforestation, polluted waters, and an ever-expanding population. Select a problem that concerns you and prepare an argumentative essay according to the guidelines discussed in topic 4. Give thought to narrowing your topic to a manageable length.

11

Works for Further Reading and Analysis

Responses to Reading: Summary, Analysis, Synthesis

In Chapter 1 we noted that there are several reasons for reading, for using a text of this sort in a writing course. One of those reasons is that reading leads to writing. One kind of written response to reading is, as you observed in Chapter 10, the refutation. You disagree with someone's argument and prepare a response, an analysis of the flaws in the original argument and a counterargument that expresses your view on the topic. In the world of argument you can see that reading leads to writing.

Summary. But the refutation is only one of several ways to respond to what we have read, or, more accurately, it blends several more basic responses that we can usefully examine as separate purposes. One purpose is *summary,* the simplest response to reading. To write a fair refutation you need to represent the original argument with accuracy; that means you must read with understanding *and* be able to restate, briefly and clearly, the key elements of the argument you have read.

A variation of straight summary is the combination of summary and evaluation that we find in book reviews, for example. The reviewer gives us an idea of the work's content and judges how well the work has fulfilled its purpose. Evaluation that has any usefulness needs to go beyond a simple assertion of liking or disliking what one has read. For example, if, in response to a book review assignment in your psychology class, you select a difficult work to review, you will not have produced a useful review if you write that you did not like the book because it was too hard to read. The fact that you did not like the book is probably irrelevant. What you must judge is whether the book speaks appropriately to its intended audience. If the book is aimed at psychologists, not students, then your reading difficulty is explained and should be a part of your evaluation only as a warning that nonspecialists may find the book challenging to read. A good evaluation draws on summary and analysis to make an informed judgment.

Analysis. To prepare a refutation, you also need to look at the specific parts of an argument to see what elements of logic and evidence you will challenge: you need to prepare an *analysis* of the work. There are many ways that we can analyze a piece of writing; looking at the parts of an argument is only one possibility. To contrast the works of two writers is to analyze their differences—differences in content, point of view, or style of writing. To examine a writer's use of metaphors is to analyze one element of that writer's style. The questions under the heading "Examining Strategies and Style" after each work in the first ten chapters are questions that call for your analysis.

Synthesis. Finally, when doing research we read widely on a topic and draw on that reading, bringing it together in a *synthesis,* a blending of information and ideas from several sources with our ideas and previous knowledge of the topic. Although developing a synthesis is intellectually demanding, it is an essential skill to develop. To read only one source on a topic is to have only a narrow understanding, perhaps even an incorrect understanding. We do research—study many sources—as a check against error and as a way to a broad perspective. If you are in the market for a stereo, you do not walk into the nearest electronics store and buy the first one you see. You compare units for price and features. You read the brochures, and perhaps an article in a consumer's guide. You also talk to friends to learn about their equipment. Then, bringing all of this information together and weighing it in your mind, you decide what stereo equipment to purchase. You have reached a synthesis. What follows are guidelines for writing and examples of summary, analysis, and synthesis.

Summary

Whether it is paragraph length or a few pages, a *summary* is a condensed, nonevaluative restatement of a writer's main ideas.

To prepare a good summary, read carefully and then follow these guidelines for writing:

1. Maintain a direct, objective style without using overly simplistic sentences.
2. Begin with the author's thesis and then present additional key points.
3. Exclude all specific examples, illustrations, or background sections. However, you may want to indicate the kinds of evidence or methods of development used.
4. Combine main ideas into fewer sentences than were used in the original article or book.
5. Select precise, accurate verbs (*asserts, argues, concludes*) rather than vague verbs (*says, talks about*) that provide only a list of ideas. Pay attention to word choice to avoid such judging words as: "Jones then develops the *silly* idea that . . ."

With these guidelines in mind, read the following summary of Isaac Asimov's "Science and the Sense of Wonder" and consider why it needs revision.

Summary #1

In "Science and the Sense of Wonder," Isaac Asimov quotes Whitman's poem "When I Heard the Learn'd Astronomer." He says that Whitman's view of science is convenient and agrees that the night sky is beautiful. Asimov then talks about what he sees in the night sky—planets and the stars that are really suns. He then says that the Milky Way—our galaxy—has more stars in it than we can see, and beyond it are many galaxies that we can't see either. All of this was discovered after Whitman died.

We can agree that the writer of this summary has read Asimov's essay, but we can also assert that the summary lacks focus and may even be misleading in places. The writer has gone through the essay, picked out some ideas, and strung them together. One result is no clear statement of Asimov's main idea. Another result is the implication (in sentence 2) that Asimov agrees with Whitman's view of both the night sky and science, a misrepresentation of Asimov's position. Here is a much-improved version.

Summary #2

In "Science and the Sense of Wonder," Isaac Asimov challenges Whitman's view that scientists, reducing nature to charts and numbers, miss the beauty of nature. Asimov, quoting Whitman's poem "When I Heard the Learn'd Astronomer," uses the astronomer and the beautiful night sky as his examples. He argues that it is the sky of the astronomer that produces the greater sense of wonder and awe. When we understand what we are looking at—not bright lights but planets and suns—and when we understand just how huge the "sky" really is—not just our own galaxy but thousands of galaxies—we will recognize that Whitman's view was "a stultified and limited beauty." Asimov concludes that modern science has given us a vision almost beyond our ability to imagine.

Analysis

The process of analysis is not new to you. You have found chapters on process analysis and causal analysis in this text. The process of comparison (or contrast) is also analysis, as explained above. To establish some guidelines for writing analysis, let's consider one paragraph in an essay that analyzes a writer's style.

Suppose your thesis is that the writer uses connotative words, clever metaphors, and ironic understatement to convey her attitude. You will need a paragraph on each element of style: word choice, metaphors, irony, and understatement. Follow these guidelines for each paragraph.

1. Have a *topic sentence* that conveys the paragraph's subject and ties the paragraph to the essay's thesis.
2. Quote or paraphrase to present *examples* of the element of style, at least three examples taken from throughout the work.
3. *Explain* how the examples support the paragraph's topic sentence and hence your thesis. This is your analysis, the "glue" that holds the paragraph together and makes your point.
4. Use the correct tense. Analyze style in the *present tense.*

Here is a sample paragraph from a style analysis of one of Ellen Goodman's articles.

Analysis

Perhaps the most prevalent element of style present in Goodman's article, and a dominant characteristic of her essay style, is her use of metaphors. From the opening sentences through to the end, this article is full of metaphors. Keeping with the general focus of the piece (the essay appeared on Thanksgiving day), many of the metaphors liken food to family. Her references include "a cornucopia of family," "chicken-sized households" and "a turkey-sized family," people who "feast on the sounds as well as the tastes," and voices that "add relish to a story." She imparts that a politician can use the word "family" like "gravy poured over the entire plate." Going to the airport to pick up members of these disjointed American families has become "a holiday ritual as common as pumpkin pie." Goodman draws parallels between the process of "choosing" people to be with us and the simple ritual of passing seconds at the table. Indeed, the essay's mood emphasizes the comparison of and inextricable bond between food and family.

Synthesis

There are many reasons for drawing on two or more sources to develop your own piece of writing, and there is more than one way to acknowledge sources to readers. But what you must do, whether with a formal pattern of documentation or informally including details of author and title in your essay, is *always* let readers know where ideas and information not original with you have been found. Follow these general guidelines for creating synthesis.

1. Have a clear topic sentence in each paragraph. Material from sources is used to support an idea; it is not just "filler."
2. Combine information/ideas from several sources. If you devote each paragraph to only one source, you are writing a series of summaries. You are not synthesizing.
3. Put most of the borrowed material in your own words. When necessary, use brief quotations.

4. Make the sources of your borrowed material absolutely clear throughout. Use introductory tags; guide your reader through the material.
5. Explain and discuss the material. Do not just dump material from sources on your reader. The result is a list, not a synthesis.

The following paragraph, part of a documented report on theories of dinosaur extinction, illustrates one student's command of synthesis. (The essay concludes with a "works cited" page that provides complete bibliographic information for sources.)

Synthesis

Of course, the iridium could have come from other extraterrestrial sources besides an asteroid. One theory, put forward by Dale Russell, is that the iridium was produced outside the solar system by an exploding star (500). The theory of a nearby star exploding in a supernova is by far the most fanciful extraterrestrial theory; however, it warrants examination because of its ability to explain the widespread extinctions of the late Cretaceous Period (Colbert 205). Such an explosion, Russell states, could have blown the iridium either off the surface of the moon or directly from the star itself (500–01), while also producing a deadly blast of heat and gamma rays (Krishtalka 19). Even though the theory seems to explain the traces of iridium in the mass extinction, it does not explain, as Wilford points out, why smaller mammals, crocodiles, and birds survived (220). As Edwin Colbert explains, the extinctions of the late Cretaceous, although massive, were selective (205). So the supernova theory took a backseat to the other extraterrestrial theories: those of asteroids and comets colliding with the earth.

The works that follow in this chapter are either famous or likely to become so. They also demonstrate the use of a number of the rhetorical strategies discussed and illustrated in this text, including narration, description, definition, contrast, and argument. Finally, they provide opportunities for exciting—and challenging—reading and for practicing summary, analysis, and synthesis.

"The Story of an Hour"

KATE CHOPIN

Now a highly acclaimed fiction writer, Kate Chopin (1851–1904) enjoyed a decade of popularity from 1890 to 1900, and then experienced critical condemnation followed by sixty years of neglect. Chopin began her career after her husband's death, having returned to her home in St. Louis with her six children. She saw two collections of her stories published—*Bayou Folk* in 1894 and *A Night in Acadie* in 1897—before losing her popularity with the publication of her short novel *The Awakening* in 1899, the story of a woman struggling to free herself from years of repression and subservience. "The Story of an Hour" depicts another character's struggle.

After reading, you will want to be able to summarize the story and analyze elements of the story to respond fully to it. Use these questions to aid your analysis:

1. What do the details of the scene outside Mrs. Mallard's window have in common? How do they help us understand what she experiences in her room?
2. How does Mrs. Mallard change as a result of her reflections in her room?
3. Are we to agree with the doctor's explanation for Mrs. Mallard's death? Explain the story's conclusion. What term describes the story's ending?

Knowing that Mrs. Mallard was afflicted with a heart trouble, great care was taken to break to her as gently as possible the news of her husband's death.   1

It was her sister Josephine who told her, in broken sentences; veiled hints that revealed in half concealing. Her husband's friend Richards was there, too, near her. It was he who had been in the newspaper office when intelligence of the railroad disaster was received, with Brently Mallard's name leading the list of "killed." He had only taken the time to assure himself of its truth by a second telegram, and had hastened to forestall any less careful, less tender friend in bearing the sad message.   2

3   She did not hear the story as many women have heard the same, with a paralyzed inability to accept its significance. She wept at once, with sudden, wild abandonment, in her sister's arms. When the storm of grief had spent itself she went away to her room alone. She would have no one follow her.

4   There stood, facing the open window, a comfortable, roomy armchair. Into this she sank, pressed down by a physical exhaustion that haunted her body and seemed to reach into her soul.

5   She could see in the open square before her house the tops of trees that were all aquiver with the new spring life. The delicious breath of rain was in the air. In the street below a peddler was crying his wares. The notes of a distant song which someone was singing reached her faintly, and countless sparrows were twittering in the eaves.

6   There were patches of blue sky showing here and there through the clouds that had met and piled one above the other in the west facing her window.

7   She sat with her head thrown back upon the cushion of the chair, quite motionless, except when a sob came up into her throat and shook her, as a child who has cried itself to sleep continues to sob in its dreams.

8   She was young, with a fair, calm face, whose lines bespoke repression and even a certain strength. But now there was a dull stare in her eyes, whose gaze was fixed away off yonder on one of those patches of blue sky. It was not a glance of reflection, but rather indicated a suspension of intelligent thought.

9   There was something coming to her and she was waiting for it, fearfully. What was it? She did not know; it was too subtle and elusive to name. But she felt it, creeping out of the sky, reaching toward her through the sounds, the scents, the color that filled the air.

10   Now her bosom rose and fell tumultuously. She was beginning to recognize this thing that was approaching to possess her, and she was striving to beat it back with her will—as powerless as her two white slender hands would have been.

11   When she abandoned herself a little whispered word escaped her slightly parted lips. She said it over and over under her breath: "free, free, free!" The vacant stare and the look of

terror that had followed it went from her eyes. They stayed
keen and bright. Her pulses beat fast, and the coursing blood
warmed and relaxed every inch of her body.

She did not stop to ask if it were or were not a monstrous joy 12
that held her. A clear and exalted perception enabled her to dismiss the suggestion as trivial.

She knew that she would weep again when she saw the 13
kind, tender hands folded in death; the face that had never
looked save with love upon her, fixed and gray and dead. But
she saw beyond that bitter moment a long procession of years
to come that would belong to her absolutely. And she opened
and spread her arms out to them in welcome.

There would be no one to live for her during those coming 14
years; she would live for herself. There would be no powerful
will bending hers in that blind persistence with which men and
women believe they have a right to impose a private will upon
a fellow-creature. A kind intention or a cruel intention made
the act seem no less a crime as she looked upon it in that brief
moment of illumination.

And yet she had loved him—sometimes. Often she had not. 15
What did it matter! What could love, the unsolved mystery,
count for in face of this possession of self-assertion which she
suddenly recognized as the strongest impulse of her being!

"Free! Body and soul free!" she kept whispering. 16

Josephine was kneeling before the closed door with her lips 17
to the keyhole, imploring for admission. "Louise, open the
door! I beg; open the door—you will make yourself ill. What
are you doing, Louise? For heaven's sake open the door."

"Go away. I am not making myself ill." No; she was drink- 18
ing in a very elixir of life through that open window.

Her fancy was running riot along those days ahead of her. 19
Spring days, and summer days, and all sorts of days that
would be her own. She breathed a quick prayer that life might
be long. It was only yesterday she had thought with a shudder
that life might be long.

She arose at length and opened the door to her sister's im- 20
portunities. There was a feverish triumph in her eyes, and she
carried herself unwittingly like a goddess of Victory. She
clasped her sister's waist, and together they descended the
stairs. Richards stood waiting for them at the bottom.

21   Someone was opening the front door with a latchkey. It was Brently Mallard who entered, a little travel-stained, composedly carrying his grip-sack and umbrella. He had been far from the scene of the accident, and did not even know there had been one. He stood amazed at Josephine's piercing cry; at Richards' quick motion to screen him from the view of his wife.

22   But Richards was too late.

23   When the doctors came they said she had died of heart disease—of joy that kills.

"A Hanging"

GEORGE ORWELL

George Orwell (1903–1950), the pseudonym of Eric Arthur Blair, was a British essayist and novelist best known for his political satires *Animal Farm* (1945) and *1984* (1949). He is also important as the author of "Politics and the English Language," the essay that set the standard for the analysis of doublespeak in political language. In the following essay, published in *Shooting an Elephant and Other Essays* (1950), Orwell displays his skill in observation and in capturing the telling details of a scene.

What happens will be easy to discern from your reading. More importantly, you want to concentrate on what Orwell wants us to understand about the event, about what it means to be human, and to act inhumanly. Pay attention to the telling details, most especially the significance of the dog's behavior, the prisoner's behavior, and the narrator's reflections. Also analyze Orwell's use of metaphors to aid description.

1   It was in Burma, a sodden morning of the rains. A sickly light, like yellow tinfoil, was slanting over the high walls into the jail yard. We were waiting outside the condemned cells, a row of sheds fronted with double bars, like small animal cages. Each cell measured about ten feet by ten and was quite bare within except for a plank bed and a pot for drinking water. In some of them brown, silent men were squatting at the inner bars, with their blankets draped round them. These were the condemned men, due to be hanged within the next week or two.

One prisoner had been brought out of his cell. He was a   2
Hindu, a puny wisp of a man, with a shaven head and vague
liquid eyes. He had a thick, sprouting mustache, absurdly too
big for his body, rather like the mustache of a comic man on the
films. Six tall Indian warders were guarding him and getting
him ready for the gallows. Two of them stood by with rifles and
fixed bayonets, while the others handcuffed him, passed a
chain through his handcuffs and fixed it to their belts, and
lashed his arms tight to his sides. They crowded very close
about him, with their hands always on him in a careful, ca-
ressing grip, as though all the while feeling him to make sure
he was there. It was like men handling a fish which is still alive
and may jump back into the water. But he stood quite unre-
sisting, yielding his arms limply to the ropes, as though he
hardly noticed what was happening.

Eight o'clock struck and a bugle call, desolately thin in the   3
wet air, floated from the distant barracks. The superintendent
of the jail, who was standing apart from the rest of us, mood-
ily prodding the gravel with his stick, raised his head at the
sound. He was an army doctor, with a grey toothbrush mustache and a gruff voice. "For God's sake, hurry up, Francis," he
said irritably. "The man ought to have been dead by this time.
Aren't you ready yet?"

Francis, the head jailer, a fat Dravidian in a white drill suit   4
and gold spectacles, waved his black hand. "Yes sir, yes sir," he
bubbled. "All iss satisfactorily prepared. The hangman iss
waiting. We shall proceed."

"Well, quick march, then. The prisoners can't get their break-   5
fast till this job's over."

We set out for the gallows. Two warders marched on either   6
side of the prisoner, with their rifles at the slope; two others
marched close against him, gripping him by arm and shoulder,
as though at once pushing and supporting him. The rest of us,
magistrates and the like, followed behind. Suddenly, when we
had gone ten yards, the procession stopped short without any
order or warning. A dreadful thing had happened—a dog,
come goodness knows whence, had appeared in the yard. It
came bounding among us with a loud volley of barks and leapt
round us wagging its whole body, wild with glee at finding so
many human beings together. It was a large woolly dog, half

Airedale, half pariah. For a moment it pranced around us, and then, before anyone could stop it, it had made a dash for the prisoner, and jumping up tried to lick his face. Everybody stood aghast, too taken aback even to grab the dog.

7   "Who let that bloody brute in here?" said the superintendent angrily. "Catch it, someone!"

8   A warder detached from the escort, charged clumsily after the dog, but it danced and gambolled just out of his reach, taking everything as part of the game. A young Eurasian jailer picked up a handful of gravel and tried to stone the dog away, but it dodged the stones and came after us again. Its yaps echoed from the jail walls. The prisoner, in the grasp of the two warders, looked on incuriously, as though this was another formality of the hanging. It was several minutes before someone managed to catch the dog. Then we put my handkerchief through its collar and moved off once more, with the dog still straining and whimpering.

9   It was about forty yards to the gallows. I watched the bare brown back of the prisoner marching in front of me. He walked clumsily with his bound arms, but quite steadily, with that bobbing gait of the Indian who never straightens his knees. At each step his muscles slid neatly into place, the lock of hair on his scalp danced up and down, his feet printed themselves on the wet gravel. And once, in spite of the men who gripped him by each shoulder, he stepped lightly aside to avoid a puddle on the path.

10   It is curious; but till that moment I had never realized what it means to destroy a healthy, conscious man. When I saw the prisoner step aside to avoid the puddle, I saw the mystery, the unspeakable wrongness, of cutting a life short when it is in full tide. This man was not dying, he was alive just as we are alive. All the organs of his body were working—bowels digesting food, skin renewing itself, nails growing, tissues forming—all toiling away in solemn foolery. His nails would still be growing when he stood on the drop, when he was falling through the air with a tenth-of-a-second to live. His eyes saw the yellow gravel and the grey walls, and his brain still remembered, foresaw, reasoned—even about puddles. He and we were a party of men walking together, seeing, hearing, feeling, understand-

ing the same world; and in two minutes, with a sudden snap, one of us would be gone—one mind less, one world less.

The gallows stood in a small yard, separate from the main 11 grounds of the prison, and overgrown with tall prickly weeds. It was a brick erection like three sides of a shed, with planking on top, and above that two beams and a crossbar with the rope dangling. The hangman, a greyhaired convict in the white uniform of the prison, was waiting beside his machine. He greeted us with a servile crouch as we entered. At a word from Francis the two warders, gripping the prisoner more closely than ever, half led, half pushed him to the gallows and helped him clumsily up the ladder. Then the hangman climbed up and fixed the rope round the prisoner's neck.

We stood waiting, five yards away. The warders had formed 12 in a rough circle round the gallows. And then, when the noose was fixed, the prisoner began crying out to his god. It was a high, reiterated cry of "Ram! Ram! Ram! Ram!" not urgent and fearful like a prayer or cry for help, but steady, rhythmical, almost like the tolling of a bell. The dog answered the sound with a whine. The hangman, still standing on the gallows, produced a small cotton bag like a flour bag and drew it down over the prisoner's face. But the sound, muffled by the cloth, still persisted, over and over again: "Ram! Ram! Ram! Ram! Ram!"

The hangman climbed down and stood ready, holding the 13 lever. Minutes seemed to pass. The steady, muffled crying from the prisoner went on and on, "Ram! Ram! Ram!" never faltering for an instant. The superintendent, his head on his chest, was slowly poking the ground with his stick; perhaps he was counting the cries, allowing the prisoner a fixed number—fifty, perhaps, or a hundred. Everyone had changed colour. The Indians had gone grey like bad coffee, and one or two of the bayonets were wavering. We looked at the lashed, hooded man on the drop, and listened to his cries—each cry another second of life; the same thought was in all our minds; oh, kill him quickly, get it over, stop that abominable noise!

Suddenly the superintendent made up his mind. Throwing 14 up his head he made a swift motion with his stick. "Chalo!" he shouted almost fiercely.

15   There was a clanking noise, and then dead silence. The prisoner had vanished, and the rope was twisting on itself. I let go of the dog, and it galloped immediately to the back of the gallows; but when it got there it stopped short, barked, and then retreated into a corner of the yard, where it stood among the weeds, looking timorously out at us. We went round the gallows to inspect the prisoner's body. He was dangling with his toes pointed straight downwards, very slowly revolving, as dead as a stone.

16   The superintendent reached out with his stick and poked the bare brown body; it oscillated slightly. "*He's* all right," said the superintendent. He backed out from under the gallows, and blew out a deep breath. The moody look had gone out of his face quite suddenly. He glanced at his wrist-watch. "Eight minutes past eight. Well, that's all for this morning, thank God."

17   The warders unfixed bayonets and marched away. The dog, sobered and conscious of having misbehaved itself, slipped after them. We walked out of the gallows yard, past the condemned cells with their waiting prisoners, into the big central yard of the prison. The convicts, under the command of warders armed with lathis, were already receiving their breakfast. They squatted in long rows, each man holding a tin pannikin, while two warders with buckets marched around ladling out rice; it seemed quite a homely, jolly scene, after the hanging. An enormous relief had come upon us now that the job was done. One felt an impulse to sing, to break into a run, to snigger. All at once everyone began chattering gaily.

"Science and the Sense of Wonder"

ISAAC ASIMOV

Born in Russia, Isaac Asimov (1920–1992) became a naturalized American citizen and famous both as a scholar and writer in physics, biochemistry, astronomy, and genetics and as a science-fiction author. In addition to having written over 200 books, and many more articles and short stories, Asimov was for years associate professor of biochemistry at Boston University School of

Medicine. "Science and the Sense of Wonder" first appeared in the *Washington Post* on August 12, 1979.

Since Asimov is writing in reaction to Whitman's poem, your analysis needs to begin with the poem. Consider: What is the poem's situation? What does the speaker do? What attitude toward science does the poem convey? What attitude toward nature? Now reflect on Asimov's response, using these questions to direct your thinking:

1. Asimov puts down Whitman's attitude toward science as "very convenient." Why?
2. When Asimov looks at what we call stars, what are some of the details that he understands in what he sees?
3. Can you summarize the information about the heavens that the author provides?
4. Has Asimov convinced you that Whitman didn't know how much he was missing? Why or why not? Whose view of nature most closely resembles your own?

One of Walt Whitman's best-known poems is this one: 1

When I heard the learn'd astronomer,
When the proofs, the figures, were ranged in columns before
*   me,*
When I was shown the charts and diagrams, to add, divide
*   and measure them,*
When I sitting heard the astronomer where he lectured with
*   much applause*
*   in the lecture-room,*
How soon unaccountable I became tired and sick,
Till rising and gliding out I wander'd off by myself,
In the mystical moist night-air, and from time to time,
Look'd up in perfect silence at the stars.

I imagine that many people reading those lines tell them-   2
selves, exultantly, "How true! Science just sucks all the beauty out of everything, reducing it all to numbers and tables and measurements! Why bother learning all that junk when I can just go out and look at the stars?"

That is a very convenient point of view since it makes it not   3
only unnecessary, but downright aesthetically wrong, to try to

follow all that hard stuff in science. Instead, you can just take a look at the night sky, get a quick beauty fix, and go off to a nightclub.

4   The trouble is that Whitman is talking through his hat, but the poor soul didn't know any better.

5   I don't deny that the night sky is beautiful, and I have in my time spread out on a hillside for hours looking at the stars and being awed by their beauty (and receiving bug-bites whose marks took weeks to go away).

6   But what I see—those quiet, twinkling points of light—*is not all the beauty there is.* Should I stare lovingly at a single leaf and willingly remain ignorant of the forest? Should I be satisfied to watch the sun glinting off a single pebble and scorn any knowledge of a beach?

7   Those bright spots in the sky that we call planets are worlds. There are worlds with thick atmospheres of carbon dioxide and sulfuric acid; worlds of red-hot liquid with hurricanes that could gulp down the whole earth; dead worlds with quiet pock-marks of craters; worlds with volcanoes puffing plumes of dust into airlessness; worlds with pink and desolate deserts—each with a weird and unearthly beauty that boils down to a mere speck of light if we just gaze at the night sky.

8   Those other bright spots, which are stars rather than planets, are actually suns. Some of them are of incomparable grandeur, each glowing with the light of a thousand suns like ours; some of them are merely red-hot coals doling out their energy stingily. Some of them are compact bodies as massive as our sun, but with all that mass squeezed into a ball smaller than the earth. Some are more compact still, with the mass of the sun squeezed down into the volume of a small asteroid. And some are more compact still, with their mass shrinking down to a volume of zero, the site of which is marked by an intense gravitational field that swallows up everything and gives back nothing; with matter spiraling into that bottomless hole and giving out a wild death-scream of X-rays.

9   There are stars that pulsate endlessly in a great cosmic breathing; and others that, having consumed their fuel, expand and redden until they swallow up their planets, if they have any (and someday, billions of years from now, our sun will expand and the earth will crisp and sere and vaporize into a gas

of iron and rock with no sign of the life it once bore). And some stars explode in a vast cataclysm whose ferocious blast of cosmic rays, hurrying outward at nearly the speed of light, reaches across thousands of light years to touch the earth and supply some of the driving force of evolution through mutations.

Those paltry few stars we see as we look up in perfect silence (some 2,500 or more on even the darkest and clearest night) are joined by a vast horde we don't see, up to as many as three hundred billion—300,000,000,000—to form an enormous pinwheel in space. This pinwheel, the Milky Way galaxy, stretches so widely that it takes light, moving at 186,282 miles each *second*, a hundred thousand *years* to cross it from end to end; and it rotates about its center in a vast and stately turn that takes two hundred million years to complete—and the sun and the earth and we ourselves all make that turn. 10

Beyond our Milky Way galaxy are others, a score or so of them bound to our own in a cluster of galaxies, most of them small, with no more than a few billion stars in each; but with one at least, the Andromeda galaxy, twice as large as our own. 11

Beyond our own cluster, other galaxies and other clusters exist; some clusters made up of thousands of galaxies. They stretch outward and outward as far as our best telescopes can see, with no visible sign of an end—perhaps a hundred billion of them in all. 12

And in more and more of those galaxies we are becoming aware of violence at the centers—of great explosions and outpourings of radiation, marking the death of perhaps millions of stars. Even at the center of our own galaxy there is incredible violence masked from our own solar system far in the outskirts by enormous clouds of dust and gas that lie between us and the heaving center. 13

Some galactic centers are so bright that they can be seen from distances of billions of light-years, distances from which the galaxies themselves cannot be seen and only the bright starlike centers of ravening energy show up—as quasars. Some of these have been detected from more than ten billion light-years away. 14

All these galaxies are hurrying outward from each other in a vast universal expansion that began fifteen billion years ago, when all the matter in the universe was in a tiny sphere that exploded in the hugest conceivable shatter to form the galaxies. 15

16   The universe may expand forever or the day may come when the expansion slows and turns back into a contraction to re-form the tiny sphere and begin the game all over again so that the whole universe is exhaling and inhaling in breaths that are perhaps a trillion years long.

17   And all of this vision—far beyond the scale of human imaginings—was made possible by the works of hundreds of "learn'd" astronomers. All of it; *all* of it was discovered after the death of Whitman in 1892, and most of it in the past twenty-five years, so that the poor poet never knew what a stultified and limited beauty he observed when he "look'd up in perfect silence at the stars."

18   Nor can we know or imagine now the limitless beauty yet to be revealed in the future—by science.

"Declaration of Sentiments"

ELIZABETH CADY STANTON

Elizabeth Cady Stanton (1815–1902) was one of the most important leaders of the women's rights movement. Educated at a local academy and then the Emma Willard Seminary in Troy, NY, Stanton studied law with her father before her marriage. An active reformer in the abolition and temperance movements, she later focused her attention on women's issues. At the Seneca Falls Convention in 1848, Stanton gave the opening speech and read her "Declaration of Sentiments." She founded and became president of the National Women's Suffrage Association in 1869. "The Declaration of Sentiments," patterned after the Declaration of Independence, lists the grievances of women suffering under the tyranny of men.

Keep the Declaration of Independence in mind as you read Stanton's version and use the following questions to guide your analysis.

1. What do women demand? How will they achieve their goals?
2. How have women been restricted in education, in work, if married, and psychologically?
3. What charges made by Stanton continue to be legitimate complaints, in whole or in part?

4. Consider: Do we need a new declaration of sentiments for women? If so, what specific changes would you list? Do we need a new declaration of sentiments for other groups? If so, who? For what reasons?

When, in the course of human events, it becomes necessary 1
for one portion of the family of man to assume among the people of the earth a position different from that which they have hitherto occupied, but one to which the laws of nature and of nature's God entitle them, a decent respect to the opinions of mankind requires that they should declare the causes that impel them to such a course.

We hold these truths to be self-evident: that all men and 2
women are created equal; that they are endowed by their Creator with certain inalienable rights; that among these are life, liberty, and the pursuit of happiness; that to secure these rights governments are instituted, deriving their just powers from the consent of the governed. Whenever any form of government becomes destructive of these ends, it is the right of those who suffer from it to refuse allegiance to it, and to insist upon the institution of a new government, laying its foundation on such principles, and organizing its powers in such form, as to them shall seem most likely to effect their safety and happiness. Prudence, indeed, will dictate that governments long established should not be changed for light and transient causes; and accordingly all experience hath shown that mankind are more disposed to suffer, while evils are sufferable, than to right themselves by abolishing the forms to which they were accustomed. But when a long train of abuses and usurpations, pursuing invariably the same object evinces a design to reduce them under absolute despotism, it is their duty to throw off such government, and to provide new guards for their future security. Such has been the patient sufferance of the women under this government, and such is now the necessity which constrains them to demand the equal station to which they are entitled.

The history of mankind is a history of repeated injuries and 3
usurpations on the part of man toward woman, having in direct object the establishment of an absolute tyranny over her. To prove this, let facts be submitted to a candid world.

4   He has never permitted her to exercise her inalienable right to the elective franchise.

5   He has compelled her to submit to laws, in the formation of which she had no voice.

6   He has withheld from her rights which are given to the most ignorant and degraded men—both natives and foreigners.

7   Having deprived her of this first right of a citizen, the elective franchise, thereby leaving her without representation in the halls of legislation, he has oppressed her on all sides.

8   He has made her, if married, in the eye of the law, civilly dead.

9   He has taken from her all right in property, even to the wages she earns.

10   He has made her, morally, an irresponsible being, as she can commit many crimes with impunity, provided they be done in the presence of her husband. In the covenant of marriage, she is compelled to promise obedience to her husband, he becoming, to all intents and purposes, her master—the law giving him power to deprive her of her liberty, and to administer chastisement.

11   He has so framed the laws of divorce, as to what shall be the proper causes, and in case of separation, to whom the guardianship of the children shall be given, as to be wholly regardless of the happiness of women—the law, in all cases, going upon a false supposition of the supremacy of man, and giving all power into his hands.

12   After depriving her of all rights as a married woman, if single, and the owner of property, he has taxed her to support a government which recognizes her only when her property can be made profitable to it.

13   He has monopolized nearly all the profitable employments, and from those she is permitted to follow, she receives but a scanty remuneration. He closes against her all the avenues to wealth and distinction which he considers most honorable to himself. As a teacher of theology, medicine, or law, she is not known.

14   He has denied her the facilities for obtaining a thorough education, all colleges being closed against her.

15   He allows her in Church, as well as State, but a subordinate position, claiming Apostolic authority for her exclusion from

the ministry, and, with some exceptions, from any public participation in the affairs of the Church.

He has created a false public sentiment by giving the world   16
a different code of morals for men and women, by which moral
delinquencies which exclude women from society, are not only
tolerated, but deemed of little account in man.

He has usurped the prerogative of Jehovah himself, claim-   17
ing it as his right to assign for her a sphere of action, when that
belongs to her conscience and to her God.

He has endeavored, in every way that he could, to destroy   18
her confidence in her own powers, to lessen her self-respect,
and to make her willing to lead a dependent and abject life.

Now, in view of this entire disfranchisement of one-half the   19
people of this country, their social and religious degradation—
in view of the unjust laws above mentioned, and because
women do feel themselves aggrieved, oppressed, and fraudu-
lently deprived of their most sacred rights, we insist that they
have immediate admission to all the rights and privileges
which belong to them as citizens of the United States.

In entering upon the great work before us, we anticipate no   20
small amount of misconception, misrepresentation, and
ridicule; but we shall use every instrumentality within our
power to effect our object. We shall employ agents, circulate
tracts, petition the State and National legislatures, and en-
deavor to enlist the pulpit and the press in our behalf. We hope
this Convention will be followed by a series of Conventions
embracing every part of the country.

"Patterns"

AMY LOWELL

Educated at private schools and widely traveled, Amy Lowell
(1874–1925) was a poet and critic. Her most important critical
work is a study of the British poet John Keats. Lowell frequently
read her poetry and lectured on poetic techniques, defending
her free verse and the work of other modern poets. As you study
"Patterns," probably her best-known poem, use the following
questions as guides.

1. What is the situation of the poem? Who is the speaker, where is the speaker, and what has the speaker just learned?
2. What does the speaker imagine doing, along the garden paths, that now will not take place?
3. What do the garden paths and the speaker's gown come to represent? What patterns are repressive or destructive?
4. Is "Christ!" in the last line an oath, a prayer, or both?

I walk down the garden paths,
And all the daffodils
Are blowing, and the bright blue squills.
I walk down the patterned garden-paths
In my stiff, brocaded gown.   5
With my powdered hair and jewelled fan,
I too am a rare
Pattern. As I wander down
The garden paths.

My dress is richly figured,   10
And the train
Makes a pink and silver stain
On the gravel, and the thrift
Of the borders.
Just a plate of current fashion   15
Tripping by in high-heeled, ribboned shoes.
Not a softness anywhere about me,
Only whalebone[1] and brocade.
And I sink on a seat in the shade
Of a lime tree. For my passion   20
Wars against the stiff brocade.
The daffodils and squills
Flutter in the breeze
As they please
And I weep;   25
For the lime-tree is in blossom
And one small flower has dropped upon my bosom.

[1]Whalebones were used to make stiff corsets for women.—Ed.

And the plashing of waterdrops
In the marble fountain
Comes down the garden-paths.   30
The dripping never stops.
Underneath my stiffened gown
Is the softness of a woman bathing in a marble basin,
A basin in the midst of hedges grown
So thick, she cannot see her lover hiding,   35
But she guesses he is near,
And the sliding of the water
Seems the stroking of a dear
Hand upon her.
What is Summer in a fine brocaded gown!   40
I should like to see it lying in a heap upon the ground.
All the pink and silver crumpled up on the ground.

I would be the pink and silver as I ran along the paths,
And he would stumble after,
Bewildered by my laughter.   45
I should see the sun flashing from his sword-hilt and
    buckles on his shoes.
I would choose
To lead him in a maze along the patterned paths,
A bright and laughing maze for my heavy-booted lover.
Till he caught me in the shade,   50
And the buttons of his waistcoat bruised my body as he
    clasped me,
Aching, melting, unafraid.
With the shadows of the leaves and the sundrops,
And the plopping of the waterdrops,
All about us in the open afternoon—   55
I am very like to swoon
With the weight of this brocade,
For the sun sifts through the shade.

Underneath the fallen blossom
In my bosom,   60
Is a letter I have hid.
It was brought to me this morning by a rider from the Duke.

"Madam, we regret to inform you that Lord Hartwell
Died in action Thursday se'nnight.[2]
As I read it in the white, morning sunlight, 65

The letters squirmed like snakes.
"Any answer, Madam," said my footman.
"No," I told him.
"See that the messenger takes some refreshment.

No, no answer." 70
And I walked into the garden,
Up and down the patterned paths,
In my stiff, correct brocade.
The blue and yellow flowers stood up proudly in the sun,
Each one. 75
I stood upright too,
Held rigid to the pattern
By the stiffness of my gown.
Up and down I walked.
Up and down. 80

In a month he would have been my husband.
In a month, here, underneath this lime,
We would have broken the pattern;
He for me, and I for him,
He as Colonel, I as Lady, 85
On this shady seat.
He had a whim
That sunlight carried blessing.
And I answered, "It shall be as you have said."
Now he is dead. 90

In Summer and in Winter I shall walk
Up and down
The patterned garden-paths
In my stiff brocaded gown.
The squills and daffodils 95

[2]Seven nights; hence a week ago.—Ed.

Will give place to pillared roses, and to asters, and to snow.
I shall go
Up and down,
In my gown.   100
Gorgeously arrayed,
Boned and stayed.
And the softness of my body will be guarded from
    embrace
By each button, hook, and lace.
For the man who should loose me is dead,
Fighting with the Duke in Flanders,[3]   105
In a pattern called a war.
Christ! What are patterns for?

"Grant and Lee: A Study in Contrasts"

BRUCE CATTON

A student at Oberlin College, a Navy gunner's mate in World War I, a reporter, an information officer for the federal government during and after World War II, and the first editor of the *American Heritage* magazine, Bruce Catton (1899–1978) may be America's best-known historian of the Civil War. Catton's interest in the Civil War was sparked by the tales of old veterans in his hometown and continued in wide reading, particularly of soldiers' diaries and memoirs. Between 1950 and 1978, Catton published fourteen books and many essays on the Civil War. *A Stillness at Appomattox* (1953) won a Pulitzer Prize for history and the National Book Award. Catton was awarded the Presidential Medal of Freedom in 1977. The following famous essay on the Generals Grant and Lee was first published in *The American Story,* a collection of essays written by historians for general readers. You can use the following questions to aid your analysis of Catton's contrast.

[3]Area in Belgium and France where heavy fighting occurred during World War I.—Ed.

1. How do Lee and Grant differ in background? In personality? In their views of society and goals for America?
2. What was each general fighting for?
3. What traits do the two men share?
4. What made their meeting at Appomattox "one of the great moments of American history"?

1   And that, perhaps, is where the contrast between Grant and Lee becomes most striking. The Virginia aristocrat, inevitably, saw himself in relation to his own region. He lived in a static society which could endure almost anything except change. Instinctively, his first loyalty would go to the locality in which that society existed. He would fight to the limit of endurance to defend it, because in defending it he was defending everything that gave his own life its deepest meaning.

2   The Westerner, on the other hand, would fight with an equal tenacity for the broader concept of society. He fought so because everything he lived by was tied to growth, expansion, and a constantly widening horizon. What he lived by would survive or fall with the nation itself. He could not possibly stand by unmoved in the face of an attempt to destroy the Union. He would combat it with everything he had, because he could only see it as an effort to cut the ground out from under his feet.

3   So Grant and Lee were in complete contrast, representing two diametrically opposed elements in American life. Grant was the modern man emerging; beyond him, ready to come on the stage, was the great age of steel and machinery, of crowded cities and a restless, burgeoning vitality. Lee might have ridden down from the old age of chivalry, lance in hand, silken banner fluttering over his head. Each man was the perfect champion of his cause, drawing both his strengths and his weaknesses from the people he led.

4   Yet it was not all contrast, after all. Different as they were—in background, in personality, in underlying aspiration—these two great soldiers had much in common. Under everything else, they were marvelous fighters. Furthermore, their fighting qualities were really very much alike.

5   Each man had, to begin with, the great virtue of utter tenacity and fidelity. Grant fought his way down the Mississippi Val-

ley in spite of acute personal discouragement and profound military handicaps. Lee hung on in the trenches at Petersburg after hope itself had died. In each man there was an indomitable quality . . . the born fighter's refusal to give up as long as he can still remain on his feet and lift his two fists.

Daring and resourcefulness they had, too; the ability to   6 think faster and move faster than the enemy. These were the qualities which gave Lee the dazzling campaigns of Second Manassas and Chancellorsville and won Vicksburg for Grant.

Lastly, and perhaps greatest of all, there was the ability, at the   7 end, to turn quickly from war to peace once the fighting was over. Out of the way these two men behaved at Appomattox came the possibility of a peace of reconciliation. It was a possibility not wholly realized, in the years to come, but which did, in the end, help the two sections to become one nation again . . . after a war whose bitterness might have seemed to make such a reunion wholly impossible. No part of either man's life became him more than the part he played in their brief meeting in the McLean house at Appomattox. Their behavior there put all succeeding generations of Americans in their debt. Two great Americans, Grant and Lee—very different, yet under everything very much alike. Their encounter at Appomattox was one of the great moments of American history.

When Ulysses S. Grant and Robert E. Lee met in the parlor   8 of a modest house at Appomattox Court House, Virginia, on April 9, 1865, to work out the terms for the surrender of Lee's Army of Northern Virginia, a great chapter in American life came to a close, and a great new chapter began.

These men were bringing the Civil War to its virtual finish.   9 To be sure, other armies had yet to surrender, and for a few days the fugitive confederate government would struggle desperately and vainly, trying to find some way to go on living now that its chief support was gone. But in effect it was all over when Grant and Lee signed the papers. And the little room where they wrote out the terms was the scene of one of the poignant, dramatic contrasts in American history.

They were two strong men, these oddly different generals,   10 and they represented the strengths of two conflicting currents that, through them, had come into final collision.

11   Back of Robert E. Lee was the notion that the old aristocratic concept might somehow survive and be dominant in American life.

12   Lee was tidewater Virginia, and in his background were family, culture, and tradition . . . the age of chivalry transplanted to a New World which was making its own legends and its own myths. He embodied a way of life that had come down through the age of knighthood and the English country squire. America was a land that was beginning all over again, dedicated to nothing much more complicated than the rather hazy belief that all men had equal rights, and should have an equal chance in the world. In such a land Lee stood for the feeling that it was somehow of advantage to human society to have a pronounced inequality in the social structure. There should be a leisure class, backed by ownership of land; in turn, society itself should be keyed to the land as the chief source of wealth and influence. It would bring forth (according to this ideal) a class of men with a strong sense of obligation to the community; men who lived not to gain advantage for themselves, but to meet the solemn obligations which had been laid on them by the very fact that they were privileged. From them the country would get its leadership; to them it could look for the higher values—of thought, of conduct, of personal deportment—to give it strength and virtue.

13   Lee embodied the noblest elements of this aristocratic ideal. Through him, the landed nobility justified itself. For four years, the Southern states had fought a desperate war to uphold the ideals for which Lee stood. In the end, it almost seemed as if the Confederacy fought for Lee; as if he himself was the Confederacy . . . the best thing that the way of life for which the Confederacy stood could ever have to offer. He had passed into legend before Appomattox. Thousands of tired, underfed, poorly clothed Confederate soldiers, long-since past the simple enthusiasm of the early days of the struggle, somehow considered Lee the symbol of everything for which they had been willing to die. But they could not quite put this feeling into words. If the Lost Cause, sanctified by so much heroism and so many deaths, had a living justification, its justification was General Lee.

14   Grant, the son of a tanner on the Western frontier, was everything Lee was not. He had come up the hard way, and embod-

ied nothing in particular except the eternal toughness and
sinewy fiber of the men who grew up beyond the mountains.
He was one of a body of men who owed reverence and obei-
sance to no one, who were self-reliant to a fault, who cared
hardly anything for the past but who had a sharp eye for the
future.

These frontier men were the precise opposites of the tide- 15
water aristocrats. Back of them, in the great surge that had
taken people over the Alleghenies and into the opening Western country, there was a deep, implicit dissatisfaction with a
past that had settled into grooves. They stood for democracy,
not from any reasoned conclusion about the proper ordering of
human society, but simply because they had grown up in the
middle of democracy and knew how it worked. Their society
might have privileges, but they would be privileges each man
had won for himself. Forms and patterns meant nothing. No
man was born to anything, except perhaps to a chance to show
how far he could rise. Life was competition.

Yet along with this feeling had come a deep sense of be- 16
longing to a national community. The Westerner who developed a farm, opened a shop, or set up in business as a trader
could hope to prosper only as his own community prospered—
and his community ran from the Atlantic to the Pacific and
from Canada down to Mexico. If the land was settled, with
towns and highways and accessible markets, he could better
himself. He saw his fate in terms of the nation's own destiny.
As its horizons expanded, so did his. He had, in other words,
an acute dollars-and-cents stake in the continued growth and
development of his country.

"A Game of Catch"

ROGER ROSENBLATT

A former senior writer at *Time* and then editor of *U.S. News &
World Report*, Roger Rosenblatt (b. 1940) has continued his career in journalism as a regular contributor to magazines and
newspapers. He is also the author of several books, including

Life Itself: Abortion in the American Mind (1992). "A Game of Catch" appeared in *Time* on July 13, 1998. Rosenblatt is admired for his lyricism and reflections on life. As you read, watch for the sentence patterns that shape his lyrical style and observe his use of metaphors. Use the following questions to aid your understanding of Rosenblatt's essay.

1. How is the game of catch similar to parenting?
2. Why is it important to have moments of silence when parents and children are together?
3. How can games serve as a metaphor for life?

1   Summer is the season for it. I dream and see the children when they were children, one at a time, standing on a lawn or on a playground, waiting for the ball to reach them. Their hug-me arms waver in the hot, wet air, as if they are attempting to embrace something vast and invisible. Their eyes blink in the sunlight. They stagger and stumble.

2   It's hard to learn to play catch. In the beginning, you use your arms to cradle the ball against your chest; then you use both hands, then one. Soon you're shagging flies like Willie Mays and firing bullets across your body like Derek Jeter, not having to think about the act.

3   They do not call it a game of throw, though throwing is half the equation. The name of the game puts the burden on the one who receives, but there is really no game to it. Nobody wins or loses. You drop the ball; you pick it up. Once you've got the basics down, it doesn't matter if you bobble a ball or two, or if you can't peg it as far as you once could, or if you have to stare and squint to pick it out of the sky.

4   Or so I tell myself as I groan out of a chaise in response to my son's "Dad, wanna play catch?" He is our third, the last in a line of catch players, the two before him having grown up and out. We stand about 60 feet apart. He gives me the better glove, and we begin.

5   I loathe the leaden drag in my arm, the lack of steam in my throw. Live, I look like a slo-mo replay. But I can still reach him.

6   He, of course, is a picture of careless and fluid engineering. He doesn't even look at the ball (I didn't either at his age). It is just there in his hands, and then it's gone again. We go back and

forth in an essential gesture of sports. A ball travels between two people, each seeking a moment of understanding from the other, across the yard and the years. To play a game of catch is not like pitching to a batter. You do not throw to trick, confuse or evade; you want to be understood.

The poet Richard Wilbur once visited a poetry class that I was in, and he told a girl who had figured out a line of his, "It's nice to have someone catch what you're throwing." 7

A game of catch is an essential gesture of parenthood too, I believe, when families are working well. Everyone tosses to be understood. The best part of the game is the silence. 8

After the recent heartbreaking shootings in the schools, people on TV said parents ought to talk to their children more, which seems sensible and true. But they should also find situations in which talk is unnecessary and they can tacitly acknowledge the mystery of their connection, and be grateful for it, in silent play. Nietzsche said there is nothing so serious as a child at play. He could have added, "or a grownup either." 9

I throw. He catches. He throws. I catch. The ball wobbles so slightly in the bright stillness that one can almost count the stitches. 10

I loved playing baseball as a kid, and then I hated it. Not half bad as a pitcher when I was 13, I threw my arm out, and my idiot coach said, "Pitch through the pain," and I did. I was never able to throw hard after that. Maybe it was a bit of good luck. The advantage in later years, when I became a player of the game of catch, was that I was all motion and no speed—a change-up artist with nothing to change up on—so that the children could study the mechanics of throwing and anticipate making a catch without too much fear. 11

Once I happened to be on the field at Yankee Stadium before game time when the players were warming up. Wade Boggs and Don Mattingly tossed a ball between them without a trace of effort, bodies rearing up and pivoting gently in a casual parody of a pitcher's full windup toward the plate. Every easy toss was delivered at a speed greater than a good high school fastball pitcher could generate. *Thwack, thwack, thwack* in the leather. And the silence between the men on the field. It was interesting to note that even at their level, this was still a game of catch. 12

13   We do what we can as parents, one child at a time. We take what we get in our children, and they take what they get in us, making compromises and adjustments where we are able, making rules and explanations, but for the most part letting things happen, come and go, back and forth. The trick, I think, is to recognize the moments when nothing needs to be said.

14   The heat and silence of the day fit us both like a glove. I toss the ball in looping arcs. He snaps it up as if waving it away, then tosses it back on a line, with much more on it. So we continue until our faces glow with sweat, and the sun drops, and we are touched by the shadows of the trees.

"Learning to Brake for Butterflies"

ELLEN GOODMAN

Ellen Goodman (b. 1941) has been a syndicated columnist since 1976. Her columns appear in over 250 newspapers, and many have been reprinted in collections. She has won a Pulitzer Prize for distinguished commentary. Although Goodman has written many thoughtful columns during her career, among her most memorable are those written from her summer home in Maine, reminding us of our need to slow down and reconnect to the natural world. She is a master of understatement, clever word choice, and the unusual metaphor. Use these questions to aid your analysis of the following column, published August 27, 1994.

1. How does Goodman use details effectively to establish a contrast between work and vacation?
2. Observe Goodman's pairs of contrasting words.
3. Find and explain two of the author's metaphors.
4. Write a thesis statement for the essay.

1   Casco Bay, Maine—I arrive here coasting on the fumes of hi-octane anxiety. The split-second timing of my daily life has adhered to my mood like a watch strapped to a wrist.

2   Behind me is a deadline met by the skin of my teeth. A plane was late. A gas tank was empty. A boat was missed.

The carry-on baggage of my workaday life has accompanied   3
me onto the island. An L. L. Bean bag full of work, a fax machine, a laptop with a modem. I have all sorts of attachments
to the great news machine that feeds me its fast-food through
the electronic stomach tube.

Fully equipped this way, I tell myself that I can get an extra   4
week away. And so I spend that week wondering why I cannot
get away.

For days I perform the magic trick unique to my species. My   5
head and my body are in two different places.

Like some computer-generated animation, my body is on an   6
island where the most important news is the weather report.
My head is on the mainland of issues, ideas, policies. My body
is dressed in shorts, T-shirt, baseball cap. My mind is in a suit,
pantyhose, heels.

I am split across the great divide between this place and the   7
other. Neither here nor there. The desk chair is full, the ham-
mock empty. On the road, I am able to see the brown-eyed Su-
sans and Queen Anne's lace only in my peripheral vision. My
focus remains elsewhere.

I feel like a creature of the modern world who has learned   8
to live much—too much—of the time on fast-forward and to
pretend that it is a natural rhythm.

What would Charlie Chaplin make of these Modern Times?   9
Our impatience when the computer or the ATM machine
"slows" down, or when the plane is late? The way many of us
have to do two things at once, to ratchet up our productivity,
that buzzword of the era, as if life were an assembly line?

In some recess of this modern times mind-set, I thought I   10
could be on vacation and at work. Instead, these two masters
wrangle for custody over me and I learned that there are two
things you cannot do at once: something and nothing.

But finally, this morning, walking down the country road at   11
a distracted, aerobic, urban speed, I brake for butterflies.

I am aware suddenly of four monarchs in full orange and   12
black robes at their regal work. They have claimed a weedy
plot of milkweeds as their territory.

As I stand absolutely still, these four become eight and then   13
12. My eye slowly adjusts to monarchs the way it adjusts to the

dark or the way you can gradually see blueberries on a green bush.

14   There are 20 butterflies harvesting a plot no bigger than my desk. Here are 30 in a space smaller than my office. The flock, the herd, has followed its summer taste buds onto my island the way native tribes once came here for the clams. They leave as suddenly as summer people.

15   The monarchs allow me, a commoner, to stand among them in the milkweeds while they work. I feel foolishly and deliciously like some small-time anthropologist, some down-home Jane Goodall,[1] pleased to be accepted by the fluttering royals.

16   I am permitted to watch from inches away. For half a minute, one monarch chooses my baseball cap as his throne. For half an hour I am not an intruder but part of the native landscape.

17   I remember now the lines of poetry I read in the icy dead of last winter. After watching two mockingbirds, spinning and tossing "the white ribbons of their songs into the air," Mary Oliver wrote, "I had nothing/better to do/than listen./I mean this/seriously."

18   Such moments are rare in our world of Rapid Eye Moments. We have been taught to hurry, to scan instead of read, to surf instead of watch.

19   We can go from zero to 100 miles an hour in seconds—but only by leaving the natural world in the dust.

20   We pride ourselves on speed—and forget that time goes by fast enough. The trick is to slow down long enough to listen, smell, touch, look, live.

21   At long last, the faxes and phones and ties all disconnect. And for a summer afternoon, surrounded by monarchs, I know this: I have nothing better to do than watch. I mean this seriously.

TOPICS AND GUIDELINES FOR WRITING

1. Select any work in this chapter other than Asimov's "Science and the Sense of Wonder" and write a one-to-two page summary of the piece. Follow the guidelines for summary given

---

[1]Anthropologist who has spent many years studying chimps in Africa.—Ed.

in this chapter's introduction. Pay close attention to word choice and to verb tense.

2. Select any work in this chapter and prepare a review of the piece. That is, combine summary and evaluation. Keep in mind that your purpose in evaluating is to judge how well the work fulfills its purpose, not to express, simply, your personal response to the work.

3. Obtain a copy of the Declaration of Independence and prepare a comparative analysis of that piece and Stanton's "Declaration of Sentiments." How are the pieces similar? How do they differ? Consider both wording and content.

4. Analyze Chopin's use of irony in "The Story of an Hour." What is ironic about the story's ending? How does irony help to develop the story's theme?

5. Analyze style in Orwell's "A Hanging," Rosenblatt's "A Game of Catch," or Goodman's "Learning to Brake for Butterflies." Whichever work you choose, select three or four elements of writing that are significant in shaping the writer's style. (Consider, for example, word choice, sentence structures, metaphors, repetition, irony, and understatement.) Organize your analysis by the elements of style you choose; be sure to illustrate and explain each element of style.

6. The essays in this chapter, in various combinations, offer comments and perspectives on a number of topics. Orwell and Rosenblatt and Stanton make observations about what it means to be human. Chopin, Stanton, and Lowell provide a feminist perspective and examine the most subtle kinds of tyranny. Stanton and Catton examine American life: freedom, justice, and the American dream. Reflect on one of these broad subjects, narrowing and focusing your thoughts into a thesis for an essay. Develop your own ideas on the topic in part by using some ideas/details from two or more of the essays in this chapter. Identify the sources of borrowed material informally in your essay by providing author and title of the work.

Glossary

Alliteration Repetition of initial consonant sound in two or more words. For example, the *first frost*.

Allusion Reference to lines or characters from literature or mythology or to figures or events from history. For example, if someone describes you as "an old *Scrooge*," then, like the character in Charles Dickens's *A Christmas Carol*, you are not generous with money.

Analogy An extended comparison of two things that are essentially not alike with several points of similarity (or difference) established to support an idea or thesis. Liane Norman (Chapter 4) draws an analogy between students and squirrels to make a point about students.

Analysis The division of a work or a topic into its component parts. To analyze a writer's style is to examine the various elements that compose style, such as word choice, sentence structure, use of figurative language. (See also **Causal analysis.**)

Argumentation A form of thinking and writing in which reasons and evidence are presented to support a position on an issue. (See Chapter 10.)

Audience The readers of a piece of writing. Hence, as a writing concept, the expected or anticipated readers to whom a piece of writing is directed. A sense of audience should guide a writer's choice about approach, content, and tone for a piece of writing.

Brainstorm Prewriting strategy for generating material on a subject by jotting down all ideas and examples or details that come to mind.

Causal analysis The examination of a situation by division into and study of its several causes, or its pattern of conditions, influences, and remote and immediate causes. (See Chapter 9.)

Character Any person in narrative and dramatic works; also, the personality traits that together shape a person's "character."

Characterization The description of a person, either a real person or one from fiction or drama. A detailed characterization includes

478

physical appearance, speech and behavior patterns, personality traits, and values.

Chronology   The arrangement of events in time sequence. A narrative or historical account organizes events in chronological order. A process analysis explains steps in their appropriate chronology.

Classification   A pattern of thinking and writing in which a subject is divided into logical categories, and then elements of the subject are grouped within those categories. (See Chapter 7.)

Cliché   Overused, worn-out expressions, often metaphors, that were once fresh and clever but should now be avoided in writing, except as examples or to reveal character. I'm *fit as a fiddle, hungry as a bear,* and *head over heels in love* are examples of clichés.

Coherence   A quality of good writing marked by a logical ordering of statements and by the use of words and phrases that guide readers through the material and show them how the writing hangs together. Some techniques for obtaining coherence include repetition of key words, use of pronouns, and use of transition words and phrases.

Colloquial language   Language used in conversation but usually avoided in writing, especially in academic and business writing, unless used purposely to create a particular effect.

Comparison   A pattern of writing in which similarities between two subjects (two schools, two jobs, two novels) are examined. (See Chapter 4.)

Complex sentence   Sentence containing at least one dependent or subordinate clause and one independent clause. For example, "When you come to a term about writing that you do not know, [dependent clause] you should look it up in the Glossary [independent clause]."

Compound sentence   Sentence containing at least two independent clauses. For example, "A comparison develops similarities between two like things [first independent clause], but [coordinating conjunction] a metaphor expresses a similarity between two unlike things [second independent clause]."

Conclusion   The ending of a piece of writing; it gives the reader a sense of finish and completeness. Many strategies for concluding are available to writers, including restating and emphasizing the significance of the thesis, summarizing main points, and suggesting a course of action. Writing needs to conclude, not just stop.

Connotation   The suggestions and emotional overtones conveyed by a word. Selecting the word with the appropriate connotative significance allows writers to develop subtle shades of meaning and to convey their attitudes.

Context clues   The words or sentences surrounding a word that help readers to understand the meaning of that word.

Contrast   A pattern of writing in which differences between two subjects (e.g., two schools, two jobs, two novels) are examined. (See Chapter 4.)

Definition   Explanation of a word's meaning. It can be provided in a sentence or expanded into an essay. (See Chapter 8.)

Denotation   The meanings of a word, often referred to as a word's dictionary definitions. For example, a *house* is a building used primarily for private living. A *home*, however, also connotes family, love, and security.

Description   Details appealing to the five senses that help readers to "see" the writer's subject. (See Chapter 3.)

Details   Specific pieces of information that range from descriptions of people and places to statistical data and that are used by writers to illustrate and support ideas and general points.

Dialect   Variations in grammar, sentence patterns, and word choice that mark the particular use of a language by one group.

Dialogue   Exact words spoken by people introduced in essays or by characters in literature. The words are always set off by quotation marks, and a new paragraph is started to show a change of speaker.

Diction   A writer's choice of words. Levels of diction refer to the degree of formality or informality in word choice.

Division   A pattern of thinking and writing in which large and/or complicated subjects are separated into parts for clear and logical discussion. (See Chapter 7.)

Effects   The consequences or outcomes of events. Effects are often a part of causal analysis when writers examine both what has produced a given situation and what that situation will lead to. Writers also analyze only effects, explaining both immediate and long-term consequences. (See Chapter 9.)

E.g.   Abbreviation of the Latin words *exempli gratia,* meaning "for example."

Essay   A short prose work presenting the writer's views on a particular topic.

Evidence   Facts and examples used to support the thesis or proposition in an argument.

Example   A specific illustration used to develop a thesis or general idea. (See Chapter 6.)

Fable   A narrative written (or told) to teach a moral or lesson.

Fact A statement that is verifiable by observation, measurement, experiment, or use of reliable reference sources such as encyclopedias, atlases, and almanacs.

Fiction An imagined narrative; a story. "The Story of an Hour" by Kate Chopin is fiction. Essays are nonfiction.

Figurative language Language containing figures of speech that extend meaning beyond the literal. A metaphor, for example, is a figure of speech.

Illustration The use of examples to develop and support a thesis. (See Chapter 6.)

Image The recreation in words of a sense experience. Vivid images enrich descriptive writing.

Imagery All the images in a work. Also, a cluster of similar images creating a dominant impression in a work.

Introductions The openings of essays; one or several paragraphs that seek to get the reader's attention and interest and to establish the writer's subject. Many strategies for good introductions are available, including using a startling statistic, stating the thesis, providing an interesting, relevant quotation, asking a question, and giving a brief anecdote or example. Introductions to avoid include sweeping generalizations that range beyond the paper's scope and purpose and statements such as "In this essay, I plan to discuss . . ."

Irony In general, the expression of incongruity or discrepancy. *Verbal irony* expresses a discrepancy between what is said and what is meant. *Dramatic irony* expresses a discrepancy between what a character says or does and what readers understand to be true. *Irony of situation* develops a discrepancy between what we expect to happen and what actually happens.

Jargon Specialized terms of a particular profession or subject area. Jargon often has a negative connotation, a reminder to writers that jargon should be avoided in essays written for general audiences who will be unfamiliar with the terms. Always define specialized terms that must be used.

Metaphor A figure of speech in which a comparison is either stated or implied between two unlike things. (E.g., "this *bud* of *love*" or "*Life's* but a *walking shadow.*")

Narration The account, usually in chronological order, of a historical event or a story (fiction). Also, a strategy for developing the main point of an essay. (See Chapter 2.)

Occasion The situation or circumstances in which a writer produces a particular work. Writers are often motivated to write in response to an event or to their reading.

Order   The pattern in which the parts of an essay are arranged. This text explains many of the patterns available to writers.

Paradox   A statement that seems contradictory but can be understood to be true, usually by taking one part of the statement figuratively rather than literally. For example, "The more money I make, the less I have."

Part by part   A structure for comparison or contrast that arranges by points of difference rather than by the subjects being compared.

Point of view   The perspective or angle of vision from which a story is told. Sometimes the term is used to refer to the grammatical "person" used in essay writing, that is, the first person ("I," "we"), the second person ("you"), which is rarely used except when giving directions, or the third person ("he," "she," "they"). The fiction writer's choices are: *first person* (a character tells the story using "I"), *omniscient* (the all-knowing narrator), *limited omniscient* (through the eyes of one character but in the third person), or *objective* (reporting only what can be seen and heard, not what characters are thinking).

Process analysis   A pattern of writing that takes the reader through the steps or stages necessary to complete a task, perform an activity, or accomplish a goal.

Purpose   One's reason for writing. General purposes include to inform, to explain, and to persuade.

Refutation   A form of argument in which the primary purpose is to counter, or show weaknesses in, another's argument. (See Chapter 10.)

Reporter's questions   Traditionally the questions *who, what, where, when,* and *why* are considered those a journalist should answer about each story covered. Essay writers can also use these questions in planning a topic's development.

Rhetorical question   A question raised by a writer when the writer believes that readers will see only one possible answer—the answer the writer would give.

Sarcasm   Bitter or cutting expression, often ironic.

Satire   Work that ridicules the vices and follies of humanity, often with the purpose of bringing about change.

Setting   The physical locale of the work. Can be presented to create atmosphere as well.

Simile   A comparison between two essentially unlike things that is stated explicitly by using connectors such as *like, as,* or *seems.* For example, "I wandered lonely *as* a cloud," written by William Wordsworth.

Simple sentence A sentence containing only one independent clause. For example, "A simple sentence contains only one independent clause."

Style A writer's selection and arrangement of language.

Summary A brief, objective restatement of the main ideas in a work.

Symbol An object, character, or action that suggests meanings, associations, and emotions beyond what is characteristic of its nature or function. A rose is a flower, but a rose symbolically represents love and beauty.

Theme The central idea (or ideas) that a work embodies.

Thesis The main idea of an essay. It is often but not always expressed in a *thesis sentence.*

Tone The expression of a writer's attitude (e.g., playful, bitter).

Transitions Words and phrases that show readers how ideas in a work are related or connected. For example, *in addition, for example, however.*

Unity A characteristic of good writing in which everything included relates to the work's main idea and contributes to its development.

Whole by whole A structure for comparison or contrast that organizes by the two subjects being compared rather than by their specific points of similarity or difference.

Index

Acknowledgments

Gaye Wagner, "Death of an Officer," *American Enterprise,* May 1995. Reprinted with permission from *The American Enterprise,* a national magazine of politics, business, and culture.

Sandra Cisneros, "Eleven," from *Woman Hollering Creek,* copyright © 1991. Reprinted by permission of Susan Bergholz Literary Services, New York. All rights reserved.

Excerpt from *Among School Children* by Tracy Kidder. Copyright © 1989 by John Tracy Kidder. Reprinted by permission of Houghton Mifflin Company. All rights reserved.

Amy Tan, "Lost Lives of Women," copyright © 1991 by Amy Tan. First published in *Life* Magazine. Reprinted by permission of the author.

From *Even the Stars Look Lonesome* by Maya Angelou. Copyright © 1997 by Maya Angelou. Reprinted by permission of Random House, Inc.

"Africa," *Time* (February 23, 1987). Copyright © 1987 Time, Inc. Reprinted by permission.

Reprinted with permission from *The Undaunted Garden: Planting for Weather-Resilient Beauty* by Lauren Springer. Copyright © 1994. Culcrum Publishing, Inc., Golden, Colorado USA. All rights reserved.

Doris Lessing, "My Father," from *A Small Personal Voice.* Copyright © 1963 Doris Lessing. Reprinted by kind permission of Jonathan Clowes Ltd., London, on behalf of Doris Lessing.

Kim Lavecchia, "A Relaxing Retreat." Reprinted with permission.

Nancy M. Sakamoto, "Conversational Ballgames," from *Polite Fictions,* copyright © 1982. Permission granted by the author.

"Education," from *One Man's Meat,* text copyright 1939 by E. B. White. Reprinted by permission of Tilbury House, Publishers, Gardiner, Maine.

Jonathan Kozol, "A Tale of Two Schools," from *Savage Inequalities* by Jonathan Kozol. Copyright © 1991 by Jonathan Kozol. Reprinted by permission of Crown Publishers, Inc.

Diane Ravitch, "Girls Are Beneficiaries of Gender Gap." Reprinted with permission of *The Wall Street Journal* copyright © 1998 Dow Jones & Company, Inc. All rights reserved.

Judith Viorst, "Boys and Girls: Anatomy and Destiny." Reprinted with the permission of Pocket Books, a Division of Simon & Schuster from *Necessary Losses* by Judith Viorst. Copyright © 1986.

Liane E. Norman, "Pedestrian Students & High Flying Squirrels," from *Center.* Copyright © 1978. Reprinted by permission from The Center for the Study of Democratic Institutions, Los Angeles, CA.

"Marks," from *The Five Stages of Grief* by Linda Pastan. Copyright © 1978 by Linda Pastan. Reprinted by permission of W. W. Norton & Company, Inc.

Denisse M. Bonilla, "The Faded Stain." Reprinted with permission.

Jack McGarvey, "To Be or Not to Be as Defined by TV," *Today's Education* (Feb./Mar. 1982). Permission granted by B. Fischer, editor.

Suzanne Braun Levine, "Caution: Children Watching," *Ms.* (July/August 1994). Copyright © 1994 by Suzanne Braun Levine. Permission granted by the author.

Gloria Steinem, "Sex, Lies, and Advertising." Copyright 1997 by Gloria Steinem. Used with permission.

Caryl Rivers, "The Issue Isn't Sex, It's Violence." Copyright © *The Boston Globe,* 9/15/85. Reprinted with permission.

Pico Iyer, "In Fact, We're Dumbing Up." Copyright © 1999 by Time Inc. Reprinted by permission.

John Skow, "Lost in Cyberspace." Copyright © 1999 by Time Inc. Reprinted by permission.

Dave Barry, "The Barbie Problem." Tribune Media Services, Inc. All Rights Reserved. Reprinted with permission.

John P. Aigner, "Putting Your Job Interview into Rehearsal," *The New York Times* (October 16, 1983). Permission granted by The New York Times.

"How to Give Orders Like a Man," from *Talking from 9 to 5* by Deborah Tannen, Ph.D. Copyright © 1994 by Deborah Tannen, Ph.D. By permission of William Morrow & Co., Inc.

Suzette H. Elgin, "Improving Your Body Language Skills," from *Genderspeak,* copyright © 1997. Reprinted by permission of John Wiley & Sons.

Carol Krucoff, "Restoring Recess." Copyright © 1999 by Carol Krucoff. Reprinted with permission.

"When You Camp Out, Do It Right," by Ernest Hemingway. Reprinted with permission of Scribner, a Division of Simon & Schuster, from *Ernest Hemingway, Dateline: Toronto,* edited by William White. Copyright © 1985 by Mary Hemingway, John Hemingway, Patrick Hemingway, and Gregory Hemingway.

Garry Kasparov, "The Day That I Sensed a New Kind of Intelligence," *Time.* Copyright © 1996 Time Inc. Reprinted by permission.

Katherine McAlpine, *"Plus C'est la Même Chose."* Reprinted with permission from the January 1, 1994 issue of *The Nation.*

"Friends, Good Friends—and Such Good Friends." Copyright © 1977 by Judith Viorst. Originally appeared in *Redbook.* This usage granted by permission of Lescher & Lescher, Ltd.

Judith Martin, "The Roles of Manners," from "Who Killed Modern Manners" by Judith Martin, originally published in *The Responsive Community,* Spring 1996. Copyright © 1996 by Judith Martin, reprinted by permission.

Franklin E. Zimring, "Hot Boxes for Ex-Smokers," *Newsweek* (April 20, 1987). Permission granted by the author.

Curt Suplee, "The Science and Secrets of Personal Space," copyright © 1999, The Washington Post Writers Group. Reprinted with permission.

"There's Three Kinds of Teams," from *Managing in a Time of Great Change* by Peter F. Drucker. Copyright © 1995 by Peter F. Drucker. Used by permission of Dutton, a division of Penguin Putnam Inc.

Ralph Whitehead, Jr., "Class Acts: America's Changing Middle Class." Copyright Ralph Whitehead, Jr. Used with permission.

James Thurber, "The Secret Life of Walter Mitty," from *My World—and Welcome to It.* Copyright © 1942 by James Thurber. Copyright © renewed 1970 by Helen Thurber and Rosemary Thurber. Printed by arrangement with Rosemary A. Thurber and the Barbara Hogenson Agency.

"On Friendship," from *A Way of Seeing* by Margaret Mead and Rhoda Metraux. Copyright © 1961, 1962, 1963, 1964, 1965, 1966, 1967, 1968, 1969, 1970 by Margaret Mead and Rhonda Metraux. By permission of William Morrow Company, Inc.

John Ciardi, "Is Everybody Happy?" *Saturday Review* (May 14, 1964). Permission granted by Omni Publications International Ltd.

"Entropy," by K. C. Cole, *The New York Times* (March 18, 1982). Copyright © 1982 by the New York Times Co. Reprinted by permission.

Robert K. Miller, "Discrimination Is a Virtue," *Newsweek*, (July 31, 1980). Permission granted by the author.

E. J. Dionne, Jr., "Personal Worth." Copyright © 1998, The Washington Post Writers Group. Reprinted with permission.

Stephen King, "Why We Crave Horror Movies." Reprinted with permission. Copyright © Stephen King. All rights reserved. Originally appeared in *Playboy* (1982).

Amitai Etzioni, "Duty: The Forgotten Virtue," *The Washington Post* (March 9, 1986). Permission granted by the author.

Robert B. Reich, "To Lift All Boats." Copyright © 1999 by Robert B. Reich. Used with permission.

Robert J. Samuelson, "Enough Blame to Go Around." Copyright © 1999 Newsweek. Reprinted with permission.

Rosalind C. Barnett & Caryl Rivers, "Family Values Go to Work." Copyright © 1999 The Washington Post.

Keith Albow, "When Parents Are Toxic To Children," *The Washington Post*—Health Section, (May 28, 1996). Permission granted by the author.

Linda J. Waite, "Social Science Finds: 'Marriage Matters,'" from *The Responsive Community*, Vol. 6, 155:3, Summer 1996. Reprinted with permission.

Langston Hughes, "Dream Deferred" from *Collected Poems* by Langston Hughes. Copyright © 1994 by the Estate of Langston Hughes. Reprinted with permission of Alfred A. Knopf Inc.